BY MAX LERNER

It Is Later Than You Think

Ideas Are Weapons

Ideas for the Ice Age

The Mind and Faith of Justice Holmes

Public Journal

Actions and Passions

America as a Civilization

The Unfinished Country

Education and a Radical Humanism

THE AGE
OF
OVERKILL

A PREFACE TO WORLD POLITICS
BY

Max Lerner

19   62

SIMON AND SCHUSTER · NEW YORK

Second Printing

LIBRARY OF CONGRESS CATALOG CARD NUMBER: 62–19077
MANUFACTURED IN THE UNITED STATES OF AMERICA
BY H. WOLFF BOOK MANUFACTURING COMPANY, INC.

TO THE MEMORY OF
MY DAUGHTER

PAMELA LERNER SCHOFIELD

(1932–1961)
WITH UNENDING LOVE

Still are thy pleasant voices,
thy nightingales, awake;
For Death, he taketh all away,
but them he cannot take.

—WILLIAM JOHNSON CORY

Contents

FOREWORD: THE ENCHANTED WOOD   9

I. *The World of Overkill*   17
1. *The Anatomy of a System*   19
2. *The Deterrence World*   23
3. *A Moving Balance of Terror*   28
4. *The Deadly Spiral*   33
5. *"Don't Touch Me"*   38
6. Hic Sunt Dracones   41
7. *The Intolerable, the Impossible, and the Faustian Question*   47
8. *The Passing of Classical World Politics*   51

II. *Power Center and Power Cluster*   53
1. *"Imperialism Is Dead, Long Live Empire!"*   55
2. *Ideas About Imperialism*   57
3. *Empire as Power Cluster*   61
4. *Power Center as Energy System*   67
5. *The Ice Age and the Political War*   73
6. *Neutralism and the Ghosts*   79
7. *Grandeurs and Miseries of Empire*   83

III. *Grand Design as Political Religion*   95
1. *Grand Design*   97
2. *The Two Faces of Revolution*   99
3. *Domination and Accommodation*   102

4. *The Daemon and the Locomotive*   104
5. *Reason of State and Reason of History*   114
6. *Winds of Communist Doctrine: Mystique, Dogma, and Distortion in Marxism*   116
7. *Armed Doctrine and Political Religion*   127
8. *The Intellectual as Fulcrum of Political War*   132
9. *A Stick, a Plan, a Myth*   137

IV. *The Undeveloped World*   141

1. *The Identity Revolutions*   143
2. *Modernization: The Leap into the Stormy Present*   149
3. *Two Designs for Growth*   153
4. *Overtake and Take-over*   163
5. *Self-Determination: Wilson versus Lenin*   168
6. *Color, Heroes, and Elites*   174
7. *A Parcel of Polities: The Unreadiness Effect and Personal Rule*   180
8. *Fire and Form in Developing Societies*   188

V. *The Viable Society: Elite, Élan, Ethos*   195

1. *The Ordeal of Leadership*   197
2. *Power, Decision, and Identity*   204
3. *Commanding and Creative Elites*   209
4. *The Education of a Democratic Elite*   219
5. *The Death and Life of Civilizations*   230
6. *Élan as Vision and Drive*   236
7. *The Battle of the Ethos: Life Style and Personality Type*   241

VI. *Beyond the Power Principle*   251

1. *Beyond Power—To What?*   253
2. *Dialogue Against Death*   259

Contents   5

3. *Negotiation Without Illusions*   264
4. *The New Federalists*   270
5. *UN: The Dynamism of the Order Principle*   279
6. *Toward Collective Will in an Open World*   287
7. *Fear and Conscience in Atomic Man*   295
8. *Death Urge or Life Force?*   301

A NOTE ON READING   309
A NOTE OF ACKNOWLEDGMENT   319
INDEX   321

THE AGE
OF
OVERKILL

Foreword

THE ENCHANTED WOOD

THIS essay, in and beyond the power principle as it operates in world politics, is written in the mood of the Greek myth of the Gorgon head, at a time when many fear to face the harshness of reality lest it turn them to stone. It is meant as a picture of the world today, which the American people and their leadership must confront, along with the leaders and people of the free-world and Communist power clusters, and the leaders of the new and largely uncommitted nations of Asia and Africa. I have tried to depict the forces which have broken loose in that world, and what they are doing to the contours of the familiar landscape of world politics. And I have tried to suggest how a world leadership, at once prudent and courageous, imaginative and sane, may be able to grapple with these forces.

While written by an American, mainly from the perspectives of American and European scholarship, the book was planned and largely written abroad. I wrote it—or it wrote itself—in the sustained intellectual excitement of two highly eventful years spent in India, Southeast Asia, the Middle East, Western Europe and the United States.* As writer and observer, I have had to watch world politics for more years than I care to think. In the process I have, like others, worked out a set of priorities—call them "principles" or "theories" if you wish—to serve as guidelines for my thinking. None of us has the luxury of experiment in the vast laboratory of world affairs, which, alas (or perhaps happily), is not a real laboratory, because you cannot achieve a rollback of time and start over again with a new set of variables as with a new set of white mice. That is why the student of world politics can never learn from experiment, but must be content with experience. But the trouble is that the actors who play the leading roles—the commanding elite, whether on stage or behind the scenes—are rarely reflective enough to strike through the mask of appearance, to the meaning of what they are doing; while the thinkers and writers rarely have to sweat out a decision on which power and destiny, life and death for millions, may turn.

* See A Note of Acknowledgment at the end of the book.

9

The resulting split, between the rulers who have to make their choices without the benefit of theory and the intellectuals who write their little Republics without the necessity of choice, has not been a happy one. What makes it worse is that both, and especially the intellectuals, get too entangled in their rituals and too committed to their Establishment (even the sharpest dissenters develop their own Establishment) to keep their eyes open and their brains cool. It is the submission of the intellectuals to the official government line or party line, which Raymond Aron has called the opium of the intellectuals, that forms their true "treason."

I cannot pretend to be wholly immune from such disabling and distorting influences. As a teacher, however, I have been compelled to develop a theoretical frame of my own. As a working journalist I have also had to take the daily risk of committing myself on one great issue after another, not as a decision maker with power, but as a commentator with some public responsibility for my judgments. The pages that follow are an effort to get a fresh view of the whole terrain of world politics in an age of nuclear diplomacy and world political war.

2

What makes the present era of world politics authentically a new one is the convergence in it of a complex of forces which create a new pattern. I count five major forces loose in our contemporary world—a lethal nuclear spiral, in which obsolescence moves so fast as to create a new "weapons generation" every three or five years; the emergence of two world power clusters and alongside them a loose world bloc of formally unaligned states; the heightening of revolutionary nationalism, bringing with it a nation-state explosion in a rapid sequence of identity revolutions and a new set of national-socialist states; a world political war, fought out on a number of non-military battlefields, largely in terms of a war of ideas; the emergence of the United Nations as a world forum and force, along with a growing anxiety as to whether it can keep pace with the need for a system of world collective security through a world authority.

In consequence of these forces we are witnessing the beginning of the end of classical world politics. For we live in an age of potential overkill, of power surplus rather than the power scarcity which marked the classical era. Because of the overkill factor, both of the great world power clusters are having to keep their power drives in check for fear of sparking a nuclear war. The democratic bloc is caught between the flames of revolutionary nationalism and the crumbling of the old order in the developed countries, unable to use the new weapons to deal with either. The world Communist bloc is caught between a Grand Design which it is reluctant to abandon and the danger of a nuclear war which it dare not precipitate.

The balance-of-power principle has been replaced by a balance-of-terror equilibrium, which (except for possible accidents) provides some measure of security from month to month and from year to year; but no new frame has yet been shaped within which a long-run security from war can be assured to any degree. The impending diffusion of nuclear weapons makes the chances of their use more probable with each passing month. Everywhere in the world there is a daemonic drive which carries nations and empires along toward unseen ends by means whose consequences have not been calculated. In the Communist world a new "reason of history" has been added to the old Machiavellian "reason of state," and an internal rivalry between Russia and China for leadership of the world Communist bloc makes both of them compete for the role of fomenting and supporting revolutions in the drive toward Communist world empire.

On the continents of Asia and Africa a set of newly independent nations have emerged out of identity revolutions, grasping at the principle of total national sovereignty exactly at the moment when the sovereignty principle is proving barren and dangerous for the world as a whole. Most of these recently liberated peoples are not likely for some time to achieve their economic independence or even effective government. Yet the compulsion toward rapid industrial development, by techniques borrowed from the older Western societies, is developing new economies which are being turned against those societies, while a largely unrecognized new form of imperialism is standing by, ready to replace the outworn ones.

The technological revolution, which is changing the traditional societies of Asia and Africa into imitations of the technical cultures of Volgagrad or Pittsburgh, is in turn transforming those cultures. The old Soviet class state of the industrial proletariat is becoming a new party state of a scientific-military elite, just as the American is becoming a state largely dependent upon a corporate-military-governmental elite. The new burdens and dangers of an age of overkill have reawakened the revolutionary impulse (in terms of limited, peaceful revolution), even in the older nations, and have brought with them the imperatives of a new leadership, new creative elites, new educational disciplines, and a new élan.

In the world political war which dominates so many of the international policies of our time, each of the power clusters is having to face tensions and conflicts within its own system and having to resolve problems of unity and order within its own domain. Whatever happens to the tug-of-war between Russia and China, to the efforts toward a Common Market and a political federal structure in Europe, and to the idea of an Atlantic Partnership, is likely to affect the outcome of the political war and perhaps point to the beginnings of a world order.

An earnest search has begun for a principle of world order which can replace the chaos of balance-of-power politics in a world of nation-states caught up in a common peril. It has become clear that the old power principle is no longer adequate to create a frame of order, or rather—since that power principle never was adequate for this purpose—that its disorders now involve too high a price for the world to pay. The problem is not to shape new power alignments or to hew out a new world empire, since neither of them can avoid continuing fragmentation and war. Nor is the problem one of discovering a new principle of order between nations, since the time has past for internationalism as such. A disarmament dialogue, taking place simultaneously with a diplomatic dialogue to resolve major political disputes between the world blocs, might buy some time for the crucial process, which is that of building a transnational frame of order.

This does not and should not require either a world state or a world society. But its minimum base must be a consensus of world law in the area of military aggression, operating through a world police force with a monopoly of nuclear weapons, administered by a world agency with a trained group of officials who do not think in the blinkered terms of national loyalties. This cannot be achieved either by a revolt against science or by a syndicalist revolt of the scientists themselves, but by the people and their intellectual (including scientific) and political leaders, all of them infected by a new and radical morality.

This is a still-distant goal, and the path ahead is not wholly clear, but what is clear is that any deep death urge within man himself must reckon with a counterbalancing life force. The world can move—is already moving—beyond the power principle of national and bloc rivalries and beyond the nuclear weapons toward a frame of order which will not dispense with power but will outlaw aggressive national and ideological military power, subordinating it to the power necessary for a collective world security.

3

In these terms my basic theme—my idea line, as it were—moves. One thing I have avoided striving for is descriptive completeness. No segment of this book deals with any of the moot territorial problem areas and friction points of our time. The reader who wants a summary of the problems of Berlin, Hungary, Albania, Laos, or the situation in Cuba or the Congo or Angola, must go to other books, where he will doubtless find more to his purpose. Mine is not intended as a descriptive book but as an analytical one. When I term it, in the subtitle, "A Preface to World Politics," I mean it as an orientation in the new forces loose in the contemporary world, and in the ideas and concepts which will help us grasp what they are, how they work and what their impact is likely to be.

These are the molds into which the reader will, I hope, be able to pour the molten metal of events as they happen in the coming years. While I have of course used contemporary events as the starting point and as illustrative material for my analysis, later events should serve the same purpose equally well, and—if the analysis is correct —even better. The obsolescence rate of books on our changing world is as rapid as the obsolescence rate of the weapons that are setting the pace for the change. I shall have more than achieved my aim if readers of this book a decade or fifteen years from now will feel that it has some meaning for them, and serves to organize the experience of their time tolerably well.

I have tried to get away from a number of the shopworn terms that have plagued the discussion of world politics. I single out one for special comment. There is a tendency, in the Anglo-American liberal tradition, to lean heavily upon the concepts of "the public" and "public opinion." I don't know whether there is one public or many—I suspect that there are many—but I do know that to speak of their "opinion" as counting in world politics is to deal with an anemic concept.

What counts rather is their convictions, thoughts, ideas, ideals, loves, hates, apathies, despairs, fears, hopes, myths, dreams, mystiques, nightmares, delusions, obsessions, actions and passions. When you think of the great symbolic political enactments of our time,

whether in Moscow or Washington, Paris or Rio de Janeiro, Buda-
pest or Havana, Lhasa or Vientiane, Algiers or East Berlin or Saigon,
the conceptual vessel "public opinion" seems too shallow to contain
them. Much the same is true of other hallowed terms like "liberal-
ism," "conservatism," "Left" and "Right," "West" and "East," "capi-
talism," "socialism," "dictatorship" and "democracy"—all of which
I have either left severely alone or used only in some deliberate
and specific sense.

If the reader finds some of my own terms labored and repetitious,
I can only plead that every fresh angle of vision generates its own
sometimes barbarous but necessary vocabulary. The nuclear strate-
gists have discovered the need for a new terminology in writing of
their own narrower concerns, as have the space scientists. Surely
each of us working in the broader field of world politics can do some-
thing to make this vocabulary more precise. The political war re-
quires such conceptual revision as much as does nuclear war; so do
the new imperial power clusters with their power centers, the new
political economy of the undeveloped world, the inner dynamics of
strength in the rival nations, the new supranational formations.

4

Sir James Frazer has made familiar to all the "sacred grove" in
which the succession to the Kingship of the Wood was settled by
mortal combat. In a sense, world politics has become such a grove,
with dense thickets and nettled problems; but what is immured in it,
awaiting extinction, is not the sacred king but the precious heritage
of humanity itself.

Yet no one has imprisoned humanity in this grove, to convert it
into a collective grave. No one holds it there captive against its will.
One might say that it is the human animal who holds himself cap-
tive by his inner nature, inevitably and irretrievably; but to sustain
this theme one would have to see human nature inherently as
springing from sin, leading to doom and saturated with death, and
I am neither theologian nor psychoanalyst enough to plunge into
these Stygian depths.

My own vision may be only a little less gloomy, but it is not a
pessimism beyond redress. I see the sacred grove as a web of en-
chantment—man-made, culture-shaped, tradition-ridden—in which
the dragons who hold man in thrall are the social contrivings of man
himself. It is in the nature of this enchanted wood that the very

ideas and passions which start by liberating man may end in imprisoning him. I see it almost as a medieval painting of a bestiary in which animals of every kind roam, including the fabled unicorn and hippogriff, all under a spell, all casting a spell.

I am speaking, of course, of the hold that ideas, myths, dreams and fictions have upon men's actions and beliefs. In Asia, Africa, the Middle East, Latin America, one can see the hold of one set of these myths and ideas upon the newer nations caught in the enchanted wood. One can see the hold of a different set of them upon the members of the Communist and free-world power clusters. I have said that the ideas and passions which start by liberating man may end by imprisoning him, whether the prison be the cult of history or of property or of pride in national identity. I should add with equal force, however, that the very dangers and dilemmas that seem to doom man may end by showing the way to freedom. This, at any rate, is the perspective from which I write, impressed not only by the death urge in men but also by the life force which the recoil from the vision of death is beginning to release.

If this were to prove true, it would be proof that man may indeed be moving beyond the power principle while embodying it in his new fumbling constructions. It would be one of the thrilling escape stories in human history, far more exciting than the tales of derring-do of prisoners of war in the dead idyllic days when war was still a tolerable experience.

CHAPTER I

The World of Overkill

1. *The Anatomy of a System*
2. *The Deterrence World*
3. *A Moving Balance of Terror*
4. *The Deadly Spiral*
5. *"Don't Touch Me"*
6. Hic Sunt Dracones
7. *The Intolerable, the Impossible, and the Faustian Question*
8. *The Passing of Classical World Politics*

The World of Overkill

1. The Anatomy of a System

AT THIS moment of history, when we have the sense of a world dying and another coming to birth—and all of us are thus to be reckoned the twice-born—we must seize and size up the dying system to understand what is being born. It is easy enough to talk of the *ancien régime* and of the "passing of the old order," but what is it that is passing? Not capitalism or socialism, and certainly not nationalism; the old imperialism, yes, but not empire; not class or status; not freedom and not tyranny, although freedom is gravely in jeopardy; not God or man, although man himself feels threatened and has grown anxious about God; not love or the fruits of it; not hate or greed or fear; not work or the sense of beauty, nor the imaginative release that makes both possible. True, all these—and others—have been affected by the convulsive changes of our era, but they are not central to its change.

The world that is dying is the classical system of world politics. At various points in recent history, enthusiastic prophets have announced the death of the nation-state. Yet it is not the nation-state that is dying, but its untrammeled sovereignty and the historic pattern of relations between nation-states; not power, but the traditional use of it and the dangerous national base of its present forms; not ideology, but the harnessing of power to the uses of ideology. It is a total system which is passing.

I want, therefore, to ask what the elements of the system are, and what is happening to them. The interaction of nations in peace and war has become so familiar to us that we have not wholly succeeded in defining it with any precision as a going system. Curiously, we talk of *classical economics,* including international economics, both as a body of thought and as a pattern of action, but we do not give the same definiteness to *classical politics* in world terms. Both emerged at roughly the same stage of history—out of Renaissance Europe, with its new national states and national economies. Yet one working pattern, that of classical economics, has succumbed, while the other still lingers, although it has now been undercut.

19

In an early book of mine I asked "Who Killed Adam Smith?" *
—but behind the frivolous form of the question was the reality that
classical economics had succumbed to three revolutions: the industrial revolution, the Marxist revolution, and the welfare-state revolution. Strikingly, the classical system of world politics survived
all three of them. As technology added to the power, it added also to
the power hunger of nations. Revolutionary Russia rejected what
Marx called "bourgeois capitalism" and Lenin called "imperialism," but along with later Communist nations she adapted herself
—despite her Grand Design of "permanent revolution"—to the
classical pattern of world politics. The democratic welfare state has
worked with zeal to stabilize the going international system in order
to achieve stability at home.

The crucial difference between the two concepts was that the
core of classical economics was wealth, while the core of classical
politics is power. In the case of economics, with the acquisition of
wealth at its heart, one could cling to a self-regulating system, but
only so long as the naïve cult of self-interest could still sustain an
economic order. In the case of classical politics, with power at its
heart, there could be no question of *laissez faire* and self-regulation
unless the balance-of-power principle is viewed as an automatic self-
regulatory mechanism; power was the arbiter as well as the prize,
and there was nothing to replace unless it was power itself.

Let me set down quite summarily the premises and principles of
classical world politics, viewing it in its fullest bloom, at the moment when it has been fatally undercut.

1. It is a system based on *power and the uses of power*—for order,
for mastery, for war and for peace, even for the international law
which limits its own use. Everything else may be challenged and
doubted in this system, but not power; it is the prime mover, and it
is also the goal toward which everything in the system gravitates.

2. If its ruling passion is power, then its underlying assumption is
the principle of *power scarcity*. There is a close parallel here with
classical economics, whose underlying premise was the scarcity of
wealth which makes men strive for the largest possible share of the
available wealth. The premise of classical world politics is the scarcity of power which makes nations eager to get power—and always
more power, unceasing and unstinting.

3. The animus of classical politics is prescriptive, competitive,

* *It Is Later Than You Think* (New York: Viking, 1938; rev. ed. 1943).

hostile. The aim of each state is not only to acquire more power for itself, but to prevent enemies and competitors from acquiring more —or any. Thus, along with the idea of power, *the idea of the enemy* is central to the system. The world becomes a world of enemies and potential enemies, and of allies and potential allies who may help against the enemy. Hence the alliance system, and hence also classical diplomacy and war.

4. Given the constant presence of the enemy idea, the characteristic psychology of the classical system is jungle *suspicion and fear,* along with the secrecy that accompanies both. The characteristic ethos is the amoral reliance on "reason of state," which justifies the use of any means to achieve the maximum security and power that are the ends of the state.

5. Toward these ends the state, in the classical system, values certain *sinews of strength:* geography (territory, natural resources, strategic boundaries), population (human resources), arms and armies, a favorable balance of trade and payments, and the channeling of investments to increase national power. The emphasis is on tangible and objective sinews of strength, and there is a contempt for ideas, ideals and other intangibles. The only exceptions to this are "national honor," national prestige, the civic education of the young, and (what the class state added) the elements for propaganda and psychological war. The whole structure of imperialism may be viewed as an extension of this search for the sinews of national strength, which means that it is not the "last stage of capitalism," as Lenin professed to see it, but an integral stage of classical world politics, whether capitalist or communist.

6. The fact about the classical system most taken for granted, and needing to be examined, is that it is *a world of nation-states.* Any entity which is less than a nation-state or is not yet a nation-state has no standing in it; hence the constant pressure toward nationalist movements and the carving out of new nations. Once a people has taken its place in the world of nation-states, its further drive may be not toward internal freedom nor toward democracy but toward self-sufficiency, in economic and military terms. Everything else is subordinated to that drive.

7. With nationhood goes the idea of *national sovereignty.* Once a nation is formed, its law and authority come from a single source (whether sovereign or people), and it can recognize no superior law and authority. The whole classical political system is pervaded by the sense that sovereignty must be jealously guarded against a hostile world bent on challenging or diminishing it.

8. Every system needs a dynamic to make it go. The dynamic of classical world politics has been the idea of *national interest,* which is based on the premise that there are power goals on which most of the members of a nation-state can agree, whatever their own interest or ideals, and that these goals give the nation its identity and set it off from the other nations.

Historically the real cleavage on the issue of national interest has been not on *whether* to pursue it but on *how* to pursue it best. Students of Machiavelli know that he laid bare the anatomy of power and did not moralize over it. But they also know the difference of mood and thinking between his *Prince* and his *Discourses.* Some have said that there were two Machiavellis; but if so, the difference between them lay only in the redefinition of the national interest. In the *Prince* it was the realistic pursuit of the Prince's (that is, the nation's) power; in the *Discourses* the question was raised of the kind of society for which the power of the state was established and maintained, and the sources of strength in it.

Here in a kernel is the whole struggle between the "realist" and the "idealist" schools of world politics. The "idealists" do not reject the idea of the national interest, but affirm that it can best be pursued toward goals more humane and by means more subtle than naked national power. In the course of a debate in which someone had referred to Turkey as England's "permanent friend," Lord Palmerston is reported to have replied, "My Lords, England has no permanent friends, England has no permanent enemies, England has only permanent interests." This was a realist speaking, and no more classic formulation of the classic doctrine could be asked for.

9. Every system requires not only a dynamic to make it go but also a balance wheel to keep it from being destroyed by going too far. The balance wheel of the system of world politics is the *balance-of-power principle.* Much abused and misunderstood, this means only that when any nation or alliance gets so much power as to overweigh and threaten its rival, the rival must move in turn to offset this power and at the least restore the balance. This is a matter not of choice but of necessity, inherent in the system itself.

Like classical economics, the classical system of world politics is thus an *equilibrium system.* As in the case of Adam Smith and classical economics, there is a providential Grand Design which operates through a Higher Selfishness; each nation, by following its own good (national interest), thereby promotes the good of the world, preventing war by restoring the balance of power. Thus the "unseen hand of God" operates to promote God's purposes on earth—not the God of Battles, note, but the God of Design. The trouble with this theology is that in trying to prevent any nation or alliance from amassing a superior war power, the rival nation or alliance in restoring and then transforming the balance must be ready to resort to war, and many times it has done so. The history of the classical system is replete with instances of wars which came in an effort, often high-minded, to prevent war.

10. This brings us to the final element of the system—*war as a principle*. The phrase "war as an instrument of national policy" has come into common use, but it seems to suggest that it is a matter of choice for any group of leaders.

What the Germans called *Machtpolitik*—power politics—has always been good for attack by humane commentators. But the fact is that there is no other politics possible in the classical system than power politics, and no means for restoring the power balance except at the risk of war. War is an instrument not of national policy but of the classical system of world politics. While usually regarded as undesirable and even deplorable, war follows logically not only from the premise of power scarcity (which leads a nation to strain every nerve to pile up more power), but even more from the principle of power balance. It has become therefore a tolerated part of the system, even when it is deemed intolerable.

2. *The Deterrence World*

ONE OF THE TERMS that have come to be accepted in the vocabulary of military leaders is "overkill factor." It denotes surplus killing power, expressed in the ratio between what is actually available for use against a population target and what would be necessary as a minimum to destroy it. In the spring of 1960 each of the two Great Powers was reported to have an atomic stockpile capable of killing every man, woman and child in the world many times over. Each had thus based its military plans on the "principle of overkill."

Doubtless the overkill factor has since sharply increased, but the phrase itself is strikingly symbolic. I use it with some extension of meaning to express the broader idea of surplus killing power today, and how that idea has pervaded the actions and passions of the Age of Overkill. This book aims in part to explore the consequences of the overkill weapons for world politics, both in the power principle itself—in conventional and nuclear diplomacy and in the political war—and in the need to go beyond the power principle.

The most far-reaching consequence is that the underlying premise of classical world politics, that of *power scarcity,* no longer holds true. It is being replaced, at least in the case of the nuclear nations, by the premise of a *power surplus.* Nor does "surplus" quite convey the full meaning of what has happened. It usually implies that you have more of something than you want or need. But the great powers, with their enormous margin of overkill, have far more power than they can or dare use, without risking their own destruction. They are thus caught in the paradox of their own excess killing power.

In my view, the "great decision" about dropping the fateful bombs over Japan, made chiefly by President Truman and War Secretary Stimson, was itself a blind error in overkill; the war could probably have been ended without that concrete lesson in extirpation, perhaps by a demonstration of the bomb's lethal power in an unpopulated area. We are now fairly certain that the political leaders of Japan were thoroughly tired of the war well before Hiroshima, were anxious to sue for peace and had even sent a probing envoy to the Russians, without result. A demonstration use of the bomb, perhaps over some atoll, accompanied by an ultimatum, would surely have knocked Japan out of the war, spared the agony of Hiroshima and Nagasaki and still saved the million American casualties which the American war leaders estimated as the cost of a reduction of Japan without the bomb. The trouble was that President Truman was never told about the whole Manhattan Project until after Roosevelt's death, and the atomic scientists who signed the Franck Report, urging the unwisdom of an actual use of the bomb, were never able to reach either Roosevelt or Truman. The decision, judged ethically, was a blunder of good men having to make up their minds in the dark. Thus, the atomic-weapons era began with a grimly accidental act, in the sense that it was never thought through with the participation of all concerned or with a knowledge of the relevant facts.

Since that time the weapons race has heightened its pace with febrile speed and with a breath-taking rate of obsolescence. The scientists and generals have come to reckon the advances of each period of roughly five years, or even less, as a new "weapons generation"; on each side, men are zealously inventing, building and testing whole arrays of weapons, which they then discard without use in order to replace them with others invented, built and tested as zealously and with as much uselessness. Despite the curtain of secrecy thrown over the process of scientific and technical problem solving on each side, the results of the solution find wide publicity, precisely because each technical advance in overkill is translated into the threat of its use, either to dissuade the other side from using its weapons or as part of the game of nuclear diplomacy. It is a little like a mock prize fight, in which each fighter telegraphs his punches and pulls them back without landing them. Thus far the war has been kept a symbolic rather than an actual one, with each advance in nuclear warheads and missile delivery systems scarcely concealed from the intelligence units of the rival camp.

The point of this symbolic war, or nonwar, lies in the principle of deterrence and in the balance-of-terror concept which underlies it. Libraries are being written on the deterrence principle, and its nuances are many and complex. The vocabulary of deterrence has largely replaced that of "national defense" in the recent writings. General Pierre Gallois, a stanch champion of peace through deterrence, points out that during the years of the Age of Trinitrotoluene (TNT), from the battle of Crécy to Hiroshima, there were hundreds of wars. As a consequence, the task of military planners was to prepare against their very probable contingency. Their task in the Age of Deterrence is to prepare weapons which will convince the enemy that it is futile and useless to employ theirs, and that any such use will have to reckon with swift punitive sanctions.

With the coming of missiles in the middle 1950s, both the possible suddenness of the first strike and the speed of retaliation were heightened, and a new time dimension of response decisions, measured by hours and even minutes, was introduced. With the testing of multimegaton weapons (50-megaton weapons have been tested, 100-megatons are in view, and there is talk of gigaton, or 1,000-megaton bombs) the destructive power both of the attack and retaliation have been stepped up. As I write, both sides are at work on antimissile missiles, H-bombs that do not need A-bombs to trigger them, missiles made of materials not detectable on radar screens. Technologically, no end is in sight. Thus the major type of deterrence is directed at and through these large overkill weapons, which have a potentiality not only for direct destruction but also for death by radiation.

Nor does deterrence stop with destructive weapons. The knowledge that one side has developed effective defensive weapons, like antimissile missiles, is also calculated to deter the opponent's use of his offensive ones. The same applies to a good civilian-defense stance, with readiness to evacuate the vulnerable populations and completion of tolerable shelter programs for them. And, since the competing world power systems are not merely nations but power clusters, deterrence may operate to fend off not only attacks against oneself but also (as in the case of the Soviet Union's designs on Western Europe) provocations or attacks against one's allies. Finally, it may operate to induce a certain stability in the power-and-terror balance by cautioning against trigger-happy decisions and by putting a premium on rational decisions and weapons controls, thus reducing the chances of accidental war.

This is the strange new world in which we find ourselves: a world of buttons existing to be pressed at need, with the underlying premise that they will not have to be pressed if one threatens clearly enough to press them; a world of peace to be achieved through the promise of nuclear terror; a world bedecked with the new vocabulary of "credible first-strike capability," "second-strike [retaliatory] capability," "escalation," "reciprocal fear of surprise attack," "calculated pre-emption," and even "striking second-first"; a world in which chance must be all but squeezed out, through "fail-safe" built-in controls of the weapons systems, with crucial decisions reserved for a few men at the top; a world of constant wariness and suspicion, of a death's-head game in which each side is bent on convincing the other that it has the means and the will to destroy him utterly before it is itself utterly destroyed, that it is powerful enough to instill terror, yet prepared enough to feel none. Only thus, it is argued, will the weapons so arduously conceived, placed on the drawing board and brought into the stockpiles remain unused. Out of this nettle, deterrence, we presumably pluck this flower, safety.

Out of this deterrence world have come weapons systems to meet each deterrence need, and the arts and strategies of using them for war and peace, for psychological attack and defense, for upsetting and restoring the power balance, for help in the political war, even for inducing concessions in the frustrating, intermittent arms-control dialogue. Out of it has come a refined communications theory, running in terms of the "signals" that are sent from one camp to the other, and of the explicit and implicit understandings between them. So many implicit conventions are being built up concerning the use and nonuse of the new weapons systems, both in actuality and as threat, that a newer and more terrible "conventional" warfare is being shaped, to take its place alongside the old-time nonnuclear high-explosive warfare.

Finally, out of the deterrence world has come what is called a "games theory," which has been the focus of considerable intellectual energy from mathematicians, physicists and military and political theorists, and the target of considerable moral resentment from a number of impassioned if tender-minded humanists who cannot tolerate the reduction of world destiny and human survival to the calculations of a game. The two principal sources of this new theory are the simulated situations of the traditional "war games" and the transposition of the mathematical theory of games into the military-political matching of wits and threats involved in deterrence theory. The final product, however, is drastically unlike its sources, in requiring knowledge and sophistication drawn from a number of exacting disciplines—history, politics, economics, psychology, sociology, mathematics, probability theory, even psychoanalytic theory. As a result, the traditional military strategists have been replaced by a new breed of men—intellectuals like John Von Neuman, Herman Kahn, Thomas B. Schelling, Henry Kissinger, Donald Brennan, Oskar Morgenstern, Albert Wohlstetter, Glenn H. Snyder.

The deterrence system is thus a bundle of paradoxes whose crowning paradox is this: while the psychic fears and needs which feed the building of the deterrent power on each side are basically nonrational, the operation of the deterrence principle in preventing war depends on an almost flawless rationality on both sides. Thus, the pressures build up because men are fearful, but their resolution is premised on the assumption that their fear leads them to be rational—which is not always the case. This, I take it, is the logic of Henry Kissinger's half-serious, half-tongue-in-cheek proposal that the push button which the President of the United States would have to press, to release a retaliatory strike, be made automatic, to operate under certain preconditions without the President's intervention; this would wholly strip away the human and possibly irrational element of Presidential decision, eliminating a twilight area conceivably subject to influence, and thus eliminating a temptation for enemy nuclear blackmail.

Kissinger's suggestion illumines, as it is meant to, the imperative of rationality in the deterrence system, if it is to operate with safety. It thus exposes the total profile of a dehumanized weapons race, threatening always to end in a dehumanized war, and preventable only by the robot principle of wholly rational, dehumanized decision. In the world of deterrence, there is nothing that a political leader can decide, that cannot—given the proper feed-in of information—be decided more safely by an electronic brain.

3. A Moving Balance of Terror

SEEN THUS, the deterrence world contains an inhumanity which has led a number of critics to condemn the whole idea of deterrence and condemn along with it the new breed of military writers who have committed themselves to the study of what is surely the strangest form that the art of war has ever taken in its whole history. This is, it has been suggested, a little reminiscent of the kings who, identifying a messenger bringing bad news with the news he bore, ordered him killed. There are a number of critics who have felt thus about the games theorists, and whose moral sense is shocked by the seeming coldness with which these writers have approached the problem of adequate defense systems. The ground of the animus against them seems to be that, while it may be necessary to maintain nuclear weapons until a way of breaking the arms impasse is found, there is something immoral about envisaging the use of un- usable weapons and thus tolerating the intolerable and (as Kahn has put it) "thinking about the unthinkable." What may be moral if you approach the Gorgon head with averted gaze becomes presumably immoral if you stare at it directly without fearing its power to turn you to stone.

I suggest that the real quarrel of the critics is less with the relentless anatomists of the deterrence system who draw the nakedest implications from it than with the world power struggle itself and the basic inhumanity of the military technology it has had to employ in an age of rapid technological advance. One must nevertheless add, on the debit side of the account of Kahn and Company, that they are better when viewed as defense strategists than when viewed as peace strategists. The difference lies in orientation. If you are oriented toward fail-safe invulnerability against attack and bend every effort in that direction, your imaginativeness will be expended on modes of immunity and offensive power, on "credible first-strike capability" and "counterforce capability." This may be as it should be, provided that the military strategist does not mistake his role and assume the mantle of the peace strategist, professing to find in the practical necessities of temporary defense a permanent principle

of peace and a new principle of safety in a new age. The orientation
of the peace strategist is toward breaking out of the deadly missile
spiral, and accordingly his imaginativeness is expended upon
modes of taking the peace initiative, of turning rigid attitudes into
flexible ones, of dispelling the miasmic atmosphere of suspicion,
paranoid fears, and repressed anxieties which become schizophrenic.
This too is as it should be, provided the peace strategist does not
mistake his role for a military one.

The failure of the military strategists thus far has been a lack of
imaginativeness in their premises; they tend to undervalue the possibilities of the UN, of calculated risks in disarmament agreements,
of deliberate steps in a peace initiative, of denuclearized zones.
They live in a world a good deal like that of Emperor Jones, in the
O'Neill play, filled with jungle fears and suspicions. The failure of
the peace strategists, in turn, has been their inability to assess the
true nature of the Communist intent and mentality, their lack of a
political (as well as a military) tough-mindedness, their tendency to
act as if the history of weapons advance and of Communist advances toward world power simply had not taken place and had
not created an actual situation to be reckoned with. What Amitai
Etzioni (in his *Hard Way to Peace*) has called the "working-
toward effect" is a different one for each of the two groups. In the
case of the defense strategists it is toward relative immunity from
attack—at least toward deterrence stability. In the case of the peace
strategists it is toward a psychological break-through in the glacial
mold of rigidity. The trouble is that not only is there a stalemate
between the Communist and free-world forces, both in power systems and in weapons systems, but there is even a stalemate between
the military strategists and the peace strategists in their working-
toward effects. If the second stalemate could be resolved, perhaps
the first might be.

Certainly, the military strategists, whatever the illusions of some
of them, have not found a new principle of safety in a new age. The
most brilliantly resourceful of them, in his logical sharpness, his
fertile typologies of possible policies and possible consequences, his
vivid historical and conjectural "scenarios" as new forms of the old
"war games," his insistence on facing the Medusa head of the unthinkable, is Herman Kahn. Be it said to his credit that he has few
illusions about finding safety, either for America or for the world,
in the shifting and always potentially explosive deterrence equa-
tions. The problem he sets is always a desperate time problem:
How to reach the year 2000, or even 1975, without an annihilating

war.* There hangs over his work some of the grotesquerie one finds, for example, in the poetry of Thomas Lovell Beddoes, arising partly from the discrepancy between the ebullient, imaginative flow of Kahn's mind and the death's-head grimness of his subject matter. One might wish that he had, in Hans Morgenthau's phrase, more of a "tragic sense of history," † but his sense of detachment is appropriate enough for the unrelenting quality of his analysis.

The essence of the contemporary tragedy, seen in power terms, is that the overkill weapons have made the classical balance-of-power system archaic, but in the absence of anything to replace it the balance-of-power system has been carried over in a more terrifying form. The traditional pursuit of a new balance has always been dangerous, involving arms races, territorial pressures, diplomatic adventures; with nuclear and biological overkill weapons, it should clearly have become too dangerous to continue. Yet it has continued, for the very simple—or very complex—reason that neither side has dared to abandon it, since to abandon it might mean laying oneself open to nuclear war or nuclear blackmail. Hence the tragedy of the deterrence trap.

The world is still operating, then, *within* the power principle, even though weapons technology has undercut the classic form of the power principle. One can recognize in the new form the old principle of seeking to achieve a power equilibrium by overtaking —and outstripping—the potential enemy, in arms, in resources and in allies, only to be overtaken and outstripped by the enemy in turn. Since a new name was required for the new situation, Winston Churchill supplied it—or at least popularized it—when he said, in his farewell speech in the House of Commons, that the old *balance of power* had been replaced by a *balance of terror*. Whether he had a nostalgia for the classical system, or a startling foreknowledge that the old realities would live on for a time in their novel form, Churchill's phrase bridges the distance between an era stumbling to its death and one struggling to be born.

There has always been a desperate note in the efforts to achieve a power balance in order to nail down a peace-by-equilibrium. Obviously, it can never be achieved for long, since each side strives not for balance but for advantage. It is like a series of perchings and

---

* His *Thinking about the Unthinkable* (1962) takes better account of arms control, the UN and political negotiations than did his *On Thermonuclear War*.

† That it is not wholly absent should be clear from such phrases of his as the "Doomsday machine," and from his haunting query, "Will the living envy the dead?"—although his answer to his own question was in the negative.

flights of a bird; the perchings are brief, the flights unpredictable. It was always hard to maintain a stable balance of power, since the forces of disequilibrium were always in motion to alter one or the other side of the balance. It is even harder to maintain a stable deterrence, or a stable balance of terror, although that is what responsible leaders yearn for. The point is that it was never any- thing but a moving balance of power, and it is now a moving balance of terror; and the terror is not only a deterrent terror for the enemy, but a purging terror for all of us.

There is a tendency to use "deterrence" and "balance of terror" loosely as synonyms. I prefer to draw a distinction. Deterrence is the threat of the use of power-in-being to dissuade an opponent from the use of his. Its universe is that of intent, capability, and will to act (credibility). It may be tactical (limited in area and in the weapons intended), strategic (encompassing in both), or all- out, depending on the extent and nature of the war that is en- visaged. But basically it is a concept of weaponry, of offensive and defensive power, including civil defense and evacuation capability as elements.

I see the balance-of-terror concept as a broader one, being not only a weaponry concept but a total power-and-resources concept, including not only the warmaking potential, but the total sinews of strength on each side which may count in the political as well as in the military decisions. While the military men in the period of class- ical world politics used the balance-of-power concept as a narrowly military one, it always was broader, to include the territorial eco- nomic, political, psychological and moral factors which counted on each side for a war showdown. As its inheritor, the balance-of- terror concept takes over its scope, although the crucial showdown element—war itself—is now a matter of terror anticipated and in- tended rather than conventional death-dealing power. Where the showdown once dealt in calculable terms it now deals in incal- culable ones, where it was once formal it is now formless—hence the terror element—but the moving balance itself was, and is, an inclusive one, taking in the whole domain of credible and actual capability for the political war in its bearing on the weapons war.

Thus, containment and "massive retaliation" have been regarded as past strategies of the free-world power cluster, now replaced by the deterrence strategy. Both of the earlier strategies were elements in the broad politico-military policy of seeking to maintain a mov- ing balance of power. One of the fallacies of containment lay exactly in the failure to see that a moving balance could not be achieved by a static policy. "Massive retaliation" was in intent a forerunner of deterrence by terror, warning the Russians that any use of atomic power would be met by full-scale force; but in fact it was undercut by the Russian H-bomb almost as soon as announced, and it became a doctrine of appropriate counterforce.

Nor can there be a "stable" deterrence, by the same reasoning that made the "containment" of an irrepressibly moving force a contradictory term. The "minimum" or "limited" deterrence dear to the middle and late 1950s was always in process of being pushed toward the unlimited form, in the sense that the "reciprocal fear of surprise attack" tends constantly to maximize the achievable deterrent force. The "multi-stable deterrence" of the Kennedy administration, at present writing, has a better chance of winning a breather of stability, if only because the advance is pushed on every weapons and political front—the stool has a better chance of balancing when it has many legs rather than one. I want however to note the opposing view as Hans Morgenthau has put it: that nuclear deterrence can be stable, provided there is technological stability (a big proviso); but that multi-stable deterrence is inherently unstable since it is a mixture of an ever-changing variety of ingredients.

When we add, to weaponry itself, the stabilizing effects of arms-control efforts and of continuous political negotiations, the chances of some stability in the moving equilibrium grow somewhat better. But if you add the fronts of the political war, you reach the larger balance-of-power effect, which can be a protracted shifting equilibrium for some time, with the balance-of-terror effect always there to focus the total calculus on the showdown.

I am clearly including in the broader concept of a moving equilibrium not only the balanced (and balancing) terror of the weaponry but also the balanced (and balancing) power of the two great power clusters. The balance of terror tends thus to be bipolar, although the current polycentrism of the Communist cluster (Moscow-Peking-Belgrade) and also of the free-world cluster (Washington-Paris-London-Bonn) makes it more complex than that. While I have emphasized the constant effort of each side to outstrip the other, and thus the dangers to a stable balance, the concept of the balance of terror would have little meaning if the stabilizing forces were not authentic ones. I count among these the dialectic of the weapons race itself, by which each new weapon evokes an anti-weapon, and the common fund of technology flows like a not easily dammed stream into both channels. I add the element of clear expression of intent, without which the highly rational process of deterrence could not operate. I add further whatever progress arms control can make, whether at the nuclear or at the conventional-weapons end of the stick. I add the economic rivalry, both in weapons budgets and in economic aid, which strains the rival economies; and finally the underlying passion for peace among the people on both sides, despite the chauvinism and expansionism of particular groups.

4. *The Deadly Spiral*

I ADD A NOTE on metaphors which are meant to represent the nature of the current global struggle. "A world ends when its metaphor has died," Archibald MacLeish says in one of his poems. The spent metaphor of our era is the Machiavellian one of world politics as a chessboard on which the Prince, as sovereign head of state, moves his counters about while other sovereign heads of state move theirs in intricate amoral splendor. The fullness of sovereignty has since been eroded, and the apocalyptic vision of nuclear war has made the amoral leader dangerous to world politics rather than its type figure, as was Machiavelli's Prince. I am not saying that power politics has ceased to be practiced, or even that it is dispensable within the frame of our time, but only that the chessboard metaphor is dead because power politics can no longer maintain world order.

As for the metaphor of a balance-of-power equilibrium, with its implied image of power as something to be weighed on a precarious set of scales, it is (I have suggested above) not dead, but transfigured in the new garments of terror. In the world of Talleyrand, Metternich, Disraeli, Bismarck and Winston Churchill, it was understood that the risk of a moving balance of power was war, and a man could take the risk without fear of going mad. In the later world of Stalin, Truman, Khrushchev and Kennedy, a new mood developed, changing the moral and political landscape on which the scales were poised and making them the scales of terror balanced against terror. It occurred to me, watching a Broadway play called *Two for the Seesaw,* that this metaphor might be apter than the scales, since it allows for an activist role in the love-hate, antagonism-cooperation duel. Certainly America and Russia seem caught on a seesaw, which yields a temporary ascendancy to each in turn as it swings high with some new weapons break-through or political victory, only to be thrust down again by the ascendancy of the other. But even the seesaw metaphor is already obsolescent, betrayed by the impending diffusion of atomic capability, which is spreading the power of decision over atomic war beyond the polar nations.

The commonest metaphor, at least in popular speech, is that of the race, in which each runner strains to outdistance the other and break the tape first. From this came the notion of the "missile gap" after the two Eisenhower terms—an image which was politically effective in the 1960 Presidential campaign, although it turned out to be dubious later. The trouble with the race-and-lag metaphor is that it assumes a victory for one or the other runner—a scarcely tenable assumption in our time; even the notion that one can outdistance the other for long without the race and stadium blowing up seems untenable. Thus, the race metaphor, by assuming that each runner has control over himself and his strength and pace, does no justice to the fact that both are trapped in a race which neither can win and which spells doom for both unless they can end it.*

In my own thinking, the metaphor of a *spiral* has been helpful in representing both the urgency and the helplessness of both contestants. As each of the two major power clusters improves either its weaponry or its world political position, it brings a heightening of resentment, tension and fear in the other, which in turn serves to spur even more heroic efforts toward bigger bombs and missiles, more invulnerable antimissile defenses, more desperate research into BCR (biological-chemical-radiological) weapons, tighter alliances, closer ties with the uncommitted nations, more far-reaching aid programs, more resounding voting victories in the UN.

What makes this not a race but a spiral is that not only a weapons rivalry is involved, but a complex relationship between a number of interacting factors which heighten each other and worsen the whole situation, in what the psychiatrists call a "syndrome." It is the syndrome aspect which makes me call it a *deadly* spiral. To simplify the web of interacting elements, one might think of a

* It is the can-win and can't-win aspect of the struggle which has led to the setting-up of a number of games, premised on one or another assumption, in the current writings on "games theory," of which Thomas B. Schelling's *The Strategy of Conflict* strikes me as the best. But games theory is more than metaphor playing. It is a calculus of possibilities. One of those possibilities, I should add, is that in some sense one of the sides *can* win something in the race, especially if a weapons advantage can be transformed into a political advantage in the political war, and result in a victory without a showdown of killing. This is of course the logic of hope in the Soviet strategy.

three-way interaction between weapons rivalry, political warfare and the whole fear atmosphere. An increase of the first, as in massive nuclear testing, or a substantial gain or loss in the second, as in the Hungary uprising, the U-2 incident, the Bay of Pigs adventure in Cuba, and widespread famines in China, tend to heighten the third —which in turn sets in motion new imperatives in the other two.

This, then, is the deadly missile–fear–political-war spiral. Putting it thus has the merit of not narrowing the struggle down to merely a weapons rivalry, and of bringing in the whole landscape of the political war, and the psychological matrix as well. To focus on the bomb or the missile alone means to see the weapons rivalry in a vacuum, removed from the complex living tissue of the world organism. The revolutionary nationalisms are a fact in the contemporary world; so is their exploitation in the world political war; so is the Grand Design within which Communist strategy operates; so is the rise of a new technological-military elite in every nation and power system; so is the political war and the prevalence of mistrust and fear. It is the sum of these facts, interacting with the fact of nuclear and BCR weapons, which has generated the deadly spiral.

The spiral effect involves a high degree of cumulative self-generating energy toward a reluctantly willed goal. Take for example, in the deterrence system, the way limited (minimum) deterrence tends always to become "credible first-strike" deterrence, which in turn is always in danger of becoming overdeterrence, or a miscalculated show of strength. I am not suggesting, however, that this happens in a political or psychological vacuum, through some mystique of the weapons themselves; it happens in the context of fear, tension and political warfare, which I described above. It is exactly because of this context that the bugbear of the military theorists, the "escalation" of a limited and localized war into a big general one, is always possible. I go farther and say that the escalation principle does not start operating only when a small war starts; it is present from the beginning and is inherent in the whole spiral, whether you call it escalation or (more complexly) the cumulative self-generating spiraling effect.

What makes the whole pace dizzier is the principle of obsolescence and archaism. Here again I do not restrict obsolescence to weapons or even to whole weapons systems. The idea of "weapons generations," of which the scientists speak, is a dramatic way of expressing the fact that weapons which seemed dazzlingly new five years ago have today become archaic, and those which are new today will be archaic in five years. The weapons themselves seem to be calling the turn: their logic of development pre-empts much choice on what to do about them. In fact, something like a weapons culture (as Ralph Lapp puts it) is emerging. But weapons strategies also become archaic, as do the larger world political strategies in which they are imbedded. Thus, there may be an interaction of archaisms: the "leapfrogging" strategy of the Communists, in place of their rim-nibbling strategy, made containment archaic; the Russian H-bomb development made massive retaliation archaic; the Russian and Chinese food failures, and then the Cuban, punctured a hole in the myth of inevitable Communist triumph, and even in the mystique of Russian science used as a strategy; the guerrilla warfare in Laos and South Vietnam killed the monolithic phase of nuclear deterrence and confirmed a multideterrence strategy for the free-world power system.

Haplessly there are no obsolescences of fear, but a continuum of varying intensity, depending on the mood of the negotiations dialogue and the varying fortunes of the political war. I must note, however, that at no time in history has there been anything comparable to the interaction of psychological elements in today's world power struggle. Thus, nuclear diplomacy, in the sense of missile rattling and vaunting of lethal nuclear capabilities, has become a recurring feature of the Russian political warfare, in the effort to drive wedges through NATO, scare the faltering members of the American power cluster, and reassure the faltering members of the Russian. Defense Secretary McNamara has developed the doctrine of an overwhelming counterforce which will spare Soviet cities if the Russians will spare American cities, but is capable of wiping out cities and populations and missile sites together, with something left over. Thus he has unwaveringly responded to Russian threats and boasts with a hair-raising recital of American retaliatory punitive power and survival power and a deflating appraisal of the Russian death-dealing claims. The spectrum of colorful psychological warfare shades from threats into blackmail—the ultimate threat of annihilation unless the specific demands are met on a specific occasion. Thus, while threats and boasting are chronic to the nuclear psychological warfare, blackmail is best seen as a calculated part of a particular episode, whether in a conjectural "game" or "scenario" in games theory or in some actual, future historic occasion.

I have spoken of escalation, obsolescence, threats, boasting, blackmail, all of them interacting elements in the missile-fear spiral. I might add the secrecy neurosis and the spy-hunting neurosis, the

dread of surprise, the arts of "chicken," and finally the formless-
ness of fear itself.

The secrecy neurosis is prescriptively Communist, flowing from
the conspiratorial experience of Communist movements and internal factional struggle, and from the closed society of Communism;
it also has national roots in Russian and Chinese history. Not only
is it a hindrance in getting effective inspection for arms control,
but it also leads the Russians and Chinese to hug suspicions long
after there is any substance in them. The spy-hunting neurosis is
common to Russians and Americans. The Russians, with their own
far-flung espionage organization, have learned to spot espionage and
dramatize it in episodes like the trial of the U-2 pilot, Francis
Powers; the Americans, in addition to their spy and counterspy
agencies, generated a do-it-yourself spy-catching organization in the
McCarthy era and seem bent on repeating that sorry performance
through local vigilante groups like the John Birch Society and
other outcroppings of paranoid fear and frustration. Needless to
add, the Russians, too, have their hysterical and paranoid groups.

There is a sense in which espionage, as a way of discovering and
estimating your opponent's capabilities, is a stabilizing element in
the deterrence system. In the farthest reaches of intelligence the
sky-and-spy satellites have replaced much of the earlier and more
pedestrian spy apparatus. What would be unsettling is the dread
that even these surveillance machines could not give an adequately
early warning of approaching missiles. This dread of an exposed
and helpless nakedness to destruction is part of the formless fear
I spoke of above. Whole civilian populations have thus become
hostages, with the added nuance that efforts toward civilian defense
may seem fruitless or may even be interpreted by one's opponent
as evidence of intransigence, with the resulting blackmail of destroying them without a chance of warning. I speak of civil populations because the pervasive fear is theirs. The military leaders are
more worried by an attack without warning which will get through
to their missile sites and nuclear forces.

This is the climate of fear. When President Roosevelt said in
his first inaugural, "The only thing we have to fear is fear itself," he
implied that fear could be faced and disposed of; but in the case
of the missile spiral, fear is the central psychological element of
the whole process, and to separate it from the rest and dispose of it
is exactly what is so hard. Even courage, in which Roosevelt saw
the resolution of the fear of the Depression era, becomes in the
context of the missile spiral a new element of danger. Both Lord

Russell and Herman Kahn, grim antagonists in the battle of strategies for the Age of Overkill, agree that the deterrence struggle can
be likened to the game of "chicken" played by delinquent boys with
souped-up jalopies. In this game it is the boy who dares to dare, in
the calculus of near-collisions, bluffs and brinkmanship, who may
either bring disaster or come off the victor. Thus, daring plays into
the hands of terror, and a cloud of fear envelops all. If the spiral
is ever broken it must be by the pooled intelligence of the contestants, not by either their fear or their bravado. The intelligence
which is required can be mustered only by men with a sense of the
tragic entrapment in which they are all caught.

5. "Don't Touch Me"

IT MAY SEEM to the reader that the old system of classical power politics, which was expelled at the door, has come back through the
window, with a new death's-head grin on its face, and that we are
now back where we were in the balance-of-power era, with a new
front on the house of death, but with war still functioning as the
final arbiter of the destinies of nations—war as it never was envisaged by Machiavelli, Marx, Clausewitz, or any of their successors.

Yet this is again only a half-truth. The fact is that, ever since the
Age of Overkill began at Los Alamos and Hiroshima, there has not
been a war of atomic weapons. A historical diversion may be in
order here. How has it happened, we may ask, that the atomic weapons have remained unused for seventeen years (at present writing)
after their first use? By every standard of social and political science,
this ought to be an easy question to answer, yet it is one of the hardest. If we knew the answer, we might know how to continue the warless atomic era, at least for a longish stretch.

The basic question is how much of it was due to the deterrent
effect of the weapons themselves, how much to self-restraint, how
much to a reciprocal feeling-out of the postwar redistribution of
power, how much to implicit understandings of what would be permitted and what would not be tolerated on either side.

Clearly the deterrence principle did not operate straight off. There
was a brief period after World War II when America had exclusive
possession of atomic power. Nothing in Marxist theory, nor for that
matter in the Machiavellian theory of classical power politics, will
quite explain why President Truman and his chiefs of staff failed to
use the threat of their monopoly advantage to clear Russian Com-

munism off the world stage or to prevent Chinese Communism from entering it. By Machiavellian precept, a prudent prince, after combining with a weaker enemy to destroy a stronger one, then turns to destroy his former ally, now doubly vulnerable by the fact of being weakened and at a weapons disadvantage. By Marxist theory, the greatest of the "capitalist-imperialist" powers—prosperous, far from exhausted by its war effort, relatively unaffected by manpower losses —should have had few inhibitions about hemming in or wiping out the greatest of the "socialist" powers. At the very least, the Americans could have undone the military-political miscalculations which Chester Wilmot, in his impressively argued study *The Struggle for Europe,* assigned to the Allied treaty-makers, and could have forced the withdrawal of Russian power from its new Eastern European territory before it could entrench itself. It is not clear whether the American failure to act thus was due to humanist scruples or to Truman's continuation of the Roosevelt policy of candor and friendliness toward Stalin, or to an ignorance of the true nature of Russia's expansionist Grand Design. The fact is that the American conscience or ignorance, or both, did operate. Whether Stalin would have acted similarly in the same monopoly position is anyone's guess, but everything in his record speaks against it.

By the time Russia got its first atomic weapons the coalition honeymoon was over and the cold war was well under way. American energies in it were directed toward containment (Truman Doctrine) and economic aid (Marshall Plan). Russian efforts were directed toward consolidating Communist power in Eastern Europe and testing Western tenacity in the Berlin blockade. But both before and after the Russians broke the atom secret, by espionage and technological will, neither side used the nuclear violence available to it. The Americans may have been tempted during the years of their monopoly; certainly there was a preventive-war school of American strategic thinking, but it never became persuasive. Even aside from humanitarian scruples, one may ask realistically what America would have done with a radioactive sixth of the globe's surface. By the time both camps developed the H-bomb, it was too late for preventive war by either. The terror element had begun to operate.

Even before the terror element, however, some inhibition operated to keep each side from the final act. Neither the Allied intervention in Greece nor the Communist seizure of Czechoslovakia led to open war between Russia and America. The Berlin blockade and the Western airlift might have done so, but Stalin withdrew. He might have carried out the subjugation of the Yugoslavs when Tito

was expelled from the Cominform in 1948, but again he faltered. The West in turn had its chance for intervention during the great East German strikes of 1952; it did not dare, despite the cries for a "liberation" policy from those who felt that containment was not enough.

In the Korean War, when direct Russian intervention might have meant a world conflict, Russia refrained and the war was kept limited. In the Indochina crisis America in turn was tempted to massive intervention, but finally held back. In the Formosa crisis of 1955, the Chinese failed to win Russian assurance of nuclear support and had to hold back from the ultimate test. The year 1956 was a dangerous one, when the Polish and Hungarian revolutions and the Suez crisis might have led to nuclear war. Of the three, Hungary was the litmus-paper test: the West had high stakes in a successful revolution of a Communist satellite, and a measure of Western military support might have spelled success for the revolution. But the Russians showed that they meant business and were ready for massive war and its consequences in a crisis involving their whole imperium. After that test the principle was clear on both sides, and the second Formosa crisis, the second Berlin crisis, the Sino-Indian border crisis and the sealing of East Berlin and East Germany were further illustrations of the central principle.

How shall we state it? To call it deterrence is to miss the nonmilitary complexity of it. For the fact is that it was not only the fear of war which caused the withdrawals from the brink. Each side was feeling out both the new limits of territorial commitment after the postwar redistribution of power, and the limits of tolerance beyond which neither side dared go. The recital of litmus-paper points, testing the deadly serious earnestness on each side, should have made clear that despite the terrors of modern war there are some issues where one side or the other has a breaking point. It is the point at which, in effect, it says *Noli me tangere*—Don't touch me! Thus far and no farther!

Thus, the American response to the Berlin blockade in 1948–49 and to Russian pressure in 1961 made it clear that the Berlin issue was a showdown issue. In the Polish and Hungarian revolts, the Russians in turn made it clear that Moscow's hold over the satellites was a fighting issue and that a "rollback" policy by the West would lead to trouble. In the Suez war there was a widespread, perhaps mistaken, belief that Russia had threatened a resort to nuclear weapons. Nor can there be much doubt, whatever America's final policy toward Castro's Cuban regime, that any direct Russian military intervention which the Americans regarded as a threat to their security would be considered a fighting issue.

I have spoken of the *don't-touch-me* imperative, because too often we talk and think as if the deterrence principle operates in a historical and political vacuum. It doesn't. It operates, as I suggested earlier, within the total frame of political war between the two great power systems. In this political war there is a constant probing of each other's power intentions and commitments. Sometimes the political war becomes a military one, as in Korea, Algeria, Laos and South Vietnam, and then there is always the danger of its getting out of hand, like a jinni that has escaped from its prison-jar. But remember that the Korean and Algerian wars, both unconscionably protracted, did not "escalate" into a nuclear one because neither was a don't-touch-me area; and the guerrilla fighting in South Vietnam was a safety-valve affair, in which both sides could push hard on principle, without much danger of starting something they could not end.

In the probing process, the don't-touch-me areas and issues mark out the limits of tolerance on each side. Much has been said for and against the principle of ambiguity—that of allowing your opponent to guess what your response will be to his provocation—but any ambiguity on the score of the don't-touch-me areas would be a fateful risk to take. It is clarity, rather than ambiguity, which works for peace (or a "stable deterrence") on such issues. Yet it does contain an element of danger in the very fact of its encouraging a commitment so firm that it may become overrigid, or a defense stance from which there is no retreat. There is also a danger that in the name of don't-touch-me commitments one of the power centers will take what amounts to a blackmail position, counting on wresting concessions through the appearance of intense emotional involvement with the area or issue. Thus one gets back, as always in the deterrence universe, to the point where a force whose impact on the whole is a stabilizing one becomes an unsettling one.

6. Hic Sunt Dracones

THE SPECTER that haunts the world, or at least the heads of state and the chiefs of staff of the present nuclear powers, is the prospect of a widely diffused nuclear technology. There are today ten nations spending over a billion dollars a year on a military budget, and twenty-five spending between a hundred million and a billion.

The diffusion of nuclear weapons has not gone as fast as was expected in the late 1950s, but it seems highly likely that by 1970 all ten of the nations in the billion-dollar class will have nuclear capability, and perhaps four or five of those in the hundred-million class. As long as Russia and the American-British-French complex were the only power entities with nuclear striking power, each could pace the other, watch over the other, and in a grim paradoxical way even control the other. But what will the chances be for a self-adjusting equilibrium when at least a dozen nations will have the power to turn the bi-polar weapons struggle into a free-for-all nuclear melee? What happens then to safety-by-deterrence? What happens when the "nth nation"—the marginal one that topples the balance—gets nuclear power?

The crucial problem involves the locus of decision. Where there are only two decision centers the idea of a balance of terror can operate tolerably, since the leaders at each center have their attention focused on each other and the world's attention is focused on both. But with a dozen centers of nuclear decision, the diffusion is not only one of weapons but of attention and controls. A Russia which has a monopoly of nuclear weapons within the Communist power system may continue to have the final word in doctrinal and power struggles within the system, even when a rival Communist power like China arises to dispute its primacy. But when China can make its own nuclear weapons, and perhaps East Germany and Czchoslovakia as well, there is no longer a focused control. This applies equally to the free-world power systems. In 1962 the American leaders became intensely disturbed by the French bid to become an independent nuclear power, fearing that France's atomic weapons might be provocative without being strong enough to act as a deterrent force. America would be equally disturbed if Germany or Japan, Brazil or Mexico or Spain were to achieve nuclear capability. And it applies even more to nations in the "neutralist bloc," such as Egypt, India and Yugoslavia.

The fact is that Russia and America have been, since World War II, basically conservative power systems—conservative in the sense that they are both *"have"* nations rather than *"have-nots,"* and it is in their interest to keep the world in which they are dominant from being blown to pieces or poisoned by radiation beyond viability. But among the ten or more nuclear nations in the near future there are almost certain to be a number whose leaders are political gamblers and overreachers, ready for adventure even at the risk of widespread destruction.

The calculus of consequences of nuclear diffusion is not merely a matter of unbased fears in an age of atomic jitters. It turns on the convergence of two revolutionary forces: a revolutionary weapons technology and a revolutionary world. "If men were angels," wrote James Madison in Number 51 of the *Federalist Papers*, "no government would be necessary." But one need not dream of a polity of angels in order to regard the calculable future with a measure of confidence. Even if the tolerably *un*angelic men who sit today in the seats of the mighty among Russian and American policy planners were to continue in their present condominium over world politics, one could look toward the future with some measure of confidence. But as the weapons are diffused, the unangelic will have to reckon with the paranoid, the schizophrenic, the megalomaniac.

There will be greater danger that nuclear or biological weapons will be used as blackmail, or that some impetuous move of a frustrated leader and nation will bring a chain reaction of massive war, or that the inadvertent will become the ungovernable. There is a greater chance also for what has been called a "catalytic war," in which a small third nation, either by accident or design, sets in motion an incident which catalyzes a war between the great powers. All the nationalist passions of a world revolutionary nationalism, in which untried states and leaders come to exercise sovereignty, will complicate the processes of world power politics. With limited war budgets the tendency, for older as well as newer states, will be to get great striking or deterrent power as cheaply as possible. And all the present difficulties of achieving a meeting of minds for arms control will become even more difficult.

I have thus far spoken of diffusion as the first and most urgent danger of a nuclear war in the calculable future. I add to it a number of other possibilities, more or less urgent.

There is the possibility of war by accident or inadvertence—by a blunder out of jittery overreaction to an enemy move or out of failure of communication between nuclear powers. This danger has increased with the advent of missiles. We must remember that war has become highly mechanized, that alertness to danger and readiness of response are the prime qualities being stressed in the war machine, and that human beings remain fallible. Nevil Shute's widely read novel, *On the Beach*, which may be taken as a layman's documentary of how the nuclear war may come, adopts the blunder-of-overreaction method.

The possibilities of accident have often been discussed in the

recent literature on deterrence and arms control. A weapon-carry-
ing plane might accidentally plunge into enemy territory at a
moment of tension between the two nations; even if it crash-landed
in territory belonging to an American ally close to Russia, like
Thailand or Turkey, the Russians might believe it had been intended for them. A trigger-happy colonel or commissar might give
the wrong order in the brief push-button interval between the
sighting of enemy craft and the verification of their nature. There
was a classic episode when an American watcher mistook a flock of
geese on the radar screen for a fleet of Soviet bombers and raised
an alarm which fortunately was corrected in time. There was
also a 1952 episode when sighted vapor trails, a careless observer,
a telephone line failure and a flight of B-47's off course, met in
weirdly improbable convergence, alerted the Air Defense Command
and the Joint Chiefs of Staff and even awoke President Truman;
and a less serious 1962 episode which brought Strategic Air Command planes out on the runways. Military alertness, usually a virtue,
becomes a disease when it can inadvertently trigger the collision of
two massive weapons systems poised for response to attack. The
danger of war lies less in a planned surprise attack than in an un-
planned overreaction to the fear of such an attack. When a heavy
premium is placed on "reciprocal pre-emptive surprise"—on antic-
ipation of the enemy's move before it can deliver a knockout
blow—who can exclude the element of blunder arising out of atomic
jitters?

This leads to a third possibility—the escalation of a limited or
brush-fire war into a nuclear war. The United States has rejected
its stance of the 1950s, with the excessive reliance upon nuclear
weapons, which left the free-world power system powerless to answer
fomented insurrections and guerrilla wars on their own level. In its
place has come a pluralist system which (in Defense Secretary
McNamara's words) "insures a response graded by degrees, by
geographical and political area, and by target type, as would be
appropriate to the type and extent of an enemy attack." This is
technical language for saying that a great-power system today
must be as prepared for small wars as for large, and may better
avoid the large ones by being ready to fight the small ones. There
is even a persisting dream (Edward Teller is the latest to champion
it) of using clean small ("tactical") nuclear weapons in limited
wars, which are kept limited by readiness to use the greater nuclear
deterrent. One can pay tribute to the McNamara doctrine of pluralist defense readiness and of the small war as safety valve, without

forgetting the real dangers of escalation. Small wars are always teetering on the brink of becoming big ones. The Korean War for a time trod a dangerous marginal line between small and big. The Indochinese war came close to nuclear intervention. It would be difficult to think of a Middle East war, after Suez, as a safely limited one. And if open war broke out between China and India, in the mountain fastnesses of Ladakh, Bhutan, Sikkim or Nepal, it would doubtless start as a war of limited arms deployed on an impossible terrain—but would it end thus? If the more destructive weapons are at hand, and if one state is hard pressed, it will use them, whatever the theorists may say.

The fourth, and most likely, source of a nuclear war is one which arises from the mutual probing of vital security interests and must thus be called a war of miscalculation. I have already spoken of the nerve-end issues and the don't-touch-me areas of power sensitivity. We live in the precarious interval between the historic past when a nation could pursue its national security without irreparable disaster for the world, and the not impossible future when its national security will have been merged with the collective security. It is in this interval that the leaders of great nations must canvass their minds as to where they will draw the line of nuclear tolerance, and calculate where their opponents are likely to draw their own line. A crisis situation could thus arise over a Berlin, a Formosa, a Cuba —wherever one of the world power centers feels that its vital security interest has been intolerably threatened. All nuclear diplomacy becomes thus an exercise in brinkmanship, and life in the modern world becomes a matter of watching two wrestlers at the edge of a pit of darkness.

I have spoken of the dangers of a nuclear war arising from *diffusion of weapons,* from *inadvertence* or *blunder,* from *escalation,* from *miscalculation.* A fifth and final, although not the most likely, danger flows from a deliberate decision to wage a *preventive or pre-emptive war.* By the nature of the deadly weapons-fear spiral, there is a not negligible temptation on each side to seize some moment of temporary weapons superiority or world political position and strike a surprise blow. Conceivably this decision might be made even by the leaders of a nation who know they are at a weapons disadvantage, but who feel their relative armed strength or world political position slipping further, see no prospect of the tide turning, and count on the element of surprise to equalize their disadvantage. From the danger standpoint, it is indifferent whether the propulsion comes from a swaggering sense of present strength or from the fear of being further outstripped. It may be rationalized by sheer national interest, or by some theory of national destiny, or, as in the possible case of Communist China, by the theory of an inevitable showdown with the "capitalist-imperialist" world, made more palatable by the prospect of a "beautiful civilization" which can be constructed on the ruins of this one.

I do not want to leave the impression that such a deliberate decision could come only from madmen because it could never be to a nation's authentic interests to start a war which might mean the suspension of history for several generations. It is possible for a group of leaders, caught in the deadly spiral, to find the line hazy between a tough-minded readiness for defense and an overtough (and overfearful) readiness for striking first. This is where the much discussed "self-fulfilling prophecy" becomes relevant: Those who persistently prophesy that the enemy will strike first may generate the conditions where he does; actually, the fearer-phophesier may even rationalize himself into making the first strike, on the ground that otherwise his enemy will get an intolerable advantage. In fact there is a sense in which there is an element of pre-emptive war in the decision of any groups of national leaders to start a war. In all the sources of war danger I have mentioned, there is the added element of the involvement of a strategic elite of military, scientific and corporate or party leaders whose vested ideas have become entangled with the deadly spiral, even if their vested interests can be shown to be free of it.

Thus, the balance of terror must reckon with the margin of error, miscalculation, blindness. The medieval cartographers, before the great voyages of discovery and exploration began to chart the sea courses and open the continents, marked on their maps what was known about the earth. But in the still unknown portions they would sometimes put the motto *"Hic sunt dracones."* What I have set down above amounts to the same kind of warning about the still-uncharted areas of future destructiveness. "Here are dragons." Here are some of the ways—categorized with a detachment which falsifies my own sense of concern and recoil—by which the fearful may in fact occur, the feared come true.

Since we fear most what we must face and we turn away from it because of its fearful character, it follows that we must face what we fear.

7. *The Intolerable, the Impossible, and the Faustian Question*

FEARS BREED wishfulness, and the reliance upon the balance of terror as a sure form of safety-through-stalemate strikes me as largely wishful blindness. The reasoning is that a suicidal war which will destroy humanity is intolerable to contemplate and therefore it will not take place.

Perhaps I shall be permitted a personal note here. For a time during World War II, I was a correspondent with the American First Army and then with the Ninth. It was conventional warfare, in the idyllic prenuclear era. Four years after the war's end, in 1949, I returned to Germany and went inevitably to the crematorium at Dachau, where 283,000 people—mostly Jews—had been gassed and burned. As I sat in the big furnace room at Dachau, with the furnace open and the names of victims scrawled later by loved ones on the walls, I thought about history and the human condition. I tried to puzzle out how a segment of a great people, with a towering intellectual tradition and a heritage of philosophy, science, theology, had committed these enormities, while the rest either had preferred not to know about them, or—knowing—had felt complacent or helpless.

There was no answer to the puzzle, but there was a moral: The intolerable is not by that fact impossible. A number of times in history the intolerable has happened. It can happen again. I have set down some of the ways in which it may, conceivably, happen. I have also said that for the first time in human history men have bottled up a power (that of overkill) which they have thus far not dared to use.

But to say that it is surplus power is not to say that it will remain bottled up. The fact that governmental leaders have thus far not dared to use it does not mean that they will not dare use it in the future. True, its use would be absurd, but there is an even greater element of the absurd in politics than in the rest of life. Thus far the restraint in abstaining from this surplus power of death has been a matter of leadership, will, moral recoil. But there still are no built-in controls to guard against possible failures of leadership, will and morality in the future.

To find the hope for peace in an illusory picture of a warless world since World War II is simply unhistorical. Actually, the generation after Hiroshima was a generation of war turbulence. Europe saw a civil war in Greece, an uprising in Hungary, an army coup in Turkey, and tension over the Saar, Trieste, Berlin. The Middle East saw revolutions in Egypt and Iraq, the absorption and later the breaking away of Syria, an Arab-Israeli war, the short but intense Sinai and Suez campaigns, civil war and the landing of American forces in Lebanon. Asia saw civil war and revolution in China, an international war in Korea, communal riots and bloodshed in India and Pakistan, colonial wars in Indochina and Malaya, a revolution in Nepal, tension over Kashmir and over the Sino-Indian border, tension over Formosa and the bombardment of the offshore islands, an uprising and its suppression in Tibet, student riots and revolt in South Korea, guerrilla war in Laos and South Vietnam. Africa saw colonial wars in Kenya and Algeria, a bloody clash over the Bizerte base in Tunis, violence in the Belgian Congo, repression in South Africa and Angola, flaring unrest across the continent. In South America revolutions and coups have continued to be endemic, with notable episodes in Guatemala, Colombia, Venezuela, Argentina, Peru, the Dominican Republic and Cuba.

Thus this era is as crowded with violence, tension and bloody encounters as almost any in history. The moving forces behind them can be so isolated: the bursting of an old social order; the opening of whole continents to the impact of Western science and technology and to Western ideas of class conflict, independence and nationhood; the flaring of revolutionary movements which borrowed these ideas and techniques from the West, but turned them passionately against the West; the march of Communist power, equipped with a Grand Design, imbued with a conviction of its inevitable victory, and aided by Soviet arms and revolutionary propaganda; the clash of this expansive force with an aroused will to resist on the part of the democratic world; the explosion of new nation-states within a triple frame of conflict—a weapons spiral, a short-of-war political struggle, and a battle of propagandas.

Given this violence and turbulence, it is a near-miracle that the dreaded over-all war has not broken out—at least, not yet. To some extent it was due to self-restraint on the part of leaders and people among the nuclear powers and a saving suicide-recoil in the spirit of the age. Russia had Stalin and Khrushchev as leaders during most of the period; both of them were shrewd and ruthless, but the first was power-intoxicated toward the end, while the second had a conservative strain amidst his energy and bluster. America had Truman and Eisenhower; the first was brisk and decisive within limited perspectives, the second was vague and at times inattentive to the great demands of his job, yet possessed of a passionate will to peace. China had Mao and Liu, revolutionaries with an implacable will, more intent on transforming China and making it a great power than on achieving peace, yet also subject to the inhibiting strains and tensions of an internal power struggle with Russia inside the world Communist system. As for England and France, under Churchill, and De Gaulle and the lesser men, economic and political reconstruction and the flowering of new creative energies kept them preoccupied with problems of a different sort. But mainly the inhibitions were due to the destructiveness of the weapons themselves— apart from the self-restraint of the leaders—and the warning signals put out by each side against excessive encroachment on the nerve-end areas. In this sense the balance of terror has in fact worked in the generation since Hiroshima: overt military aggression has been contained, large-scale violence has been averted.

It was thus an era of wars, but of limited wars. It was an era when men fought with limited weapons while contriving unlimited ones, an era in which they carried out underkill while they prepared or strove for the weapons of overkill, an era when the leaders of the nuclear powers were caught between lethal weapons which they dared not use and positions from which they could not bring themselves to recede. "If you do that, we'll do this," each warned the other, as if to underline the fact that both were caught in a mutual embrace of attraction and hostility which neither dared to break. If we ask, "Whom will the deterrent deter?" the answer must be, "Only those who play the game." Deterrence deters only so long as both sides know the game thoroughly—as the medieval knights knew the rules of the tourney, or the Japanese No players the traditions of their dramatic form—and act out their roles accordingly.*

But what happens when a nation comes into the nuclear phase and scorns the rules? Not necessarily out of inhumanity, but perhaps out of a conviction that it is a special carrier of humanity, a historically chosen vessel entrusted with a mission more sacred than the life or death of a number of people at a particular time, and therefore immune to the general recoil from nuclear weapons? When the People's Republic of China assumes membership in the Nuclear Club, will its leaders accept the rules thus far operative among the

---

* For a discussion of unilateral disarmament and various forms of a psychological "peace initiative," along with the prospects of arms control, see Chapter VI, especially Section 2, "Dialogue against Death," and Section 7, "Fear and Conscience in Atomic Man."

members? The apothecary in *Romeo and Juliet* is told that "the world is not thy friend, nor the world's law." Excluded from the UN, kept from rounding out territories they have regarded as rightfully their own, the Chinese Communists have felt alienated from the world community. They have put their reliance on the strength of their own collective will rather than upon any mutuality with either the Russian or the free-world system. But the will involved is unilateral, rather than the world will required for the collective security and survival of humanity as a whole.

Amidst these perspectives one cannot know how man will stumble along the Stations of the Cross on his thorny path to peace. But the fact is that, up to now, he has not fallen and still survives.

Consider what this means. One might frame an allegory along the lines of the great tradition of the Magus, before and after Faustus. The achievements of science today cannot be boxed within a compass any narrower than the Faustian bargain itself: What is your heart's dream? You shall have it.

Call up an apparition such as fascinated Marlowe and Goethe, when the Devil came to Faustus to strike the Faustian bargain. Suppose some daemon had come to man and said, "Here is your heart's desire, the dream you have been dreaming. This is what all your imaginings were about. This is what your philosophers have speculated on, your young men have dreamed of, your scientists have charted in the long vigils of the night. This is what your mathematicians have calculated and your poets have spun in their gossamer visions. Here is your utmost dream, your Helen, your gleaming city of the mind. Here it is, yours to possess and command. You have wanted the ultimate of power and mastery. Now you can put it into execution, and destroy those whom you hate, and incidentally the world, too. What are you going to do about it?"

Will the historian of man's bloody road record that at this moment, when the Faustian question was put to man, instead of grasping for the power he had dreamed about—man faltered? He will have to record, of course, that man had to pay a heavy price—how heavy we still do not know—for the gift of power he craved. But he will add that, in that act and in that moment of faltering, man moved beyond the power principle.

8. *The Passing of Classical World Politics*

I DO NOT CLAIM here that the principle of overkill has abolished or will abolish war, or that it has eliminated the operation of power within the frame of world politics. Freud pointed out, in *Beyond the Pleasure Principle,* that to move beyond something does not mean to leave it wholly behind; it may even mean to carry it along, but no longer as the decisive principle.

The operation of power by the sovereign state in a constellation of sovereign states, with all-out war as the final test of strength, was the decisive principle of the classical system of world politics. That is no longer possible if either the nation-state or the world of nation-states is to survive, even with diminished sovereignty.

The nation-state will continue to function as such for some time, not knowing that its base has been eroded. The alliance system will continue in feverish motion both in the form of the big ideological blocs and the smaller alliances in the Middle East and in Africa. The jungle of fear and hatred will continue to be a jungle, and the concept of the enemy will be kept alive, as a spur both to individual pugnacity and to national cohesion. The balance of power will continue to be pursued as an ideal for world equilibrium, in the transmuted form of the balance of terror. The deadly spiral of weapons rivalry will grow deadlier before it starts to unspiral. There will be alternating chills and fevers of the cold war and of warmer wars, and there will be brash talk of settling everything by the split-second decisiveness of a nuclear strike.

Yet it won't do. If there is one clear fact in the contemporary world it is the powerlessness of power when charged with overkill, and the failure of viability of a world of nation-states. War, which may have made some sense in the past, has now become the acme of the senseless. Like a frog whose head is severed but which still keeps jumping for a time, the classical system of world politics continues to behave with all the outward traditional forms. Yet it has been effectively undercut in its essence, because it can no longer provide a frame either of peace or of order for the world.

The alternatives become, then, either a new system which can provide that frame, or chaos.*

---

* For a discussion of these alternatives, see Chapter VI, "Beyond the Power Principle."

CHAPTER II

Power Center and Power Cluster

1. "Imperialism Is Dead, Long Live Empire!"

2. Ideas About Imperialism

3. Empire as Power Cluster

4. Power Center as Energy System

5. The Ice Age and the Political War

6. Neutralism and the Ghosts

7. Grandeurs and Miseries of Empire

CHAPTER II

Power Center and
Power Cluster

1. "Imperialism Is Dead, Long Live Empire!"

THE new weapons of the new age do not exist either in a power
vacuum or in a social and idea vacuum. They are wielded—by
whom? Mostly by the two great world empires of our time, which
are in part power masses and in part organizations of social energy.

An old world dies hard, even while a new one is being born. In
our anguished time the death throes and birth pangs are obscured
by the splitting of the world into two or perhaps three segments, and
by the dramatic struggles and maneuverings between them. We
might say that there are two and a half power systems today: The
free-world system, the Communist system, and the neutralist nations
which have little military strength and do not add up to a power
system, refuse virtuously to align themselves with either grouping,
but nevertheless seem to feel compelled to vote and act together
like a bloc, thus making a necessity out of their virtue.

I do not quite agree with the title of John Strachey's able book
The End of Empire. I should prefer to say that while a Copernican
revolution has indeed taken place in the history of imperialisms,
we are witnessing in our time not the end but the transformation
of empire.

The "end of empire" is the end of European imperialism as it
flourished since the eighteenth century, but mainly between 1870
and 1914, and it marks a shift of imperial axis. But it is not an end
of big power systems confronting and interacting with smaller ones
and with each other. Nor is it wholly an end even of imperialism,
since the aggressive expansion of power (which is the core meaning
of imperialism) continues. Put most simply, what happened was a
shift of axis from an imperialist Europe, which exploited and
developed the resources of the other continents, to a setup in which
the nuclear powers—America and Russia, both outside Europe—
became the big empires, while China with its incipient power and
its 700 million people strained to overtake them.

55

There was a second shift, not geographical but political. The struggle for larger domains and dominations is no longer primarily economic, as it seemed at the time when John A. Hobson and Lenin himself studied it in its classic form. When Communist Russia entered the world arena, the struggle became political and ideological —political, since it concerned the polity to be spread; ideological, since the weapons in the struggle became largely the ideas about the polity and its society, and the stakes of the struggle became the destruction or survival of one of the societies and its system of ideas and values. I should add that in the 1950s the drive toward empire became the drive of a nuclear as well as of a political and ideological imperative. The importance of being a great empire today rests on being a nuclear power with a capacity to build nuclear deterrents and enter into the charmed circle of the nuclear stalemate.

Let me say straight off that I distinguish between *imperialism* (at least in the old sense) and *imperium*, or empire. "Imperialism" has become a bad name, but bad or good it needs precise definition. I use the word to mean the aggressive expansion of power—the conquest or colonization, the exploitation or administration, of one people by another without consent. I might add, as a footnote, that this usually resulted in the enrichment of the exploiting nation or of groups within it, at the expense (although not necessarily the impoverishment) of the exploited. I use "empire" (*imperium*) to mean an actual, going power system, however it may have been built up—whether as a product of imperialism, or by ways less violent and exploitative; whether constitutionally, or by revolution or war. Any great historical power mass must be seen as imperium, or empire—Babylonian, Persian, Greek, Roman, Chinese, Mogul, Spanish, French, Dutch, British, German, Japanese, Russian, American. Every imperium is likely to be the end product of a process of imperialism, although the accretions of power may come by relatively innocuous ways, with a measure of consent.

Perhaps the difference can best be put by saying that in the old imperialisms of 1870-1914 the dominant forces were armies, proconsuls, missionaries, travelers, adventurers, archaeologists, ship captains. The empires of today must still reckon with armies, but mainly they are governed not by these men but by scientists, missile men, propaganda experts, specialists in planning and aid, technologists of every sort.

This is the Copernican revolution to which I have referred. It represents the new conditions for the survival of power masses in the world, in the interval between the classic system of nation-state-*cum*-imperialism which is dying and the transnational system of a world authority which has not yet been born.

Nothing in the past half century has aged more quickly than the once vigorous system of imperialism. If "imperialism" is applied only to what the British, French, Belgians, Dutch and Germans did in Africa and the East during the halcyon days of the "white man's burden," then we have indeed come to the end of the era of classical imperialism, although not of empire.

One thinks back to Winston Churchill's stubborn assertion, in November 1942, about empire. On being asked about British war aims, he answered, "We mean to hold our own"; and he added, "I have not become the King's First Minister in order to preside over the liquidation of the British Empire." But the fact is that after the war was over India did become free, and so did Burma and others. The British, French, Dutch, Belgian and Portuguese empires are now on the way out as empires; they have become historical relics.

The Russian and American empires are in the center of the stage, and waiting in the wings there may be an emerging Chinese empire —provided that it does not meet with further mishaps on the way like the famines and industrial breakdown of the early 1960s.

2. *Ideas About Imperialism*

IMPERIALISM and empire are as old as history, but the theories of both are a phenomenon of modern self-consciousness. As one might expect, there has been a lag between the reality and its shadow, between imperialism and the analysis of it. Yet, there are also evidences that the idea has created a reality to correspond to it, and to some degree the shadow has brought the substance into being.

John Hobson was a gentle, scholarly Englishman in the Manchesterian tradition who believed in an international system of free trade, free thought, and self-government for all. Lenin was a tough-minded, ruthless Russian revolutionary, with a commitment not to freedom for anyone or anything but to the liberation of humanity through a dictatorial proletarian class rule. One of the strange fateful partnerships of history was forged when Lenin, finding that Hobson related imperialism to the evolution of capitalism and its search abroad for the raw materials it needed, and for markets for the products of its machines it could not sell at home, seized upon

Hobson's analysis, annexed it and used it for his own purposes. Transmuted by Lenin's powerful mind it became, in his own book, *Imperialism: The Highest Stage of Capitalism.*

Both men saw the grinning death's head of finance capitalism behind the Great Power rivalry for resources and markets on the dark continents. Other theorists saw militarism as the driving agent which conscripted the economic systems and classes to its purposes, and some were certain that there was an alliance between the militarists and the industrialists. Still others put their emphasis upon the racist idea of the ethnic and cultural superiority of some particular stock, and therefore of its divine right to subject other and inferior stocks to its sway and lord it over a broad swath of the earth.

Most of these theories are more satisfying aesthetically, as self-contained constructions, than in any correspondence to social reality. The trouble with the Hobson-Lenin theory is that it turns the inherent nature of capitalism upside down in order to make it fit the premises of the theory. Any study of the classic case of pre-nineteenth-century imperialism—that of England and its American colonies—will reveal that it arose not out of the free-market needs of capitalism but out of the logic of a highly controlled precapitalist mercantilism. One has only to read the sections on the American colonial empire in Adam Smith's capitalist classic, *The Wealth of Nations,* to understand why the artificial contrivances of colonialism were anathema to the spirit of the new capitalism. True, the entrepreneurial class which came into power in Adam Smith's day used the doctrines of capitalist liberalism as the vestments of its power, and it was willing to seek profits wherever they might be found, even with the risks and rigors of distant climes. If greed is the essence of imperialism, then the necessary greeds were there. John Maynard Keynes once defined the capitalist spirit in terms of "a congeries of possessors and pursuers," and this cluster of eager seekers for pecuniary advantage were willing to annex profit-as-loot just as avidly as they annexed profit-as-managerial-returns.

The rub comes when the risks are no longer individual but national. The spirit of capitalism had historically been relatively peaceful rather than military, seeking to expand and conquer by the lure of affluence rather than by the sword. Businessmen as a class have had little stomach for the imperialist adventures which entail war and bring with them losses, liquidations, confiscations and hated governmental controls. The classic historic evidence of this is to be found in the American record. If America is the purest

distillation of the capitalist spirit in modern history, one would expect it to have been the supreme illustration and proof of the
Hobson-Lenin theory. But it is exactly on the rocks of the American
experience that the theory founders. Except for a brief inglorious
spell in the Philippines, in Cuba and in Hawaii at the turn of
the century, and for the "dollar diplomacy" of the 1920s, America
has stayed clear of the classic imperialist trauma. This is due not
to any superior virtue on the part of the American power groups,
but to the comparatively empty continental expanse which lay
around them almost for the taking, and to their reluctance for extra-
territorial adventures which might fail to pay off and would merely
mess things up for them at home.

The Hobson-Lenin thesis about the classical imperialism is based
on the twin doctrines of class struggle and capitalist accumulation,
and on the link between them. Presumably it is when the dialectic
of class struggle has reached the stage of a mounting surplus of
profits which cannot be channeled into the home market because of
the impoverishment of an exploited proletariat, that capitalism
seeks investment in backward areas and is willing to pay the price of
imperialist wars in order to safeguard those investments. The American example suggests that a high-consumption economy can be
tolerably content with the home market and with capital export,
without having to colonize or rule distant areas or involve itself in
colonial wars.

This does not mean that American business groups have refrained
from seeking to extend their own corporate empires beyond the
American national borders; the export of capital is a fact of a certain stage of capitalist development. But it need not flow from the
class struggle or issue in imperialist wars. In the American case,
while there is a democratic class struggle for the division of the
national product, the industrial workers have shared in the expanding high-consumption economy, and have found a way of living
with the middle class, and absorbing and influencing its mentality.
The investment of capital—whether in the other Americas of the
Caribbean and South American areas, or in Western Europe or in
Middle East oil or the China trade—has had consequences dramatically different from the colonial conquests and settlement of the
tropical areas by the British, French, Belgians or Dutch.

Unquestionably capitalist accumulation seeks profitable investment, and it may even (as in the case of the "dollar diplomacy" of
the 1920s) try to invoke military sanctions as safeguards, especially
where the area has been historically regarded as out of bounds for

the nationalist rivalries of the European powers. But while this kind of power complex, involved with investment export, presents political problems of its own, it has been the target of American liberal criticism and must be judged in its own context. We are unlikely to get fruitful results by confusing or identifying it with the nationalist imperialisms of Europe, which have a different context and which derive from the frustrations of a high-consumption economy rather than from its overflow, and from the claustrophobia of nations with a narrow economic base, as contrasted with the rich resources of a continental expanse.

This furnishes the clue to what is perhaps the most searching analysis of imperialism in the literature. Joseph Schumpeter, an Austrian economist who taught at Harvard in his later years, placed his stress on the psychological sources of European imperialist movements in countries whose political ambitions and hungers had outrun their resources, and for whom the drama of national glory had to be enacted on a broader stage with exotic trappings of empire. His subtle mind saw that the blame which Lenin and Hobson had placed on the financiers and the class of big entrepreneurs, belonged elsewhere. In his *Imperialism: a Sociological Analysis,* he links the energy needed for imperialist adventures with the religious fanaticisms that historically have come either with missionary religions like Islam and Christianity, or with the "civilizing" fanaticisms of movements which seek to bring the light of a superior culture or race to the inferior ones.

In recent times this fanaticism has come not from the traditional religions but from the new political religions of fascism and Communism. In the first case Schumpeter's reasoning would place the death's-head mask of imperialism not on the class of finance capitalism but on the amorphous middle class, alienated from production and from life, insecure, panicky with status panic, wreaking its frustrations upon helpless minorities. In the case of the Communists his argument (he wrote before the Russian Revolution) would place it upon a new dominant elite, which in the name of an exploited proletariat seeks new areas to conquer for its political religion of a classless Utopian world society.

It helps to clarify imperialism if you start with its types, something the Marxists with their single-key approach have scorned. There are *economic* imperialisms whose motive force is primarily trade, investment and profit. There are *military* imperialisms, for the glory of a conqueror and his conquering mission. There are *religious* imperialisms (conquerors with a sword for the glory of

God), by those who have a pipeline to His truth. There are *ideological* imperialisms (conquerors with a book or a doctrine), which may hold to their doctrine even amidst the dangers of overkill. Cutting across these categories one may speak (as Reinhold Niebuhr does) of *nationalist* imperialisms, which operate by the classical methods of power politics; and *universalist* imperialisms, which may be military, religious or politico-religious, but transcend the limits of power politics and have in them a strong mixture of the Utopian and the messianic.*

There is a musty, dusty tang to the Hobson-Lenin doctrines and their successors now, mainly because what they condemned or celebrated is archaic. The old theories still crop up in current writings, as in the Palme Dutt-Paul Baran thesis that the non-Communist countries cannot commit themselves to economic aid because their own high living standards depend on exploiting the undeveloped countries—a view that John Strachey makes a shambles of, in one of the best murder cases in the literature.†

But this already suggests that the inheritors of the old theories are now hunting different game. With the passing of the classical system of imperialism and the rise of the undeveloped world, the axis of discussion has shifted from one to the other. The controversies now rage around economic development, which is as it should be.‡ The danger is that in our recoil from the outmoded theories on imperialism we may forgo the chance to analyze the nature, sources and consequences of the imperium, or the imperial power cluster.

3. Empire as Power Cluster

THE OLD IMPERIALISM, then, is dead; but a new imperialism has emerged—the Communist brand—which may be called a *doctrinal* imperialism, adapting for it Edmund Burke's description of the French Revolution as an "armed doctrine." The old alliance system too is dead; in its place have come new power clusters which serve the same function as the old alliances, but are more realistically geared to the demands of the new world power confrontation. The dynamic of the old imperialisms was more or less naked

* For an analysis of the doctrinal-religious drive behind Communism as a power system see Chapter III, especially sections 4 through 7.

† See his *End of Empire* (1959), Chapter XIII, "Non-colonial Empires," pp. 195-203.

‡ See Chapter IV.

force, whether military, political or economic, while that of the new doctrinal imperialism is a mixture of anticolonialism, revolutionary nationalism, and Communist commitment, cemented by party cohesion and military force where necessary. The dynamic of the old alliance system was a jockeying for position among equals who found themselves in roughly the same community of interests or community of fears and greeds. The dynamic of the new power clusters is still a community of interests or of fears or greeds, but the members are not equals except in rhetoric—they form a loose grouping, of greater or lesser degrees of mutual dependency, around a power center.

I use the term "power center," because it focuses on the power nucleus at the core and its relation to what is around it. Thus the United States is a power center around which are grouped almost all the nations of the hemisphere, those of Western Europe, and others as far away from the center as Thailand, Pakistan, the Philippines and Australia. The Soviet Union too is a power center; around it are grouped the Communist satellites of Eastern Europe, and other nations from Cuba to China and North Vietnam.

Within these clusters there are epicenters of power, each with its own constellation, inside or outside the larger constellations. Thus China is a power center inside the larger cluster of world Communism, just as Russia is, with an extraordinary tension of dependence and hostility between them. The Chinese have a power cluster reaching from Albania to Laos. India is a power center despite the fact of its neutralism, or perhaps *because* of it, since it not only exercises a cultural sway over Southeast Asia but has a strong voice in the neutralist UN voting bloc. The United Arab Republic is a power center inside the Arab power cluster; Nigeria and Ghana are competing power centers in the new Africa; France and Britain are power centers of the nations in the British Commonwealth and the French Community, which even in independence maintain ties with London and Paris.

The idea of a power center has no meaning without the idea of *power cluster* around it. I prefer this concept to that of *alliance,* which belongs in the context of the classical system of world politics. I prefer it also to that of *coalition,* which is a wartime military grouping, and to that of *bloc,* which is mainly useful for voting behavior in a world parliamentary body like the UN.

Thus power center and power cluster are integral to each other and aspects of each other. A nation may be strong and viable, like Germany, Japan or Italy today; but without the penumbra of power that spreads beyond its borders it is not a power center. If the fascist allies had won World War II, Italy would have had a minor power cluster around it from Spain to Ethiopia and beyond, Japan would have had a "coprosperity sphere" throughout Eastern Asia and the Pacific, and Germany might have lorded it over half the world. Having lost, these three nations are powers without being power centers. One should add, however, that the economic power of West Germany is making it a potential power center for whatever European economic and political community may emerge in the years ahead.

Nor does only naked strength count, whether military or economic. I have spoken of India as a cultural and ideological power center, although its military might is not great and its economic burdens are heavy. The reach of the Catholic faith, despite Stalin's taunt about the Pope not having any divisions, makes Rome a power center without any formal political sovereignty. Tito's Yugoslavia has no power cluster of satellite nations around it, yet the Yugoslav idea—of a going workers' socialism, fused with an independent nationalism—is still a potential rallying point for Communist parties and nations of the future. By the same reasoning, Castro's Cuba—if it does not succumb to revolt, invasion and civil war—has a potential future as an agitational center for a Communist power cluster challenging that of the United States in the American hemisphere. In fact, even the Communist power cluster, with its Moscow center and its epicenters in Peking and perhaps Belgrade, gets its strength not only from the armies, resources and economies of Communist states, but from the eighty-one Communist parties over which Moscow and Peking exercise control. Power in the contemporary world struggle does not depend on contiguous territory, nor need it always involve sovereign governments. It derives as much from the capacity to build a network of propaganda and influence on a world-wide scale, and to channel directives for thought and action through them, as it does from the traditional power instruments of the states.

This disengagement of power from its historic military and political sources is part of the transformed landscape of world politics. It is at once a cause and a consequence of revolutionary nationalism, whose victories would have been impossible without the spread of the idea of national liberation on the "winds of change," and whose continued potential for revolutions threatens the power of the existing power systems. The dissolving force of ideas is such that there are no longer established power centers, only receding and emerging ones—those which are losing their hold on power, and those which are gaining a hold. A power cluster, whether American, Russian, Chinese, British, French, Indian, cannot think of itself in terms of an Establishment, but only in terms of a new grouping of resources and ideas which must either strengthen its appeal to the world or go down to defeat. Thus dynamism is not a monopoly of any particular political movement or creed, but has become an imperative of power survival in the world.

It is these conflicting and competing dynamisms which form the world political war, and exert pressures toward cohesion that corrode a good deal of the traditional image of national sovereignty. In the days when the nation-state was the unit of order and decision, one could speak of its sovereignty without too wry a smile at the gap between rhetoric and reality. Today that is scarcely possible. If sovereignty has much meaning, it has come to reside not in the nation-state but in the power cluster of which it forms a part. Hungary or Rumania, North Korea or North Vietnam, or East Germany, have little that could be called sovereignty since they are satellite states. The case of South Korea or Thailand, of Iran, Kuwait or Yemen, of Guatemala, of Togo or Gabon, is different, since these are client states with far more freedom of movement. Yet each nation of both groups shares its sovereign functions with the power cluster of which it forms a part, and which affords it an umbrella of protection against the storms of outer danger and internal disaffection.

One of the knottiest problems of analysis is whether the power clusters are in essence nationalist or ideological.* The classic form of this problem is the question that troubles historians of the growth of the Soviet and Chinese empires: Have Lenin, Stalin, Khrushchev, Mao Tse-tung been primarily nationalist or ideological leaders? Have they been spurred by the drive to add to the power and glory of Russia or of China, along the traditional lines of expansionism in each country, or did they have springs of motivation not to be paralleled in the history of the great Russian Czars and the Chinese dynastic rulers?

---

* For a further discussion, within the frame of Communist theory, see Chapter III, Section 4, "The Daemon and the Locomotive." One should note, despite my emphasis, that the relation between nationalism and doctrine is a shifting one in the history of Soviet conduct, as Hans Morgenthau has pointed out in a number of recent articles. The pragmatic bent in all three Russian leaders— Lenin, Stalin and Khrushchev—led each to shift from one to the other with shifting circumstances. See Chapter III, Section 3, "Domination and Accommodation."

While I do not underrate the nationalist motif in either instance, especially in an era of revolutionary nationalisms, I tend to see the newly emerging power clusters primarily as doctrinal. True, they use the traditional elements of national sentiment, as they use every other available resource. True also, a Russian or Chinese leader, an American or French leader, cannot get out of the skin of his national identity, or wholly break out of the pattern of the history and style of the nation of which he forms a part. This was truer of Stalin and De Gaulle than it was of Lenin and Franklin Roosevelt. Yet even in the extreme cases of nationalist leadership, as with Stalin and De Gaulle, while their impulses may have been deeply nationalist, the frame within which they had to operate was doctrinal. What I am saying is that Stalin could not have carried through his crash program of industrialization, or his annexation of new countries in Eastern Europe, if he had used only the appeal of Russian power and grandeur. He had to use the appeal and myth of the Communist idea. And even De Gaulle, with all his talk of French national grandeur, could have done nothing in holding together the residual power of the French Community if he had not used the idea of freedom, economic growth, and cultural greatness as his principal dynamic.

Thus, it is not only the Communist empires which are "ideological," but every power cluster, in the sense that its appeal is no longer to the greatness of a single nation but to the survival and growth of an idea. What American leader could hold together the power cluster of the Latin American and West European countries around the United States as a power center if he were the leader only of an American nationalism? Nor is this merely a matter of rhetoric. The hard fact is that the crucial decisions made at the power center must be made with some participation by the other partners, in the interests of the cluster as a whole. In the extreme case of Russia and China, the Communist power cluster, during 1961–62, broke in two and became polycentric. The split may prove a temporary rift, may deepen and widen into a chasm, or may remain an uneasy and unresolved split.

But the very difficulty of guessing at the outcome underscores the continuing flux of relations in all power clusters. Nor can the American power center take for granted its relations with free-world peoples in Europe, Latin America or Asia: it must constantly refashion the connecting links. There is an important difference, however, between the power situations. In the case of free-world relations a complex polycentric power cluster is possible without hostility. The movement toward a Coal and Steel Community, a Common Market, a Euratom or even a United States of Europe, is bound to sharpen the focus of a European power center. The same is true of the growing regional consciousness of the Latin-American nations, which are unlikely to remain content with Washington as their power center, but will probably develop their own—perhaps with the Mexican-Brazilian-Argentine triangle as its focus, much like the British-French-German triangle in Europe. But both the European and Latin American power groupings are likely to be cases of cooperative rivalry with the United States power center, rather than the antagonistic rivalry which applies to Moscow, Peking and Belgrade.

One reason for the antagonistic rivalry may be in the nature of Communist doctrine: Russia and China each has a Grand Design, and thus each is universalist in its inherent drive and will not feel fulfilled until it has achieved world power, or at least power over the Communist world. Thus, the differences in the power-cluster rivalries within the free world and the Communist world reflect the differences between the internal power struggles of open and of closed societies.

It is in this universalist sense that one may apply to the world Communist movement the often-suggested term, "Third Rome." The first Rome aimed at a political and administrative empire over the world, the second Rome at a religious empire. The "Third Rome" seeks to combine them, using the drive of a political religion, but consolidating every conquest through political and administrative forms. It is worth noting that the idea of a "Third Rome" comes out of the history of Pan-Slavism as a movement, and was part of pre-revolutionary Russian history before Lenin turned the political religion of Communism into a totalitarian movement aiming at world power. The United States has also at times been thought of as a new Roman empire and the inheritor of the Roman organizational genius. But what it has lacked thus far is the capacity to turn its sense of doctrinal mission, which has been present in its history from the start, into a political religion.*

One of the best instances of its ineptness in this area is the American willingness to use "the West" as descriptive for the power cluster which opposes world Communism. To the revolutionary nationalisms of Asia, Africa and the Middle East, where

---

* On the concept of the "Contemporary" (in Spengler's sense)—what today corresponds to Greece, to Rome, to the barbarians—see my *America as a Civilization* (1957), Chapter II, Section 2, and Chapter XII, Section 7.

so much of the decision in the world political war will lie, "the West" has overtones not only of provincialism but of imperialism as well. When Americans come to understand how deeply doctrinal the weapons of power as well as the stakes of power must be, and how world-wide in scope both of them must be, they will be extremely chary of a term so repugnant to at least two thirds of the world.

The Communists speak of their movement as "socialist" and "proletarian." Only a term as radical as these—terms like "freedom" and "democracy"—can meet their challenge. I find "free world" the most usable, being world-wide in its scope, with both goal and method converging upon freedom, so that it suggests the total spread and inner spirit of its power cluster, whether the nations involved be West or East, and whatever the degree of their development toward democracy.*

4. *Power Center as Energy System*

IT IS TIME NOW to examine the power center itself and ask how it came to play its present role and what forces shaped it to its destiny. Each imperium is to be seen crucially as an energy system, drawing in and storing up social energy, attracting the energies of others toward itself, using its energy to extend its reach and power.

We may get at it best historically. America started on its great adventure in nation building at a time when revolutionary nationalism had barely begun and when mass democracies did not exist. It had to improvise whatever ideas and techniques it did not borrow from Britain and Western Europe. It started with a huddle of scraggly colonies, an economy kept deliberately colonial by its imperial masters, a few ships and wharves, a continental expanse barely explored and mostly unsettled. In little more than a century and a half it grew to its present position among the powers of the earth. It had land and rich resources, some people with skill and brains, isolation between two oceans, and a wild sense of its destiny

* Let me stress that the use of the term "free world" to apply to states like Spain, Portugal, Iran, Turkey, Nationalist China, South Vietnam, South Korea and others does not imply any belief that civil liberties and democracy operate in them. This applies also to a shifting number of Latin-American military regimes. But they are not committed by doctrine nor linked by power ties to a totalitarian power cluster. They are independent, in the sense that their regimes can and do change. Whatever power tyrannies they have are their own, not those of the Communist power cluster. As long as this is true they have a chance to move toward internal freedom.

and mission that must have seemed preposterous except to those who possessed it and whom it possessed.

What brought it to its present height? Not arms. Wealth? In part, yes; America got its start in industrial growth from the Industrial Revolution of Europe, but carried it farther and faster than Europe did, becoming the most developed high-consumption economy in the world. Yet to say that it was wealth is question-begging, since what we have to answer is exactly why America was able to turn its resources into wealth when other nations with resources could not and did not on the same scale. What America had was the European tradition of science and technology, on which it improved; and a continent to which to bring people; and the people who came to it, with skills in their hands, ideas in their heads and fires in their bellies; and the burning hungers for social equality, and the career open to talent.

America thus became a great power mainly by drawing to its shores the human material out of which wealth and creativeness flow, and on which in the end all power structures rest, and by finding somehow the springs which released the energies of the people who came. All the rest of the history of America's expansionism—the twists and turns in diplomatic relations with Europe, the Young Warhawks of 1812, the proud "Keep Out" doctrine of Adams and Monroe warning Europe away from the Americas, the thrust southward and the war for Texas, the dreams of the Pacific Northwest and of a passage to India, the caravan trains across the continent, the merchant vessels sailing the seas toward every point of the compass, the brief spread-eagle strutting in Cuba and Hawaii and the Philippines, the shabby adventures in Caribbean "dollar diplomacy," the struggle between isolationism and interventionism, the two world wars, Hiroshima and what lay after—all the rest are more or less important footnotes to this basic text. America became the kind of power mass it became, not by armies of conquest and colonization, or by the legerdemain of world maneuver, or by the conspiracy of capitalists and politicians, or by the mystical dreams of intellectuals, but by drawing to its shores people who could build a dynamic open society.

One should add that while America imported its human resources over the centuries, it also became a great exporter of capital and technology. It thus emerged as the greatest industrial and financial power among the democracies, and in two world wars it had to come to the help of the European cultures from which it had been born and had derived its leading ideas. It was a curiously reluctant role. A President called Woodrow Wilson, with a strong humanist bent, found himself drawn into military involvement, both in the American hemisphere and in Europe, strongly against his will. It is now clear that American power came to the aid of the Western alliance not only to keep the seas and markets free for American enterprise, as some of the historians have emphasized, but because the defeat of the British and French would have meant a drastic setback for an open American society as an energy system.

This applied even more sharply when America assumed the leadership of a coalition, which included Soviet Russia, to prevent Hitler's dream of a thousand-year Nazi world domination from coming true. Even more than a Europe controlled by a dynastic Germany, a Nazi world imperium would have meant the crushing of American freedoms and dynamism. After World War II, American resources had to turn to the aid of a war-ravaged Western Europe, and American arms had to protect the non-Communist world from the thrust of Communist power. These were not a people or ruling group eager for the chance to spread their power and build an empire. It was only after agonizing debate, and with the hesitations and self-doubt that accompany the democratic process, that America assumed its present world role. Some nations are born to empire and dream of it, some achieve empire by sheer collective will, and some have empire thrust upon them. America belongs to the last.

And Russia? The trajectory of its rise to world power is as dramatic as anything in the history of power. Czarist Russia came on the stage of world history in the mid-sixteenth century, with Ivan the Terrible, and became a great power in Europe with Peter toward the close of the seventeenth century. During the whole of the eighteenth and nineteenth centuries, when St. Petersburg as a capital kept a window open on Europe, Russia was not only one of the prime actors in the great enactments of the classical European alliance system, but was fertile to the utmost in literature, music, drama and dance. It was a great power before Lenin, if only by its vast spaces, its population, its armies, its role in the alliance and balance-of-power system, and its impact on the chancelleries of the world. It was expanding Eastward, becoming an empire with internal colonies. It was also moving toward becoming an industrial power.

Lenin and his revolutionary elite bridged the former gulf between the Russia of the educated elite and the Russia of the masses, welded the two Russias into one, rescued Russian society from its downward spiral of inefficiency and corruption, shifted the axis of power from an elite of birth to one of ability and drive, pushed the economy by a drastic effort of collective will more rapidly toward industrialization, and gave the new society the added weapon of propaganda and the dedication of a party elite. They did not make Russia a Great Power, since it had been one, but they soon made it a more powerful Great Power and of a different kind, with different methods and with a new design for world politics which upset the equilibrium of the old.

When they started on their improbable adventure, toward the end of what they regarded as an imperialist war which would shatter the imperialist system, the Communists seemed (like the leaders of the American Revolution) to have little to build with: an exhausted and demoralized army, a wretched administrative apparatus, an economy which had come to a creaking halt, and a loose collection of federated regional peoples of diverse ethnic languages and descents, straining to secede. The revolutionary surge outside Russia on which they counted, especially in Germany, did not come, and the Russian leaders had to settle down to the hard task of setting their own revolutionary house in order. They rebuilt the administrative system, fashioned a new army and diplomatic corps, consolidated and expanded the economy, found ways of holding together the ethnic areas which were breaking away from the center, forged a party and a doctrine-in-action which would serve at once as cohesive and expansive forces.

That they brought this off is an achievement ranking with any of the chapters of empire building in the past. I call it empire building because from the start it should have been clear that the Communist leaders were shaping an economy, an army, a party apparatus, a bureaucracy, a doctrine and propaganda system, in order to build a new proletarian imperial power mass. The Revolution was itself part of a doctrine that cut across national boundaries and saw the world as its arena. Lenin made it clear in every statement that the world revolution could count on using the new class state as an instrument of revolutionary class war toward a world imperium. Even the doctrine of "socialism in one country," which Stalin intended as a counterdoctrine to that of the "permanent revolution," did not mean that he had abandoned the idea of a proletarian imperium, but only that he wanted a stronger industrial and military base at home before pushing external revolutions.

From the moment when the author of *The State and Revolution* and of *Imperialism: The Highest Stage of Capitalism* came to power, a new force of incalculable consequences was introduced into classical world politics, which was later to combine with the Hiroshima bomb to undercut the system itself.

In their thrust toward empire the Communist leaders, as children of the Western heritage, were determined to use every weapon the West had developed, including science, technology, industrialization, diplomacy, even armies. True, Communist doctrine had been antimilitarist and antipatriotic, since the Communists regarded war as an instrument of imperialist struggle, and patriotism as a cloak for imperialist rivalries. But the Soviet leaders were drawn into military involvement beyond their expectations. Despite the Communist vision that armies would be dissolved along with the police and the whole apparatus of state force—a vision which even a hardheaded leader like Lenin shared—it didn't take long for military reality to break into the Communist dreamworld. When Trotsky laid down the portfolio of Foreign Affairs to become Minister of War and confront the civil war, he rebuilt the army under the slogans of the defense of the "Socialist Fatherland." World War II was termed, under Stalin's orders, the "Second Patriotic War." After the war the presence of the Red armies in the liberated areas of Eastern Europe was as important as propaganda in setting up the new Communist regimes.

It is clear now, however, that the ultimate reliance of the drive for empire was on Communism as an energy system. The Communist leaders called on the two energy sources where they had a natural superiority over America—their collective revolutionary will and their new political religion, which was to be spread over the world by the revolutionary cadres of propaganda and subversion. World revolution was always part of Communist doctrine, and the engineering of subversion part of Communist practice. But it is one thing to pursue an aim in distant prospect—pie in the sky tomorrow—as Marxist partisans and theoreticians had done in every garret and café of Europe since the Manifesto. It is quite another to see the distant prospect become an attainable goal. Foreshadowed in the late 1920s when Stalin offered aid to foreign revolutionary movements on the basis of Russia's new industrialized military strength, this reached its decisive stage in the fateful stretch between 1945 and 1950. In that stretch the war-as-revolution paid off in the East European satellite states and in the final success of the Chinese Revolution as a conquest of power over the world's biggest population mass.

Once the distant prospect became a calculable possibility, perhaps even a probability, the pace of the Russian thrust toward world empire was quickened. The same period, 1945–50, witnessed the Russian quest of the atomic bomb. By the time Stalin died and Khrushchev came to power, the main lines of the Communist drive to empire had become clear and confident.

If we read the history of empire in terms of the symbolic events of the collective will, the first event in the Russian Communist story was the skillful touch-and-go turning of the democratic (March) revolution into the (November) revolution of a dictatorship state. From the moment when Lenin arrived at the Finland Station in St. Petersburg to take command of the Bolshevik cause, to the time when his new regime repulsed the interventionist armies, the Communist elite aimed constantly at turning theory into action and used their steel will to fashion a party state as a new instrument of history.

The second event in what has now become the legendry of Communism was the successful defense of Stalingrad. At that moment, when the future of the Communist world imperium teetered on the edge of survival, the probabilities seemed heavily on Hitler's side: not only did he have the advantage of a prepared surprise assault, but he had counted on widespread disaffection with the regime dominated by the Great Russians. Had he exploited this effectively, the Nazis might have won Russia by the inner collapse of resistance rather than by arms. But they threw away their chance. Infected with the madness of their racist dogma they treated the Ukrainians, Poles and other Slavic populations within Russia as subhuman material, fit only for use as serfs—and the Russians had no desire to return to the bitter memories of serfdom. Thus Stalingrad stood as the final test of the collective Communist will.

The third event was the break-through of Russian science in the Sputnik rocketry. It marked the first time that the Communist world had overtaken the West at its own game of science; Russian propaganda played it up as portent of greater wonders still to come, and offered it to the new nations as a vicarious triumph for them over the West and a revenge for the whole colonial past.

These symbolic events mark the progress of an empire in the consciousness of the Russians themselves and of the world. The Russian imperium as an energy system is contained within them.

One important difference should be noted between the two energy systems. I have said that in the building of the American imperium the critical energies came from the suction force exerted by the American legend upon people from every part of the world, and the technology, science and industry which these people developed. In the building of the Soviet imperium this suction force did not operate. While Moscow became a Mecca for foreign Communists and for many students from undeveloped countries, people did not come in masses to the Soviet Union, despite the clear shortage of manpower for the economic task forces. In fact, even in a "worker's paradise" like East Germany, they had to be kept from leaving, through a lesser or greater array of force, with the Berlin Wall serving as the final symbol of the Communist encirclement of their own people.

In another sense also, the movement of energy was *out of* the Russian imperium, instead of—as in the classic days of the building of the American imperium—*into* it. Soviet Russia had come into being by the application of theory and strategy to a revolutionary situation. It could not help expanding its power by the export to other revolutionary situations of theories, strategies, and cadres of trained and committed men. With each new revolutionary success abroad the imperium spread, and it consolidated its strength as a total world energy system.

5. *The Ice Age and the Political War*

THESE TWO GREAT contemporary empires clashed in what came quickly to be called the "cold war," reflecting the world's pervasive glacial mood. There was a time of hope toward the end of World War II, when the Western leaders thought a bipolar world struggle could be avoided. The familiar portrait of the three principals at Yalta recalls the mood as well as the men: Churchill, with his jaunty air of confidence, planted squarely in the reality principle; Stalin, with the stiffness of a Georgian peasant, his eyes averted as if to say he had no need to outface you; Roosevelt, valiantly optimist, ready to treat the Communists as if they were merely tough Tammany politicians or filibustering Southern Senators, with the pallor of death already on his features, the famous cape over shoulders so frail they seemed ready to dissolve into nothingness.

The secret Yalta promises about Manchuria and Poland represented (at least for Roosevelt and Churchill) a gamble, an assumption and a hope. The gamble was that the Russians would go through with their commitments. The gamble failed. The assumption behind the gamble was that the Russians would concentrate on rebuilding their shattered country and give up their Grand Design of world conquest. Again, the assumption failed. The hope was that Stalin would continue to work with Roosevelt and Churchill and prevent the coalition world from splitting into two hostile worlds. The hope failed.

America in 1945 was faced with a new situation—a world in which the older empires, especially the British, French and Dutch, could no longer hold onto power, leaving a vacuum into which the Communists could move with their Grand Design for world power. An obscure and untried man named Harry Truman had to bear the burden of history and fight out the great duel with Stalin. He made some hasty, weak decisions on Eastern Europe, and when added to the trust of the Russians displayed by Roosevelt, Hopkins and Eisenhower, they led to the first big victory of the Communist power cluster: from East Germany and Poland to Albania, Eastern Europe became Communist. The cold war was on.

President Truman made two moves to meet the Communist drive toward world power. He adopted George Kennan's idea of the containment of Communism; and, by applying it in the form of the Truman Doctrine, he kept the Communists from occupying Greece. Even more important, he placed American resources at the disposal of Western Europe through the Marshall Plan, formulated by a creative group in the State Department. Not only physically in ruins, Europe was sick economically, and there was a hovering sense of impending social and moral collapse. The broadest-gauged and most generous move of statesmanship in the history of American foreign policy, the Marshall Plan was a turning point in the political (cold) war. It worked. The internal energies of the European economies were released for a new cycle of prosperity.

But then the question arose whether they might not prove to have been fattened up only to be raided and annexed by the military force of the Russians. True, the Communists were devoting much of their energy to the nationalist movements of the undeveloped world, but the prize of a developed Europe was one that tempted them. In a ballad of high-spirited raiders by Thomas Love Peacock there are some lines which express their situation:

> The mountain sheep were sweeter
> But the valley sheep were fatter.
> We therefore deemed it meeter
> To carry off the latter.

Hence NATO, with its bridge of weapons stretching over the Atlantic, for the defense of the revived Europe against aggression.

There is little question that the Russians started the political war when they decided to push ahead unilaterally in Eastern Europe and when they cynically used their espionage to help their scientists in the technology of the atomic weapon. But NATO nailed it down. To this must be added the shift in policy when America abandoned its attempt to deindustrialize and decartelize West Germany, and decided to help rebuild its economy and power. It was clear to the Russians that a German-American alignment was to become a crucial foreign policy posture for America. The Russian response was the Warsaw Pact, the tightening of the screws on the satellites, and the war of nerves of Stalin against Tito. The fateful sequence was on, of rigidification in the political war, interacting with the deadly weapons-fear spiral I have described.

We live by symbols, and the seeker after them can find at the end of World War II a vivid symbol of what was to come. It was the town of Torgau, on the banks of the Elbe, where the victorious American and Russian armies, advancing from opposite directions, met—in the middle of Germany, in the middle of Europe, splitting that creative continent in two. "This symbolic event," writes John Lukacs,* "marks the supreme condition of contemporary history that has remained essentially unchanged ever since. That supreme condition is not the Atomic Bomb and not Communism; it is the division of Germany and of most of Europe into American and Russian spheres of influence. The so-called cold war grew out of this division."

I fear this overstates the case, mistaking the symbol for the cause. If it were not for the Grand Design of Communism the cold war would never have begun. On the other hand, if it were not for the nuclear bomb and the way it has transformed the world into a community of fear, the cold war would at some point have turned into a hot one. Thus the cold war, including the splitting of Germany and of Europe, is effect and symbol rather than cause of the contemporary world crisis. It is a symbol of passions which keep the two world power systems from abandoning the struggle for power, and the fear which keeps them from the final overkill test of strength. The cold war has continued into our own day in the form of the political war because the passions and the fears have also continued.

If Torgau was a symbol for the start of Europe's split, Berlin became the symbol of its continuance. The decision of the Allied lead-

* See his evocative book, *A History of the Cold War.*

ers to divide Berlin into zones and leave it as an enclave inside Eastern Germany was a fateful one, because it left both sides in the cold war with an unbearable burden and an unending mission. Stalin sought to end it by his effort to drive the Western forces out of Berlin in 1948-49, but Truman responded with the Berlin airlift and called his bluff. Khrushchev in his turn put pressure on Berlin in 1959-60 and in 1961-62, and again the pressure was resisted. The result was stalemate with a built-in set of provocations to end it, but also with a built-in fear of responding to the provocations.

There was a difference between European and Asian conditions with respect to their defense in the political war against an encroaching Communist empire. Western Europe, shorn of its former imperial splendor and burdens, has witnessed political, social and economic resurgence of strength. Within this frame NATO has functioned as a shield of freedom from foreign invasion or intervention. Its crisis came when the problem of its defense was caught in the deterrence trap, and when the decisions about the use of the deterrent weapons had to be located across the Atlantic. Yet the European social structure remained relatively strong. If European politics seem at times febrile, it is because Europe is inherently a seismograph that records every intellectual, political, aesthetic and moral tremor in the world. But the nations of Asia, and this is even truer of Africa, have no strong social base to receive either aid or arms. Their invasion doors open inward, not outward. Their disaffected young men—whatever the sources of disaffection—tend to become guerrillas, to train under Communist-nationalist leaders, to follow Communist-nationalist slogans, and no formal Russian or Chinese invasion armies are necessary.

By its nature the political war is an interlocking of rivalries short of a shooting war, with a containing action by each side against the encroaching actions of the other. While much of its emphasis is on military aid and on politico-military alliance, economic aid has been one of its more enlightened instruments since the Marshall Plan. But neither military nor economic aid has any special virtue in itself, except as it is part of a frame of order. Europe had, and largely still has, this frame of order; Asia and Africa, where the traditional societies are being so drastically uprooted, do not have it.

Feeding the political war are a number of factors—historical, geographical, technological, economic, social, political, moral—all of them bearing on the inner life and character of the nations involved in it. There is, of course, a degree of truth in Nehru's phrase, "the cold-war mentality," which implies that it is an arbitrary and willful aberration of the imperial leaders (especially of the West). But the phrase simplifies the reality. For if the political war is willful, it can presumaby be set right by will; if it is irrational, it can be corrected by reason. There are some who regard it as the product of a double standard of morality, in which case it could be resolved by a resolution of the moral problem.

I find all these approaches too easy because too rationalist. The political war will not yield to good will, right reason, pure morality, because it grows out of the interacting fears, aggressions, defensive sets, and irrationalisms of two power ganglia locked in a monstrous mutual embrace. Nor is it, I might add, hostile in its totality. There is an aspect in it of "my dearest enemy," with each side finding the other a cherished outlet for its own inner aggressions. One is tempted even to adapt for the cold war the idea that Stendhal used in his book *On Love*—that of "crystallization." Once in love, the lover is driven to refer everything that happens around him to his central passion, so that every event is crystallized to enhance the beloved and underscore the strength of the love. So, too, with the events which are pressed into the shape of the world rivalry and become crystals of the glacial political contest.

The prospect is thus of an ice age of world political war which will last at least another generation, until the aggressions and fears which come out of the convergence of overkill weapons, ideological fervors and national characters will have been diminished by the political and arms-control dialogue. When that happens it will be time to transform the containment principle of a mutually poised murderousness into a principle of world collective security.

I speak of *political war* as a better term than *cold war* for the great struggle of our time between the world power clusters. "Cold war" implies primarily a war of nerves, which is only one phase of the total struggle; it implies also a permanent freezing of power relations between the contestants, which simply is not true. One great fact of the power struggle is exactly its fluid character, with shifting battle lines and varying fortunes of war, and with the real possibility that the tide of battle may flow so strongly in one direction as to bring about a political conquest without a single missile being fired. One might call the struggle a "war of ideas," since the idea component is so important; yet that too is only a fragment of the total pattern. The weapons and strategies range from arms and military alliances, trade, technical and economic aid, and espionage, to propaganda, cultural and technical missions, student interchange, diplomacy, leadership, education, relations with the elites, the sustaining of an *élan,* the effort to surround an entire civilization with a particular cultural *ambiance* and even to create an emerging type of "new man." *

There is no single adjective which can convey the total range and depth of this array of weapons and strategies, unless it be the traditional term "political, which suggests in some measure the idea of the total polity. Hence I shall be speaking of the broader struggle not as *cold* warfare but as *political* warfare. Yet I hope that there remains in the term some of the quality of the interlocked agonies of imperial struggle which the term "cold war" was first meant to convey.

If I am right in my definition, the political war is a product of three converging factors: the postwar vacuum of power, both in Europe and within the new nations, created by a wave of revolutionary nationalisms; the Communist intent to exploit it in both areas; and the free-world response to both the vacuum crisis and the Communist power drive. How have the fortunes of this political war gone, and what has happened not only to the Communist challenge and the free-world response, but to the vacuum itself?

One is tempted to say that the axis of the political war has shifted from Europe to the undeveloped world. But it would not be quite true. The European vacuum has been filled by strong economies, effective governments, movements toward economic and political unification. Yet the continuing tug of war over Berlin shows that the struggle for Europe goes on, although the form it now takes is more closely linked with the deterrent strategies of the overkill weapons. Despite the high stakes which the undeveloped world offers, Europe remains the decisive battleground; with its great cities, its high cultures, its developed economies, it is the tempting prize for one camp, and the don't-touch-me showdown security area for the other. If it were not for the ocean span between them, one would say that Europe and America together form the heartland of the free-world power system, and that neither dares allow the other part of the heartland to be laid waste. The current evidences of a European renaissance only make the prize more tempting, converting it into a target for nuclear diplomacy and even blackmail, while they also harden the resolve to conserve it.

In the areas of the anticolonial nationalist movements the vacuum is a dominant fact of political life, and the struggle on both sides

---

* On this range of themes, see Chapter V, "The Viable Society: Elite, *Élan,* Ethos," which is—from my own angle of vision—a discussion of resources and strategies in the political war.

is to fill it, using the weapons of aid, pressure and prestige to influence the new leadership and shape the new political forms. For a spell the intensity of the revolutionary nationalist struggle itself, in each country, seemed to fill the vacuum. But once the new nation is established, with an untried governing elite, with everything still to be done and with scarcely any traditional forms for doing it, the vacuum returns. The policy of neutralist noncommitment is an understandable one for keeping the contending power systems at arm's length, gaining time for the new governing elite to find its bearings, and putting it in a strong bargaining position where it can play off the contenders against each other. But it would be a mistake to believe that this policy is more than a makeshift. Far from resolving the intensity of the political war, it serves to redouble it by making the battle a continuing battle for stakes which are never wholly yielded. Even more important is the fact that the vacuum arises out of a once traditional society whose roots have been torn up, a once stable if impoverished economy which is now in explosive growth, and a once accepted set of arbiters in every realm of power and belief who have been displaced without being replaced. Thus, it is the unquiet vacuum within which the fires of a consuming political war rage.

Thus also, in a curious way, the figure necessarily changes from ice to fire. It may be that an ice age will settle over the human spirit, but if so it will come at the end of a fierce political war which employs every weapon and engages every energy of the contestants.

6. *Neutralism and the Ghosts*

ONE OF THE FALLACIES of a bipolar view of the world, which develops out of the political war, is the feeling that nothing exists except the two great contenders and their contest. What this view omits is the idea and practice of neutralism as a force outside the two big power clusters. During the 1950s there was considerable hope that a bloc of uncommitted nations could hold the balance between the two camps, isolate them as ugly and dangerous quarreling children, outvote one or the other at the UN, mediate between them when their rigid postures threatened nuclear war, and compel them by sheer moral weight to see the error of their ways and to mend them.

But this hope has been thinned out. In a world of overkill weap-

ons mounting in destructiveness, the effective role of the neutralists
has been severely limited. They have had no impact thus far upon
the missile spiral and disarmament. They are too caught in their
own nationalist disputes to be able to tender their good offices in
settling the disputes of the giants. The moral force they invoke
against the aggressions and urgencies of others they may themselves
repeatedly betray in aggressive episodes of their own; after the Indian annexation of Goa it was hard to take seriously the repeated
moral lectures delivered by Krishna Menon at world conferences. It
has grown increasingly clear that neutralism is often little more
than a rationalization of a difficult geographical or political position in which it would be dangerous to choose sides.

The man most responsible for the neutralist idea is Jawaharlal
Nehru. The Indian mind delights in the balancing of contradictions,
and Nehru conceived of his international posture as a balancing
posture. He is himself a "double" man: a man of the East in his pacifism and his rejection of the urgencies of the moment, in his sinuous-
ness and his subtlety; a man of the West in his intellectual training
and his socialist conditioning. As it happened, India reached nationhood in 1947, just when the political war in Europe reached its
most glacial phase. Understandably, Nehru tried to stay clear of
political or moral commitments to either of the two great power
centers.

The fact was that China and Russia were giant neighbors who
could crush India, and that no arms build-up could yield quick
results in resisting them. But Nehru, an intellectual, felt he had to
build a doctrine to house his necessity, and he went back to Gandhi's doctrine of *satyagraha,* or "truth-force," fashioning out of it
the idea of nonalignment. The basic idea went beyond the tactical
need of the new nations; but most generally it was that peace could
never be brought about by armed or economic force, or by political
pressure, but only by the force of morality. Unfortunately, it didn't
work out. The tragedy of Nehru's policy was that he tried to apply
the force of morality to his neighbor, Communist China, in the
form of the *Panch Sheel* (Five Principles) and, for his pains, got a
chunk clawed out of India by the Chinese dragon. After first breach-
ing the *Panch Sheel* by an invasion of Tibet, the Chinese army
invaded and annexed Indian territory itself in the form of a sizable
portion of Ladakh. The map of Asia flamed up, and the principle of
Panch Sheel lay in ashes, and with it Nehru's strategy of relying on
morality as a guiding principle in world politics.

As a principle of keeping a new nation from becoming embroiled in the polar contest for world power, neutralism is grounded in reality. Sukarno and U Nu adopted it in Asia, Nasser in Egypt, Nkrumah and Toure in Africa, Tito in Eastern Europe, each of them with concrete political motives. But when neutralism, as a politics of morality, was applied unilaterally it proved disastrous. As embodied in *Panch Sheel,* morality was a one-way street; India observed the Five Principles, while China contemptuously scrapped them. While neutralism as noncommitment was fairly effective in the relations with distant power centers, neutralism as a politics of morality-without-force toward a neighboring power proved to be a failure. Power without morality is imperialism. Morality without power is helplessness in a world of the Communist Grand Design.

The neutralist paradox lies in the fact that the uncommitted country can remain uncommitted toward the Great Powers, but not toward its neighbors. Hence, it must arm itself, often massively, against that neighbor. Ironically a neutralist leader like Nasser arms himself as fully as a committed leader like Ayub Khan of Pakistan. In Nehru's case a measure of pacifism went along with the neutralism, yet even India was pushed toward a greater arms effort by the Chinese aggression. Nehru long shrank from any extensive arms deal with either camp on the ground that arms carry commitments. But it is the essential paradox of every new nation which seeks to adopt neutralism that its economic as well as its military needs are always pushing it away from the balancing posture toward commitment. The statesmanship of neutralism is the statesmanship of the tightrope walker.*

Lacking effective power, the smaller neutralist nations which are not linked with one of the great power clusters must look for ultimate protection to the United Nations. But when Dag Hammarskjöld in the UN crisis of 1960, appealing from Khrushchev's crippling proposal for a triple Secretariat, called for the support of the small nations who would be the first victims of a UN paralysis, he got little response from the neutralist bloc. Its leaders had not learned the lesson that the best moral position needs power to sustain it, and that in the absence of adequate power of their own, the immediate and potential power of the UN is the only safeguard for their neutralism. This is a way of saying that the principle of noncommitment cannot be limited to a nation or a bloc, but must be embodied finally in a world authority which operates with detach-

* The Chinese aggressions first forced India into buying helicopters and planes from the West, and as I write (1962) Krishna Menon as Defense Minister is discussing a deal with Russia for MIGs and a plant to build them in.

ment as arbiter and policeman. The fear of getting involved in the cold war has led the neutralists to avert their gaze from it or wish it away, rather than to get at the roots of its continuance, which are (as I have suggested) a social vacuum within the new nations and the vacuum of authority in the world at large.

These are some of the realities and illusions of neutralism in our time. There remains what has been, for a number of neutralist nations, the most dangerous illusion of all—the belief that by avoiding commitment they can safely ignore the fact of the Grand Design of world Communism.* The basic premise underlying the neutralist attitude is that both houses are equally plagued, both contestants equally power-hungry, both dynamisms equally dangerous. But to view both these power clusters—one which can profit only from world order, while the other explores what gains it can make out of constant disruption of order—with a plague-on-both-your-houses detachment, is the fatal flaw in the neutralist position.

It would be thus even if the neutralist cards were not stacked from the start against the free world. This history of imperialist injustice has left a heritage of hatred, and the anticolonial slogans and passions operate uniformly to cripple one camp in the world political war and help another. But the fact is that the cards *are* stacked, and along with the inherent expansionism of world Communism this makes the actual impact of neutralism different from its formal rhetoric.

Thus, the neutralist nations live in a world haunted by ghosts, the ghosts of past colonial atrocities and past imperialist oppressions. I have suggested that the classic imperialism is dead and has been succeeded by an era of imperium. Yet the ghosts continue to haunt the new nations, which have freed themselves from their former masters but not from their memory-obsessed and fear-haunted world.

The nationalist movements of liberation fed on real grievances and sought to free their people from real oppressions. Once the liberation has been achieved, no new passions arise to replace the old ones, yet the need for passions persists. Thus, the carry-over of the old slogans and stereotypes into the new vacuum makes the educated elite a vulnerable prey for the ideological partisans who know how to use them. They need talk only of imperialism on the one hand and of poverty and inequality on the other, and the link between the two is easily forged in minds made ready for the forging. Where once the imperialism of the West was held responsible, with justice, for the unfreedom of a people, it is today still held responsi-

---

* See Chapter III, "Grand Design as Political Religion."

ble, with massive injustice, for the poverty and inequalities of the society and for every other ill attending life in it.

Thus, ghosts have their uses, and it does not take a brilliant propagandist to use them. The irony is all the greater for the fact that even the best leaders of the new nations, clear-eyed in vision and realistic in intent as they may be, usually cannot resist going along with the tide. They find it expedient to compete in the use of anti-colonial slogans as a protective mask even for policies which aim at resisting Communism; they may be driven to a neutralist stance because only thus can they defend their substantive policies.

So much for the irony of it. The tragedy of it cuts even deeper. For the tragedy is that the ghosts of the old imperialism often keep the educated elite, and the mass of people to whom and for whom they speak, from recognizing the real and present danger of a new imperialism—until it is too late for the recognition. Not often are a people and its leaders aroused from their ghost world as rudely as Nehru and the Indian people were aroused by the Chinese conquest of Tibet and invasion of Ladakh, or Toure and the Guineans by the discovery of a plan for the take-over of power. Usually the Communists operate more subtly and less nakedly in the world political war. They scarcely need to move armies across borders, since it is easier and more effective to move agents, trained party functionaries and "advisers"—those who can best set fire to the inflammable material already available in each nation.

But when the point of no return comes, the ghosts are sent scampering because they are no longer useful. The nationalist slogans are replaced by slogans of Communist world unity. The newly found freedom gives way to the iron discipline of a party controlled from abroad, and Communist power is consolidated beyond redress. It is then that the full reach of the tragedy becomes clear. But at that point it is too late.

7. *Grandeurs and Miseries of Empire*

EVERY SOCIAL SYSTEM has a style by which it lives and dies, a characteristic mode of behavior which reveals itself daily in every phase of life but is more sharply shown in its great crises. There is a style for the great power clusters as well.

In the early phases of modern empire, when Europe burst its bounds in discoveries, explorations, and colonization of distant lands from the sixteenth to the nineteenth century, empire was dynastic, gaudy, and frankly acquisitive—although usually in the name of God and the extension of His sway. A second phase of empire, starting in mid-nineteenth century, marked the convergence of capital export with Great Power rivalry in the rifling of the still dark Continents in an age of high finance and high adventure. Here again the style was at once exploitative and demonstrative, with a good deal of imperial fanfare in the grand manner of proconsuls and rajahs, along with the grubbier realities of double-entry book-keeping plus swollen annual returns on the initial investment.

The current phase, in the age of nuclear-doctrinal empire, is more ambiguous in its style. It is schizoid, caught between the accumulation of unparalleled power, which might have been used with a swaggering assertiveness, and the fear of actually using it. No imperial leader, although master of untold missile power, even hints of using it except with unending obeisances to disarmament, peace and his hopes for turning nuclear swords into industrial plowshares. Nor do the economic leaders of any empire dare to speak of their imperial economic interests except with the dreariest unction about helping to develop the undeveloped world.

Yet, membership in the Nuclear Club remains one of the hallmarks of empire. The France of De Gaulle, for example, strove hard to develop a nuclear weapon, partly at least as a symbolic replacement for the loss of the colonies and of French imperial prestige. Great Britain, which had to watch its empire become a loose collection of Commonwealth loyalties, found its resources unequal to the costs of the deadly weapons spiral and gave it up, thus becoming dependent on American missile power, with a further loss in imperial prestige. China, which made a "Great Leap Forward" that didn't leap, seems ready to squeeze its underlying population and risk its disaffection, in order to end the bitterness of continuing—amidst its tensions with the Russians—the ward of Russian missile power.

This suggests another hallmark of empire: the burden and privilege of extending an "umbrella of protection" to regional or doctrinal allies, dependencies, wards, client states, or satellites. America has held an umbrella over a scattering of regimes from Spain and Greece eastward to Japan, from Mexico to the southern tip of Argentina, and (through NATO) over the whole of Western Europe. The Russians hold it over their Asian allies, perhaps over Cuba, but mainly over Eastern Europe. Europe, in fact, once the home and source of imperial grandeur, has virtually ceased to exist in terms of military self-sufficiency, half of it coming under the American (NATO) military umbrella, the other half under the Russian.

The nuclear history of the French is especially interesting. Under the Fourth Republic, with the Communists forming the largest party in the Chamber of Deputies and always ready for a political coup, the danger that shared atomic secrets might fall into Communist hands hung like a shadow over American military planners. With the army coup of 1958 and the creation of De Gaulle's Fifth Republic, this worry was replaced by a fresh one. With his belief in French *grandeur*, De Gaulle was furious at the Anglo-American *entente* inside the free-world power system and insisted upon sharing equally in the nuclear secrets and the big decisions. He had his own reading of history, his own evaluation of the sources of Soviet conduct, his own attitude toward NATO, the UN, and the doctrinal weapons of the political war, his own vision of the future and its shaping. When the American leaders refused to share their nuclear technology with France, De Gaulle pushed for his own nuclear deterrent, however expensive, and he refused to work with NATO's forces wholeheartedly unless the French controlled their own missiles and warheads inside NATO. Despite the massive disparity between American power and French power, De Gaulle was a formidable center and obstruction inside the power cluster. He has sought to woo the West Germans and the Italians, and win them over to his dream of a loosely federated Europe which will use its independent nuclear deterrent (along with its economic unity) to stay clear of both the great power clusters.

To military aid the new imperial style must now add economic aid, not only to allies but to reasonably friendly unaligned states as well. To be sure, West Germany, Czechoslovakia and Poland have all entered the network of nations dispensing aid without becoming empires. It is not one factor or another alone, but the convergence of economic aid, military protection, nuclear power, and symbolic standing in the world struggle which makes up the criteria of the imperial power systems.

This is a long way from the classic imperialism which, in theory, arose out of the surplus value from exploited labor at home and led to profits from the surplus value of labor applied to colonial resources. The new imperial style has taken on the burden of economic aid, not in the hope of profit or exploitation, but for the political strengthening of a power complex. And once caught in the rivalry of loans, grants, barter deals and investments, neither of the great empires of today can manage quite to extricate itself.

Nor is the imperial role in diplomacy an easy one. The power center of today must continue to use all the old modes of diplomatic action and intrigue while playing a role in highly publicized summit conferences and the UN. Its leaders try to lay down public directions of policy, even while tensions within the power system may threaten to tear it apart, and they must reconcile the conflicting national interests of the cluster members and the prima-donnalike personalities of their associates in leadership. It must seek total knowledge of what the rival empire is doing, in order to guard against total surprise, yet it must retain the element of surprise in all its maneuvers. It must therefore practice espionage—on land and sea, in the air through reconaissance planes, in the stratosphere through observation satellites—even while it maintains correct relations and disowns sternly any intelligence agent luckless enough to get caught. And all the time it must send satellites and spaceships into orbit, shoot dogs and monkeys and men into interstellar space, and train them not only for the rigors of the journey but for survival there and for the new mode of life it entails.

It must send out an army of technicians, consultants, linguists, aid specialists, cultural emissaries. It must develop skills in propaganda and psychological warfare, even while it professes a committed belief to the strategy of the truth. It must worry about the morale of its young people and the quality of the educational systems which shape their minds and ethos. It must prepare a succession of grand tours for prime ministers, presidents, heads of state, in which the right countries are visited at the right time, handing out the right amount of money and credits, visiting dams, steel mills and hospitals, laying wreaths, addressing parliaments, speaking to the sensibilies of the country and to the larger reaches of the world.

Nor does this task end with these ardors of diplomacy and travel. There are also the burdens of the internal cohesion of the power cluster: to keep it from being split by factional struggles over policy and doctrine; to keep it from becoming disaffected because of decisions which are either too strong for the self-image of its members or too ineffectual for their sense of security; to channel aid where it is needed, without either starving or humbling the recipients; to find a common political language which all the members can speak, while ministering adequately to the divergencies of national interest and identity; to split the enemy, while keeping oneself from being split; to prevent changes in internal politics in any member state from weakening or destroying the cluster as a whole.

The empires which, in their own day, had a comparable éclat, with comparable grandeurs and burdens, have had to develop a more muted style in our time. Of the residual empires carrying over from the past, the Belgian, Dutch, German, Portuguese and Italian are all but gone. The British and French remain in a truncated form. Both of them have had to learn, terribly late, the difficult arts of dissolving an empire, sometimes (as in Algeria) too slowly and too bloodily, sometimes (as in the abrupt British withdrawal from India and the Belgian withdrawal from the Congo) too hastily once the decision was made, but always with the drive to cut losses, salvage the salvageable, and re-form a working partnership with the new nations.

These exercises in a dissolving and re-forming empire mark an effort to retrieve past errors and redress ancient wrongs. Although Churchill refused to preside over the dissolution of an empire, yet he and his successors, Attlee and Macmillan, had to, and did. The same is true of De Gaulle, a ruler so imperial in mien that history should have given him a greater power base on which to stand. He achieved with native grace the art of keeping the aura of power while surrendering its sinews. The British genius for constitutional makeshift fortified by custom was never shown to better advantage than in the Commonwealth. The French grand manner, even in a time of agonized withdrawal, was never more brilliantly deployed than by De Gaulle.

This was a gift denied to the Belgians, Dutch and Portuguese— partly because of the difference between them and the others in educating their colonial peoples and making them part of their culture. While the British in India and Burma educated only a small percentage of the population, they shaped a civil service elite which served as a transmission belt not only for British rule but also for the English language and literature, for English history, for the British university tradition and culture. So effectively was this built into Indian institutions and the Indian mind that it survived the bitter struggle for independence and has remained part of Indian life today. The elite in the French colonies came to the magic world of Paris and never broke away from its thrall, even when they burst the political and economic bonds by which the French had held them in subjection. The linkage with the French literary and cultural tradition serves to tie many of the new African states in a residual alliance with Paris. The Dutch in Indonesia never succeeded in establishing such ties, or perhaps never tried, out of fear that an educated colonial elite would soon cease to be colonial. The same was true of the Belgians in the Congo and of the Portuguese in Angola. The result was the loss of empire without redress or result.

It is worth noting that the contemporary American imperial style was shaped by a nation which was not particularly hungry for imperial power. The interventionist "dollar diplomacy" phase of American foreign policy in the 1920s, when the United States Marines had the crude task of "protecting" American investments in the nations to the south, was a style decisively rejected in the 1930s, by the same elements of the American mind and conscience which rejected the *laissez faire* ethos in the American economy. As a rule, the expansionist American groups have been *immobilistes* at home, while those pushing for dynamic action at home have opposed economic exploitation abroad. I should add that there are crosscurrents to complicate the picture: American isolationism, once a movement of anti-imperialist liberals, became in time the last refuge of *laissez faire* reactionaries, and many once "Continentalist" liberals—who went back to Jefferson for their inspiration, and whose slogan could have been "Look homeward, Empire"—found themselves finally embroiled in an internationalism which could not escape two world wars and the Korean War. But the beginning of clarity here is to distinguish between the drive toward an active American international role and the drive toward an American imperium. They have not been the same either in motive or in political direction; yet the imperium has come, not in a "fit of absence of mind" (as Sir John Seeley described the building of the British Empire) but as a byproduct of world involvement.

In a society saturated with power, Americans have not felt the psychic need of wreaking their power frustrations abroad. Except for the Dulles phase of American diplomacy, the philosophy of *or-else* has rarely been part of the American style. It has stayed clear of making the most effective use of the weapons of propaganda and political warfare, partly out of a lack of political sophistication, partly out of a distaste for politicizing instruments like advertising and public relations that seem to Americans best insulated in business. The spreading of the faith, in a political sense, seems alien to them.

The whole of American history has put stress on will, but it has been on the individual rather than the collective will, on personal choice rather than disciplined group commitment. This has led Americans repeatedly to take cumbersome, costly and roundabout methods of reaching their goals, and it has given the Russians an inside-track advantage in the imperial race. While Americans have prided themselves on their scientific achievement, they have thought of it as something for individual or corporate exploitation, not as an instrument of state policy. The central planning of scientific research for national goals, an integral part of the Communist political style, is being achieved in America only after a considerable lag. And the drive toward a world imperium which will fulfill the "scientific" laws of history is alien to the American imperial style.

One may ask what has happened to the historic American revolutionary national style and why it has not been transferred to the current world political war. No one can doubt the authentic revolutionary tradition of America. It produced the first modern revolution against colonialism and imperialism, and the first organically revolutionary modern society. In land tenure, separation of church and state, freedom of speech and press and thought, the rights and habits of association, the rule of law, the rights and practice of political opposition, and an egalitarian idea which has acted as a dissolvent for too-rigid class strata, America has led the way for other revolutionary peoples. Yet for a time America turned its back on this tradition and presented itself—strangely to a world of exploding revolutionary nationalism—as a *status quo* system of power.

Slowly, all too slowly, American policy makers have become aware of this contradiction between tradition and practice, and are seeking to adapt the tradition of constant experimental change to the realities of a world political war and of a struggle between power systems. They are also seeking to combine the necessities of a power system with the tradition of Constitutional consent. The result is a constitutional imperium which is emerging in the free world, unparalleled in history, still in the earlier stages of its fashioning, largely unwritten and even unacknowledged, with incalculable changes still ahead, which strains the capacity of its leaders for practical political invention.

The problems of this constitutional imperium are not easy ones. Its member nations are constantly rent apart by national pride, rivalries and interests, and by the need to respond to popular fears or passions at home. Some are democratic, some authoritarian, some military dictatorships. They cannot, as the Communist dictatorships can, keep their internal conflicts from public knowledge. They are subjected to a constant critical barrage from within, they are torn by debates, their young people are vulnerable to pacifist movements, their intellectuals are often drawn to the Left. Their sensitive men and women are ravaged by crises of conscience about the overkill weapons. Their heads of government may change frequently, their regimes are unstable, their politicians seem like barrels of writhing snakes, their parliamentary wrangles may become shambles of violence. The democratic power cluster of our era is caught between new imperatives and time-honored institutions (the nation, civil liberties, the rule of law, democracy) which were shaped under simpler social conditions in the classical system of world politics. But there is no suicide imperative within it.

One merit the democratic world has: It can pool its science and technology and to some extent even its leadership talent. Power systems in our time are made by science and must command science. The republic of knowledge knows few national barriers, but in the empires of secrecy there are always secrets to be kept from nations or shared with them. By pooling their working teams of scientists, the members of a constitutional imperium can move faster in the deadly weapons race than alone. They can also, by constant consultation, present a unity of decision to the Communist system and the world which would be impossible without working understandings that have become almost political conventions. The time will come when the NATO nations will also interlock their system of educating and training the intellectual elites upon whose social intelligence even more than on science and technology, the survival of an open society depends.

Something of the same sort may happen in the realm of political leadership.* The American power center, which has had thrust upon it the burdens of free-world leadership, has had neither the long British and French tradition of political experience nor the Communist method of tempering its leadership in the fiery furnace of party struggles. But something is emerging which is almost a pooling of leadership resources and the rise of a kind of *rotating leader* for the free-world system. Franklin Roosevelt clearly dominated the anti-Nazi war coalition; when Roosevelt died, Winston Churchill stepped into his place, and while the active free-world protagonist in the duel with Stalin was President Truman, it was Churchill's "Iron Curtain" speech at Fulton and his balance-of-terror farewell speech in Parliament which became guidelines for the free-world strategy. After Roosevelt and Churchill, neither Eisenhower nor Macmillan could quite fill their place, and for a time Charles De Gaulle moved his gawky, bristling personality, his sharp-edged mind,

---

* For a further discussion of the burdens of free-world leadership, see Chapter V, Section 1, "The Ordeal of Leadership," and Section 2, "Power, Decision, and Identity."

and his habit of command into the vacuum they left. With President Kennedy, the commanding free-world leadership, inside the frame of the working constitutional imperium, moved back to America.

In building their imperium the Communists have used their revolutionary dogma and tradition to the hilt, presenting themselves as anticapitalist, antiprivilege, anticolonial, antifeudalist, antibourgeois, antiracist, and comprehensively anti-*status quo*. Yet Russia too is caught—torn between the new burdens of empire (aid, development, competitive armaments and disarmament, the fear of nuclear war, "summitry") which turn it in a conservative direction, and the logic of Marxist doctrine, combined with pressures from other Communist states, which turn it in a revolutionary direction. This may partly account for the alternating moods of rough and smooth, bluster and moderation, brutal and honeyed language, missile rattling and disarmament proposals, *or-else* threats and negotiating offers, which have characterized the Russian foreign policy line and driven both its opponents and the faithful into despair.*

In fact, there is even a suggestion by a British psychologist, William Sargant, that these alternating positive and negative signals are based on the conditioned-reflex psychology of Pavlov and are intended to "brainwash" the Western mind and break down its resistances, much as the methods of alternating kindness and cruelty did with Pavlov's historic experimental dogs. It is a theory with some merit, but I should regard it not as the main text of the Russian imperial style but as a footnote to it. The main text can best be studied in the tension between the Communist doctrine of world revolution and the burdens of empire for Russia in a real world. That provides impetus enough for the alternating moods, without dragging in Pavlov and his dogs.

One advantage the Communists do have in confronting the problems of unity and discipline in their power system: Their leaders don't have to worry much about student demonstrations, parliamentary melees, newspaper attacks. Yet, while the police state, rooted in the fear of force and the mystique of revolutionary success, is not easily overthrown, it exerts an adverse propaganda-by-deed to negate the propaganda of the word. There is always the harsh fact of the practice of Communism-in-action to belie the promises of Communism-to-come in non-Communist states. Thus, there is from

---

* For an elaboration of this theme, see Chapter III, Section 3, "Domination and Accommodation."

the start a tension between the Communist regimes (in power) and the Communist parties that are striving for power.

The tensions inside the power cluster of the Communist world are even greater than those inside the democratic world, partly because the Communists are more conditioned toward the importance of doctrinal factionalism, partly because they are nations on the make and in a hurry. There are tensions of nationalist Communism which split off Yugoslavia from the Soviet power system and almost lost it Poland and Hungary. There are rivalry tensions for position in the empire, and doctrinal tensions—on strategy and tactics, on economic policy, on "hard" and "soft" lines toward the democratic world—as witness the strains between Russia and China. To resolve these tensions there is constant negotiation and discussion at party congresses, with the Soviet leadership as something more than *primus inter pares*. Despite the wishfulness of free-world opinion, I suspect that these tensions operate within the larger frame of the Communist community of interest; the Communist leaders know that they must hang together or they will hang separately, and necessity makes some kind of cement, even if not always a good one.

The case of China illustrates the burdens of Communist empire.* As a recent commentary has put it, "China's troubles are Russia's troubles, and her triumphs are Russia's troubles too. When she is weak she must be helped; when she is strong, she is an incubus of massive proportion." The Russian bear has a dragon by the tail, and it is not a paper dragon. Its militancy and menace are directed not only at the free-world power system but at the Soviet as well. Nor are the national differences between the giants of the Communist power system very different from the doctrinal differences inside Russia and China themselves. Communism is a doctrinal movement, with a doctrinal strategy, faith and goal; it is doctrine, and the consequences of doctrine, which both divide it and make it cohere. This also helps to explain why the Communist imperium has not followed the free world in setting up a semiconstitutional structure for resolving tensions and reaching decisions; where a doctrine and a party exist which are already transnational, they can dispense with constitutional inventions.

Thus, the power centers of each of the antagonist worlds have to operate within a double set of limits. One is the limiting fear of re-

---

* For further discussion of this, in the frame of the doctrinal controversy over coexistence or war, see Chapter III, Section 4, "The Daemon and the Locomotive." See also Chapter VI, Section 4, "The New Federalists."

leasing the forces of overkill; the second is the limits set by the other members of the power cluster.

Hungary and Cuba each illustrates an aspect of these limitations upon the power center. Hungary dared assert its aspirations toward its own brand of socialism, or perhaps even a national Communism different from that of the Kremlin leaders; and its daring was dissolved in blood. The dissolution had to be accomplished ruthlessly and with dispatch—ruthlessly in order to set an example to other members of the Soviet empire; with dispatch so that the episode would not remain a protracted symbol of how democratic the "People's Democracies" actually are. It was not an abstract "world opinion" that worried the Russian leaders but concretely the morale of the people in Communist countries who are driven hard to achieve rapid industrialization and must endure coercions that cannot be stretched too far. In this sense, even a totalitarian regime must reckon with the outer limits of its power; and one which is also a power center—as the Russian regime is—must reckon with those limits in the minds of the people of the member states as well as its own.

The invasion of Cuba illustrates a similar theme of limits, but in the context of the free-world power system. As a matter of power the United States could launch an overwhelmingly effective invasion of Cuba. The chance that an invasion-in-force would mean a nuclear war with Russia was not decisive, since Russia was unlikely at the time to go to war over Cuba. President Kennedy was inhibited not by the Russians but by the Latin-American states. His dilemma was that a full-scale invasion might be held comparable to Russia's conduct in Hungary and would shock these states beyond redress, while a course of nonintervention in Cuba would lead to protracted and intolerable Castro-Communist interventions in other vulnerable Latin-American countries. He chose a middle course—intervention without adequate air cover—which was carried out with amateurish ineptness. Only afterward did he understand that either of the other courses would have been preferable. In justice to Kennedy, it should be added that the Bay of Pigs episode ran counter to a larger hemispheric policy which was then in the making and later emerged—a policy of common action by the Organization of American States, along with Alliance for Progress aid, which in turn is linked with internal social reforms in each nation where vested class interests or governmental indecision had produced an inflammable situation. The surge of anti-United States feeling after the Cuban intervention was a heavy price to pay for the American blunder.

But the episode was useful in showing that the leader of a democratic power center cannot behave as if it were only his own people and his own national interests he has to reckon with.

To say that the new broad strategy within an informal constitutional power system is difficult whether in Latin America, in Europe or in Asia, is not to say that it is impossible. There are some who avert their gaze from the fact and operation of power in world politics; they prefer to believe that the free world as a power system simply does not exist, that the effort to keep it cohesive must always be approached on tiptoe, that only political rhetoric and economic aid are permissible, and that the assertion of power is somehow sinful. This is tender-minded thinking, of a species which has made little sense at any time after Machiavelli, Hobbes and the authors of *The Federalist,* and it makes even less sense now, in the face of the ruthlessness and guile of the Communist power system.

Ideological factors are still of great importance. This is not the end of ideology in world politics, any more than it is the end of empire. But ideology derives its importance from the fact that it is a form of power, and not from its being antipower. The duty toward power which the national leader must face at the power center itself, and which he cannot delegate to any subordinate—that duty is as true of the larger power cluster as it is of the nation-state.

CHAPTER III

Grand Design as Political Religion

1. Grand Design

2. The Two Faces of Revolution

3. Domination and Accommodation

4. The Daemon and the Locomotive

5. Reason of State and Reason of History

*6. Winds of Communist Doctrine: Mystique,
Dogma and Distortion in Marxism*

7. Armed Doctrine and Political Religion

8. The Intellectual as Fulcrum of Political War

9. A Stick, a Plan, a Myth

95

CHAPTER III

Grand Design as Political Religion

1. Grand Design

THE power of the Communist world is wielded by revolutionaries who take history as their frame and world domination as
their goal. Ever since the Russian Revolution the world has had to
reckon with an inner daemonic force which has left no corner of a
continent untouched and has become the political climate of our
time. When I speak of the Grand Design, I mean an over-all Communist purpose which is at once a theory of history, a strategy of
action and a political religion that gives the individual Communist,
from the peak leader down to the newest doctrinal recruit, the conviction of being linked with history as part of something larger than
himself and the immediate moment.

There is nothing new about the fact of a Grand Design. Each of
the great conquerors in the past has had one of his own. Alexander
the Great was the son of an ambitious princeling in a poor moun-
tainous region, the pupil of Aristotle who tried to teach him how a
king might become a philosopher even if a philosopher could not
be a king.* But Alexander went beyond both his father and his
teacher. A traveler in India today will find areas reached by the conquering tide of Alexander's armies and of Greek culture. Aside from
his boldness of imagination and sweep of will, Alexander's power
lay in his vision of a cultural Grand Design which ignored ethnic as
well as political boundaries. Unlike the other Greeks, he disdained
to regard Asian peoples as barbarians, and wherever his armies
swept they affected a fusion of native and Greek cultures. Yet his
heirs fell out with each other, his world empire lasted scarcely beyond his death, and his Grand Design dissolved like a dream.

At the core of Caesar's vision was the conviction that most men
are neither heroes nor warriors but want a framework of peace
within which to live out their lives. He extended the reach of

* For the relation between the two, see the Introduction to my edition of
Aristotle's *Politics* (Modern Library).

97

Roman law as a frame of world order, and opened Roman citizenship to many whom he conquered. *Sum civis Romanus* became a badge of belonging to the great going concern of Roman power and order. But in the face of the rude challenge of new peoples, the Romans experienced a failure of nerve, and Edward Gibbon traced in melancholy detail the story of how the Grand Design fell apart, attended in its fall by the Byzantine softness and cruelty of the praetorian emperors.

For a time the Middle Ages had the idea of a universal church, held together by religious faith where arms and law had failed. But this too broke up, under the thrust of the idea of militant nationalism. The two great modern efforts, before Stalin and Mao Tse-tung, to carry through a Grand Design of world power were Napoleon's and Hitler's, and both of them used revolutionary nationalism as a frame for world conquest. Coming in the wake of the French Revolution, Napoleon inherited its revolutionary *élan* but added his own characteristic design. For the first time in modern history he put a nation under arms and sought to use it for a thrust at world power. He came close, not only by the sweep of his sword but also by the force of the legend he made of himself. But in the end he failed, because the idea of power, even of revolutionary power, was not enough to hold down a world that hungered for the power of an idea.

Of all these Grand Designs, Hitler's dream of establishing a Nazi world empire for a thousand years was the most ambitious. Starting with his march into the Rhineland, he won a succession of victories, right through the collapse of France and the near-conquest of Russia. He came close to success. When he got the news of the French surrender, in the historic railway car in the forest at Compiègne, he danced a little jig of triumph—the triumph of a man who was more of a revolutionary than any of the conquerors who had gone before him. But it was a revolution of darkness, a throwback to the primeval in man. What gave his little jig a grisly reality was the convergence of three far-reaching ideas, those of nationalism, socialism and racism. The cement that held them together went beyond each into the dark regions of the human heart. Hitler had discovered the power of the irrational, and with it he tried to build a structure of power for himself. In the end he failed, as the Japanese leaders failed even more ingloriously in Asia, but he set the stage for the Communist effort to carry through a Grand Design.

While Hitler saw himself as the sole architect of his dream of power, Lenin's theory of history made the individual leader less important than the campaign of history. Although an activist, he was nonetheless an intellectual, immersed in the literature of the Marxist prophets, viewing himself as an instrument in the fulfillment of their vision. He had no illusion that he could set up a world Communist structure in twenty years, but on the other hand he did not limit its life, once set up, to a thousand. He had no doubts about the inevitability of Communist triumph, provided that the strategy and tactics of its leaders were correct; but once the triumph came, he saw it as the fulfillment of a historic scheme which would have to be fought out for generations, war by war and battle by battle.

Stalin worked with massive patience, and with his own ferocity of purpose, in the same spirit. Khrushchev has indicated his own time scheme and his sense that the day of world triumph may be near. Taunting his opponents in the free world, he has said, "We will bury you"; and again, "Your grandchildren will live under socialism"—that is, under a world Communist system. The strength of the Communist Grand Design lies in its combination of doctrine, pragmatic sense of power, and resourcefulness in political warfare, and in its strategies of a political religion. Above all else it lies in the extent to which it has become identified with the revolutionary temper and with the inevitability of revolutionary triumph.

2. *The Two Faces of Revolution*

REVOLUTION HAS PLAYED the dominant role in world history from the American and French revolutions to the present moment, when what was once the particular passion of the vanguard nations has become the world climate for all. The great revolutionary enactments of modern history—the British revolutions of the seventeenth century, the American and French in the eighteenth century, the abortive European revolutions of 1848 and the tragic French Commune of 1870 in the nineteenth century, the Russian and Chinese revolutions and the Indian and lesser revolutionary nationalisms of the twentieth century—have shaped the tradition within which revolutionaries of today think and dream and act.

The Russians and the Chinese have entered a prescriptive claim to the revolutionary tradition, as if it were a monopoly of those who use terror to set up a one-party state and a closed society. The free world has unhappily, by silence and default, let the claim go unchallenged, despite the fact that until 1917 the great modern revolutions were European or American, and largely democratic; and even Marx in one aspect of his thought had absorbed that tradition. It was Lenin who broke away from it with finality, and the Communists have since associated the revolutionary tradition with only one phase of it. The curious fact is that many in the free world have carried over to Communist revolutions the emotional attitudes which have historically clustered around democratic ones. We still think of every revolution as if it were like the British and American and French, in establishing a people's freedom. That is why many liberals feel a political romanticism in identifying with every revolution, and feel guilty if they don't. They fail to understand the change that has come over the face of revolution.

Actually, revolution has two faces. One kind of revolution—apocalyptic, fanatical, terrorist—has always used purges and conspiracies and devoured its children. The other has aimed at liberty, and even when such revolutions have temporarily had to suspend liberty as a means, they have restored it as soon as possible upon achieving a new equilibrium in a new rule of law. The basic difference is between the constitutional revolutions, which aim to overthrow a tyranny and establish an open society, and on the other side the revolutions which aim to overthrow a regime, whether of freedom or oppression, and replace it with a closed society and a tight dictatorship. In the first category are the American and French revolutions (despite the Reign of Terror in the latter, and the Bonapartism which ended it), and in our own time the Indian and other democratic or military nationalist revolutions. In the second are the Russian and Chinese revolutions and those which have followed in their wake, in the spirit of the Communist movers and shakers, and manipulated by them.

The first type I call *revolution limited*. It was through limited revolution that the British in the seventeenth century transformed their absolute monarchy into a constitutional one. They did it through the Cromwellian revolution, which was bloody and protracted, and through the bloodless Glorious Revolution of 1688. The survival of the monarchy was a formal matter; the crucial one was the achievement of freedom, and it was the element of continuity with the past that made the bloodless revolution possible. The American Revolution, which proved to be the forerunner of anticolonial revolutions in our own time, was also a constitutional one.

The French Revolution was the first to bring in the element of an unlimited revolution, although it was a hybrid of both types. Rousseau strove to liberate mankind from the institutions that oppressed it in every area of human life. "Man is born free," he wrote, "and yet everywhere we see him in chains." But in preparing the ideas which were to strike off their chains, he failed to think about limiting the means. It was left to Robespierre, Marat, and the others of the French "Five," to show what this meant in action. Thus the liberal French Revolution already carried within itself the seeds of the totalitarian revolutions in Russia, Germany and China—of Lenin and Hitler and Mao Tse-tung. It is to this second type of revolution that Danton referred when he said that "revolution devours its children." This has been true of the Chinese Revolution, but not of the revolutions in India, Burma or Israel. It is true of the revolutions in North Korea, North Vietnam, and the Castro revolution in Cuba, but not of those in Tunis, Nigeria, Mexico or Venezuela.

Marx himself was torn between the idea of freedom and that of ruthless terror. In one aspect of his thought—that of democratic socialism—he absorbed and expressed the humanist tradition of Western Europe and America. This is why there have been two heritages of Marx's thinking—one the humanist heritage of the British Labour Party, the Scandinavian Socialist parties, and the parties and regimes of the democratic Left in Asia and Latin America; the other is the heritage of Russian and Chinese totalitarianism.

Until 1917 it was not clear in which of these two directions the main stream of Marxism would go. Lenin was the turning point. He too distinguished between the two revolutions. He called the first the "bourgeois revolution" and the second the "proletarian." But he saw them both as part of the same revolutionary process, and he insisted that no revolution could be considered completed until the constitutional phase had been replaced by the proletarian. This second regime Lenin defined as one in which the workers, through their dictatorship, refuse to share power with any other class. One could similarly define the present Communist vision of a new world order, the Grand Design, as one in which Communism refuses to share world power with any other social system. Lenin's historic question, *Kto kovo?*—Who whom?—expresses the principle of *revolution unlimited* in its most naked form. It is the principle of absolute force in the political jungle.

When Lenin was once asked, "What is socialism?" he answered, "Socialism is Soviets plus electrification," and then again, "Socialism is accounting"; he was saying in effect that Communism is whatever is needed to industralize and plan the economy. Communism was thus the strategy of modernization. But that is only one side of it. In the early days of the Russian Revolution the head of the Cheka, Dzerzhinsky was urged to spare a victim on the ground of justice. "We

don't want justice," he answered, "we want to settle accounts."
Dzerzhinsky's settling of accounts was closer to the spirit of revolution unlimited than Lenin's "accounting."

Stalin also was the embodiment of the ruthlessness of a regime
which does not regard any means as excluded. This ruthlessness in
the internal regime was bound to reflect itself in Stalin's foreign
policy. He treated heads of other Communist states as if they were
members of his own party apparatus at home. Khrushchev tells us
that Stalin showed him a letter he had written to Tito at the time of
the break from Russia in 1948, and how Stalin had boasted, "I will
shake my little finger and there will be no more Tito. He will fall."
After telling about this in his speech denouncing Stalin's crimes and
his cult of personality, Khrushchev added, "You see to what Stalin's
mania for greatness led." He was saying that Stalin had mistaken his
own stature for the shadow of history. But is there not the same
"mania for greatness"—I should myself call it "overwill," or "overreach"—in the whole of Communism when seen as a revolution unlimited? Khrushchev's condemnation of Stalin's crimes came from a
man who had maintained silence until that time, and who could
never wholly wash away his complicity in them. While Russia has
since then become a relatively conservative power and Soviet industrialization has set in motion far-reaching internal changes, it
would be rash to say that Khrushchev has abandoned either the idea
of revolution unlimited or his zeal for the Grand Design.

What a contrast between this historical record and the idealized
picture that the romantic revolutionaries still carry about in their
tender-minded imaginations! Albert Camus's remarkable book,
L'Homme révolté, points out that much of the strength of Communism lay in enabling the young Europeans to feel allied with the
powerful and inevitable forces of history. It gave them a less lonely
and isolated sense. From their self-pity as victims they were ready,
like a juggernaut, to roll with history over the bodies of thousands
and millions.

3. Domination and Accommodation

THERE IS A natural history of revolution which applies to both types
of it—a progression of more or less marked phases through which
revolutions pass, from fanaticism to stability, or perhaps from im-
maturity to maturity. It has become a truism to point out that the
Soviet state in Russia has grown into a conservative great power,

while the Chinese Communist state, more than thirty years younger, is roughly where Russia was in the middle 1920s. It is still resentful at not being accorded recognition, vituperative in utterance, intolerant and contemptuous toward its opponents, harsh in police-state methods, and drastic in its efforts to refashion Chinese society into a honeycomb of barrackslike communes.

This time differential has its importance. But in seeking the sources of the differences between the Chinese and Russian revolutionary mentalities, and the common elements as well, I prefer a different approach. I start from the proposition that the Marxist revolutionary state, born out of a fanatical hostility to the democratic world, never wholly loses that hostility. Yet it is constantly being pushed toward an equilibrium of some sort, in the form of a practical working relation with the world. I call these two impulses the *domination effect* and the *accommodation effect*.

The first is governed by the urge to take vengeance and destroy, the second by the urge to belong and be recognized. The first is ruthless, implacable, dogma-conditioned, power-obsessed. It is "militant" Communism, throws its weight about and behaves as if the front were everywhere. Its motto is "We or they"; its question is the jungle question that Lenin asked, "Who whom?" It believes that a showdown war is inevitable between the Communist and democratic worlds, that until then the feud between them is unhealable, and that in it any method goes. It seeks always to reach and pass the point of no return, confident that what lies beyond can always be transcended, and that there will never be any need for retracing its steps. It believes in tight discipline of Communist parties and in police-state controls against opposition and dissent within each state. It uses every revolutionary situation and every war as a revolutionary leap forward in bringing another segment of the world under Communist domination. It is even willing, for the moment, to confront the possibility of a nuclear war in the same terms, if not deliberately toward the same end.

The accommodation effect is adaptive and pragmatic. It accepts international law in a world of nation-states, works within the United Nations, uses the channels of diplomacy, talks of "summits" even when it does not intend to go through with them. Its slogans are at various times those of a "Popular Front," "collective security," "coexistence," "*detente*." Instead of stressing inevitable showdowns, it carries on political warfare in rivalry with the non-Communist world, seeking to appeal to the revolutionary movements and nations of the newly opened continents. It stresses Communist economic growth, shifts its policy emphasis at home to consumer goods, boasts of the "overtake" achievements of Communism in science and technology, holds forth the promise of the good life under Communism, and talks repeatedly of the inevitable Communist triumph.

The efforts to embrace both these phases of the revolutionary Communist state has accounted for the dilemmas of Soviet policy and the alternation of emphasis between them. One could write the history of Soviet Russian conduct largely in terms of a kind of commuting between these two drives inside the Communist state and the Communist mentality. There are, of course, other factors which loom larger in their immediate impact. The historian must reckon with the social consequences of industrialization, with the logic of the internal development of a Communist economy, state, society, as these confront the tasks that the leaders have set for them. He must also reckon with the personalities of the individual leaders and the power clashes between them. But what is unique to the nature and behavior of the Communist state is the conflicting demands of the accommodation effect and the domination effect.

The policy alternations of the free-world power system are real enough, partly because of leadership and opinion changes, partly through changes in the world power balance. But it does not have, either in doctrine or in inner dynamic, the same exigent drive toward a world imperium and is not caught in the same bind as the Communist system, between its two impulses.

4. The Daemon and the Locomotive

THIS IN-AGAIN-OUT-AGAIN alternation of strategies has grown increasingly more difficult to maintain in an age of overkill. The Communist leaders are faced by a crisis of long-range choice. Will they pursue their unlimited aims through unlimited means, with the overwhelming probabilities of a destructive and self-destructive war? Or will they abandon their unlimited aims because the unlimited means have become prohibitive in human and political cost?

The Soviet leaders seem to have chosen the second course. If this is so, then it marks a victory of the overkill principle over the Grand Design, and of the reality principle over the Utopian dream of a Communist world. If they want to support this policy, the Communist leaders can quote Scripture. Lenin, with his intense realism, may have seen that revolutionary science might some day set limits within which revolutionary politics would have to work. At any rate, that is how his name was invoked, at a Lenin Day celebration in 1960, by the veteran Communist bureaucrat Otto Kuusinen:

> The classics of Marxism have never denied the fact that new types of weapons not only can bring about a radical change in the art of war but can influence politics as well. For instance, Engels wrote about it in *Anti-Dühring*. And Nadezhda Krupskaya tells that Lenin foresaw that the time will come when war will become so destructive as to be impossible.

Thus, for the first time in Communist history, unlimited war as an instrument of unlimited Communist expansion is ruled out. The logic is clear enough: If a major war has become "so destructive as to be impossible," then the Communist theory of an inevitable major showdown between "socialism" and "capitalist imperialism" has also become impossible.

This does not exclude the *appearance* of an unlimited intent, either as part of the nuclear deterrent strategy or as part of the strategy of political war. As an observer at the Paris non-summit conference (or summit nonconference) of 1960, I watched Nikita Khrushchev at his unending press conference, raging at the Philistine capitalist leaders, calling the journalists "bastards," rattling the missile power of the Soviets, and threatening all and sundry with the condign punishment of the days of wrath to come. The calculated indignation, heightened perhaps by a self-infection, took on credibility when you remembered that this was a man possessed of an idea. It was the idea of transforming the world, by force or fraud, by persuasion or terror or death, into an ideal world-state run by a dictatorship of the disciplined and dedicated proletarians. To make it further credible, one saw a man presumably awakened from a temporary dream of peace and competitive coexistence, now determined on prodding the historic inevitability of Communist triumph by every weapon at his command.

Earlier in the year I had attended a midnight press conference held by Chou En-lai in New Delhi, after a fruitless week of talks with Nehru. As he spoke, he was clearly moved by a passion and a dream. The passion was for the recognition of the "existing realities" of the boundary situation—*after* the Chinese *fait accompli* of occupying Longju and a chunk of Ladakh—as the basis for negotiation. The dream was the Grand Design of a Communist Asia under Chinese control, within a broader Communist world imperium. This was a True Believer, representing an elite group which had never succumbed to the temptations of the *détente* but was willing to face the consequences of dying and killing for a cause. This group, even in its period of seeming relaxation of discipline (the "Policy of the Hundred Flowers"), had never been deflected from the pursuit of its ultimate purpose.

The differences between the Russian and Chinese situations may serve as a commentary on how careful the observer must be, neither to take too seriously the rhetoric of the Grand Design, nor to assume that the overkill weapons have dispelled it into thin air. While the Russian *élan* was largely transformed from a religion into a church, and the Soviet Union itself into one of the possessing and therefore conservative powers, the Chinese elite remained a tutelary Old Guard seeking to indoctrinate its people with a quenchless belief in their world destiny. The Russian leaders were sitting on top of a power pyramid which a nuclear war would destroy; but the Chinese firm was still "Revolution Unlimited," still exploring the rickety commune structure to find one which could survive a nuclear war, and confident in a population of 700 million, which would remain the world's largest, whatever happened to the rest of the world. The Russian leaders were still wary of how far the weapons race might swing the world into the arc of destruction; the Chinese leaders, still lacking the nuclear weapons, were more matter-of-fact in accepting them in their pursuit of a Communist imperium.

The Chinese periodical *Hung Ch'i* (Red Flag), theoretical organ of the Central Committee of the Chinese Communist Party, announced on Lenin Day, in April 1960, that

> until the imperialist system and the exploiting classes come to an end, wars of one kind or another will always appear. . . . Communists must make two preparations: one for the development of the revolution, and the other for nonpeaceful revolution. . . . They must master wherever possible more and more of such new techniques as atomic weapons and rocketry.

As for the risk of world annihilation, *Hung Ch'i* was not daunted. Out of the wreckage of the war would come "a civilization thousands of times higher than the capitalist system and with a truly beautiful future."

One might take the case of China as a reassertion of the Communist daemon—the mystique of an inevitable world triumph and of the collective will to achieve it. This would argue that the Communist world elite is not yet ready to give up the domination effect and fall back upon accommodation, and upon settlements reached in the political war; that the risks of nuclear war could not yet turn it away from the dynamism of Communism-as-religion. But running counter to this view there is the massive fact of the Soviet abstention from nuclear crisis threats except as deliberate deterrent policy, the emphases upon opportunist policy rather than dogma, and the increasing Soviet reliance upon political war rather than upon weapons.

This does not, however, dispose of the Communist daemon or of its dangers to world peace. Its operation may be clearer if we add to the principle of overkill, a corollary principle of "overreach." All power tends to overstep its limits, and every decisive wielder of power is tempted to push it not only as far as it will go but experimentally farther. As with every human enterprise involving will and calculation, the exercise of power has a generative principle within it by which it feeds on itself and adds accretions of will to the will already there. History is full of instances where the sober calculation of limits did not operate in time to check the will-to-power and the conqueror became the "overreacher." The Greeks used this in their concept of *hubris* as material for their tragedies. The Elizabethans, who had a sensitive feel for power and its limits, also saw its tragic involvements: the idea of the overreacher, Harry Levin has suggested, was at the center of Christopher Marlowe's tragedies as at the center of his life.

While the overreachers in the past have often been dictators without doctrine, the characteristic overreacher of our time has been the ideological leader bent on building an empire—a Mussolini, a Hitler, a Tojo, a Stalin.* Mussolini and Hitler overreached themselves when they took on the Soviet power cluster as well as the democratic one, as did Tojo and the Japanese war lords when they tried to carve out a Pacific-Asian naval and land empire on a narrow base of resources and population. Stalin almost overreached himself by allowing the war power of the Nazi Reich to grow while he strove to divert the Nazi fury in another direction. But what has happened today is that overreach has intermeshed with overkill and must reckon with suicidal dangers. The overreacher today knows that he is bound to get messed up with a nuclear war if he pushes beyond the margin of tolerance set for him by his adversaries.

I note in passing that the overkill principle is serving the cause of world Communist power both badly and well. Badly, because if

---

* For further discussion of the overreach principle in its bearing on the survival of civilization today, see Chapter V, Section 5, "The Death and Life of Civilizations."

it were not for nuclear weapons there would be room for a succession of nonnuclear wars, big and small, which would be of advantage to Communist expansion. For war of any sort today has revolutionary consequences: it dislocates the power structure, places weapons in the hands of men who would otherwise not be able to get them, lights the fires of nationalist consciousness, ravages the land, uproots the traditional social structure, leaves misery in its wake, and thus leaves the area riper for revolutionary overturn. An era of such wars might well have the consequences in other world areas that it had in Eastern Europe after 1945. If it were not for the threat of H-weapons, the Communists might conceivably by this time have overrun the European mainland, the better part of Southeast Asia and the Middle East, and even portions of Africa. But in an age of overkill, war becomes a form of dangerous adventurism, even for a Communist regime. Moreover, by putting the reliance of the most advanced forms of warfare upon small, highly technical units rather than upon mass armies, the nuclear age has ended the era of the nation-in-arms and inaugurated one of elite warfare—which cuts the advantage that the manpower resources of China and Russia would otherwise give them.

But the overkill principle has also served the Communist cause well, in dispersing the necessary Western bases for deterrent attack, thus stretching the democratic imperium, making it costly and vulnerable, forcing it to rely on military pacts, and exposing it to a campaign of Communist political warfare.

In the clash between the dangers of overkill and the thrust of the Communist daemon, only one rational answer seems possible: that the daemon must limit itself, lest the Communist leaders find the world they coveted for the global enactment of their drama of transformation a world of radioactive ashes. Marxism has always been fond of historical "contradictions"; the final ironic contradiction is that the symbolic victory of the Communist system in the rocket weapons race used a science so dangerous that even a world triumph over the opposing power system is purchasable only at the risk of unthinkable war—unthinkable, but again (as I put it earlier) not impossible. In that sense the great crisis of our time is not a crisis of the democratic world, but a crisis of Communist decision as to whether the daemon in it can be contained.

But can it? Remember that it is exactly the daemonic force—the preconscious of the Communist mind—from which not only the fierce drive of Communism has come, but also a good deal of its creativeness. There are few historic instances of causes which have demanded and evoked more from their true believers, in terms of discipline, personal sacrifice, ruthlessness, subordination of human feeling, self-denial, unquestioning obedience to the party doctrine, and the repressing of ethical standards in the interest of a "higher" morality flowing from the cause itself. George Kennan has pointed out how deep an impression the "early Bolshevik personality" made upon the American, British and French unofficial observers who watched the new revolutionary regime in action during its first years. Observers who traveled with the Eighth Route Army of the Chinese revolutionaries during its great retreat were likewise impressed by the austerity of life and the rigors of discipline among leaders and followers alike.

There is a sado-masochistic element here which goes deep to the neuroses of our time, a wild satisfaction in the abandonment of personal choice and in the imposition of authority over others, which accounts for a good deal of the evocative force of the movement. But there is also an element of appeal that goes beyond the neurotic. At the core of it is the heady sense of an irresistible movement which gathers up men and ideas in its course, and sweeps toward a victory of purpose in an otherwise purposeless world. Much of this is only rhetoric, but the Communists have in many cases come to believe in their own legend and have been caught despite their cynicism—perhaps because of it—in the search for meaning.

This may shed some light on the much debated question of the extent to which the strength of Communism lies in its nationalist as against its doctrinal elements, and the extent to which Soviet policy has been Communist or Russian, and Peking policy Communist or Chinese.* Many have contended that the continuities of Russian history and national psychology are more important than the immediate urgencies of Communism, and that it is simply Peter the Great who reappears—fiercer, more cunning, and with a domain writ large on world history—in Lenin, Stalin and Khrushchev. Nehru and other Indian leaders have felt that it was the Chinese expansionist tradition, and not the Communist doctrine and dream, which was behind the invasion of Ladakh.

Put in the form of a clear choice between the two forces it is a meaningless dispute. One cannot understand either Russian or Chinese society today except as the convergence point of Communist doctrine and strategy with the national tradition and character.

* For an earlier discussion, see Chapter II, Section 3, "Empire as Power Cluster," and Section 7, "Grandeurs and Miseries of Empire."

But in each case the dynamic element is Communism, acting on the history and society as raw material, seeking out the elements of both that are most plastic and permeable, infusing them with its implacable quality of will, laying siege to the more resistant elements (like the Chinese doctrine of "face," or the tenacity of the Chinese family) and in time storming them. This is not to say that the struggle between the two forces is not a fierce one. Even in the Baltic and East European satellites, where the problem of mastery ought to be compassable, there has been a silent struggle between the Moscow-trained party bureaucrats and the nationalist Communist heretics—a struggle which only the repeated interventions of Moscow's armed authority have kept the nationalist forces from winning.

One must remember that the only emotional force which has mustered a daemonic strength comparable to Communism has been nationalism. Perhaps the best way to put it is that the Communist hold has been strongest where the daemon of the Communist idea and the mystique of the nationalist idea have been mutually inflammatory. This is true in China, where a small leadership elite established itself improbably on a family-based, gentry-led, dynastic tradition. It is true also in Russia, in North Korea and North Vietnam; it has been weakest where the two ideas have been in conflict, as in Poland or in the Kremlin's failure to hold on to Yugoslavia.

At a party at one of the East European embassies (so goes the legendry of the foreign correspondents at Moscow) Nikita Khrushchev propelled himself across the floor on his hands and knees, announcing to the guests, "I am the locomotive of history." Whether it actually happened or not, it is psychologically true of Khrushchev and forms an interesting footnote to the traditional Marxist theory about the dynamic of history.

The essence of that theory is that history unfolds by a dialectical process in which the changes in the modes of production bring about changes in the relations of production; that the determining factors are broadly materialist, which in terms of our time means broadly economic; and that it is the class struggle directed and disciplined by conscious leadership, which furnishes the dynamic element in historical change. When Khrushchev calls himself the locomotive of history he means not to reject the Marxist tradition, but to add a gloss to it. He personalizes a process which Marx means to be an impersonal one, although clearly he meant to assign a role to leadership in this impersonal process—the role of grasping the nature of the historic forces in working with them.

It was Lenin who made the great theoretical leap on this score, in *What Is to Be Done?*, by demanding of the leadership elite that it take action in the name of the working class. In Lenin's thinking, the crux of revolutionary leadership lies in timing, boldness and decisiveness—in knowing when the revolutionary situation is ripe, and in taking action as a commander would in battle, without hesitations and never with any half measures. Given this approach, it was inevitable that Lenin should regard the issue as closed after the elite group had made its decision through "democratic centralism," and should meet dissent from "the enemies of the people" with repression and terror. Lenin has sometimes been sentimentalized as a "democratic" Communist whose native impulse toward permissiveness was frustrated by the difficulties that beset him, and whose humanism was turned upside down by Stalin's preference for ruling through terror. Certainly he was a freer and less tortured personality than Stalin. But the machinery of coercion was an inherent part of an intellectual universe which ran in terms of the class-struggle dynamic, of the role of leadership in the process of historic change, and of a cleavage between the vanguard champions of the people and the feudal, bourgeois and counterrevolutionary enemies of the people. This was true also of Stalin and has remained true of Khrushchev.

What it amounts to is that, while a certain sequence of historic change is impersonal and inevitable, it must be prodded by particular persons, and its inevitability is made actual by their decisions. Those decisions moreover must inherently involve coercion, since the holders of power in the old regime do not willingly give up their power, and even proletarian leaders may hold to erroneous views of the course of history and its strategies. Marx himself spoke of the proletarian class as "the midwife of history," implying that the process of revolutionary change was as natural as birth, needing as in birth a helping hand. But, with Lenin and Stalin, the intermediary became not the workers as a class but their leadership elite, speaking and acting for them; and in practice, the methods they used unavoidably included force and violence.

Thus, Khrushchev's locomotive of history comes at the end of the progression of doctrine and emphasis. It is worth noting that Khrushchev has become in himself the single carrier of the historic role which Marx assigned to the total working class and Lenin thought of as operating through a small leadership elite. Khrushchev as a locomotive chugs across the floor of history in behalf of revolutionary change in other countries and under other skies than those of the Soviet Union. The assumption is that they are given a chance through Khrushchev's decisions to fulfill their role in history.

But where does this leave Russia itself? If the dialectic of history operates in Laos and Cuba, in India and Iran and Guinea, it must operate in Russia as well.

Yet I suspect that Khrushchev's self-image as a locomotive over-accents the individual leader's role, partly because world changes, converging with Communist objectives, severely limit the leader's freedom of action, partly because Russia is subject to internal changes as well. Take as an example the Trotsky-Stalin controversy over spreading the world revolution, which seemed to take the rival forms of the doctrine of "permanent revolution" as against that of "socialism in one country." They were different strategies toward the same end, a Communist world; Stalin preferred to build a solid power base in Russian industrial and military strength, to use it more effectively when the time came for revolutionary intervention. Trotsky held that while you had to build Socialism in Russia you could not complete it unless you had expanded it abroad. Stalin won. But in order to carry out his strategy he had to reverse himself in his economic policy; where he had once fought Trotsky's plan for ruthless development of heavy industry at the cost of forced collectivization of agriculture, he had to take it over; in the end, after World War II, he also embraced the strategy of world revolution by military expansion, grabbing Eastern Europe at his first chance and telling Milovan Djilas that wherever the Communist armies went they necessarily imposed the Communist social system. It is likely that Trotsky, had he won power, would have come out with policies not very different from these.

As for internal change, the fact of Russia as a Communist society does not mean that history is completed there and has stopped moving. True, the Communist answer is that with the establishment of Communism the class struggle will resolve itself, and that historic change will operate on another level. But Russia too is moving. It is not exempt from the deep, if silent, changes which are the consequences of technological advance. I don't go along with the school which holds that the quality of Khrushchev's role is due to technological and class changes in Russia. The logic of this, carried further, would mean that Stalin, had he lived, would have become an anti-Stalinist, and in responding to the dialectic of internal social change he would have relaxed the police-state rigors. Projected into the future, it would mean that such a Stalin regime would be-come (as Isaac Deutscher says Khrushchev's will) in its own way as free as the American and British. Freedom granted at the sufferance of a leader with unlimited power is not a freedom that can be predicted as part of a process of historic change. To assume that the new classes, generated by technological and industrial change, will be able to make their needs and demands felt despite the will of the ruling elite is to reckon without the coercive strength of whatever "locomotive of history" happens to be in power.

Yet it is perilous to omit the larger frame of ongoing social change within which men like Stalin and Khrushchev have to work. The process of rapid industrialization, the access of new goods, the availability of new technology, the mushrooming of new industries and cities, the necessity for new skills and education— all of them on a massive scale, and all with a pace of urgency be-yond anything that Marx, or even Lenin, could have dreamed— are bound to bring new classes and elites into being in Russia, with new attitudes, new aspirations and claims, new limits of tolerance. This is the real dynamic of history, and every leader works both against these forces and with them, in varying combinations of resistance and prodding. Stalin, had he lived, would eventually have had to reckon with this dynamic, whether or not he would have been flexible enough to adjust to it.

To speak of the *dynamic* is to imply a general theory of imper-sonal and personal elements in social change; to speak of a *locomo-tive of history* is a heightened way of singling out the role of an activist leader in the total process; to speak, as I have done earlier in this chapter, of the *daemonic* in Communism is to seek a term for the inner drive—arising partly out of the self-generated propul-sions of the doctrine, partly out of the habits of mind of Communist leaders and people—which cannot be reduced to rational terms. Communist behavior cannot be understood without all three, and without adding to them the *mystique*—whether of history itself, or of the role of science in it, or of revolution—which gives to Com-munist thinking the hazy edges of submissive belief.

Several questions obtrude themselves. First, why don't the Com-munists apply all these elements of the historic process to Russia itself? By his own reckoning Khrushchev performs for the still "un-liberated" peoples a function of prodding and expediting revolu-tionary social change which no one is permitted to perform for the Russian people themselves; in fact, no one is permitted to acknowledge even that the revolutionary dynamic is at work inside Russia. The answer is that it would be dangerous to the power of the Communist commanding elite to apply their own doctrine to their own situation.

Second, what is there to stop the daemon of Communism, driven by its inner propulsions and fed by its mystique? Nothing, except the dangers to which it exposes Communist power through over-kill weapons, and the recoil of people and leaders alike from that danger, and the resistances from both the free world and the un-committed world, and the revolution of rising expectations within Communist societies which sets life-goals more likely to be achieved in an open world of diverse societies than in a struggle for un-limited ends by unlimited means.

5. Reason of State and Reason of History

To GET SOME further insight into the probable future of the daemon of Communism, it may be well to probe its inner nature. This must be sought in the history of ideas in the Europe of the eighteenth century and perhaps further back.

It was the eighteenth-century French social thinkers—the "Proph-ets of Paris," in Frank Manuel's phrase—who developed the idea of history as an impersonal force justified in mowing down the in-dividual in pursuit of a larger good for "humanity." The dominant ideas of the eighteenth century were those of History, Progress, Posterity and Humanity; out of them was shaped the triad of slo-gans—Liberty, Equality and Fraternity—which was blazoned on the banners of the French Revolution. Marx and Engels, as the chil-dren of the European Enlightenment, inherited the underlying ideas as well as the embattled slogans. Communist practice has made a mockery of the slogans. There is a considerable measure of equality, not of wealth but of poverty, and little fraternity, and al-most no liberty to be found in China; and the relaxing of police-state controls which followed Khrushchev's denunciation of Stalin proved to be only a limited freedom, in the interests of consolidat-ing the Khrushchev regime.

But the underlying ideas have had their lasting impact in the doctrine that there are laws in history which can be traced by ob-jective study; that History itself is an animate, if impersonal, force, a moving actor in the flux of events; that Progress is inevitable and that its prospects and possibilities are unending; that the overriding question about men's acts is less their essential nature than whether they are done for Humanity; and that the final judgment will be delivered by Posterity.

The bearing of this on international politics, and especially on the armed doctrine of Communism, is readily apparent. If you start from a theory of the state, as Machiavelli did, and also the German thinkers of the nineteenth century who built on him, then your rationalizing of arbitrary state action will be the form of reason-of-state (*raison d'état, Staatsräson*). But if you start, as Marx and Engels did, following the tradition of the eighteenth-century thinkers, with a basic "scientific" theory of history and its inevitabilities, then you will end with reason-of-history (*raison d'histoire, Geschichtsräson*). In that event, you will not reckon the cost in human life as decisive. "The Cheka," said one of its early directors, Dzerzhinsky, "cannot reckon with whether or not it will inflict injury upon private individuals, but must concern itself with only one thing—the victory of the Revolution over the bourgeoisie." History would have to ride like a juggernaut over the individual life, in order to establish the foundations of the future. Posterity was to be not only the judge of the acts of statesmen and executioners alike, but also their justification, since it would be the beneficiary of the progress thus achieved.

The role that reason-of-state played for the statesmen of the classical system of world politics, in covering both their aggressions and blunders, is now being filled for the revolutionary elites by reason-of-history. Doubtless the Russians who gave and carried out the orders for mowing down the young Hungarian nationalists believed that in suppressing the "counterrevolutionaries" they had history on their side. The Chinese leaders were doubtless also convinced that history would thank them for supplanting the outworn feudal institutions of Tibet with the dynamics of China's "Great Leap Forward," for having decimated the lamas and replaced the lamaseries with "houses of ideological rehabilitation." One must remember that the very term "counterrevolution" itself refers to a movement whose crime lies in daring to oppose the onflowing stream of history.

Once you have justified your acts by reason-of-history there remains a further step in formulating the daemon. The eighteenth-century idea of the use of knowledge for progress was based on the premise that nothing is outside the reach and competence of man. The science of the nineteenth and twentieth centuries seemed to confirm this premise. But along with it came the crucial corollary: If nothing is beyond man's reach as a goal, in his striving to serve

Progress and Humanity, then nothing is excluded as a means. Anything goes—honor and honesty, the plighted word, the recognition of the identity of another person or another nation, parental and filial ties, love and loyalty and the integrity of thought. These are only items to be transcended in the march toward the final goal. The Grand Design of Communism, with the Communist daemon at its core, is part of another Grand Design: the sense of being allied with History and of having a pipeline to the secrets of Progress.

Anything goes; nothing is excluded. The consequences of this doctrine, derived from the "totalitarian liberals" of the eighteenth century, distorted by the overreachers of the twentieth, are written in the annals of our time. You will find them in the destruction of the European Jews and in the history of the German death camps; in the forced collectivization of the Russian peasants in the 1920s; in the sadisms of Stalin, so egregious that Khrushchev's own belated condemnation of them gave only a hint of their reach and nature; in the repression of the Hungarian revolution; in the ruthless means used in consolidating the Chinese Communist regime.

Perhaps the best verdict on those who sought, sometimes with the idealism of True Believers, to link the elevated ideals of eighteenth-century European man with the twentieth-century doctrine of "Anything goes," was given in a scrupulous sentence of a nineteenth-century man, Alexis de Tocqueville: "He who seeks in Liberty anything other than Liberty itself is destined for servitude."

6. Winds of Communist Doctrine: Mystique, Dogma, and Distortion in Marxism

OF ALL THE Utopian elements in Communist doctrine, the role of science as a torchbringer for humanity has been the most relevant for the situation today. "The natural sciences," wrote Marx in 1844, "have prepared the emancipation of humanity, even though their immediate effect may have been to accentuate the dehumanizing of man. . . . They will become the basis of a *human* science, just as they have already become—though in an alienated form—the basis of a really human life." When Marx spoke of the "dehumanizing of man" and of "alienation" he meant that capitalist industrialism had turned labor into a commodity, and the worker into a counter to be bought and sold, and had cut man himself off from his inner potential for human flowering. He did not foresee that democracy would move toward new economic and social forms to counteract the rigidities that beset any successful system, and would give human potentials a better chance to develop, while alienation would be carried farther in the "socialist" societies than in the democratic ones. He would have been stunned to discover that man would become an object for manipulation by the cynical and idealist leaders alike—in the name of history and in the interests of a Communist world imperium.

Science has become for the Communists at once a means, a value and a religion. The seeds of the cult of science in Marxism are already to be found in Marx's prediction above, that the natural sciences would lead to the "emancipation of humanity." Here Marx was again working with the heritage of the eighteenth-century thinkers. "Fontenelle led men gently," writes Kingsley Martin, "from faith in Christianity to religious skepticism, and from religious skepticism to a new faith in science." The religion of revolution and the religion of science were closely intertwined, and both of them were linked with the daemon of the Communist mission. Speaking in London in April, 1960, Konstantin Fedin, Secretary of the Union of Russian Writers, asserted that in Russia literature and science are equally expressions of the human spirit. "Surely our scientists have enough passion, inspiration, dreams— and Russia is not giving up its dreams to anyone."

The dreams were given a fillip by Russian successes in missiles and rocketry. It was almost as if the heady experience of shooting at the moon in the heavens had given the Communist leaders a renewed belief, by an infectious carry-over, in their ability to shoot at the moon of a world imperium. The Utopian passion for the "liberation of humanity," the cult of science and its possibilities, the refusal to recognize the existence of what must lie outside the scope of human will, the release of long-repressed hostilities, the giddying sense of vaulting power—these were fused into a new psychological pattern of propaganda and belief.

This is all the more striking because it carries the tradition of Marxist thought to a new and unexampled degree of subjectivism. In attacking the succession of Western thinkers from Plato to Hegel, Marx wrote that "the philosophers have only *interpreted* the world, in various ways; the point, however, is to change it." As Hannah Arendt has pointed out, it was not so much Hegelian idealism that Marx stood on its head, but the relationship of thought and action in themselves. He wanted to deal only with the objective universe as the ultimate reality, and with action based upon that universe, but he was caught by having to work within the philosophical tradition while seeking to overthrow it. The action of revolutionaries cannot go through unless it is contained within a frame of ideas about history and its direction, and about social change and its means and purposes. Thus, the effort to jump out of this frame was as futile as an effort to jump out of his own philosophic skin.

By every Marxist canon of judgment, the scientist belongs with the philosophers who have merely studied and interpreted the world, while it is the revolutionaries who do change it. But to give science as important a role as the Russians are now doing is to contradict this canon, and to acknowledge the historic reality of science, either as idle or purposive curiosity, or as a condition of technical advance. It is to accept, as crucial, the men who formerly were regarded as coming along with the changing forces of production in a kind of package deal.

But at whatever psychic cost, the paradox of the subjective becoming the creative is one that the Communist leaders have had to swallow. They may try to explain it away by attributing to science in a Communist state a superior efficacy, flowing from a greater sense of social purpose and a more committed release of energy. But this scarcely resolves the basic intellectual problem. If the most creative forces are those of science, if the intellect and will can be used to create new modes of technological power for war and peace, then why cannot similar efforts of intellect and will be used throughout history? Why might they not change the structure of power in a Communist society itself, perhaps even in Russia? And if the good life to which science drives is the objective of the best effort in a society, then what is to stop the explosive idea that there may be other and better social forms for achieving the good life? What I am suggesting is that there are consequences which flow from turning science into a mystique. This may work to give young people in the farthest reaches of the world a sense of being part of an irresistible new order. But it opens up a new corridor of possibility for the young people in the Communist society itself, exposes them to the corrosive impact of ideas, gives a new prestige to the life of the mind when used not only by commissars and Politburo giants but also by working intellectuals. By bringing subjectivism back into the universe from which Marx had sought to exile it, the mystique of science brings about a transvaluation of Communist values.

The Marxist doctrines have moved far from the original fierce but humanist indictment by Marx of the alienation of man from man. They have moved also from the breath-taking perspectives of history he brought together out of the past and projected into the future; from his laying bare the extent to which the whole society moves to the puppet strings of money, power and class; from his mapping out a strategy for the conquest of power by the lowliest so that men could become brothers, and so that man might transform his own nature in the course of transforming his society. What was it that the Communists, speaking and killing and dying in the name of Marx, yet using him for their own purposes, did to the legacy they took over from him?

The first thing that strikes you in studying the past half century is the continuing relation between doctrine and policy, between ideology and social reality—what Marx himself called the *unity of theory and practice*. This raises the ghost of the controversy over the sources of Soviet conduct. Those who say that the Russian leaders have been guided throughout by the Marxist-Leninist canon will have difficulty in accounting for its wild variations of policy, even in a single regime like Lenin's, Stalin's or Khrushchev's, always in the name of the same body of theory. On the other hand, those who attribute all of Communist policy to the impulsions of naked power and opportunism will miss the attraction of the theoretical frame within which these impulsions operate. The relation between doctrine and policy is open for anyone to trace who is willing to follow the twistings and turnings in all their tortuous fascination. This means that a good history of the Soviet Union should go along with a good history of its Communist Party and a good intellectual history of the fate of Marxist doctrine in Russia. But in this web of relationship the gleaming red filament is that of the practical necessities of situation and action, not the intellectual rigors of doctrine.

Some of its opponents persuaded themselves wishfully that the Communist doctrine is rigid and its absorptive power is therefore lacking. But the facts are against them. The Russians and Chinese, in varying degrees, have been able remarkably to absorb into their intellectual scheme the new facts of a developing world, and to adapt their doctrine to a changing social reality. It is true that Communism is "dogmatic" in the sense that it lives by dogma. But in the early years of the Revolution, Lenin said: "Our doctrine is not a dogma but a guide to action." And a hardheaded, resourceful Communist leader like Khrushchev, at once power-minded and realistic, has managed to make the letter of the dogma and his own political needs intermesh, adapting his policy to the mold of the doctrine, and using the appropriate texts from the Marxist founding fathers to nail it down. He uses the dogma as a stick with which to beat his opponents inside and outside the party and the nation. Maybe this is only pragmatic politics, to be found in any power structure. Maybe it is a characteristic of Russian or Chinese energy, spending itself over thousand-year stretches of history, refusing to be pent up within the too-narrow confines of doctrine. Maybe it is only what shrewd men have done under any social system, even when they wore the too-tight garments of a dogma. Whatever the cause, the fact is that both Communist Russia and China have proved highly adaptable regimes.

The Communist may thus turn out to be, despite his dogma, the adapting man. This may help to explain the failure of either the Russian or the Chinese regime, after the conquest of power, to develop any original theory or theorists. Since Lenin and Trotsky, the Russians have had only men of action (Stalin, Malenkov, Beria, Molotov, Khrushchev) struggling for power within a changing frame of events. Stalin was touted by his sycophants as a theorist on the nationalist question and on the language controversy, but his contributions scarcely survived his death. In China, Mao Tsetung is depicted as having transformed Marxism from a European to a nativist (Asian) form. Certainly he is responsible for some original ideas about guerrilla warfare and for merely formalistic and hortatory ideas, such as, "Regard the enemy disdainfully in strategy; regard the enemy seriously in tactics." But, despite his claim to be a theorist on Lenin's level, he comes closer to Stalin as a man of action. In neither regime does the climate of even relative intellectual freedom exist for the development of another Marx or Engels, Saint-Simon or Sorel, Hobson or De Leon, Kautsky or Hilferding or Rosa Luxembourg, Plekhanov or Lenin or Trotsky, who were allowed to mature in the social soil and climate of Gemany, England, France, America and Czarist Russia.

Thus Communist practitioners have diminished the gap between Marxist doctrine and Communist action, but in diminishing it they have sought to fit the doctrine to the needs of action and power, whatever distortions resulted for the doctrine, rather than to govern the action by the directives of the doctrine. An American will understand this process best by the ways in which the judicial interpretation of the Constitutional text is turned and twisted and expanded to accommodate itself to desired social action. Yet the judges of the Supreme Court do not always pretend that nothing is happening to Constitutional doctrine. To a greater or lesser degree they are aware, as someone like Cardozo or Holmes was explicitly aware, of the nature of the judicial process. They do not delude themselves with the belief that the law is standing still, and they do not tell the people fairy tales about its eternal sanctity. They are more or less candid craftsmen working with the materials of social flexibility. The keepers of the Soviet doctrine, however, must insist that they are living up to the letter as well as the spirit of the sacred texts, even while they are repeatedly stretching both beyond recognition.

The uses to which ideas are put by later generations are often drastically different from the intent of their creators. Recognizing this fact of the history of ideas, I want to ask what Karl Marx, humanist as well as revolutionist, would make of the two great-grandchildren of his brain and vision—Russia and China—were he to live in either of them today? The chances, of course, are strong that in either of these proletarian states he would be one of the first to be purged. But I want to set down quite summarily the major distortions of the Marxist idea as he might see them in current Communist theory and practice.

I see six such major distortions of the original vision of Marxism:

1. *The prestige of the military principle.* Although himself (like Engels and many other civilians with a repressed power drive) a military writer of sorts, Marx would be shocked at the power and splendor of the place of the military principle in both societies. Instead of the revolution-from-within which he envisaged, the larger number of Communists states—except for Russia and China themselves—have been won for Communism by the social disloca-tions of war, the use of Communist-trained guerrillas and guerrilla leaders, and in some cases the presence of Russian and Chinese armies. The use of arms as a short cut to revolution has merged with the éclat of Russian achievement in weapons development to give prestige to the military within the structure of state power. In China there is a cluttering array of marshals in the top policy group: a similar array of Pentagon men in the American decision elite would raise a deafening clamor both at home and abroad. In Russia, while one recalls the burly, be-medaled Marshal Malinovsky at the 1960 Paris summit conference, dogging Khrushchev wherever he went, in an unparalleled twin act of substance and shadow, the generals have been held under civilian control as a matter of policy. The real reach of the military principle in Russia must be found in

the orienting of every resource and policy toward war power. For Marx and Engels, military tactics were of importance to revolutionary groups in seizing power, but how would they feel about a Communist state whose leaders make the capacity to wage destructive war the burden of their speeches on high state policy?*

2. *The cancer of the satellites.* Marx sought always to dominate the Socialist International, but his image of it was of an association of equal parties from equal states; for the ruling elites of Moscow and Peking, it is the image of a system of central suns and satellites. Whatever may be true of the exploitation of man by man, Communism in action has moved far toward the exploitation of nation by nation. While Marx scorned nationalist movements in backward countries but respected the cultural achievements of the developed nations, the present-day Marxists play up every revolutionary nationalism which may add territory and power to the Communist imperium; but once the conquest of power is accomplished, and a new Communist government is set up, the idea of a nationalism independent of Russian or Chinese control is rejected. The great Communist powers, which acquired their satellite states largely by arms, are ready to hold them by arms, not only against the force of arms from without but against revolution within.

Hungary and Tibet were not special cases but an inherent part of the Communist pattern. If India or Indonesia should some day be won for Communism, their regimes would bear the same relation to the Chinese that North Korea and North Vietnam have today, or that the regimes of Poland, Rumania and Czechoslovakia bear to the Russian regime. The basic distortion involved here is the violence done not so much to the idea of nationalism (which played a minor role in Marx's thinking) as to the idea of the free nation. The "liberation" of a nation in the Communist vocabulary means its freedom only in the sense that it is freed for a new kind of satellite relation. Thus the corruption of the nation idea flows from the cancer of the satellite idea.†

3. *The supremacy of the party.* It was perhaps inevitable that a revolutionary movement which began by stressing the act of faith and will of a minority should end by giving that minority a central

---

* For a discussion of the problem of the military in the undeveloped nations, see Chapter IV, Section 7, "A Parcel of Polities." For the developed nations, see Chapter V, Section 3, "Commanding and Creative Elites."

† I have not discussed above the repressed nationalities—Ukrainian, Jewish and others—within the Soviet Union itself. The wave of death sentences for "economic crimes" in 1962 has implications for the position of the Jews.

place in the final apparatus of decision. When out of power the Communist Party was never meant to be a competing group within the frame of any constitutional system; it becomes a weapon for destroying the system. When in power it changes its function and becomes an instrument for bolstering and perpetuating the system, but still on a noncompetitive basis; it shares power with no other party. In essence the party is dominant because it serves as a "steel frame" of a society which minimizes the authority of its old units (family, church, voluntary association), and it dares not let the people find new ones to take their place. The party is thus the carrier of Communist values. It uses the enforcement of doctrinal loyalty to nail down political loyalty and eliminate any effective opposition. Thus, while Marxist doctrine, once central, has yielded priority to the party as an agency of action, the party in turn has discovered that it must employ doctrinal policing to survive.

The triumph of the party and its apparatus, the vesting of power in the party secretariat, the habituation to the party line as the final test of truth—these all mean that the party and its power have become essential to the functioning of the Communist state. Marx hoped there would be a withering away of the state, but now the party has *become* the state. Under Stalin there was an interlude when he played the various agencies of Communist power off against each other—party, army, secret police, state bureaucracy, economic bureaucracy. But under Khrushchev the party came back to power. Any future Communist state must expect to come with party supremacy as a built-in principle. Truth in it will be party-line truth, and art will be party-line art; only those acts will be counted ethical which fit into the elastic ethic of "objective historical necessity"; everything will be subordinated to the party, except science, which must have freedom to function despite party dogma. Marx was himself something of a tyrant in suppressing opposition through party discipline. But while he foresaw the attrition of the state apparatus, he could not have dreamed that the party itself would flourish in power like a green bay tree.

4. *The dominant elite.* Marx and his colleagues had a vision of a society in which class power and distinctions had been dissolved and there was no longer a dominant class. "Will the downfall of the old society," Marx asked in 1847, in *The Poverty of Philosophy*, "be followed by a new class domination, expressing itself in a new political power?" His answer was, "No, the condition for the emancipation of the working class is the abolition of all classes." And he added, "There will no longer be any political power, properly so

called, since political power is precisely the official expression of the antagonisms in civil society."

No classes, no domination, no power. A century and a decade later there is a new dominant class, wielding total power, endowed with arrogance and brutality, a commanding elite holding the strategic passes to the military forces, the internal security apparatus, the industrial trusts, communication, propaganda and employment—holding them, I may add, not in its own name as a dominant class which controls the sinews of power and enjoys its perquisites, but "in the name of the proletariat." What makes this even more curious is that the factory workers have in fact surrendered the right to strike against the party and the state, and the peasants must in fact work on terms set by the dominant elite.

How far this is from Marx's dream, which encompassed the triumph of the working class as a means for the abolition of all classes! For Marx, the working class was a segment of the total proletariat, not to be confused with the proletariat as a whole. It had a curious mystique for him, because of its qualities of resentment and defiance, because it was at once a deprived and alienated class and at the same time a militant carrier of historic progress. What is left of this is not much more than the rhetoric. What was to have become a classless state through the action of the working class remains a class state, and not even a proletarian one. The men who have come to the top are the functionaries of the state trusts, the specialists in party infighting, the experts in military violence and propaganda manipulation, the top policemen, the scientists and technicians who go by the name of "toiling intellectuals."

Many of them doubtless derive from the working class and peasantry, but they have reached the top as an elite with administrative, manipulative and power skills. Even in the strategy of fomenting revolutions in other countries the emphasis has shifted from the use of working-class or even agrarian leaders as a leverage to the use of trained men with political skills. Their incentives are what they have always been in a governing class—power, prestige, the perquisites of life that come with both, and fulfillment of the self-image shaped by the society. As for perquisites, the spread of rewards in a Communist society is sweeping enough to have goaded an idealist like Milovan Djilas, in *The New Class*, into denouncing the fat men in their big limousines, with their stress on creature comforts and luxuries, with their chattering and gossiping wives, their blatant badges of superiority and their cruel contempt for those below them. Caricature? Yes, but a caricature which has pinned down a reality. The Populists (*Narodniki*) and the Leftist Socialist-Revolutionaries warned the Russian people that the triumph of such direct-action methods as Lenin's would lead to a new self-perpetuating ruling class. The event proved them right.

Yet Djilas, with his romantic Puritanism, did not quite hit the jugular. The withering fact about the new class is not that it has been corrupted by the fleshpots and the big cars, nor even that it is self-perpetuating, but that, while it is a commanding elite, it is not a creative one. It lives in an atmosphere of suspicion, recrimination, and terror. It trains young men to replace it, but it picks the safe ones, and even them it fears to educate as well as to train. The fear goes with the territory.

5. *The repressive psychology and morality.* At the heart of every intellectual system you will find a theory of human nature and a vision of possibility for the individual life. The Marxist theory of human nature was always overrational, squeezed dry of the fun and nonsense, of the sense of play and the sheer abandon of the individual life. It is a dour theory, which sees men almost exclusively in terms of their public conduct, narrowing the focus of the picture in order to provide the party and the state with a logic of total control. This obsessive need for the control of men (the psychological aspect of total planning of the economy and of the party dictatorship) leads to a double repressiveness: man becomes repressive of freedom in others, and repressive of self. There is no room for public dissent, which is regarded as a confession of disunity and therefore of weakness. The fear of dissent leads to a competitiveness in orthodoxy. Even drastic turns of policy are defended as the true way of orthodoxy, faithful to the founding fathers and the saints of the Church, while the salvaged accounts of Comintern meetings show that when the comrades were tearing each other apart with furious denunciations, each was vying with the others to establish a position squarely on the path of the True Believer.

This urge to orthodoxy reveals, better than anything else could, the ghastly insecurity of life and career in a Communist society. The heavy atmosphere of suspicion that hangs over the political jungle is not the expression merely of the "Dostoevskian" national character of the Russians. In a revolution which reached success three decades later, with the whole of Russian experience to learn from, the Chinese did not get rid of the rituals of accusation, purge, liquidation, confession and self-flagellation. If anything, they intensified them: they added to the direct coercions of the party and state apparatus those indirect group pressures which are often more coercive for being indirect. There are some who are sanguine enough to believe that these repressions will in time be eased. Such hopes have grown since Stalin's death and Khrushchev's thawing of the police state. But the repressive psychology and morality of the Russians and Chinese run deeper than the policies of a particular leader, and deeper also than police-state harshness. They reach to the individual psyche and its constriction, to court-ship and marriage and the erotic aspects of life. It is curious that a movement which promised the freeing of the individual from the shackles of bourgeois morality should have fashioned a new Puri-tanism more repressive than any since Cromwell and John Bunyan. That such a Puritanism should have coexisted with a Byzantinism like Stalin's and that of his sycophants is not wholly surprising: the repressive and the orgiastic are facets of each other, and at the breaking point one becomes the other.

But the breaking point may have a bearing on world peace. The danger of a too-constricted emotional expressiveness is that it will seek its outlets more violently elsewhere. Perhaps the true orgiastic element in Communism is that of power, not of Eros, just as in the developed democratic world it is largely channeled into the preda-tions of business life and its expense-account accompaniments. The hope of keeping Communist frustrations from becoming too de-structive, perhaps even of breaking out in nuclear war, lies in their being diverted into the world political war, until some future time when they can be diverted into a pursuit of the individual good life.

6. *The cult of instrumentalism.* I have said that the class state is the inheritor of much of the tradition of the Enlightenment. One aspect of that tradition was that the nature whose laws govern men can also, by the manipulation of those laws, be used by man. From the manipulation of nature to the manipulation of man was a "natural," if also fateful, step. It applies also to the mentality of the open societies, yet with a difference. Where individual men find their own salvation and damnation, the dehydrated purposive manipulation of man by man varies with the urgencies of the in-dividual vocation and the driving necessity of their situation; but where social engineering is the fiber of the society itself you get manipulative instrumentalism gone mad.

The Russians carried it far, but by some saving quirk of surviving wildness, in their national character, which resisted the ultimate orderliness, they escaped total instrumentalism. The Chinese, following out the mechanical ethos more systematically, carried it all the way. Their all-purpose commune, which purported to articulate social ends with human resources, was meant to be like a Chicago stockyard operation which turns the hog into pork, bacon, sausages, and sundry by-products, making use of "everything but the squeal." The fact that it has been modified and in large measure abandoned is evidence of how far overboard the Chinese went in their instrumentalism. The marshaling of Chinese children to kill off every sparrow is related, in its ethos, to the logic of brainwashing which keeps mental energy from being dissipated into heretical diversions. This is a matter of psychic economy, just as the round-the-clock work shifts, the shock brigades of human labor, the rationing of scanty calories, the communal kitchens, the hours of overtime and holidays devoted to "social" purposes, the colonizing armies sent to troublesome border areas, are a matter of "human investment." Here is a honeycomb construction of human society which omits nothing from its scrutiny and mastery—nothing but the restlessness of selfhood, the subterranean river of instinct, and the wild human dream.

The drive toward acceptance is strong in every human being, and Dostoevsky foresaw the orgy of submissiveness by human beings hungry to surrender their being to authority, as he foresaw so much else. The struggle to spread a political religion is a struggle for the annihilation of identity. In the end the adhesion to the identity of self, which wages a silent struggle beyond all the instrumentalism of the state and society, will perhaps prove stronger even than the urge to submit.

7. *Armed Doctrine and Political Religion*

WHILE EDMUND BURKE called the French Revolution an "armed doctrine," today we speak of the Communist "ideology." I am not certain that it is an improvement. One need not share Burke's views of revolution as the creator of the final evil, anarchy, to agree that in the showdown any revolutionary doctrine must find arms. But he risked forgetting that even in terms of armed strength it is the idea that counts. If you have an evocative idea fighting on your side, weapons will somehow grow in your hands; if you do not, then the weapons that your hands clutch will somehow trickle through them. Long before Burke, Francis Bacon saw that ideas can become *eidola,* or idols. In this sense of cult, Communism is a political religion before it is anything else, whether a theory, a strategy, or a manual of action. As a political religion, it cements the power of the commanding elite in existing Communist societies, just as it recruits new partisans for Communism in the twelve corners of the earth.

As a political religion Communism is, in Georges Sorel's sense, one of the social myths, which evoke actions and passions from their followers regardless of their validity. Historians of religion have noted that the great world religions—Judaism, Christianity, Islam, Hinduism, Buddhism—came onto the stage of history crowded together, in a single era of world history, and largely from the Middle East and Central Asia. No great world religions, in the sense of supernatural ones, have emerged since that time; the later centuries seemed to have lost the religion-creating capacity. But the historians of the future may see Communism as another world religion—a political and secular one, but nonetheless a myth-creating, myth-cherishing, myth-spreading religion. Much of its daemonic force, most of its push and thrust in moving toward its Grand Design, comes from that fact of being such a religion.

A number of writers, notably Sorel and Harold Laski, have noted the parallels between Christianity and Communism. Basically, the two were as different as possible. One was the religion of love, the other of power and class hate; one of humility, the other of certainty and a single-minded drive. Yet they share one trait: each tried to meet the insecurities of its era. Christianity was in its time a revolutionary idea, appealing to the poor and oppressed in the Roman Empire who had neither justice nor ease in their lives, and it offered them the prospect of equality in the next world. Communism, which derides and persecutes the Christian churches, tries to make the same kind of appeal to those who are hungry for life chances and power, and to the psychologically insecure even among the rich. It promises that they will find salvation not after death but during life, by allying themselves with history and destroying the existing power structure.

The last two centuries have witnessed a marked erosion of religious feeling, as well as an uprooting of traditional values. There has been a debate over the vacuum thus left, as to whether it can be filled by rationalism or whether a religious revival is required in order to fulfill the hunger for the irrational. The Communists have resolved this debate, in their own intellectual universe, by grasping both horns of the dilemma. They have dismissed the world of the irrational as mere superstition designed to shore up the old order against collapse, have rejected both religion and psychiatry, and have embraced a thorough-going rationalism. But at the same time they have transformed this rationalism into a religion, using the tests of social utilitarianism in all matters of intellectual and political dispute, but making that utilitarianism a gospel of faith. This comes close to the "religion of humanity" as Auguste Comte worked it out from the vision of Saint-Simon and his circle. For it was Saint-Simon who seized most vigorously on the idea that technical and social construction were the core of human progress and should therefore be the core of a new religion. Comte developed this insight into a philosophy and sociology of "Positivism," looking toward definable social values that derived from science and the natural universe rather than from superstition and faith; but he converted it, with intricate and painstaking ritual, into a faith.

The ritual of rationalism was in many ways worse than the unqualified leap into faith which it sought to replace. There was a monstrous quality about it, almost like a Black Mass; it repelled even a devotee of the life of reason like John Stuart Mill and led him to write a devastating analysis of its abdication to superstition in the name of rationalism. What Mill did not foresee was that his own brand of social utilitarianism, from which he himself was careful not to exclude the sense of beauty and the role of the creative, would in the hands of his followers become merely a blueprint of social engineering and would be squeezed dry of everything that could stir the imagination and the blood of men. Thus the vacuum which Saint-Simon and Comte tried to fill, with their incongruous combinations of faith and reason, became a vacuum again until the Communists managed to fill it with their own brand of political religion.

I should define this political religion as the total commitment which a Communist gives to a cause that demands of him faith as well as works, and the submission of reason, as well as the resourceful use of the mind, to authority. One phase of this religious commitment is the daemonic drive to world power.* Another involves the surrender of the mind and personality to life in a controlled society. A third involves a mystique of identification with the impersonal forces of history as interpreted by the personal vicars of these impersonal forces. In the case of the intellectuals there is a special thrill of identification with the lives and deaths, the sufferings, martyrdoms and triumphs of the worker and peasant classes,

* See above, Section 4, "The Daemon and the Locomotive."

which are supposed to be the carriers of history, and the vicarious sense this brings of being close to the Life Force.

But it was not only for the young intellectuals that Marxism provided a substitute for religious faith. It provided men of every class and station in life with a messianic hope for building a new Jerusalem on earth, and for achieving the salvation of all mankind within human history itself, not in some realm of essence transcending history.

I don't mean to exclude the element of the "chiliastic" from the Marxist religious canon. Every religion promises something attractive in the world to come—some, pie in the sky; some, hope of a promised land into which the faithful will enter tomorrow. Communism as a religion promised the faithful that there would be a golden age "after the revolution," when capitalism had been overthrown. Once socialism had been established in Russia, but with all the trappings of a coercive state, the promise was that some day there would be a withering away of the state and the coming of a free society where men would live as autonomous beings without the use of any state force. That promise seems as far as ever from fulfillment. In its place the Communist leader-priests now offer the promise of perpetual peace when once the hostile capitalist powers have been overthrown by revolution or overcome in a test of arms. And once this peace is established, they offer the further promise of unlimited plenty for all through the exploiting of the new technology of nuclear power.

It is here that the mystique of science joins forces with the religious promise of Communism. It always helps a religion to be able to authenticate the promise of things to come by presenting solid evidences of present miracles. The Russians offer such evidence in their break-through in rocketry and missiles. The Chinese offer it in their rapid strides in coping with illiteracy and disease, and (very imperfectly) in their efforts at rapid industrialization. Thus we come full circle. Just as Communist rationalism needed an act of faith to provide its impetus, so it ends by pointing to the triumphs of social rationalism in science and industrialization as evidence to bolster the act of faith.

But if Communism is a religion, it is one with little gentleness in it, little love, no humility; in their place are a vaulting will to power and an inner violence. R. P. Blackmur has said of Dostoevsky that "the deprivation of his nature, like the privations of his life, led him to envisage emotions as released either as an ecstasy of rage or as a rage of ecstasy." One thinks also of what Virginia

Woolf said of Joyce, that he was "a desperate man who feels that in order to breathe he must break the windows." This strain of violence, along with the obsession with the achievement of world power, is what I have had in mind when speaking of "overwill" in Communist thought and action. It is to be found best not in someone like Stalin, whose excesses of personal character and whose sullen brooding over the threats from his rivals led at one point beyond the margin of sanity, but in a man like Lenin, who was all compact of decisiveness and control.

Lenin is the best prototype of the Communist religious leader exactly because he gave everyone the feeling of being in control. Yet in the history of Marxism as a political religion it took a leap which was in essence not very different from Kierkegaard's "leap into faith." The Marxist tradition has always been opposed to the individual act of violence, whether performed by anarchists or performed by nihilists, and it has stressed instead the disciplined capture of power when the historic situation has become ripe for it. Yet nothing in the history of Marxist action is plainer than the fact that Lenin's seizure of power in the March Revolution was an act of individual will imposed upon the historic pattern, and that in the end it was an act of personal faith which, for its consolidation, demanded the unquestioning collective faith of others.

We must remember that there was a tradition of Russian Jacobinism and Blanquism—of the use of terror and of the sudden act of power seizure—just as there was a tradition of French Jacobinism and Blanquism. In Russian history the great names were those of Nechaev and of Tkachev. The latter was especially important in developing the idea of seizing political power through a band of young professional revolutionaries who had given total will and total commitment to the task.

The genius of Lenin lay in welding the Marxist tradition, which emphasized the slow ripening of the revolutionary situation, with this determined seizure of power. While Lenin talked of the maturing of finance capitalism, this was scarcely relevant to what he actually did, which had little to do with finance capitalism, especially in the case of Russia, where capitalism was still relatively backward. His leap into faith was to seize political power by convincing his little minority elite that it could be done, and then holding on to that power by clamping a machinery of terror upon the vast majority. But that machinery of terror could not have proved effective if he had not accompanied it by another leap into faith—the belief that a Communist state could survive amidst hostile capitalist encirclement, and that it could evoke enough of a commitment from its people to endure its rigors. Perhaps only Lenin could have managed to establish so thorough a dictatorship as he did, in the name of liberation, and so complete a surrender of freedom of the mind in the name of a rational society.

Of all the forces operative in the contemporary world, only nationalism is able to evoke the emotional response that can match the appeal of Communism as a political religion. In any direct encounter between the two the wagering would have to be on victory of nationalism. It has the enormous advantage of engaging the loyalties of place, language, family, cultural heritage, and usually religion as well, and of being associated with the tradition of something sacred enough to die for. It has also the advantage of unifying elements in the nation that would otherwise be in conflict, while Communism as a transnational force can only split them.

It was inevitable therefore that Communism should seek to ally itself with the force of nationalism wherever it could do so. This it has done by invoking the slogans of anticolonialism and anti-imperialism, until it is able to achieve power on its own and scrap its nationalist ally. It is at this point, at the convergence of the Communist idea with the idea of revolutionary nationalism, that Communism as a political religion becomes the most formidable weapon of political warfare.

8. The Intellectual as Fulcrum of Political War

INSTEAD OF CALLING the present era the Age of Overkill I might have called it the Age of Political War. By political war I mean the total effort, of each side—by diplomacy, by propaganda, by economic aid and trade, by rivalry in the arena of the UN, through cultural interchange and the warfare of ideas—to sustain and expand its position in the competition of the great power clusters. Note that this does not wholly exclude military aid or the making of military alliances. But what is common to all these means is that they fall short of conventional and overkill weapons—or perhaps go beyond them to something more fundamental. They fight it out on subtler battlefields, where the fortunes of struggle are shifting, elusive and, for the most part, invisible.

The boundaries between political warfare and weapons warfare are not sharply defined. Thus, guerrilla operations are part one, part the other. In fact, nuclear war, limited war, guerrilla war, revolutionary violence and political war may be seen as part of a continuum, each phase shading into the next. This is recognized in the Marxist writings. Lenin saw war, revolution, diplomacy and the battle of propaganda as interlocked. The Communists always politicized war, making a contest of political programs and visions. And they militarized political action in the sense that it must issue either in revolution or its war equivalent or sequel. When nuclear weapons became too dangerous to be used with sanity, Communism fell back on what it had long done well—revolution and political war.

In theory at least, political war is meant as a safety valve or insulation for tensions that might otherwise issue in a fighting war. Yet in reality there can be no such insulation. The Communists may carry on propaganda among students or peasants in a revolutionary situation, but they do not reap its rewards until they have organized guerrilla warfare or student demonstrations. These guerrilla or street-fighting operations, in turn, are met by the strengthening of the military arm of anti-Communist governments; by the training of guerrilla and air units, as well as by economic aid to counteract hunger and to bring modernization, and by new land legislation to deal with the disease of landlessness.

Thus, political war augments as well as resolves tensions. Both sides are constantly lighting counterfires to the fires they are fighting. As the struggle gets fiercer, the hostilities that each generates feed on themselves. Sometimes the tensions spill over into guerrilla and paramilitary operations; more often they stop short at riots and sporadic fighting. But the circle of political warfare is an endless one. Rarely do the tests of power reach any clear decision. The emphasis shifts from one part of the world to another as the over-all strategy on both shifts—from Europe to Asia, to the Middle East, to Africa and Latin America. Thus the world map of political war presents a picture of a dozen or a score of simultaneous contests of varying intensity, the focus shifting from one "crisis area" to another, and all of them fitting into a patchwork pattern of global political war.

Within this world frame the Communist strategies have been those of penetration, agitation, neutralization, Popular Fronts, partisan and guerrilla warfare, and outright revolution. Behind the alternation of radiances and rages, as the Communist line has shifted, there is the endless forward thrust, sometimes zigzagging ("one step backward, two steps forward"), never stopping, of leaders who rationalize their power aggressions in the name of history and a political religion, and followers who are forced to accept the risks and burdens because they have no choice.

During the 1950s world Communism made a radical shift in its strategies of political war. It moved the axis of emphasis away from the industrialized nations of Europe, whose regimes had rediscovered their strength and showed an impressive power of resistance, toward the undeveloped new nations of Asia, Africa and Latin America. It organized a more active economic and military penetration of the vulnerable target countries, through arms deals and shipments, large-scale barter, aid for heavy industry, and the export of technicians. Finally, it put its major stress not on the industrial or even the agrarian proletarians, but on the intellectuals.

If anything ever seemed firmly fixed about Marxist doctrine it was the revolutionary role of the working class. The Bolsheviks gained power through a small band of professional revolutionaries, mainly intellectuals, but they relied upon the cadres of factory workers to carry out paralyzing strikes and act as shock troops. They waited for working-class revolutions in the more highly industrialized countries of Western Europe to follow their example and envelop them in a circle of security. The foreign workers never responded to the call, and the supportive revolutions never came. Thus, Lenin's reliance on the advanced industrial workers as revolutionary carriers was undercut. After Lenin there was a shift in strategy from the industrial workers to the peasants. The advisers sent from Moscow to direct the earlier phases of the Chinese Revolution sought to make it into an Asian version of the Russian, and to rely ultimately upon the industrial workers, even while they equipped the Kuomintang with a high-sounding program of agrarian reform. It didn't work. Mao Tse-tung's genius lay in grasping the fact that in a heavily agrarian society the revolution would have to start with the faceless men in the fields and villages. Thus, the Chinese Revolution used not an industrial but an agrarian base, but had to recruit and train the peasants in a disciplined army before it could win power. In setting up the postwar Communist states in Eastern Europe the Russians used the same base of agrarian revolt plus an army—the Russian army in every case, except in Yugoslavia.

In the 1950s another shift took place. The emphasis turned toward the intellectuals—the youth in the universities, the instructors, journalists, lawyers and doctors, the civil servants, the younger army officers. These make up in every country, especially the undeveloped ones, the educated elite. The intellectuals are used in preparing the soil and climate of the revolutionary situation, the army officers are used in the showdown of force. This means that the Communists have been flexible enough to rethink their class-struggle dogma, and have concluded that ideas are the most inflammatory weapons and that the intellectuals as idea carriers can tear a regime or even an empire down.*

If we ask how it happened that a materialist philosophy should have turned to the primacy of the psychological and political and the value of intellectuals, the answer runs in terms of the need for a mystique. Since the Communists are being forced to a greater reliance on political warfare, they must find men who will be vulnerable to their political religion. While a supernatural religion appeals to simple folk, a political religion like Communism will naturally appeal mainly to the literates. For they deal in ideas and symbols and have largely lost their traditional religion, while the peasants and workers on whom the traditional religions still have a hold, live less in the world of ideas. It is a truism that Marx took Hegel's idealist dialectic and stood it on its head, turning it into a materalist dialectic. One might add that recent events have taken Marxist materialism and turned it topsy-turvy again, bringing it back closer to Hegel's emphasis on the historical creativeness of the idea. The Communists are thus embracing aspects of the doctrine of thinkers whom they have loudly rejected, from Jefferson to Mosca and Pareto and Weber, all of whom have stressed not the demos itself but the creative and revolutionary circuit of relationship between demos and elite.

The key, I have said, is the mystique. The politically conscious young officers fight and die for it, intellectuals live on it and dream of it. The soldier, essentially conservative, nevertheless rejects the softness of civilian life and values, and longs for a hard cause and doctrine, convinced that once power is taken he can administer it better than the civilians. The intellectuals long for meaning beyond the humdrum; they are roused by liberation slogans, identify with the suffering of the lowly, are pushovers for the simplicities of collective action and planning, and seek a father principle in a

---

* I don't mean to make the change in Communist tactic oversharp. The intellectuals were a prime target from the start. Nevertheless the change has been a real one, since the earlier emphasis on the workers and peasants is now little more than a remembered litany, while the educated elite of the undeveloped countries forms the real target.

cause which is authoritarian in structure even while its slogans are libertarian.

Hence the new strategies of Communist political warfare and the role of the intellectual as a fulcrum. These young people, with all their feeling of being champions of freedom, are actually rushing into strait jackets. The paradox of our time is the romantic revolutionary as rebel who voluntarily dons a strait jacket. In the traditional society, the career of journalist or schoolteacher, civil servant or soldier, is one way of breaking out of the bleak limited life of village and countryside. It is also a way of opening oneself to exciting new winds of doctrine. To march together down streets alive with menace and promise, to dodge policemen's clubs, to shout anti-colonial slogans and attack the symbols of American power, to get a sense of life as dangerous, but also a sense of comradeship in meeting its dangers, to fight in the hills and let your beard grow and carry a gun in the crook of your arm, perhaps to go to jail and emerge a martyr and be borne triumphantly on the shoulders of your followers, to break the conventions and defy your elders, to stand on the threshold of a new order which will count you as someone to be reckoned with—these appeals are hard to resist and dangerous to underrate.

These young people, in short, respond to the urgencies of the present and see themselves as part of the wave of the future. To be part of a going concern makes them feel less lonely, even if it means surrendering freedom to make choices, and their very identity. Filled with self-pity as victims they are ready, like a monstrous death machine, to roll with history over the bodies of others. From being victims they are ready to become executioner. The tragedy of it is that they end up, after all, as the victims.

The question remains whether the new emphasis on recruiting and training intellectuals will bring to the center of the stage a group who, by the logic of the life of the mind, may demand the actualities of freedom as well as the slogans of liberation. This is part of the anxiety of world Communism; even its political warfare is doomed to attrition by the modernizing forces which it sets in motion and by the intellectuals whom it seeks to enroll in its armies. For the idea of freedom is the most revolutionary in world history. Once you bring the intellectuals into your movement, you face the danger that they will not be content with being indoctrinated but will educate themselves.

9. *A Stick, a Plan, a Myth*

IN THE EARLY STAGES of world Communism there were many who thought it could be undone by wishing it away and by mending the old order with rhetoric, some pieces of *laissez faire* string, and a few bits of freedom plaster. They were wrong, but no wronger than those who have now gone to the other extreme, convinced that Communism cannot be kept from its final triumph, no matter what blunders it commits, no matter what forces and resources are mustered to release the free world's vigor. There is too much yammering about the "inevitable" Communist victory and the "irresistible" tide of history.

At bottom the Communists have three prime weapons—the *stick,* the *plan,* the *myth.* The *stick* is for discipline and coercion. For centuries men have found it easier to govern with a stick. The Communists have only found a more intricate model of the stick and a more elaborate rationalization for rule by it. The Communist elite has also explored more searchingly the hidden recesses of men's hunger for submission. But this hunger is not limitless, nor is it the chief fact about man. As compared with his radical impulse to freedom, it is only the darker side of the moon.

It would be a mistake to regard Communism as in itself an inherent part of the human condition. Like any other social movement it has historical roots, a definable here-and-now, and a trajectory into the future which is part of history, not permanence. The Marxists have given their own version of the historic sequence from primitive communism to feudalism to capitalism to socialism and finally to Communism in the fullest sense, and have placed themselves neatly in this sequence as the culmination and end of history. It is folly to accept their analysis of their own place in history as the final word.

There are other analyses. Karl Wittfogel has traced Russian Communism back to the Oriental "hydraulic" societies which organized a tyrannical structure of power at the irrigation center through a propertyless bureaucracy. This system moved from the Orient to Russia by way of the conquering Mongol tribes, and found congenial roots in the Russian soil. For Arnold Toynbee the absolutism of the Russian class state is the successor to the absolutism of Byzantine society. By this version the Russians inherited the main features of Byzantinism, including its centralism and its subordination of the individual to the collective will even in the Church, while the Marxist features of the contemporary absolutism were simply borrowed from Western Europe, much as Peter the Great had earlier borrowed from the West its system of modern administration, and Lenin and Stalin were to borrow its techniques of industrialism. One may accept or reject these versions of the shaping of Russian Communism, and one may wrestle with the same problems in the case of Communist China. The crucial fact, however, is that the stick with which Communism governs is man-made and time-placed.

If the stick is for discipline, the *plan* is for coordination. It was a response to the capitalist overemphasis upon the spontaneous and organic elements of *laissez faire,* and upon the "unseen hand of God" which made a pattern out of individual greeds and decisions. In reaction against this anarchy the French Utopian Socialists spun their plans for a more perfect society, while Bentham and the Philosophical Radicals added their own charts, and the German spirit from which Marx and Engels derived contributed its characteristic bureaucratic *Grundlichkeit.* Add to this the resources of recent mathematical economic theory and the logic of industrial accounting, and you get the Five-Year Plans as the symbol of collective forethought.

But there is nothing in planning as such which makes it the prescriptive property of Communism or requires the perfection of coercion which the Russians and Chinese have applied to it. Nor is it at all clear that running industry and agriculture by a party bureaucracy is the most effective way of organizing an industrial society. The breakdown of agriculture in Russia, Eastern Europe and Cuba, and the famines in Communist China, are not accidental or secondary defects of the planning machinery. They are inherent in the absolutism of the planning principle—in the effort to evoke the productive energies of men by turning them into an ant colony, forgetting that they work best when their work is linked with their creativity.

The place for socialist planning is primarily in the undeveloped economy, where capital accumulation is needed with urgency, and where there can be no later capitalism unless there is an earlier socialism which will gather and invest the capital. Even in these economies* the best case to be made out is for the rational calculating aspects and not the coercive aspects of planning. But in mass-consumption economies—as in the United States, Britain,

* For a further discussion of them, see Chapter IV, "The Undeveloped World," especially Sections 3-5.

France, Germany, Japan and to some extent Russia—the organic in the economy is more important than the coercive and bureaucratic.* The future lies not with the Communist plan, but with welfare economies which use noncoercive and limited planning and evoke the spontaneous inner energies of men.

Finally there is the *myth,* by which the Communists hope to convince the world that its future lies with Communism and that history offers no other choice. The recipe for the myth of inevitability is one part self-hypnosis, one part intellectual charlatanism, two parts political religion, and a final part the self-doubting and self-hating folly of those who are ready to succumb to the psychic intensity of the True Believers. So masochistic a disbelief by the free world in its own future is the strongest component of the Communist myth. It can be healed only, as psychiatry seeks to heal other neurotic distortions of reality, by following it back like an Ariadne thread to its sources in guilt and the need for submission and the fear of freedom.

If the *myth* is exposed in its hollowness, the chances are strong that the blunders of world Communism will help the process. The *plan* can also be countered with a less mechanical and coercive one. A democratic system, Tocqueville has said, will always find it hard to carry out a "fixed design" of its own. But what is hard is not impossible if the urgency is great enough. Then all that remains will be the *stick,* which cannot stand up against the power of the radical idea of freedom and the good life for all.

* I am speaking here of high-consumption economies in a long-range view. It is true, of course, that the current Soviet transitional stage of coerced rapid growth continues to require limitations on consumption for the purpose of overtaking the U. S. Yet one may ask whether the coercion will end with the end of the transitional phase or whether it is inherent in the Communist state, economy, and society.

CHAPTER IV

The Undeveloped World

1. The Identity Revolutions

2. Modernization: The Leap into the Stormy Present

3. Two Designs for Growth

4. Overtake and Take-over

5. Self-Determination: Wilson versus Lenin

6. Color, Heroes, and Elites

7. A Parcel of Polities: The Unreadiness Effect and Personal Rule

8. Fire and Form in Developing Societies

141

The Undeveloped World

1. The Identity Revolutions

O NE of the overarching facts today is the heightening of revolutionary nationalism as one facet of the multiple revolution of
our time. This rapid and dramatic emergence of new governments
amounts to a nation-state explosion. You get a glimpse of its measure,
pace and intensity when you attend a meeting of the United Nations
Assembly. You gaze at a patchwork of color—white and black, yellow
and brown, with every mixture of them and every cephalic index.
And you reflect that a decade ago many of these young men were
political prisoners, colonial civil servants, or university students
taking part in nationalist demonstrations, and now they are
young heads of delegations, members of cabinets, even heads of state.

It is a curiously new world struggling to be born—a world of new
nations led by new men, on age-old continents that have been lost
in the sleep of centuries but are awakening now and becoming the
new continents and are perhaps the hinge of the world's fate. To
take Africa as an instance: In past centuries Africa has been a dramatic frame within which explorers and missionaries, kings and
grandees, adventurers and absentee millionaires have pursued their
dreams, while they took for granted the population below as if it
were a piece of stage machinery, a fixture of the stage set. Today in
the still unliberated areas of Africa the poorest black man, at once
penniless and powerless, is yet more powerful than the greatest
grandee was, for he has in his sullen resentment and his unleashed
nationalist fervor the power to call a nation into being, where the
grandee could only rule a territory. In the new nations, already
established but still untried in the tasks of government, the same
black man is being wooed by both sides in the political war. Might-
ier than the tread of mighty armies, said Victor Hugo, is the power
of a dream whose hour has come.

But new questions arise. For what purposes and in what direction will this power be used? To call it "nationalism" does not
answer the question of the nature of the new nation, and to call it
"revolutionary" does not answer the question of the direction in

which it will move. To the partisan caught in the stir of the
struggle, these are bothersome questions—which is exactly the
point about revolutionary nationalism. It is enough for most of its
adherents that liberation is going on. A revolution is in process,
a people is taking its rightful place as a nation. Why ask paralyzing
questions? The insulted are now riding high. The exploited, once
at the base of the pyramid, are now in position to bid for moving
eventually to the top. What will come will come, but meanwhile
the revolutionary nationalisms continue to come into being. To the
two great power systems competing for the commitment of the new
governments, the stakes of victory are too high to admit of any
paralyzing questions.

Two common names for it are "hunger revolution" and "revolution of rising expectations." The hunger is real, and so is the pauper-
ization. It is also a fact that the expectations for a better life, as well
as for a better diet, have become part of the thinking of the new
generations in Asia, Africa, Latin America. But these are only aspects
of a more general event—that of an old world, long slumbering,
awakening to a number of simultaneous explosive revolutions, political, industrial and intellectual, administrative and social, Marxist and Western at once. This explosion engulfs class, caste and race.
It is transforming the tribal and social system, the religions, the
technologies and economies, courtship and marriage, government
and administration, the rearing of children and the education of
young men, village life and city life, birth and death and population, and the actions and passions of all. These make up the multiple revolution of our time. Nothing so convulsive, so rapid, and so
far-reaching has happened to any comparable number of peoples
in history, in any comparable span of time.

There is the *village-and-city revolution,* with the breakup of the
village economy and the traditional village society, and the migration of the peasants' sons (and sometimes their daughters) to the big
cities. Many of them, once in the city, may wander homeless and
uprooted, subject to the dehumanizing forces of a world they
never made. Yet the fact that they keep coming suggests that city
life exerts a pull on them, and that all its disabilities are more than
counterbalanced by the excitements of the freer choices it offers.

There is the *industrial revolution,* still juxtaposed with the traditional technology, on every road where trucks and cars pass oxen
and donkeys and camels, in every country where the dynamo, the
steel mill, the hydroelectric dam and the airport are planted down
near a still-uncleared jungle, or near ancient ruined temples or wells

where oxen keep going round and round with a patience born of centuries.

There is the *intellectual revolution.* Old religions are breaking up and giving way to the new religion of science and technology. Young men are hungrily devouring textbooks on engineering, on electronics or physics, on administration. New vistas are opening for students and teachers, and along with them new discontents.

There is the *political and administrative revolution,* with young and untried people trying to build new government machinery, a new administrative and legal system, and a new diplomatic service— all of them alongside surviving remnants of magic and astrology.

There is a *color revolution,* with color becoming a badge of a new pride and prejudice where once it had been a badge of servitude. This is the bitter harvest of color hatred, now being reaped after the centuries of contempt that the colored have suffered from the whites.

There is a *social revolution,* with women being freed from the veil and from their old subjection to men and venturing into new careers, with the caste system breaking up, with new modes of schooling, new techniques of child rearing, new ways of growing up and of courtship and of marriage choice, and even (I am sorry to say) new modes of dress.

The Western nations went through some of these experiences over the span of the centuries, but the newly liberated peoples are taking their full impact all at once, shaken to their center by the force of the storms, bedazzled by the grandeur of the prospects opening up before them, borrowing every possible technique from both power systems, trying desperately to develop the needed leadership and skills. Given their exacting ordeal, the wonder is not that they undergo it with anguish and failures, but that they manage to undergo it at all.

What common element ties together these aspects of the multiple revolution? One possibility is to see them as forming a triple revolution: a *colonial* revolution against imperialism; a *color* revolution against the whites: a revolution for *land and food* against the existing land tenure system. This has the merit of combining an emphasis on nationalism and class, since the themes of colonialism and color are phases of nationalism, while the theme of land tenure and distribution is a phase of class.

Although the Communists have staked out claims of close kinship with these movements, the fact is that they have not followed the

Communist pattern. Marx wrote from the angle of vision of Europe —an old Europe in which caste had given way to class, and where nationalist movements were assertions of statehood within a system of nation-states of long standing. On this issue Marx got stuck with his class fixation. Looking through the Marxist glass darkly, he perceived only faintly the anticolonial nationalisms still to come which would encase class resentments within a larger frame of race, language, caste, and leadership hungers. Lenin, after paying lip service to self-determination, fought the nationalist movements within the Soviet Union itself and finally settled for a system of federal cultural autonomy stripped of much of its meaning by the steel frame of the Communist Party in every area. The force of revolutionary nationalism in Asia gave the Communist leaders a chance to retrieve their original errors. While for a time, until the mid-Thirties, they tended to equate nationalism with social fascism when it suited their purpose, they ended by playing down the theme of class warfare and playing up that of revolutionary nationalism. Wherever the nationalist idea has collided with the class idea, whether in India or Egypt, Iraq or the Congo, the former has won out, and the Moscow-oriented Communists have accepted its priority.*

What gives the nationalist idea a seemingly irresistible quality is that it achieves cohesion by virtue of the enemy concept. It plays upon the *we-they* contrast, and thus channels the rancorous frustrations and resentments of a people into a mounting strength against the enemy symbol. At the same time it furnishes a large enough tent covering to include diverse classes, castes, religions, languages, traditions, economic interests, political viewpoints. By combining the fierceness of the independence idea with the oneness of the nation-state idea, it suspends the ordinary internal hostilities, makes folk heroes out of workaday people, and leaders out of simple men who can make others catch fire.

* In the *Communist Manifesto*, Marx wrote that in each country the proletariat must "settle accounts with its own bourgeoisie" and that the proletarian revolutionary struggle is therefore "at first a national struggle." But he was understandably suspicious of national patriotism, and as a believer in large power units he was also suspicious of fragmentizing nationalist movements. Lenin, on coming to power, had a very concrete problem of how to fight the forces of nationalist dispersal within the Soviet Union. For a survey of the developing attitudes of both men, see E. H. Carr, *The Bolshevik Revolution: 1917-1923* (1951), vol. I of his great *History of Soviet Russia*, note B, "The Bolshevik Doctrine of Self-Determination." For Lenin's theses on the national and colonial questions, adopted at the Second Comintern Congress in July 1920, directing support for "national-liberation movements" while fighting the "bourgeois-democratic" trend in them, see *The Communist International Documents*, vol. I (1956), pp. 141-144, Jane Degras, Ed.

Both the Communist and free-world leaders run the danger of mistaking and underestimating the quality of this nationalist *élan*. The Communists regard it as a necessary evil which must be endured before a class state can be set up. The democracies see it as a nasty demagoguery by half-educated men who play upon the primitive emotions of simple people, and who need to be tutored like striplings in the ways of responsible government. The idea of the "revolution of rising expectations" has at least the merit of shifting the emphasis from the anticolonial slogans and the free world's condescensions. It also shifts the emphasis from what people suffer to their image of themselves. There has been hunger in Africa and Asia, the Middle East and Latin America, for centuries. The revolutions didn't come until the people learned the gap between what they were and what they might be.

What I am getting at is the question of identity. The heart of the colonial experience has usually been held to be exploitation, the rifling of the resources of an area not for the benefit of its people but for the profit of the exploiters. The ideology of resentment leads to the diplomacy of hostility and to the politics of grievance and hurt memories. This is the characteristic heritage of the era of colonialism.

Yet something more basic than economic exploitation prepared the harvest of hate and revolution. It was the denial of identity. The worst offense the colonial settlers committed was not that they used the indigenous peoples as cheap labor but that they considered them a different and anonymous order of human beings. The regime of the Belgians in the Congo in the last quarter century of their tenure, which ran welfare services for the Congolese and cared for their health and housing, treated them as anonymous faceless ciphers in a calculus of differential advantage. Whether the colonial masters viewed the natives as children or as savages, or quite simply as "they"—undifferentiated members of a group outside the pale— they squeezed them dry of their humanity.

They brought on themselves the wrath that came. When the time came for a response, was it any wonder that it took the form of reprisal? Sometimes it was explosive and hysterical, as in the case of the excesses committed by the Congolese after independence. It was a way of saying to the former masters, "Look at me. Do you recognize me? I am the thing you ignored all these years. Now I am someone, a person. As a member of the nation, I have a past and a future. You cannot take us for granted any longer. Even if we have to chase out those who taught and exploited us, maim and kill, we shall make you recognize us as a nation. You have always referred to us as 'they.' We are no longer 'they.' We are *we*."

In the course of his life history, as Erik Erikson suggests, an individual goes through a succession of identity crises. I suggest that this applies to the life history of a people as well. For centuries the colonial peoples of Asia and Africa have had their identity submerged. They have been kept from governing themselves, from using their resources for themselves, from facing their problems and their destiny. Now, coming out of a long sleep of denial, they awaken to who they are as a nation. Every facet of their identity revolutions has been a facet of that awakening.

Their first impulse is rejection. An individual must first peel away the husks of what he is not, in order to get at the core of what and who he is. Just as he makes his first breakaway as an adolescent, rejecting his family in order to discover himself, the same theme of rejection can be traced in the identity revolutions of the new nations. They owe more to Europe than they like to think or are willing to face. Their tools and schools, their science and books, their radios and movies and press, their roads, their laws and legislatures, their cars, in many cases their language and religion, are all borrowings from their cultural parents. Even the guns with which they drive out their former masters, and the idea of nationalism itself which inflames them to use those guns, are borrowed from the West. This reminds one of Emerson's "Bramah": "When me they fly, I am the wings." In the process of rejecting the ideas and institutions of Europe and America, those ideas are the weapons by which the rejection is made. The former colonial peoples have to slay their father and banish him, by using the strength they inherited from him, much as the Americans themselves had to carry through the slaying of the European father.*

Is the true nature of these movements perhaps not *nationalist* but *culturalist?* Do these people want most perhaps to turn their backs on their former conquerors and return to their past? I agree that the influence of the new forces may be only on the surface, and that the emerging cultures are less deeply touched by them than the champions of the Westernizing drift are anxious to believe. But it is possible to overplay the culturalist emphasis. While recognizing that something deep is going on among the young Africans, especially in the search for *negritude* among the French-speaking peoples and in the researches of young African historians into the

---

* For this theme as applied to the American experience, see my *America as a Civilization* (1957), Chapter I, Section 3, "The Slaying of the European Father."

greatness of lost African cities and empires, I put less stress on the rediscovery of their past, more on the discovery of their future, and most of all on their leap into the stormy present.

2. *Modernization: The Leap into the Stormy Present*

THE ASSERTION of identity has at least one great failing: It leaves open the question of what is the unit of identity. The excess of nationalism is separatism. The recent history of India and Indonesia, of Burma, of Afghanistan and Pakistan, of the Congo Republic, testifies to the disintegrating forces set in motion by the principle of self-determination, which has no built-in method for stopping the fission process, once it is under way. The divisive forces were always there, implicit in racial, regional, tribal, linguistic, religious and historical differences, but the *élan* of the independence movement kept them in check. Once independence is achieved, the barriers against the centrifugal forces are leveled, the hostilities which were once turned outward are now turned inward, and the new nation becomes a barrel of eels. Thus, by taking a leap into the stormy present, the nation opens up again the divisive forces of the past.

The case of India and its leaders brings some of the problems into focus. There is a puzzling double fact about Gandhi: that he was at once revolutionary and reactionary. He was a revolutionary with a prayer mat and a spinning wheel. He shared with the Hindu reactionaries the dream image of the Indian village and its technology, and a scorn for the corrupting taint of the city. He shared with the modern revolutionaries the daring to demand unqualified independence, exacting it by sheer force of moral will, contemptuous of any form of physical force. He had a genius, as witness the classic salt march to the sea, for the symbolism that would reach the mind and will of the simplest man. This skill with symbols, along with his appeal to tradition and his reliance on moral force, were what tied him to the Indian masses. He talked their language, and as he moved among the villagers—asking for no more food or clothing than the lowliest of them had—he was their saint and leader, in a sense impossible for a more modernized leader. Had he lived, he might have tapped the springs of moral will and unity of all the Indians sufficiently to furnish a common base on which the new India could build. His death kept him, however, from having to face the problems of economic aid and industrialization which every developing economy has had to face.

Nehru, two thirds Western socialist and rationalist intellectual and one third Indian aristocrat and mass leader, had to make his obeisance to the past while his whole being was oriented to the modern world. Another Indian intellectual leader, Jayaprakash Narayan, has cleaved more consciously to the Gandhi tradition, insisting that India must give up the dream of bigness, whether in industry or in government, go back to the ancient village as base, and develop its own Asian form of democracy. They reflect a conflict that will be found throughout the undeveloped world, between the hold of tradition and the demands of modernization. There can be no doubt of the final triumph of modernization everywhere. Traditionalism draws its strength from nostalgia for a passing social and moral order, and from the need for rootedness. But modernization feeds upon the sense of national identity and pride, and the hunger for new experience, and the fear of being left behind by advancing life changes and life chances. As between the two it is not modernization that will lose, however tenacious the roots from the past.

The most tenacious are those which persist in linguistic pluralism, whether in Southeast Asia or in the tribal cultures of Africa. Once national independence is assured, what tends to happen is that every linguistic group feels cheated of its identity revolution unless it can make its language the dominant one, at least in its own area. Around the language there cluster the fierce prides and loyalties of religion, tradition, and the sense of local and regional place. In India the young college student training himself for a career must master English and Hindi as the languages of the modern world and the national tradition, and assume the added burden of his local language. Where the state legislature makes the local language official, there is the problem of translating the science and technology books into a language that has not been shaped to carry it. And always there is the problem of communication, in a diverse medley of tongues that have little relation to the needs of a modern going society. What applies to the centrifugal pulls of language applies even more forcibly to the more emotional pulls of religion and caste. In fact, there are careful students of Indian society who regard these fragmentizing forces as even more dangerous than the problems of food and population, since they hobble the capacity to deal with those problems. Remembering the bloody communalist and separatist struggles leading to the split with Pakistan, they are skeptical of India's capacity to survive unless it can continue to evoke a unifying leadership comparable to Nehru's.

The centrifugal pulls in Africa are the tribalist ones, linked with language and religion. With its social organization, its power resting with the tribal chief, its complex codes of what one must do or refrain from doing, its loyalties and its enmities, the tribe is the carrier of the continuities of the past. Sometimes it exacts a terrible penalty for the infraction of its codes, as did the Mau Mau in Kenya, with their blood oath and terrorism, whose strength lay in the tribal ties and taboos which are common to the rituals of secret primitive societies. Everywhere in Africa the tribal ties have an earlier hold on the people than the newer and more synthetic ties of the nation-state.

The pathos of the tribal tie is that it does not survive the dislocation of the traditional society. Frank Moraes, an Indian observer of Africa, has said that the anomie caused by the migration to the cities is more devastating in Africa than in India. An Indian villager of a particular caste will carry his caste along with him when he moves to Bombay or Calcutta and gets a factory job there. But a member of an African tribe, migrating from village to city, cannot take his tribal and religious ties along with him, since they are rooted in the soil of his locality. He is in effect detribalized, without any new connection to take the place of the one he has lost. This suggests at once the strength of the tribal structure in its own locale and the lack of any future for African tribalism as the process of industrialization moves on.

The paradox of the transition from the traditional to the modern is that the old roots are embedded in localism, which is separatist, while the new potential unities must be sought in modernization, which breaks the old connections without yet having found ties to replace them. Thus, what is rooted carries the canker of separation, while what is centralized carries anomie with it. These contradictions embody the dilemma of the young African. They also set the frame of the conflict between the power moving toward the center and power being dispersed from it to the rim. The power of the tribal chiefs and the "stool kings" was a dispersed power, while that of the new national leader-heroes is centralized. The new leaders have found it convenient to take over the territorial boundaries set by the former colonial powers, however artificial they were, because they make good administrative units. But the pulls toward a decentralized or federated state are strong, and logically such a state often makes sense in ethnic or economic terms. The sharp problem arises when one area—Sumatra in Indonesia, Katanga in the Congo Republic—has a secondary role in the centralized government although its resources make it a rich and indispensable unit.

The logic of self-determination would in such a case counsel a looser federation, except for the fact that it would lead to an endless process of fragmentation.

Where can self-determination logically stop? This cannot be settled abstractly. It was the accidents of history and the folly of the Congress Party leadership, rather than abstract logic, which led to the creation of separate Pakistani and Indian nations. Today the application of the same principles of ethnic identity and self-determination to Kashmir would dictate its adherence to Pakistan—an intolerable thought to the Indians. Logically Katanga deserves independence, but it would leave an unviable Congo Republic. The prudent policy is to end the logic of self-determination where it could endanger the survival of the new nation and, similarly, to join a number of unviable nations into an economic and military confederation.

Within this frame of present and past, of new unities and ancient divisions, we may glimpse the situation of the young leaders of the identity revolutions. They have been suddenly thrust into history, with scarcely any preparation for this role. They are young men in a hurry—tied to their nation's past, but anxious to overtake the older nations and find the blueprints for their leap into the future. They are hungry for anything that will help them to make the leap. They are proud of what their people have done, but also touchy—about their color, their country's poverty, and its limited experience. They come into history, these young men, when there is a United Nations to receive them as members and pin upon them the badge of equality with the older members. One can scarcely estimate how much this badge of belonging, the certificate of equal sovereignty, means to them.

The emotional undercurrent flowing through the new nations and their leaders is the hunger for connection, with both past and future, with their own traditions and with the established nations outside. This is why arms and economic aid cannot buy their affection. Americans who want the new peoples to identify with America must first learn to identify with them, while they respect themselves and their culture. Aid is crucial, not as a way of buying love but as a symbol of identification. The best way of establishing connection, however, is by identifying with the healthy forces which are moving from formal independence to a functioning freedom within the society, from poverty to welfare, from tribalism to nationhood, from linguistic chaos to linguistic order, from religious bigotry to religious understanding, from racism to ethnic brotherhood, from magic to reason, from provincialism to internationalism.

Yet it is hard to make the identification, since the new nations often sustain their resentments against the cultural tradition from which they borrowed the ideas for their revolutions. There is an irony in the fact that these new peoples, largely unviable because they are so fragmentized, have to be kept alive by the very nations they are sworn to hate. There is another irony as well. The nation-state explosion comes exactly at a time when the nation-state itself is being called in question and its existence imperiled by the new weapons. The quest of added sovereignties comes exactly when the old ones are finding that national sovereignty is too costly and dangerous a luxury to be maintained in a world whose safety requires its surrender to a world authority. The "white man's burden" has changed, but the black man's and the yellow man's burden remain—that of trying to sustain economically unviable states, with an untried leadership, under political forms shaped to the new tasks.

3. Two Designs for Growth

IN AN ERA when the weapons race is matched and supplemented by the aid race, a change has understandably come over the discipline of economics. In its great *classical* stage it was concerned with how capitalism as a largely automatic system functions; in its *neoclassical* stage, during the capitalist Time of Troubles, it was concerned largely with cyclical and fiscal theory, and with the controls needed to set the malfunctioning right; in its third, or what we should call the *postclassical* stage, it cuts across capitalist and socialist systems, and focuses on economic growth, in both types and in the varied amalgams of them. The whole undeveloped world has been turned into a laboratory of economic growth, where technicians from developed economies show the young apprentice nation how to carry the experiment through. The undeveloped country has become the center of attention for the economists and statesmen of the developed ones.*

Economic growth runs in terms of the idea of process, which goes

* A new vocabulary too has emerged. Where once "backward area" or "backward country" was used, they have been replaced by "underdeveloped" or "undeveloped" areas, and more recently by "developing area." I use one or the other of the latter two terms, depending upon the context.

back to the pre-Socratic philosophers, but will be found most active in the nineteenth-century Western social thought, including Marxism. Thus, growth economies are at home in both the liberal classical and the Marxist traditions, although pitifully little was available in either, before the present generation, to guide the growth lines of an undeveloped economy. These growth ideas, moreover, are being introduced largely into cultural systems where they are not at home. Whether it be the Hindu and Buddhist culture or the Islamic, the Catholic culture of Latin America, or the tribal cultures of Africa, what they have in common is a stress on permanences rather than change, on the timeless rather than the timebound. The largely Westernized Indians, for example, must do their planning in a culture which has survived the changes and chances of fifty centuries, in which time is traditionally held to be cyclical and the present moment eternal.

The idea of growth, in itself evolutionary, has become a revolutionary instrument, to be used by a new technical elite, not under the old taboos and gods, but within a new religion of science and machines and for the wild hopes based on them. They want access to the technologies that will give them power over their environment, rising levels of living, the means for educating their elites and masses, a place in the sun on their continent and in the world of nations. Hence their emulation of Russia and America, and their willingness to adopt any plan, whether democratic or Communist, which promises them these things most rapidly and surely.

The Communists offer the undeveloped country a total plan, with coercive controls, and with the growing trade and capital resources of the Communist cluster behind it. Along with it comes a warning that the capitalist powers, caught in the internal contradictions of their own economies, are fearful of allowing the undeveloped nations to build heavy industry of their own, since that will bring new rivals for the already established factories and steel mills.

Do not rely on such tainted aid, say the Communists; do not draw capital investment from sources which will put you on a dependency dole and retain you as an imperialist colony despite the forms of sovereignty. Instead, reclaim your unused labor power by planning, confiscate the capital equipment already established by the imperialists, and turn the former profits back into new investment, eliminate the "drain" which kept your country impoverished and your people on a starvation level, liquidate the feudal holdings of landlords and the strangle hold of the merchant and banker class, revolutionize agriculture by communal land use, concentrate your new investments in hydroelectric power, steel mills, and other foundations of heavy industry, exchange your raw materials and agricultural products in barter deals with other Communist countries, and make use of their backlog of technicians and technology.

The adequate answer is that the Communist path of economic glory leads inevitably to the grave for national independence, since it involves an all-out integration of the economy with Communist trade, aid and technicians, and an apparatus of state coercion which pushes the polity over into Communism willy-nilly.

One must distinguish here between the impact of aid itself and that of adopting the Communist growth pattern as a whole. India, Egypt, Iraq, Afghanistan, Ghana and Guinea have taken considerable aid from the Communists without becoming Communist-dominated. But they all had learned the art of playing one camp against the other, which is a prerequisite of gamesmanship in the economic growth of new nations. None of them adopted the growth pattern as Castro did. In each case, moreover, the ruling elite had enough gumption and strength to build up its own loyal officer corps, minimize Communist influence within the army, and even—in the case of Egypt outrightly, in Iraq virtually—outlaw the Communist Party.

The tragic case of Cuba is another matter. However Castro and his July 26 group may have begun, they ended up by adopting almost every feature of the Communist scheme for economic growth: they confiscated American and Cuban corporate holdings, nationalized banking and credit, collectivized the land, entered heavily into barter deals with the Communist bloc, made extensive use of Soviet bloc and Chinese technicians. They doubtless found considerable satisfaction in expunging all traces of "Yankee" and "imperialist" economic power from the island, but in the process they handed over economic power to a ruling bureaucracy which also had power over the state, the single party, the army and the communications system.

They were convinced that a social revolution requires heroic economic measures, at whatever cost in the temporary welfare and freedom of the people, and that no other course can achieve a social revolution. The case of Mexico casts doubt on this assumption. It went through a social revolution which included land reform, the confiscation of American and British holdings in mines, oil and railroads, the nationalization of banking and a large segment of heavy industry, a revolution in education and in the social status and welfare of the Indian villages, and a vigorous anticlerical move-ment to displace the alliance of the Catholic hierachy with the feudal elements of economic and social power. Yet this revolution, spanning two generations between 1910 and 1940, was carried through without the use of Communist power cadres and was es-tablished before the intrusion of Russian ambitions into the Ameri-can hemisphere. The United States limited its intervention to the landing at Vera Cruz and the ill-starred punitive expedition against Villa, an undertaking ordered by Woodrow Wilson, whose idealism misled him into thinking that he could use American foreign policy on the side of the revolution, instead of letting Mexico work out its own destiny. Much later the indemnity claims of the United States companies were settled amicably between the two governments, and Mexico today is an example of a postrevolutionary mixed economy whose economic growth continues at a healthy pace.

The Cuban leaders might have followed Mexico's example, but they had a Grand Design of their own for a broader Latin-American revolution. To carry this out without the old-line Communists, Castro and Guevara would have had to fashion revolutionary cadres of their own to operate in Venezuela and Colombia, Guatemala and Panama and Bolivia, Argentina and Brazil. As Marxist-Leninists of a home-grown variety, they needed the old-line Communists for these grandiose continental ambitions and dared not oust them from the trade-union leadership, the military elite, the party organ-ization posts, or the communications posts and secret police, which they chose as their strategic leverage points. This was the price they paid for the chance to make history on a grand scale. The American failure to meet Castro's demands for aid on his own terms, and the disastrous intervention at the Bay of Pigs fortified Castro in this course and led him to strip away the disguises from the economic-growth plan and the political-power pattern to which at some point he had committed himself. In the end his mistake may lie in his faith that the Soviet Union will accept his brand of Marxism-Leninism for its Latin-American bridgehead. In the power struggle between the two brands, as expressed in the conflict be-tween the "old line" Communists and the "Castro Communists," the Soviets hold the cards, because they control the economic-growth plan and the technicians on which Cuba has come to depend, how-ever ramshackle the resulting economic structure may prove.

The fact is that the economics of growth is rarely separated from the politics of power. The *economic nation* is as much an abstrac-tion as *economic man* ever was. The case of Egypt is instructive here. President Nasser's intent was to build an economic base for the spread of Egyptian power, via his version of Pan-Arabism, through the Middle East and via Pan-Moslemism through Africa; it is not unfair to say that he was more concerned with political dynamism than with economic welfare. His honeymoon with the Communist power cluster, which gave him arms and aid, ended when he discovered that the Communist armed doctrine would not tolerate any competing political dynamism, and that there could be no sharing of power with them except on terms which meant absorption by his Communist partner.

Is there a plan for economic growth which can be called *democratic* and which the more developed economies of the free world can help the undeveloped economies to achieve? The trouble is that the advanced countries do not offer enough compassable models for a struggling new nation. Yet some design is emerging, and may lead to a firmer one in the near future. I sensed a change in the Asian intellectual climate between my first trip in 1955 and my second in 1959-60. It was symbolized by the frequency with which I heard, in university and government circles, terms like "take-off," "mature economy," "social overhead," "public and private sectors," "democratic planning." It has taken a revolution in Western and Asian economic thought to come to the point where these terms have achieved currency.

The great figure in this revolution was not Marx or Adam Smith, but John Maynard Keynes—logician, philosopher, essayist, amateur of the arts, tough-minded investor and Treasury negotiator. While still a controversial name in American business and university circles, Keynes has become a name to conjure with in the undeveloped world because he stressed the possibility of democratic action to deal with cyclical fluctuations and to stimulate economic growth in both developed and undeveloped economies. In the generation after Keynes, four other economists have been able to reach the educated elite of the new nations—Gunnar Myrdal, J. K. Galbraith, Walt W. Rostow and W. Arthur Lewis. Myrdal has done much to carry over the idea of the welfare economy, of a mixed capitalist and socialist character, from the European context to the context of traditional societies in rapid change. Galbraith, by attacking the American "affluent society" for its "private luxury and public squalor"—that is to say, for lavishing upon the private sector of the economy some of the resources needed for the public sector— has turned the tables on the advanced countries and made the division into public and private sectors part of the economic norm rather than a special problem for the undeveloped economy. Rostow has framed an evolutionary scheme of economic development that is at once simple and sweeping—in fact, say his critics, simpler than the complex truth and more sweeping than the hard and tortured road of economic development warrants. He has argued that the new economies can learn the outlines and lessons of economic growth from the experience of the nations which have already traversed its path, whether in the democratic or in the Communist world. Lewis has had a direct influence on the economic thinking of Nigeria, Ghana and several other new states.

With elements of the traditional society still clinging to it, each new nation is struggling to get at the distant goal of the "high-consumption" economy, which will mean power and prestige for the elite, jobs for the bureaucracy, and the good life for all—or almost all. But each nation also, with undeveloped resources, few capital goods, and little technical and managerial skill, seems to have been catapulted into a present that doesn't work. Through dividing the total span from the traditional to the mass-consumption society into stages, Rostow makes the journey seem more possible by mapping out its course. The crucial stage is the third, or "take-off," stage, preceded by the stage of preparation for it ("preconditions for the take-off") and followed by "maturity." Rostow defines the take-off stage as "the great watershed in the life of modern societies . . . when the old blocks and resistances to steady growth are . . . overcome," when economic progress sets the whole tone for the society, and "growth becomes its normal condition." Something crucial happens at this point—perhaps the borrowing of technological knowledge, or the development of business or managerial skills, or the beginnings of innovation in both technology and management, or the building of a system of transport, or the plowing back of saving into investment at a quickened rate—and as a result the economy achieves a break-through.

The appeal this makes is clear enough. The act of winning political independence needs to be paralleled by an economic independence which will bolster the new political sovereignty. An almost heartbreaking effort is required to transform the traditional society, to gather the capital, to formulate the plan, to develop the technology, to train the young people both in industry and government, to find markets for the new nation's products and—even more important—to obtain the means for paying for the machines and machine tools which have to be imported. It is important to see, in perspective, that there is no one simple formula for the break-through into self-generating growth, that historically each of the developed countries has made its break-through in its own characteristic way, which the new nation can also do.

There is a tendency to think of economic aid in terms of past hurt and guilt, as a debt owed to the former oppressed peoples of the colonial world because of the human crimes committed against them. There is equally a tendency of the part of the new nations to assume that they have a right to a kind of moral reparations for what happened in the past. This mood may have provoked George Kennan's defiant sentence: "I, as an American of this day, cannot accept the faintest moral responsibility [for the present condition of the undeveloped nations]; nor do I see that it was particularly the fault of my American ancestors." Kennan, who has always attacked the injection of morality into international politics, is consistent in scorning a new brand of moralism whose self-flagellant quality makes little sense for Americans, who had no share in the history of European imperialism.

If the moral problem is stripped of its sickly guilt, it can still be put in terms of the human connection. The remark by William Graham Sumner—that at the banquet of life there are dinners without appetites at one end of the table and appetites without dinners at the other—sets both the problem of the human connection and the problem of a balanced world economy. C. P. Snow put the first problem in terms of the "overfed" and the "underfed." "We are sitting," he said, "like people in a smart and comfortable restaurant . . . Down on the pavement are people who are looking up at us: people who by chance have different-colored skin from ours and are rather hungry. Do you wonder that they don't like us? Do you wonder that we sometimes feel ashamed of ourselves as we look out through the plate glass?" This is a common enough sentiment among many Westerners who have seen whole families of the homeless sleeping on the sidewalks in Bombay and Calcutta and have seen destitution in village and city slum alike.

One thing that makes the struggle against mass poverty a disheartening one is the failure to deal effectively with population control. In the world of Malthus the balance between population and food supply was maintained by what he called "misery and vice" —that is to say, by famine, disease, flood, massacre, war. Since his day, the world's population has multiplied two-and-a-half times, and more than half of that increase is to be found in the undeveloped areas that cannot sustain the new hungry generations as they come crowding in. Modern medicine and sanitation have cut the death rate, especially among the newly born, while the birth rate has been scarcely affected. Thus the improvements in food raising and in industrial technology are wiped out by the increasing millions of population. Unfortunately, three streams of tendency— Catholic teaching against birth control, Communist anti-Malthusianism, and the fear in the colored areas that population control is a white conspiracy to deplete the strength of the nonwhite nations—have converged to frustrate the raising of living standards. Nor can one exclude the ignorance and isolation of villagers in areas where additional children are an economic aid to the family or a symbol of marital success. Yet, the case of Japan, where a program of population control has been carried through against all the resistances, is evidence that where the will exists on the part of the national leadership, the result can be achieved.

Beyond the human question of individual poverty, there is the more general stake in the problem of the rich and the poor nations, and in redressing the uneven balance between the advanced and the undeveloped countries. For the world as a whole, it is a healthy thing to replace the pattern of wealthy consumer economies and impoverished economies with a pattern of more or less strong and self-sufficient states, able to enter into the circuit flow of trade and ideas and move beyond a narrow nationalism to a confident world perspective. If each nation could at last make the break-through, it would cease to be dependent upon a continued flow of aid which it dare not reject and which the aiding nation dare not end, and there would be improved chances of an orderly world.

This problem of economic aid reluctantly given and sullenly received, and often used to enrich the top bureaucrats of the receiving country or to sustain life among an increasing population of the impoverished rather than effectively applied to achieve an economic break-through, is the crucial problem of relations between the advanced and the undeveloped nations. In a remarkably brief period, mainly because of the example of the Marshall Plan, economic aid has become an established feature of the world landscape, marking a quick and silent revolution in world politics.

The Russians felt they had to counter the American example, for practical reasons as well as by the logic of their anticolonialism. Their aid, wherever possible, took the form of a rough barter plus the shipment of technicians and instructors. The American impulse to help, out of a vague willingness of heart, was at first bolstered by the assumption that the way to solve a problem is to spend money on it. The weakness of this base for economic aid was that when much of this money for various reasons produced few results, and the problem showed no signs of yielding, there was bound to be disillusionment about the principle of economic aid itself.

Yet clearly, it was a valid, if limited, instrument of American policy, with four provisos: first, that the results be judged objectively rather than in terms of affection or gratitude; second, that the aid be given only for approved projects, under watchful supervision, so that it would not be siphoned off to enrich the already rich; third, that it be granted only to nations with effective governments, the strength and creativeness of the government being even more important than the quality of the economy receiving the aid; fourth, that the Americans learn the facts of life about the undeveloped world, including the fact that the receiving government may well be "socialistic."

I do not include here, as an unchangeable fact, the bleak state bureaucracies which every traveler in the undeveloped world remembers, with their post offices, telegraph services, transportation systems, their inefficiency and stagnation, their pervasive bribery and bribetaking, their fear of assuming responsibility, their tendency to play it safe and take it easy on the job. Galbraith has called this "post office socialism" and has urged the democratic planners in India and elsewhere to break through it and to refashion the public sector in livelier and freer terms. There is a vicious spiral effect here: an economy which cannot provide work for its educated clerical and middle class is compelled to find petty jobs for them in its bureaucracy, where they are underpaid and demoralized; but this kind of bureaucracy in turn plays havoc with the whole economy and slows up the pace of economic advance. The Communists tried to solve the problem, not always successfully, by a combination of coercion, fear and induced *élan*. The democratic planner cannot fall back on these supports; he tends instead to rely upon the protracted aid from the more advanced economies of the free world.

In the case of most of the new economies, there is little chance of moving toward a relatively free market without having first established a considerable measure of government control. To put it more simply, a strong public sector must come first, before there can be an emphasis on the private sector; the economy cannot move toward capitalist forms without having first established a considerable measure of state socialism or, at least, of directed or planned economy. Where there is no appreciable saving because life is lived too close to survival itself, the state must act as the agency for saving and accumulation.

Where there is little private investment the state must become the medium for public investment. Where the automatic market controls have little meaning because the market has not had a chance to operate in a traditional society, the state must decide the allocation of resources, capital investment, foreign exchange. Where little challenge for management has been developed, the state must train an economic and administrative elite and set it to work in the management of state enterprises. Where there has been apathy about the functioning of the economy, leaving the results to custom, or to God or the big landlords and merchants, the state must grapple with the planning for economic growth.

In short, if socialism in undeveloped countries means collective action in the decisions, priorities and planning which are needed to amass and assign the capital funds and machine skills for economic growth, then in that sense socialism is likely to precede capitalism. This is what Nehru called the "socialist pattern" in the Indian economy. If this pattern is orderly, flexible and strong enough, it can lead to an increasing role for the private sector without leaving the individual helpless before the power of uncontrolled private enterprise. Thus, the state bureaucracy, which has to play a decisive role in the early stages of economic growth, can in time be balanced by a market mechanism operating more freely than the state can, and by a large number of individual calculations and choices that give scope to diversity in economic life.

In the undeveloped economy it takes collective action to create the conditions for further self-generating growth, and as this growth takes place the economy can move, step by step, farther in the direction of freedom. If Western observers grasp this fact, they will know that they cannot wish away the public sector of the undeveloped economy or weep over the necessary "socialist pattern" phase of the development, and they will refrain from trying to impose their own forms of economic decision and preference upon the new countries.

Part of the confusion about democratic planning lies in the confusion of defining it. It might mean economic planning in an open society, as in Israel, whose economy has the added merit of being compassable enough to serve as the model for a number of the new states which lack Israel's democratic fiber; or as in India, where the plan made by a small government elite at the top is freely discussed at the provincial and local levels, and is sometimes substantially changed in response to criticism. But it is more likely to mean that even when the state and society are not "democratic," the necessary state controls are kept to a minimum, that the element of coercion flows from the nature of the economic task rather than from the coercive state or ideology, and that the direction of economic growth is toward greater freedom not only in the economy itself but on every level of the society. If the idea of democratic planning is used in this latter sense, it can be applied to all the new economies that have not come under Communist power. The democratic element in economic growth thus becomes a matter of direction, temper and intent, rather than a formal mechanism.

4. Overtake and Take-over

THE QUESTION about each of the developing economies is not whether it will commit itself to a growth plan, but how fast and how big. Every new nation wants a steel mill and a hydroelectric dam, something to wear in emulation of the more developed countries. They are the mink stole and diamond ring which are to give the upward-mobile nation its status among the powers of the earth. Hence all the impulse to "plan big," and all the impatience with economic advisers who counsel slower and more modest planning.

In economic terms the problem is basically one of the rate and direction of capital formation, or—put differently—of saving and investment. Some of the capital will be borrowed from other countries, some will be earned by profitable exports, some will be extracted from the population by the margin between production and subsistence levels. At every stage, planning involves strategies of development, choosing the sectors and industries where growth will have a cumulative effect throughout the economy, deciding what resources and investments to allocate where, and setting in operation the necessary plans and controls. This requires not only planning skills, but also scientific, technical and managerial. For the new nation, these skills are as important as investment capital, and even harder to develop on its own. The temptation is to turn to a more advanced nation and hand over the difficult tasks to its technicians.

The cult of the heightened tempo of growth sometimes threatens to sweep away other values, especially humanist and political ones, in pursuit of quick growth returns. It has been argued, for example, that the investment rate carries with it a built-in political structure, that when a nation sets a certain goal of capital formation at a steep annual rate of growth (say 15 per cent or more), it must automatically develop coercive state machinery to make this rate possible. This is a kind of goal-determinism: given your goal in economic growth, a lesser or greater degree of totalitarianism goes with it. It is an interesting idea, which would make political freedom a function of the rate of capital formation rather than of the habits, leadership and ethics of a people. But the implied argument—that rapid economic growth is possible only in a totalitarian state—has been disproved in economic history. The British, American, Germans, Japanese and Russians each carried through their industrialization at a high tempo, but each achieved it with a different pattern of freedom and authority. Thus, there is no iron determinism linking a high rate of capital formation with a particular political and social system. In the house of economic growth there are many political mansions.

This does not mean that economic growth is politically indifferent, but only that it is politically variable. What is needed is not a particular type of political frame, but a particular kind of effectiveness in that frame, no matter what its type. The economic breakthrough in the United States came with the development of the canal and railroad systems, which brought a food supply and manufacturers to their markets. After Commodore Perry's opening of Japan to the West, the Japanese achieved an economic breakthrough by the use of traditional centralized power. After the Hitler defeat, the Germans made a startling economic comeback with a burst of technological and managerial creativeness inside a market economy. The instance of Russia is especially illuminating. After attacking Trotsky for his program of ruthless expansion in heavy industry, Stalin cynically took over the same program, reaching a higher capital investment rate than anyone had foretold as possible. He forced the people to cut down on consumption, pushed the peasants into collectives, starved millions of them when he decided on the exchange of his scanty grain for machinery, and developed a police state, of nightmare cruelties, to crush dissent. He was in a hurry because he feared attack from abroad. His slogan "socialism in one country" should have read *"military* socialism in one country"—that is to say, enough forced industrialization to serve as a base for a strong modern army, enough military power to give a Communist state and its rulers some security and a base from which to spread world revolution.

In his grim way Stalin performed a considerable task in carrying through this program of economic growth and transformation. But his repressive police regime, while doubtless a factor in the acceptance of the economic hardships, was neither cause nor consequence of the rate of economic growth. It was largely the consequence of Stalin's own mind and personality. Even if he had gone much slower, at half the rate of capital accumulation, his regime would still have been a police tyranny. Whether you double or halve the economic growth rate of Communist China you will still have one of the most oppressive regimes in history. Double or triple the rate of economic growth in the India of Nehru, and you would still have a tolerably free society.

What happened in the case of Russia may best be described as a kind of circuit flow: the need for rapid capital accumulation tempted the new ruling group, and especially Stalin, to take the relatively easy way of a repressive police state, which was already provided in the theory of proletarian dictatorship; at the same time, the available totalitarian means made it possible to achieve the coercion needed for growth-without-consent. Within this circuit flow there is room for the working of the personal temperament and character of the top leaders, so that sadism sometimes gets rationalized as necessary policy, while a different kind of leadership might have played the policy differently. Once established, however, both the rate of growth and the totalitarian machinery take on a life of their own, and what was once a means toward an end becomes an unquestioned way of doing things.

The idea of the indifference of the political means, given the economic goal, is crucial to the strategy of overtake which the Communists are seeking to apply in the undeveloped world. "Your nations and ours," they say, "are trying—each with its own political forms—to produce goods for the people; together we can overtake the West, which has been the source of our colonial oppression." This idea of overtake has a powerful emotional appeal in the struggle for influence in the colonial world, since it fits in so aptly with the psychology of *ressentiment* and the politics of grievance. For the leaders of the new nations, the world is divided neatly into rich and poor nations, the "haves" and the "have-nots," the hungry and the sated ones. They see this division as corresponding roughly to the division between East and West, between the revolutionary world and the *status quo*. The fact is, of course, that Russia today is a rich, not a poor, nation, one of the "haves" rather than the "have-nots," a conservative society which does not want to see its pyramid of powers destroyed by war, a repressive power holding down potential revolutions within its own imperial domain. But this fact has not yet become evident to eyes unwilling to see it. Communism is identified historically with the revoultions of the poor classes and is, therefore, now identified with the revolutions of the poor nations. The Russians and Chinese are thus put not into the category of the enemy to be fought, but into that of fellow revolutionaries who will be sympathetic to the struggle. The new African leaders, passionate to expel the last residues of the white man's power and influence, seek also to overtake his economy and living standards.

The danger is that in the zeal for overtake there will be a squeezing-out of humanist values, and that the ground will be prepared for a take-over of power by cynical men and regimes, perhaps even by a new imperialism. "If the people can get bread," I heard Asian students ask, "and if we students can get jobs under a system of Communism, then what's wrong with Communism?" The assumption here, hidden even from the questioners, was that the only way to get bread or jobs is to give up freedom and to pay for them by a police state, a party-line standard of truth, a closed society, and an intellectual strait jacket for those whose role in life should be intellectual inquiry without limit.

It is hard to get out of one's mind the young Asians, Africans and Latin Americans who ask these questions—their eagerness, their mingled belligerence and bewilderment, the smoldering fire in them, their amused skepticism at what they think your answer will be. "As between freedom and bread [one might have said to them] don't assume that freedom comes second. It comes first. Suppose that they promise you bread provided you are willing to give up freedom and the struggle for it; suppose they mismanage things, get slothful or cruel with power, grow rigid and forget that economic growth comes only by creativeness—then you will find that you have neither freedom nor bread, and perhaps not life itself. What the Chinese Communists call the 'Great Leap Forward,' which is a short-cut term for the effort at overtake at any cost, is likely to prove a 'Great Leap' into darkness. If you move toward freedom, you can manage to change your rulers and institutions if they fail to get bread for you. But once you have suffered a take-over of freedom, you will find it hard to retrieve except by a long and agonized struggle."

This bread-or-freedom fallacy is not restricted to the emotional young men in the undeveloped countries. You will find it among some sophisticated older ones. I recall a conversation with a high Indian diplomat. The trouble with Westerners, he said, is that they cling to the illusion of freedom because it means something to the well-fed and the educated; it is a luxury an intellectual can afford. But the ordinary peasant in a nation that has gone through a liberating revolution—the Russian *muzhik,* the Chinese villager, the Latin American *campesino,* the Arab *fellah*—doesn't care who is in power. Regimes have come and gone on the plains, deserts and mountains where he has lived. From his angle of vision at the base of the pyramid, the governments above him are all unfeeling tyrannies. He had little voice in bringing them in and he has little chance of getting them out.

The only thing that matters, said this diplomat, is the progress that the regime makes in technology and economic growth, which will be reflected in the living standards of the peasant. True, the initial capital accumulation may have to be taken out of his pitifully meager living standard. He may sullenly resist the program which bears heavily upon him, he may be tempted to revolt or flee, the doors may have to be shut upon him, and he may even have to be starved into submission. But after the initial difficulties there will be more national income to divide, and the lowly peasant will be cut in on the gains.

Thus ran the diplomat's argument. It isolates the single factor of technology and reduces everything else in a man's life to a cipher. A peasant too is a man, deserving of freedom as well as bread, a convergence point for drives of understanding and expressiveness as well as of elementary hunger. To reduce him simply to an appetite is to show a contempt for him as a man—a contempt which often peeps out from behind the mask of the cult of the common man, which the champions of the economic motif in history sometimes assume. What was nevertheless valid in the argument was the fact that it is the deprived man at the base of the pyramid whose hunger and frustration form the dynamic of revolution and to whom the new political religions of the world make their appeal.

If hunger is indeed the nub of the problem of the undeveloped world, then it is not an East-West problem but (as Sir Oliver Franks has put it) a North-South problem. Half the world—neglected and exploited in the past, imprisoned in a net of climate, soil, race, tribalism, superstition, disease, primitive technology—is trying to telescope the transformations of centuries into a revolution of a generation. The free-world power system has the best of reasons for aiding this effort—that of a common stake in a world frame in which each nation can determine the shape its own institution will take.

5. Self-Determination: Wilson versus Lenin

WOODROW WILSON, the father of the idea of self-determination, was one of those curious figures in American democracy—an intellectual in politics. His stubborn Calvinist assurance of having a pipeline to some source of Divine guidance made him a prickly and often insufferable figure. Yet he knew what was required of his era, far better than the professionals who scorned him for his amateurism and idealism.

In World War I he saw that a revolutionary statement of America's war aims would be a more resounding weapon than any in the Allied arsenals; and at the war's end he saw with equal clarity that men were hungry for an end of all wars. His historic Fourteen Points (1917), called for the "self-determination of all peoples." With that phrase, based of course on a long intellectual tradition, but bold in its simplicity, he dug a grave for the rickety old empires of Europe still lording it over their subject peoples in Europe as well as in Asia and Africa, and he also fashioned a corrosive for other imperialisms still to come. True, he did not foresee how far-reaching would be the impact of his manifesto upon the colonial empires; the fifth of his Fourteen Points, dealing with colonial settlements, was in its explicit wording extremely cautious. But the angle of vision from which Wilson viewed his era had in it an inherent revolutionary logic that could not stop short of the total liberation of the colonial peoples. Once you embraced the principle of self-determination you could not set limits to it by continents or categories: you could not apply it to the oppressed white people living within the old empires and deny it to the oppressed colored people who made up the outlying bastions of empire.

When Wilson came to Europe on his misssion of peacemaking in 1919, he was hailed in Paris and Rome by crowds who saw in him the symbol of an era of democratic revolutions. The wildness of their acclaim was the measure of their wild dream of a world of peace in which people would choose their governments and destinies. But beyond Europe's portals stretched the lands where the dreams of nationhood were to burn even more wildly in the hearts of men more unlettered than in Europe and less experienced in the exacting arts of democracy. The words spoken by an American

President on European soil were seminal words out of which would be born a whole array of new revolutionary movements and nations. What the still-unformed leaders of Asia and Africa got from them was a dawning sense that one people need no longer be oppressed by another, whatever the writ by which it claimed its overlordship, and that every people has the right to work out its salvation or damnation in its own way.

In the same year, 1917, in which the Fourteen Points made Wilson a world revolutionary symbol, there was another figure who appeared dramatically on the European stage. After obscure years of struggle in Russia and exile in Switzerland, V. I. Lenin saw in the first Russian Revolution of March 1917 his chance to test and carry out his new Bolshevik strategy for engineering a revolution by a small, disciplined group of determined men. He sped through Germany on the now legendary sealed train, arrived at Finland Station in Leningrad, took charge of his tiny Bolshevik faction— and the rest is history. I return to the often-told story of these two men, because history in its unfolding has given importance to aspects of their work that seemed secondary at the time and has pitted them against each other sharply as symbols for the undeveloped world.*

Lenin is reported to have said, sometime in 1919, that the road to world power for the Communists lay through Asia. Certainly the Communist leaders came, in time, to understand this crucial fact. But it took a while for the realization to come through. Though he had broken sharply enough with the Marxist intellectual tradition to gamble on the chance of revolution even in a largely agrarian economy like Russia's, Lenin still faced West in his expectations for world revolution. The Russian Revolution was only the beginning; the great impetus, he felt, was to come from the more "advanced" countries of Western Europe—from Germany, France and even Great Britain. It was to the workers and the workers' leaders in these countries that his pamphlet, *Imperialism: The Highest Stage of Capitalism,* was addressed; it was they who were meant to become weary and bitter over the imperialist adventures of their ruling capitalists; it was they who were to "turn the imperialist war into a civil war" and, by capturing power in their own countries, buttress the shaky fortunes of the Soviet regime. But the hopes for Western revolutions collapsed, one after another,

---

* I owe much for this whole account of Wilson and Lenin as the two symbolic figures of this time to Arno J. Mayer, *Political Origins of the New Diplomacy: 1917-18* (1959).

and Lenin blamed the "labor aristocrats" for having grown comfortable with their share of the profits from colonial exploitation,
and the Marxist intellectuals for having perversely wrong ideas
about revolutionary tactics.

In 1920 there was a "Congress of the Toiling Peoples of the
East" in Baku, where for the first time Communist leaders gathered
to organize Asian revolt. The shifting of the axis of revolutionary
expectations was carried further at a series of anti-imperialist congresses, often held in European capitals, where a number of Asian
and African nationalist leaders met and mingled with anti-imperialist intellectuals of the West.

What Lenin did was to redefine the elements entering into the
"revolutionary situation." A matured industrialism was no longer
the crucial element; it was, in fact, even a serious deterrent, since it
carried with it a long-standing democratic tradition, and the working-class leaders could not be trusted to act under Comintern
orders. The Asian nationalist ingredients were better, since the history of repression had led to explosive resentment, and the memory
of the indignities done to the local population could be fanned
into a revolutionary flame. The problem became not so much to
turn the imperialist war into a civil war as to turn the nationalist
revolution into a Communist one. This gave a new fillip to Lenin's
classical formula of the two revolutions, which was that of turning
the constitutional (or "bourgeois") revolution into a socialist (or
"proletarian") one, by which he meant a Communist Party dictatorship. What was changed was only that the "bourgeois" revolution
was transposed into a "nationalist" one. True, some of the earlier
bourgeois revolutions had also been nationalist in character; but
what was once marginal now became central.

In many ways the new revolutionary assignment is an easier one.
After the initial nationalist revolution, with its act of liberation,
there is no strong government to be overthrown or subverted. There
is, to be sure, usually a hero-leader of the liberation movement who
heads the first government of the new nation and whose hold on
the people is somewhat like that of the traditional tribal chiefs,
with the added revolutionary charisma. The Communist strategy
must come to terms with this leader, unless it can gain control of
him early and secretly. But it does not have to confront a sustained
libertarian tradition. A people who have lived for centuries under
one or another kind of tyranny does not suffer a traumatic loss with
the imposition of a police state, as would the British or French or
Americans, the Scandinavians or the Dutch. I must add, however,

that the tribal and religious fiber of an African society, or the pacifist-humanist one of an Asian society, has posed considerable problems for the successors of Lenin.

Lenin must have seen enough of what was to come, to die with at least a dream in his political imagination. Wilson died broken-hearted, because his dream of a world polity to end wars was rejected by his own people. Yet, comparing the two futures they held out to the developing nation, it would be rash to see all the advantage on Lenin's side.

Two roads diverged for the world in 1917. One had the great advantage of historic underdog associations, along with trained cadres of organizers who could bring to a new nation the experience of decades of social adventuring. But the other road could give humanist fulfillment to the years of revolutionary travail. It had the advantage of linking the ethos of the liberation movement with that of the new regime. Liberation from a colonial oppressor makes little sense if it leads the people back to another kind of enslavement to a foreign power. The very fact which gives the world Communist movements its strength—its organized and manipulative direction from a single power center—acts as handicap in its struggle for new nations who have for generations hated being governed from another power center. They may get an inefficient and corrupt government, and their leaders may be demagogues with a dictatorial streak —but the government and the leaders are *theirs*.

While Lenin gave lip service to the principle of self-determination in the Russian system of regions and races, it was a cynical lip service, and he first made certain that the ribbed iron frame of the Communist Party made the seeming federal autonomy safe. At the Eighth National Congress of the Communist Party, in 1919, when the first postrevolutionary party program and statutes were adopted, Lenin made it clear that the Communist parties of the Ukraine, Latvia, Estonia, and the other ethnic areas would be treated as provincial units and come under the authority of the Russian party. Nor have the Communists shown any sign of extending self-determination to their satellite nations; when it was put to the test, as in the Hungarian revolution in 1956, the bid for self-determination was drowned in blood.

This is not a question of the whim of a leader, but a built-in characteristic of the doctrine and mentality of Communism. The Wilsonian principle of self-determination, on the other hand, is inherently revolutionary because it puts the burden of choice on the new nation, which must shape not only a going government for itself, but a going society as well. "To free oneself is nothing," André Gide wrote. "It's being free that is hard." Having achieved nationhood, the new nations must confront the task of self-government. If Wilson's meaning for the new nations is a deeper one than Lenin's, it is exactly because their revolutions have been identity revolutions. What Wilson offered was the chance to continue these revolutions by making the search for identity in a sense a permanent one. What Lenin offered, in the name of class war, was a closure of the search for identity and a closure, therefore, of the continuing revolutionary process. This may help to explain why, except for China, none of the recently created nations in Asia, the Middle East and Africa have embraced Communism unless they become Communist in the process of their creation. In North Vietnam and North Korea, Communism came as the product of civil war. But in all the other cases it is even, in a distorted sense, some form of the Wilsonian road which is being taken.

To Wilson's should be added the name of Franklin Roosevelt, who rounded out the idea of self-determination by showing that a democracy can adapt itself to the changes in the contemporary world by a New Deal welfare revolution. The New Deal idea has thus far been associated with developed economies, but in the sense of a democratic economic dynamism it can be transferred to the developing ones as well. This suggests that their choice for the future is between the Communist class state and the New Deal welfare state.

The case of India is crucial exactly because the effort for a new democratic welfare state is being made on the largest and most meaningful scales in India, in a third Five Year Plan shaped by democratic means. Speaking of the Ladakh border conflict between China and India in 1960, Nehru said that "on this disputed border two revolutions confront each other." He expressed, thereby, both the immediate drama of the struggle to survive against Chinese power, and the long-range symbolic importance of the Indian experiment in nation building. In giving India economic aid, the free world, especially America, Great Britain and West Germany, gambled heavily on the success of this democratic revolution, while the Communist world gambled on its failure despite the aid it extended. One sees the curious paradox of Soviet policy toward India—that of building a steel plant and training technicians for a regime whose early demise as a going concern you confidently expect, and which you hope to overthrow at the earliest possible moment.

In a world rife with insanities this would seem a prime insanity; yet, for the Russians it makes sense. It gives them a chance to present themselves as a regime granting aid without political conditions. At the same time it gives them the inside track as a successor regime—as against India's Communist Chinese neighbor—in the event of the collapse of the free Indian regime through inner weakness and the disruptive forces of language, region and religion. To hasten that process, the Russians have followed an astute course in wooing the governmental, technical and trade-union elites, in restricting Soviet aid to dramatic "impact projects," and in flooding the country with the output of their publishing houses. They are thus at once the gravediggers and the potential residuary legatees of the regime to which they give aid. They may reason that a policy of fattening the calf is not a bad one if you have a good chance some day to own the fatted cow.

The Chinese are moved to a more astringent policy by the fact of being still a "have-not" nation that cannot compete with the Russians in the aid race. Add their conviction that the Russians are selling out the Communist parties in Asia in their anxiety to work with non-Communist national leaders like Sukarno and Nehru. In terms of national identity and power struggle they cannot tolerate having the leadership of the Asian Communist movements slip from their hands. But they also disagree with the Russians on the role of time in the world revolutionary situation, unconvinced by the Russian view that time is on the side of a Communist world victory and that they can afford to wait, in India and elsewhere.

The Chinese believe that the Communist power cluster must strike when it can in each nation, before the new national identity has had a chance to strike roots in the psychology of the people. After a decade of democratic independence, the Indians are unlikely to cherish a "proletarian dictatorship" operating either from Moscow or from Peking. Even the disruptive forces I have mentioned—of language, region and religion—are deceptive, since they sink their differences in the face of a unifying threat to the nations. With each passing decade, the Communists in India may find not that the new nation is growing ripe for Communism but that it is growing ripe for a larger measure of social freedom and democratic equality. Hence the Chinese dissent from Russia's policy of aiding India, and hence China's own abrupt action on India's borders.

What I am saying is not that the disruptive forces cannot prove fateful, but that they need not be fatal to the democratic fulfillment of the identity revolutions. Even when communalism, tribalism and other centrifugal forces make the task more difficult, the essential choice remains. It is not a choice between revolution and reaction, or between growth and the *status quo;* it is a choice between the two revolutions that confront each other—between that of Woodrow Wilson, Roosevelt and Nehru on the one side, and that of Lenin, Stalin and Mao Tse-tung on the other.

6. Color, Heroes, and Elites

THE FIRST GREAT WAVE of nationalisms in the modern world came in European history, from Joan of Arc to Mazzini; and while the price that had to be paid for liberation was often blood and terror, the energies released were in the main generous and creative, and the perspectives of the liberation movements embraced the whole of humanity. In contrast, the new wave of the revolutionary nationalisms especially in Africa, tends to be jealous, exclusive, narrow in focus, often bigoted in viewpoint. There is a danger that the era they represent may be known in history not as the Great Enlightenment but as the Great Narrowing.

The most disturbing evidence of the Great Narrowing is the new nations' color consciousness, most pronounced in Africa, but also infecting Asia and the Middle East, especially since it furnishes the principal emotional cement of the Afro-Asian bloc in the UN. The attitudes of white superiority on the part of their colonial masters left the colored peoples of Africa and Asia with a color score to settle. They had learned over the centuries the color of power, and they had found that it was white. They were now to show the world the power of color. They found that by wielding the weapon of color consciousness they could play on the sense of guilt of the Western nations, on the conscience of the world as a whole, and on the color chauvinism of their own populations.

In the case of Africa, the form that militant color consciousness took was the demand that white settlers, some of whose families had lived in Africa for generations, must get out of politics. But it went farther. It demanded that the new governments must be ethnically monolithic both in leadership and in political participation, and that Africa as a matter of principle must belong to and be run by Africans only. The tragic fact here is that this is white supremacy turned upside down. One of the tricks which history has played on men and nations is that the very people who suffered most from the doctrines of racial superiority and exclusion should now adopt the same racist doctrines which had once victimized them, and now become the perpetrators of racist supremacy where once they had been its victims.

There is a double meaning to Pan-Africanism. One is the nexus of interest between the various liberation movements in Africa— the doctrine, as Louis Lomax has put it, "that none of Africa is free until all of Africa is divested of nonblack interests." Put in these terms, it means that what happens in Angola, in Mozambique and in South Africa is of central concern for the people of Kenya and Ghana and Nigeria. There can be little quarrel with this, except to say that whites have an equal stake with blacks in the liberation of oppressed people, not as blacks but as human beings.

In the second meaning, "Africa for the Africans"—the exclusion of whites from the common efforts and common benefits of life in a new African nation—Pan-Africanism is insupportable in logic, in justice or in humanity. White settlers and white soldiers were attacked in the Congo, and in the case of the Italian medical team they were hacked to pieces, not because they were particular human beings but because they were generically white. Dag Hammarskjöld was denounced because as UN Secretary General he had sent some white detachments, commanded by white officers, as part of the larger UN police force in the Congo. In a great dissenting opinion, in *Plessy vs. Ferguson,* Justice Harlan of the United States Supreme Court said that the American Constitution is color-blind. Insofar as Pan-Africanism violates this principle, it cuts away the moral basis on which the genuinely color-blind people throughout the world might otherwise support its liberation efforts.

The color of power in Africa has become black, as a total reaction against the fact that it was once white. "Racism," says Louis Lomax, "is the irritant on Africa's raw nerves—not colonialism, but that *white* people have colonized *black* people; not settler domination, but that *white* settlers have dominated indigenous *black* people; not economic exploitation, but that *white* people have exploited *black* people; not social discrimination, but that the *white* power structure sets itself apart from the *black* masses; not denial of civil rights, but that *white* people deny *black* people their civil rights." In short, it is not the moral sense, but a sense of invidiousness which stirs the passions and actions of black Africa— not the difference between right and wrong, but the feeling that the wrong people have been doing wrong, and that it is now time for the right people to do wrong in turn.

One recalls Tolstoy's sentence from *Anna Karenina:* "Everything has been turned upside down and is only now taking shape." But what a monstrous shape, given the generous potentials open to it! It is Caliban's curse upon Prospero for having kept him so long under his sway, but Caliban too is having to pay for the curse by his failure to rise to full humanity. Perhaps the worst indictment of the whites is that this angry scar which they left on their subjects, servants and victims should prove so ineradicable.

Much of the intensity of color feeling, let it be remembered, is a political coin of exchange, meant for home use in the internal political struggles and the rivalries for control of the new little empires emerging in Africa. The leaders who served their jail sentences and emerged as nationalist heroes know the value that the masses attach to a belligerent use of color symbols. They are themselves caught up in a tangle of conspicuous and competitive color rivalries, in which resentment, hate, pride and hope are mingled. Each leader finds himself compelled to outdo his rivals in bidding for these emotions, in a context in which the worst charge against a leader is that he has grown soft on the whites. Unfortunately, what is meant for home consumption becomes hard to withdraw in the formation of national policy and the taking of positions in the UN, where the one-nation-one-vote principle makes the leaders of the new African nations the most persistently wooed targets in the history of diplomacy.

The catch lies in the question of technical and managerial skills. Technology too is color-blind. The black masses, conditioned to their tribal religions in which a magical power is held to reside in certain ritual and incantatory words, believed that the word *freedom* would release for them all the things they had been denied under the regime of unfreedom. But only the magic of technology can release the potentials for the good life that lie in the still-untamed rivers and undeveloped resources of the continent. Poverty may prove harder to defeat than white power. But only with the help of the whites can the new leaders run the industries, build the roads, airlines, schools and dams, formulate the economic plans and administer the government services needed to defeat poverty. Thus the white technician must play the role in the new black governments that the Czarist officers played in the Soviet army in the early years after the Revolution—the role of being tolerated for their usefulness until their skills can be taken over and they can be dispensed with.

This may, however, prove too short and bleak a view. Technologies continue to make demands which cannot be met by color and class exclusiveness even after new elites are trained. The Russians found that they had to use scientists in developing their rockets and missiles, even Jewish scientists, and that they had to ease the political tests to which other Russians were subject. While the values of industrialism are barren enough in themselves, the discipline of the machine can corrode racism and class invidiousness as it must corrode magic. It is a long revolution on which the African peoples are embarked, and before the end of the voyage they are likely to find that the old color shibboleths are clumsy encumbrances. The archaic fires will not be enough in a world of new forces. In the process of confronting these forces, the nationalist revolutions may recapture some of the perspectives of humanism that the revolutions of Voltaire and Jefferson, Mazzini and Kossuth and Masaryk opened, not just for Europeans or for whites, but for man.

But Africa, like Asia and the Middle East, has become not only color-conscious but hero-conscious. The nationalist martyr-hero has become the national leader-hero. Primitive cultures which for centuries have personalized and dramatized the forces of magic were bound to personalize and dramatize the forces of politics. This is not the place to discuss the quality of this leadership.* But I must note how closely connected is the cult of the hero, especially in Africa, with the color consciousness I have been discussing. The African hero stands between the masses and the educated elite, a symbol of power to the elite, a symbol of connection with the masses.

It is too easy for a European or an American—or, for that matter, a Russian—to forget that African color consciousness is not only vengeance for the oppressive past, but also connection in the bewildering present. The tensions of living in an African society are as insistent as those of the modern Western city, but they operate in a different universe. Dr. T. Adeoye Lambo, a Nigerian psychiatrist, has adapted some of the practices of the native healers to modern psychiatry, and he has not shrunk from animal sacrifices, tribal dances and rituals, as elements in therapy. An anxious man who

* For the hero as founding father see the next section below, "A Parcel of Politics."

believes he has been bewitched by tribal enemies will be released from his obsession best within the frame of tribal ritual. A people who feels torn up by the roots, out of its traditional society, may find its sense of connection through assertion of their common color, as symbolized by its nationalist color-hero.

The educated elites of the new nations need a sense of connection as badly as the village and tribal masses. As a class they are largely the creation of the colonial administrators, who needed them to govern with, as they needed the tribal chiefs for indirect government. They were part of the crucial migration to the cities as centers of communication and administration. They learned the lessons of the Western revolutionary tradition better than their mentors had counted upon, and they came to scorn the tribal chiefs who continued to lend themselves to the uses of indirect rule. The British and French educational traditions proved best in establishing links that outlasted the colonial administrative needs, while the Dutch, Belgian and Portuguese systems proved least effective. But, whatever the intellectual legacy, and however much or little it has carried over, it was for the educated elite only a road to a modernism of their own.

It is a conscious part of Communist strategy to reach these educated elites by every possible appeal. The "freedom fighters" from Kenya, Somaliland, Uganda, Rhodesia and Southwest Africa who set up headquarters in Nasser's Cairo during the turn of the 1960s, were also given lavishly subsidized trips to Moscow and Peking. The courses and quarters for African students at Russian and Chinese universities are a calculated part of the Communist policy. The Chinese have the color advantage in their appeal to the racist nationalisms of Africa. The Russians, with their propaganda stress on the struggle of the "have-nots," have curiously come to be regarded as themselves "have-nots," and therefore almost as non-whites. But color nationalism has itself become a political religion, with the same overtones of liberation and righteousness that revolutionary nationalism once had. Thus, there is no vacuum left for the Communist political religion to move into. And if you add to the psychic intensity of color consciousness the urgency of self-improvement and self-enrichment, on the part of those who feel for the first time that they are coming into their kingdom, you get some measure of the new temper in Africa, and why it does not fit into the political war of the great power clusters, even while it uses that war for its purposes.

The great disadvantage under which the Communist movements operate is the envious eye they cast upon the rich resources of the continent. The stakes of the power-struggle in Africa are big stakes. They are diamonds and gold, manganese, cobalt, oil, natural gas, cotton, hydroelectric power. What is most likely to frustrate the Grand Design of world Communism in its African ambitions is that the new Africans consider themselves "have-nots," but not proletarians. Their dreams are of personal comfort, leisure, enrichment, the good life and the raising of living standards for their own people.

The educated elites of the new African nations are as middle-class as the most middle-class American Negroes. They want to live in their own houses, ride in their own cars and planes, send their children to their own universities, have their own furniture, wear their own good clothes, eat their own food, be waited on by their own servants. All the things that the whites once denied them they want to have now as their color monopoly in their own countries; but they did not struggle for them in order to surrender them to other foreign imperialists. They did not survive the ordeal of colonialism and suffer the rigors of imprisonment so that men sitting in Moscow and Peking should fulfill their dream of world power. They mean to enjoy the products of their own good earth, and where they can make its eroded stretches better they mean to take the benefits of its betterment for themselves.

Thus there may be a deep core of truth in Jean Genet's surrealist play, *The Blacks,* which recognizes the ritual murderousness of color hatred in the hearts of the Negro victims of white power, but which also asserts that once they have taken off their habitual masks —after playing the roles at once of black men and of white men— they find a wholeness in being unashamedly themselves. One may even see their racist nationalism in Africa, with all its bigotries of black supremacy, as part of this wholeness. Franklin Frazier may be right in underscoring the emptiness and normlessness of the "black bourgeoisie" in an American culture. But in the course of their struggle and triumph on African soil, much of the normlessness of a similar black bourgeoisie has been annealed. Since they no longer have the imperialists to fight as an enemy, they take on their own whites to continue the enemy role. But much as they need an enemy they need something else even more. Their sense of connection with the symbol of the city—African and Western alike—is part of the glow and wonder of modernism which has a greater hold on them than Communism or their own tribalism or even their color as a badge of belonging. Immanuel Wallerstein, protesting against the view that Africa before the whites was a vacuum, speaks of the "movement and splendor, conquest and innovation, trade and art" of the earlier African cultures. He is right, but the new ones are yearning for a "movement and splendor" of their own. Their daemonic thrust is not that of the Communist daemon I have discussed, but the pulsing beat of the modern city and modern life—rootless perhaps, but exciting—which exerts on them an almost tropismatic attraction.

7. A Parcel of Polities: The Unreadiness Effect and Personal Rule

IN A SENSE, the central problem of the undeveloped world is the pace of change, with its dislocating and dissolving effects upon the fabric of the total society. In traditional societies, the slowness of change left the underlying daily life of the people almost untouched and left the "cake of custom," which had always been part of that daily life, relatively unbroken. But with the new pace of change the traditional society has been torn up by the roots, with consequences still incalculable for every part of it. There are two phases of change—the *dislocating* phase and the *reactive* or *adaptive* phase which comes in response to the dislocating.

Edmund Burke was able to make a good case for traditionalism and slow change as the sustainer of freedom, and condemned too-rapid change as its enemy. In Asia, Africa and the Middle East, the pace of change became revolutionary, and the revolutions were able to bring liberation with them; but they largely failed to convert liberation into freedom, in the sense of the scope for individual diversity and dissent within a frame of government by consent. For the same rapid change which brought liberation from the oppressive masters also disintegrated the fabric of the society, and neither freedom nor democracy sits comfortably with chaos, while authoritarianism does.

For tyranny is as old as human history and can "work" under a variety of social situations. Democracy requires and invokes a certain pattern of human energies which takes some time to develop. A too-rapid pace of technological change, as happened when the Germans and later the Japanese took over the industrial skills of the British and Americans, puts a strain on the capacity of the society to adapt the rest of its institutional life and ways of thought to it

—which may be why both peoples developed an authoritarian imperialism.

The crux of the matter lies in the relation between rapid change in one part of the society and a slow reactiveness in the others. It is the unequal pace of change, as between the technology and the rest of the society, which produces a precarious imbalance between them, and brings about a malaise in the minds of peasant, city worker, university student, soldier or officer. In such a situation it is hard to get the consensus on first principles on which a functioning responsible government depends.

The economists have dealt with the criteria of readiness in the developing economy for some decisive turn in its development. One might do the same for the polity and speak of readiness and failure of readiness for the burdens of government—what we may call the *readiness effect* and the *unreadiness effect*.

The capacity for responsible government in the undeveloped country, it has been said, seems to grow at best in an arithmetical ratio, while the pressures upon the society grow in a geometrical ratio. Accordingly, there are crises that are never met, decisions that are never taken, dispositions that are never made, resources that are never called upon, problems that are never solved, conflicts and dilemmas that are never resolved. This should be no surprise in the case of the former colonial peoples, whose self-governing faculties were never adequately developed.

There are important differences here between the records of the colonial powers on the transition to independence and on the turnover of the governmental machinery. The great French colonial administrator, Marshal Lyautey, saw clearly what lay ahead and strove mightily to prepare for it through education and a phased autonomy. The British, who showed a genius for indirect rule through local chiefs and administrative civil services, also developed the dyarchy, with an apprentice government operating alongside the professional one. Most colonial areas passed through this phase of double rule. It has been pointed out that where it came early, the period of parallel rule was long and the turnover of government went with comparative ease; where it came late, the parallel rule was too brief and the turnover often a violent one.

In the case of India the preparation was tolerably good and the turnover would have been smooth except for the communalist hatreds between Hindu and Moslem, which were too deep to be resolved and were further embittered by leadership mistakes both in the Congress Party and the Moslem League and by the British Labour Government's unwise haste in getting rid of its burdens even under the shadow of a coming fratricide. In the case of the Congo, where the problem was handled worst, there were stormy demands for independence, with riots and ugly passions. The Belgians panicked under the mounting pressures from without and the rekindled guilt from within, and got rid of their responsibilities hastily, exactly when they should have held on to them somewhat longer in a deliberate process of phased freedom.

Given this unreadiness effect, the experience of the developing nations shows the folly of judging political systems in the abstract, viewing them as aesthetic systems with *a priori* features. What counts is the polity at the point of action. The question is not whether it is a "democracy" or not, but whether it is tolerably or badly organized for carrying through the tasks of order, power, welfare and creativeness which belong to responsible government. The criteria of a functioning democracy, seen austerely, are probably these: the *rule of law,* in the sense that those who administer the law must be subject to it, and that neither the majority of the people nor their government can ride rampant over the minority and the individual; an *administrative merit service* assigning the daily tasks of government to men equipped for them, rather than by the spoils system, nepotism or corruption; *civilian control over the military,* and (with lesser urgency) *separation of church and state,* so that neither the army nor priestly hierarchies can command the lives and liberties of men by a writ that goes beyond reason, speaking to the blood of unquestioning obedience and belief; a *party competition,* whereby choices of rulers and policies are periodically submitted to the people by at least two groups effectively organized to present them; *equal access* to opportunities and life chances, available to all, rather than to one class or religion or ethnic group; *responsibility and consent* in the interaction between leaders and people.

By these standards there are only a tiny group of functioning democracies in any austere sense. Responsible government, on the other hand, demands a good deal less. It may not offer a true party competition, and may function through a single party, in fact if not in name (as in Mexico, Japan, even India). It may not keep church and state wholly separated (note the case of Great Britain, Pakistan, Israel, the European Catholic states) and its rulers may come from the military (as in Turkey, Egypt, Pakistan, South Korea). It may exercise a censorship, more or less stringent, over its press. Its top people may be above the law, and its chief of state may exercise a personal authority. But it is responsible government if there are means by which the people express their consent and make their wishes felt; if the judicial system operates with tolerable fairness; if government is orderly without being enforced by any pervasive machinery of police terror and without a policing of thought; if there is an administrative system based on ability, and run impartially and with little corruption; and if the leadership elite considers itself responsible to the people, and to them alone, rather than to an arbitrary power outside the people or outside the nation itself.

These may seem new concepts and distinctions, but it is a new world in which governments are today compelled to operate. Never before in the nation-state system have there been fewer accepted guideposts in the conduct of the state. While the unreadiness effect applies to most developing countries when judged by the standards of mature democracies, they have proved readier for effective government and are moving toward it. In many cases, especially the African nations, the transition toward such government is under the control of the dominant party, whose leader is usually also the chief of state. But the striking fact is that what happens within the party may prove more important than what happens to the state machinery, since it is the party that must train state officials and interpret the state to the people and the people to the state, giving direction to both. The party has served some such function under Communist regimes as well, in Russia and in China and in their satellites. But there it has chiefly served the state as an integrating agency—the "steel frame" of society, as the Webbs put it. In the developing countries there is often a parallel authority of state and party, with the party not necessarily the second partner. Thus, it was not surprising that the "founding father" of Tanganyika, Jules Nyerere, should, in 1961, have given up his role of chief of state in order to devote his full energies to being the head of his party; for it is in the party that leadership is recruited and developed, and that bridges are set up between leader and demos. In the case of a progressive leader like Nyerere, who is not a fanatic and not a demagogue, a strong grass-roots party organization could mean the difference between holding power long enough to achieve his essential goals and losing it to a flashier and less scrupulous rival.

Seen within the broad frame of what I have called responsible government, a whole parcel of polities emerge as possible forms of such a government. One type is the surviving kingship—the man of old or recent royal blood who (like Haile Selassie of Ethiopia,

Pahlevi of Iran, Hussein of Jordan, Mohammed V of Morocco, Yahya of Yemen) insists on being an effective ruler as well as the titular monarch. Where such a leader has personal strength and will, a feel for picking the right administrators, and a flair for sensing and riding the tides of public sentiment, he is likely to hold on to power where other regimes fail. For he has around his head the magic encirclement of the kingship, for which a parvenu leader and his successor have to sweat and strain for generations. Bernard Shaw's fantasy of a king who became a Communist seemed whimsical in his own day, yet the example of Prince Souphanouvong in Laos, a prince who became a Communist and is a member of the ruling triumvirate in Laos, suggests that Shaw's joke had a vein of seriousness in it.

A second type is the strong and accepted civilian leader-as-father, usually the man who led the revolutionary nationalist movement to a successful conclusion in independence. The most striking examples come readily to mind: Nehru in India; U Nu in Burma (the residual leader after the wiping out of his seniors by assassination); Bourguiba in Tunisia; Sir Abubakar Balewa in Nigeria; Nkrumah in Ghana; Toure in Guinea; Jomo Kenyatta in Kenya; Senghor in Senegal, Nyerere in Tanganyika, Ben-Gurion in Israel. Among the Communists who belong in this group are Ho Chi Minh in North Korea and Castro in Cuba. Essentially, it is the regime of the founding fathers, usually of the leading founding father (however young) as was true after the American Revolution.

What the kingship regime achieves by the nimbus of traditional acceptance this founding-father regime achieves by its association with heroic struggle. The head of this regime has about him the authority of the revolutionary founder, a good deal of the tribal boss, and often more than a touch of the demagogue who knows how to reach the village mind while he knows also how to appeal to the urban crowds. Because of the mystique that derives from these combined roles he can govern in a relatively open society, with the minimum use of the stick.

A third type is the regime of the soldier as authoritarian leader, using the army which enabled him to seize power, but in turn subjecting it to his personal control as a national leader. The prototype of this soldier-leader of a new nationalist regime in the modern era was, of course, Kemal Ataturk. Its principal examples extant as I write are Colonel Nasser in Egypt, General Ayub Khan in Pakistan, General Kassem in Iraq, General Sarit in Thailand, General Gusel in Turkey, General Chung Nee Park in South Korea. In almost every case such a regime made its appeal not only through the force of the sword, but as a protest against the weakness, corruption, and confusion of tongues in a preceding parliamentary regime. Its objective is presumably national unity and order, its battle cry that of an anti-corruptionist integrity, its method that of military discipline transposed into the civilian realm. If the instances I have given come from Asia and the Middle East it is not to scant the importance of the Latin-American *caudillo* regimes.

As for the Communist regimes, it may seem strange to discuss them alongside the military dictatorships, since the latter are so strikingly nonideological. Yet, perhaps not so strange. Arnold Toynbee has spoken of the "savior-with-a-sword" and the "savior-with-a-book." Each offers salvation through a short cut. One rationalizes the conquest of power by the higher law of force, the other by the higher law of doctrine. In the perspective of the modern age the savior-with-a-sword is less dangerous than the savior-with-a-book, since the latter is part of an organized world-wide operation while the former remains local. True, the military leader who seizes civilian power may be a narcissist, an adventurer, a power seeker, a tyrant, and quite generally a nuisance. Yet his regime is likely to end with the end of his life, and it does not threaten world stability or world peace in an era of nuclear weapons.

Both the strength and the weakness of the military dictatorship lie in its being personal rule. Built around a single striking personality and his flair for power and authority, it has the strength of his personal appeal, and thus transcends and survives shifts of policy and political mood. But by that fact, he runs the danger of failing to institutionalize the reforms that he may accomplish. There is also the fact that the needs of industrialization and planning in the new nations call for suppleness and resourcefulness as well as for discipline and integrity. A Communist regime, whose leaders have been trained for decades in the arts of political survival, may find the necessary suppleness, but rarely can the military regimes find an educated elite which can run the various technical and administrative posts, unless it learns how to train officers in civilian tasks or infuse civilians with military discipline and loyalty.

All three of the regimes I have touched on, which have emerged in the developing nations, are regimes of personal rule—the leader-as-king, the leader-as-founding-father, and the leader-with-a-sword. The particular names of leaders I have given are passing names and may prove to have been written on water. Yet the categories are likely to remain, since each fills a deep need and represents an effort to find a pattern of ruling which fits the society, the time, and perhaps the personality of the man himself. All of them are rooted in traditional society, yet they usually possess a reforming zeal to reshape that society in a hurry. They also have in common an unwillingness to embrace the Communist formula and be strangled by it— even the regimes which are strongly anti-Western, neutralist in form, and seemingly close to the Communists in sympathy. For their real political religion is not that of Communism but of nationalism and industrialization. All of them, finally, have a personal flair which counts more in their political survival than their doctrine or even their program.

Personal rule is characteristic of developing polities which set the frame for developing economies. Democratic rule and Communist rule are, each in its own way, depersonalized; the democracies have put law above personal power, and the Communists have put the logic of history above personal will. But the developing countries, which are neither democratic nor Communist, must rely on personal rule to see them through the transition period between the traditional and the modern society. Classifying the new African national heroes, Wallerstein sees three types: the *flamboyant* (Nkrumah, Bourguiba); the *analytical* (Nyerere, Toure, Azikiwe); and the *quiet* (Olympio, Senghor). This is interesting; but if we broaden the frame beyond the African leaders, the typology by sources of power as I have suggested (kingship, founding-father status, army leadership) may prove more useful. It may have the merit also of linking with the personal authority of the leader a characteristic ruling elite which goes with it.

I shall be writing in the next chapter about the leadership ordeal in an age of overkill, with my focus on the great powers and the developed countries,* and much of that ordeal applies to the personal rule in the transition polities as well. But what most of the latter have in common is the poverty of their resources for government, the need to start almost from scratch in everything of importance, the pressure to build an administrative elite, the question of how to operate between the cross fire of the political war from both world power camps. The great resource that they have is the atmosphere of the two passions—or two political religions—within which all the personal leaders move and rule: the passion for nationalism (often a color nationalism), and the passion for modernism. To-

* See Chapter V, Section 1, "The Ordeal of Leadership," and Section 2, "Power, Decision, and Identity."

gether they form the medium with which they work, as political artists.

It must be obvious that the usual sharp distinction between democracy and dictatorship is not useful in these instances. When liberal commentators dismiss the whole array of these regimes as "dictatorial," they wipe out the distinction between them and the Communist regimes, and leave only a nonexistent pristine democracy as a working alternative to Communism in the undeveloped world. It would be delightful if all the new nationalist regimes could be as democratic as Nehru's India or Ben-Gurion's Israel. But alas, the political world does not spin on its peculiar axis for the delight of purists, whatever their political breed.

The actual alternatives in the new revolutionary nations are not democracy and dictatorship. They are the totalitarian class state as against personal rule. The latter fills the temporary vacuum produced by the sudden accession to power of a ruling group largely unprepared for it. This personal rule in a transition period may be of better or worse quality, but the important question is, What is it moving toward? Is it moving toward institutionalized rule, toward a rule of law rather than of the person, toward meaning which is attached to the *office* rather than the *cult* of the leader, toward a competition of ideas, toward a tolerance about color? Or is it moving toward the hardening of color lines, toward a police state which wipes out opponents, toward a single-party system extended beyond redress, toward a doctrinal rigidity which excludes the creative in the political process or anywhere else?

I suggest that while two governments like those of China and Burma, or those of North Korea and South Korea, are both dictatorships, there is a difference between what may be called the *built-in* elements of dictatorship in the Communist system and the *temporary* elements in the various systems of personal rule. In the case of China or of North Korea, you have a one-way passage to a system where totalitarianism continues regardless of the incumbents in power. In the case of Burma or of South Korea, you have (as I wrote) a personal government which is backed by the army and has replaced an ineffectual parliamentary regime, but which is meant—with greater or less sincerity—to be a transitional regime; to the extent that it succeeds in its objective of developing a society where a competition of ideas and programs can take place within a frame of national independence, it will also succeed in eliminating itself as an instrument of personal rule.

Twice a regime of military authoritarianism has voluntarily

given up its power—under Kemal Ataturk in Turkey and under General Ne Win in Burma. The latter, however, seized it again when there was danger that the weak parliamentary regime could not maintain an independent Burma in the face of Chinese pressure. The Burmese experience shows the difficulty of the efforts to give democratic government a foothold in Asia, as do also the experiences in Ghana and Guinea in Africa, and in Argentina and Peru in Latin America. In the case of the Latin-American military governments there is an added fact of great importance: the military elite is often politically representative and sometimes reformist, being drawn from every stratum in the community; and (as Keith Botsford has pointed out) it fills the vacuum of power which the Latin-American middle class has not yet been able to fill. Thus, in evaluating any of these governments, one should add to the *unreadiness effect* something that might be called the *moving-toward effect*.*

One might even say that these often shabby regimes have a radical idea. It is the idea that a struggling new nation born out of frustration and hate, torn by discords, wretched in its poverty, lacking a trained governing elite, need not necessarily become a conscript in the array of Communist regimes, and need not give up the hope of developing ultimately a tolerably open society in which the good life, with a considerable measure of freedom, is possible.

8. Fire and Form in Developing Societies

IN THE BROADEST TERMS, the problem of the undeveloped world is how to convert the undoubted fire of nationalist passions into economic, political and social forms, or—more modestly put—how to contain the fire within a frame of form. The derisory resources of most of these nations make the prospect an unpromising one. The first thing to be said is that the fire does not of itself create its own forms; there are no inevitable molds into which the life and striving of these new communities are bound to be poured. The second and related thing to be said is that technology, while it is certain to be of great importance in shaping the character of the society, does not of itself carry an ethos with it and cannot in itself decide either the culture style or the personality style of the society.

Two overrigid views have developed about the direction in which

* For use of this concept in another context see Amitai Etzioni, *A Hard Way to Peace* (1962).

the developing societies are moving. One, within the undeveloped countries, stresses technology and gives it an almost magical quality. The other, outside the undeveloped country, whether in the free-world or Communist power systems, stresses the nature of the polity and abstracts it from the society as a whole. One might call these respectively the "fallacy of the isolated technology" and the "fallacy of the isolated polity." Each commits the sin of tearing a living segment of the society out of its organic context and treating it (in Kantian terms) as an object rather than a subject.

The fallacy of the technology is an easy one to fall into, since it seems so clearly the dynamic element in social as well as economic change. The intellectual in a developing nation looks about him and sees that changes in technology have caused far-reaching changes and disruptions in the traditional (slow-change) society. He also sees that where technology has taken least hold—in the villages and the countryside, as compared with the cities, airports, oilfields, hydroelectric sites—the society remains stagnant. The American social scientist, in turn, is conditioned to see technology as prime mover, and whether he welcomes or laments the passing of traditional society, he sees technological change as cause, and social change as consequence. The view which I have discussed earlier—that political forms and liberties are irrelevant for the life of the underlying population—derives largely from this stress on technology.

I do not deny the dynamic element in technology; that should be obvious enough. But I suggest that technological change itself has to be first imagined, then sweated for. The idea of a physics of force, Spengler has said, was already in the Faustian mind, even before the modern sciences of physics emerged. The educated elite in African or Asian or Middle Eastern countries have in their minds an image of what technology can achieve for their society, and they must decide what kind of meaning modern machines and gadgetry have for them, before they can begin to think what the new technology will do to the lives of their people. Much of the technology, especially at the start, will be borrowed from the developed economies, but unless the developing nation provides education for science, and training for machine skills, it will find the technology all but useless. What I am saying is that instead of cause and consequence we think of social change as a polar field, with constant crosscurrents of interaction between technology at one pole and the style, ethos and imagination of the society at the other pole. The value of Gandhi's thinking, despite its reactionary phase, was his refusal to admit anything decisive, creative or final about the available technology. One may reject Gandhi's vision of a return to the village society, but one can scarcely reject his insistence that between technology and man it must be man who is the master and makes the choice. It is a dehumanizing thing to accept the autonomous march of the iron men as a decisive force in shaping a society.

It is this new orthodoxy of industrialism that forms the operative ideology of the undeveloped world. Some of the educated elite who lean toward socialism recognize the Western origins of the new industrial technology, and they sense that industrialization is in essence Westernization. But this does not disturb them overmuch. The question of where the new technology comes from becomes an idle question, since the machines are needed for finding that place in the sun to which they aspire. Thus, when the national identity revolution becomes a national status revolution, the fires of revolutionary nationalism become the emotional flame of industrialization.

World Communism is bent on using the forms of Communist power to contain that flame. The Communists understand the full importance of "showcase" aid and "impact" aid in exploiting technology as symbol and emotional complex. Despite their dogma of the materialist basis of life, they know that, in practice, technology does not of itself build a new society to replace the old one. It must be helped and guided in its consequences by a group of men who know the kind of polity, society, and personality structure they want to develop. That is why the Communist elite offers to direct the pace of modernization in a planned way, using the Communist parties as a vanguard for showing the way to the new social forms. The aim is to replace the shattered beliefs of the traditional society with new ones, the old loyalties (of family, kinship, system, tribe and caste) with new loyalties, and the old religions with a new political religion.

Economic aid plays a different role in developed and undeveloped nations. When aid is given to a society with stable political forms, and particularly with both a middle-class political base and an educated elite for leadership, it strengthens the political and social frame which is already there. The best instance of this was the impact of the Marshall Plan aid on Western Europe. But when such aid is given to a nation which has not yet developed a strong moral and political frame, the danger is that it will destroy the traditional society, uproot old institutions, and play havoc with the human personality. Even the case of aid to India does not disprove this. For India inherited a political fabric from the British, along with an educational system and a civil service with a habit of responsible discipline. India had also a strongly knit religious and philosophical fabric which could serve as a frame even when a strong political frame was removed.

The Communists approach this problem with advantage, because they possess a world network of Communist parties, with trained cadres whose leadership can be exported wherever needed, capable of training new and talented recruits. They also use Moscow, Peking and Prague as training centers for the educated elite who will carry out their purposes. The free-world power system cannot match the disciplined Communist parties, yet their intellectual and political capitals can be turned into vast laboratories for training the talented young men and women of the undeveloped nations in the arts of government. True, the spirit of the new African elites comes closer to the philosophy of Rousseau's "general will" than it does to that of Jefferson's "aristocracy of virtue and talent." The gap between them and the masses is great. This could lead to a personal rule for the calculable future, yet it does not mean that the soil of the society is ready for Communism. The crucial difficulty in the path of responsible government does not lie in the vulnerability of the new nations to Communism, but in the fact that mechanization and industrialization are now available to them without the long and arduous experience which other peoples have had in the conquest of the machine. Modern technology is the product of a sustained adventure in ideas and of a complex series of chapters of political and social history. Dehumanizing as the machine may prove in the advanced societies, it is stripped of some of its dehumanizing effects by the fact of these humanistic accompaniments. The difficulty in the new nations may prove to be that the machine will be all too available in itself and will not carry with it the whole complex of humanistic values which alone can give meaning to its use.

This raises the issue of the fallacy of the isolated polity. When in the 1920s Bukharin had his famous controversy with Stalin over the pace of expansion of the Soviet economy, the real issue was not an economic or technological one, but a political and social one. Bukharin believed that a society is a reality in itself, and not only as the reflection of a technology—that it is an organic equilibrium which can be thrown off into unhealth and chaos by too abrupt and violent an assertion of the will of an elite in the name of the society. He lost out in the struggle, and Stalin achieved the pace of industrialization he aimed at, but with a long-range grief for the polity and the society. Stalin aimed only at a readiness economy in a polity that could survive the coming wars and expand into a world system. He tore the polity, as he tore the economy, out of the society.

Earlier in the book, I spoke of the metaphors in which we view our world. The same question may be asked in relation to a society: By what metaphor do we view it?

One possible metaphor is that of a pyramid. If you visualize the traditional society in the undeveloped country in the shape of a pyramid, you will find at the base of the pyramid the magic, the religion, the taboos, the deepest subverbal beliefs that have held the society together over the centuries with relatively little outward change. Not far above this is another layer—that of the tribal, clan and kinship systems, the village community, the organization of caste and class. Above this in turn is the layer of technology, from the most primitive agricultural or fishing or handicraft implements, along with the economic system that goes with the stage of technology and with the village and kinship structure. Resting on this, in turn, is the organization of power, law and authority which we call the political system. Finally, toward the top of the pyramid, there is the cultural superstructure—the languages and literatures, the folklore, the drama and music, the philosophies and arts that express a civilization, and the moral codes that guide it.

I have put this as a five-level analysis of the structure of a total society. But a better metaphor is that of an intricate circuit, or a whole complex of circuits. With the folklore, philosophies and codes which form the top layer of the structure, we are, of course, back at the religion that gives the folklore its content, and the codes their sanction; and so we are back at the deepest layer of the collective unconscious (or preconscious) where we started. I used the metaphor of a pyramid mainly to emphasize the dependence of the upper layers and superstructure of a society upon the fundamental institutions at the base. But once this dependence is established, the other metaphor becomes the truer one. I think of society much as the biochemists and biophysicists today think of the brain, as a cluster of interacting circuits, in which memory, learning and experience are stored, with events and changes from the outside world producing a sequence of linked reactions, while the whole cluster is responsive to the deepest drives of man's nature. A traditional society is one which, having encased itself against most intrusions from without, has worn deep grooves in the repeated circuits of interaction, and seems therefore to be (depending on the viewpoint) either "stable" or "stagnant."

Whichever metaphor we adopt, it is worth remembering that the political system is only a segment or aspect of the total society. Try to impose upon the political system a set of codes and practices belonging to a different kind of society, at another stage of development, with very different grooves of interaction, and you may well come to grief. Nor would it be wise, in your recoil from the consequences, to conclude that there is something radically wrong either with the society which rejected the beautiful democratic system or with the democracy thus rejected. In both instances you will be light-years distant from the truth of the matter.

Neither may be inherently wrong, yet they may simply not fit together because they have not grown together organically, as a democratic polity and an open society grew together in eighteenth-century Europe and America. The prime questions are those of inner congruity and of the pace of change. This is a case where the anthropologists and psychologists may shed more light than the political theologians. Studying the whole of a society in Latin America, Africa or Asia, the anthropologists have noted that the new machines, science, schools, factories, legislatures, press and ideas may have brought their own kind of blessings to village, town and jungle, but that they have also disrupted the existing balance of the society and broken the cement that held it together. The psychiatrists, in turn, have noted the confusion and loss of values and the warping of the personality when the old cohesions are fractured and the old roots torn out of the soil, without the growth of any new ones to replace them.

Thus the *unreadiness effect,* of which I spoke in my section on polities, may be viewed, from the larger angle of vision, as an *incongruity effect.* The traditional society is unable to absorb the new elements intruded into it and incongruous with it, and it is especially unable to absorb them at the pace of change which they set and demand.

This is one of the troubles with the effort to classify the developing societies by the test of the kind of economy or polity they are seeking to establish. For example, one could classify the political economies of the new states as national socialist, military socialist, military state-capitalist, democratic state-capitalist, democratic socialist, authoritarian mixed economy. The trouble with all of them is that the labels narrow and destroy the rooted organic realities of the society itself. Thus, as Wallerstein has persuasively argued, a socialist state like that of Sekou Toure in Guinea has little to do with Marxist-Leninist "socialism," as it has also little to do with

Scandinavian or British or even Israeli socialism, although the last forms in some respects a compassable model for Guinean development.

Since there is no capitalist owning class in the recent African countries, and little if any middle class, there is no rationale for the Communist doctrine of the class struggle, and no drive to "expropriate the expropriators" or to dispossess the possessors. The whole people are in effect dispossessed, except for a tiny educated elite which is only to a small degree a "possessing" elite. The Communist parties are thus largely confined to the countries which still have large white-settler communities. "African socialism," as Toure calls it, is thus a base for what Nkrumah in turn calls the development of the "African personality." If it is meant in chauvinist terms it is too narrow. If it is meant to stress the nature of the organic society with its roots in African history, it underscores one of the great psychological facts—about the importance of the larger society of which the polity and the economy are only partial interacting circuits of energy and relation in the larger galaxy of circuits.

CHAPTER V

The Viable Society:
Elite, *Élan*, Ethos

1. The Ordeal of Leadership

2. Power, Decision, and Identity

3. Commanding and Creative Elites

4. The Education of a Democratic Elite

5. The Death and Life of Civilizations

6. Élan as Vision and Drive

7. The Battle of the Ethos: Life Style and Personality Type

The Viable Society:
Elite, *Élan*, Ethos

1. The Ordeal of Leadership

"**I** SHALL be either America's greatest President or its last," Franklin Roosevelt said during the early days of the New Deal. Exactly because everything goes faster in the Age of Overkill, men cling the more anxiously to political leaders who have this kind of confidence and resolve. This applies to world leaders like Khrushchev, Kennedy, De Gaulle, Mao Tse-tung, Nehru, and to lesser ones like Nasser, Tito, Sukarno, Nkrumah, Ben-Gurion, Castro. What it comes down to is the question of who and what will survive. Given the facts of nuclear weapons, the Grand Design, insurrection, revolution, hunger, the population explosion, no leader can any longer take for granted the survival of the nation or the power complex of which he is part. He must dare greatly in a world where indecisive leaders and timid civilizations will inherit only the grave, and where he knows that, whatever imperatives history may thrust upon him and his nation, the suicide imperative is not one of them.

A Communist leader not only must know how to loosen or tighten his police-state repressions, but also must reckon with the awakened resoluteness of a free world whose resources, talent and living standards he will underestimate only at his peril. A leader of one of the older democracies must know how to dissipate the assumption that all will be well if left alone, must fight the corrosions of greed and the desire for comfort, and invoke an *élan* to meet the zeal and ferocity of the Communist True Believers. He cannot act like a frightened Roman emperor quaking at the march of barbarian battalions. The leader of an uncommitted nation must make up in a brief span of years what his people have lost through the stagnation of centuries, must establish his nation's new status and nail down his own within it. Thus each leader, in his own type of state, is wound up like a clock ready to strike twelve at once.

The qualities called for in a people are those of fortitude and the will to survive despite the broken visions inevitable to the age, and the capacity to rebuild what may be shattered by its changes and chances. But within this frame there are additional qualities that the political leader must command. The varied nature of the age sets the varied talents he must ideally possess.

In an age of political war he will learn how to politicize every act and event. In a technical age he will rally the scientific and creative elite to the nation's standard and train them in mustering their best energies. In an age of revolutionary nationalism he will act radically, even for conservative ends. In an age of symbols he will learn to walk with ease among symbols, stirring men's minds and emotions with them. In an age of mass culture he will be close to his people, educating them to the nature of their time. In an age of political religions he will seek a cohesiveness of belief that will tie his people together.

This is somewhat idealized. The reality is much less resplendent, with smudges of workaday experiment, confusion and blunder. The leader is involved in problems large and small, all the way from big armaments, grand diplomacy and state visits, to the complaint of a peasant deputation from a collective farm, or pressures from a small industry asking for tariff protection. While he is trying to build, beg, borrow or even steal a technology on which the weapons mastery and economic growth of his nation depend, he is also messed up with an internal power struggle with opponents inside and outside his party, and is grappling with difficult conflicts of religious and ethnic groups, with linguistic rivalries, perhaps with separatist movements. Always he is wary of the loyalty of his army leaders, anxious to maintain the morale of the young men who are soldiers and retain the commitment of the young men who are students. Amidst all this he must understand that he is operating in a world that never was, on sea or land, before; that the world is new and requires a new vision.

He may develop a characteristic political style. Studying the political leaders of the two generations since 1930, one sees that their style was shaped in the convergence of tradition, crisis and personality. Churchill, in the Battle of Britain, revealed and evoked the unexpungeable stubbornness of the British national character when brought up against overwhelming odds: his style was compounded of tenacity, swagger, and a Tory feel for the abiding realities of power. Roosevelt too had a buoyancy of self-confidence that expressed the optimism of an America which held it to be self-evident that even the knottiest problems had a solution and would yield to personal salesmanship. Harry Truman's style was that of an uncommon small-town common man, with the no-nonsense briskness of one who gets up earlier in the morning than you do, so you had better not try to fool him. Dwight Eisenhower, picked by Roosevelt fatefully for his crucial war role, was as President a good man in the wrong job: he was not so much a weak leader as an *anti*leader, with an almost mystical belief in a harmony within a society, like the harmony in the natural order, which was best left alone to work out its own pattern. John F. Kennedy has still to leave his impact on history, but his style is already all but formed: with a tightness of personality, half-shy and half-arrogant, which perhaps expresses the double facet of his Boston-Irish political heritage and his Harvard intellectual surface, as of a man who has not yet decided whether history can be stormed with a tactical assault by force or whether it contains a cunning of its own which will yield only to the campaign of ideas.

Such doubts and inner conflicts do not mark the Soviet leaders. Detach yourself from Stalin's character and cause, and you will see that he carried through a great operation of sheer will, bringing Russia—by industrialization and by territorial annexation —to the status of an imperial power center, and establishing a military "socialism in one country" which would serve as a base for Communist expansionism. He was a Marxist only in the crudest sense of believing in the primacy of the economic; beyond that he believed in will rather than in dogma, and in tactical accommodation to reality rather than in received doctrine. He was cynical and vindictive, with a deadpan contempt for verbal claptrap and an almost insane suspicion of anyone who might be in a position to betray or supplant him, and with a genius for playing off his opponents against each other and destroying those who survived. He was the Great Purger who ruled by terror and lived in fear, a successor to the line of brutal Czars, all of whose power, added together, was not a tithe of his. Irreligious, he made an ikon of his power, and in bowing before it he was at once the worshiper and the god.

Nikita Khrushchev has Stalin's pragmatism, much of his cunning, his tenacity about ends and plasticity of means, his vaulting resolve to move the world as close as possible to Communist rule. But this largely self-taught peasant, at once earthy and wily, has known how to modify and modernize the police rule of the Communist state and preside over a technicized society with the aplomb of an intellectual born to the world of science and ideas. He too, like Kennedy, is caught between a kinship to power and a saving fear of using it to the full. But with the confidence of one who has survived the jungle perils of the Communist internal struggle, he has given full scope to his natural flair for the theatrically effective and has learned how to apply, in his political warfare with the democratic world, the Stonewall Jackson formula, "mystify, mislead and surprise." *

Macmillan's style, as befits a British Prime Minister presiding over a dissolving empire with a narrowed base of financial and industrial power, is characteristically a sleight-of-hand style. It is that of a leader who is most skillful when he is reshuffling his Cabinet line-ups; somehow he has managed to hold on to power longer than anyone could have foretold and has got the middle class to accept a welfare state and the workers to respond to a middle-class image of themselves; he also has managed to make an England almost stripped of modern armed power nevertheless effective in the councils of the democratic world. Adenauer, in his turn, presiding over a Germany which he led back into prosperity and world acceptance, has the style of a tyrannical old schoolmaster who wants to direct the lives of his students long after they have grown up, or of the burgomaster who overstayed his tenure because the bridge he had begun could not be trusted to his successors. History may rate him, however, as the leader who brought Germany back into the family of nations, who was able to control the German military elite, and who gave a great impetus to the idea of European union.

Perhaps the most remarkable of all, although without the impact on history of the American and Russian rulers, is Charles De Gaulle. He would be in some ways absurd, if it were not that he turns even the absurd into a "grand style" of leadership. Roosevelt disliked him, and Churchill avowed that the hardest cross he had to bear was the Cross of Lorraine. The French army officers who helped bring him back to power and founded the Fifth Republic felt themselves tricked by his Algerian policy and determined to kill him; the French intellectuals who accepted him as an alternative to the generals ended by hating him, much as he despised both them and the generals. His strength in transcending his time carried a defect with it, since, in his sureness about French destiny and his own, he let himself be cut off from every French elite—the military, the intellectual, the bureaucracy, the old-line parliamentary leaders. Yet, to

---

* Hans Morgenthau has described him aptly as a reviver of the universalistic goals of Lenin, but as a leader who is able to use the new techniques which the new power of the Soviet Union provides him with, and which Lenin could scarcely have anticipated.

an extraordinary degree he combined a feel for power with a sensitivity for words, both of them chiseled in the classical fashion. Despite his deliberate remoteness from the people, he continued to have a magic for them; it was not his authoritarian regime that lent him its authority, but his own personal authority that made the authoritarian regime work.

Almost alone among the world's leaders, De Gaulle maintained a fixed position amidst the flux and swirl of events—a position which came from both his valuing of himself and his insight into history and the political process. At their worst, these qualities led his private world to shut out the world of social reality. At their best they made him into a figure who transcended circumstance, even while he had a sharp sense of contemporary needs, saying, *"Il faut que la France épouse son temps"* (France must wed her time). He was able to refurbish the old worn words—*honor, glory, greatness*—in the face of a generation which felt cynical about them but, still, responded to the equally tattered words "history" and "revolution." With all his tough-mindedness he had a feel for the symbolic gesture, although the *grand monarque* in him disdained to use it too frequently. He was in some ways the last of the giants, closing the tradition of leadership in the grand manner, all the more an anachronism because, with the manpower, resources and technology of a slipping second-rate power, he sought effects which only a first-rate power could achieve.

One of the problems of a political style is the question of the distance between leader and people. In a situation of closeness, as with Andrew Jackson and later with Harry Truman, he is on first-name and even backslapping terms with as many people as possible and walks among them as one of them. In the distance-type leadership he is detached and relatively inaccessible, makes only rare public appearances, is willing to have legends grow up around him. One thinks of Woodrow Wilson and of Stalin. One thinks, best of all, of General MacArthur and of De Gaulle, each wrapped in a legend of his own making, so that eventually one came to expect of him only the earth-shaking utterance and act. A leader like Franklin Roosevelt could resolve the problem of closeness and distance without a clear choice, since he played the role of a father who could be either warm or distant, close or stern, as fatherly authority might demand. Gandhi, in turn, resolved the problem by being a leader-as-saint, walking among his people yet clearly removed from them by the fact of his sainthood. In the case of Khrushchev and of Kennedy there is a shuttling between the two distance roles, with Khrushchev tending toward closeness and Kennedy toward distance.

Whatever the distance between them, there must be some kind of political dialogue between leader and people. This usually involves an element of the demagogic, which keeps him in touch with people and recreates his energy. In a Communist state the leader may pit the party elite against the chaos of the mass; by speaking to the elite, he also masters the mass. In the newer nations, coming out of traditional tribal societies, the leader may wrap himself in a high-sounding, necromantic title, such as *Osagyiefo* ("Redeemer") in Ghana. In a "directed democracy" or a military dictatorship he is tempted to muzzle the press, rule without a parliament, liquidate all political parties except his own. In Communist regimes this privilege of ruling without annoyances and opposition is built into the system and dogma. Even in the democracies, the obstructions a leader encounters in the political process may be exasperating. But, whatever the temptations of rule without the strenuous dialogue, in the end it is a short cut which plays too many tricks with the art of government.

For the irritations and obstructions are to the leader what the intractable material of a craft is to the artist—the medium with which he must struggle for his effects. Even popularity is expendable; the truly confident leader knows it is something to be spent, not hoarded. He can use it in crises as a bank account to draw on, and if his people know he will confront them with the unadorned facts of their situation (as Churchill did in the Battle for Britain), it will supply an element of trust between them more precious than sycophancy. The leader, in turn, must husband his moments of decisive contact with his people. He cannot be a jack-in-the-box, jumping out in every moment of day-to-day crisis. He must keep away from the trivia of government, although not from its necessary sweat of organization, and dare to make the innovating decisions only after a period of brooding and reflection.

This means that the test of leadership rests with the relation of leader to event. It is more than merely an echo of Carlyle to say that a great leader must be not just an event-responding man but an event-creating man. The reader of De Gaulle's memoirs will find him often overconscious of his role and overdeliberate about his career. But in the hour of truth the question about a leader is whether he happens to history or history happens to him. I don't mean he must always take history by storm; he must have some knowledge of what Hegel called the "ruses of history." He cannot be in too great a hurry to lay siege to history and overcome it. He will be patient, have infinite resourcefulness of method and mood, and know when to wait, when to retreat and when to attack. Yet the dynamic must always come from within him and his relation to his people. He cannot wait for the event to furnish him with the motive power which he must alone supply.

This will require considerable ruthlessness. In every period of history, political leaders have proved ruthless, although the habit of rationalizing it by calling it "reason of state" or "reason of history" is a recent product. In his novel *Advise and Consent*, Allen Drury draws a President of the United States who lies, betrays, bribes and manipulates men, and even drives them to destroy themselves—all in the name of the higher political morality of national survival. In the jungle of Communist polity, the wiles of a democratic leader like Roosevelt (as James M. Burns depicted him in *The Lion and the Fox*) are paled by the deeds of Lenin, Stalin, Malenkov, Beria, Khrushchev and Mao. Need one add that Khrushchev has survived politically because he knew whom to betray, when to wait, when to strike? He rose on the shoulders of other men, destroying one by one those who had helped him to rise.

Thus it is inevitable, in fashioning a great political leader, that the man in him will be destroyed, and that something will emerge which is at once less and more than a man. For the purposes of his cause he may hew close to legality and to legitimacy, but he knows their limits as he knows the limits of morality, and will flout any of them when it serves him. The political leader is neither saint nor hypocrite, but a possessed man, with a daemonic possession for whose roots one must probe in writers from Socrates to Dostoevsky and Thomas Mann. He is the instrument through whom forces speak which come from outside himself and go beyond himself.

One thinks of Oedipus, who did things of which he was unaware, driven to them by his tragic destiny. The difference is that Oedipus did not understand the ambiguous meanings of what had happened to him until he put out his eyes, while the political leader cannot afford such a price for understanding. For all his cunning he is likely to be a naïve man, who plays the role assigned to him much as an actor does, without being too conscious about the hidden meanings of the lines. Thomas Mann said of the artist, in his essay on Freud, that he has a "mythical slant on life." The political leader does not see life as myth, but sees myth as life. Always he deals in the stuff of myths, but he must make this stuff the substitute for the life he must himself forgo.

Thus, he is a lonely and tragic figure. Those who interpret political myths in a wholly rationalist fashion will never understand the true nature of political leadership, especially in a time so dense with myths as our own. Like the primitive hero, the leader is a symbolic agent who lives out a number of the crucial conflicts not only in his world but in himself, in a cycle of acts which describes the progression of human life. Sometimes he may come to feel, as Lincoln felt, that the cup was too full for him. Gandhi too felt it. There was a mystery and legendry about both men, and in both cases the leader, who for many had become almost a god, was killed by a hate-filled member of his own people.

There is a symbolism in this that reaches beyond the men themselves to the nature of leadership. For, in being tested by history, the leader must bear the burden of history and of his people. De Gaulle's cry, "Frenchmen and Frenchwomen, help me," during the second Algerian army coup, was witness that he could not bear his burdens without their help, and they helped because they could not bear theirs without his direction. This nexus has a special truth in an Age of Overkill, when for the first time one can conceive of a leader giving directions from a bomb shelter in the entrails of the earth, and when a blundering step may lead to a Golgotha for nation, for leader and, indeed, for humanity.

2. Power, Decision, and Identity

THE EXPERIENCE of leadership I have described has consequences for the contemporary leader's war role. He is not the war captain of the Old Testament—"He paweth in the valley, and rejoiceth in his strength; he goes out to meet the armed men. He sayeth among the trumpets, Ha, Ha! And he smelleth the battle afar off, the thunder of the captains, and the shouting." Such a war-horse leader is no longer possible, since the full use of the military must be ruled out within any frame of sanity, and the "thunder of the captains" can be too destructive for any vision. In our own era, the leader is caught between a concern for the intangibles of political war, which is the only kind he can meaningfully pursue, and the knowledge that he must pursue it with resolute heart and will and that half measures may be more dangerous than no measures at all.

To do this he will need a sense of the timely, of timing and of time. He will have his antennae out, to get the feel of the contemporary and avoid both archaism and futurism. He will sense the moment of readiness for great actions. Most of all, he must know how to buy time in order to carry on the political struggle for commitment, and how to survive until a world will, which is tardy in the forming, can ease some of the agony of leadership.

Involved inextricably with power, the political leader will know that his efforts will be futile unless he brings with him a whole leadership generation. He will use the skills of experts—scientists, businessmen, technicians, economists, military leaders, intellectuals —and translate into political terms the expertise they furnish him. But in the end he must filter it all through the spectrum of his own vision and will. For the technician may forget what the people think and feel, or he may lack the intuitive sense of what history demands of his expert fact. But the political leader dare not forget or forgo it. He must draw on others for their specialties, but when it comes to power, which is his own specialty, he can draw (as Richard Neustadt has seen) on no one but himself—on his instinct for the people, on his sense of the past and vision of the future. He is not Chairman of the Board; he is the Number One man, operating at the end of a long tunnel, and always there to take what comes through its darkness and hold it up in the light.

A further word about power: It has been a defect of the humanist tradition to be tender-minded about power. But the great leaders, from Cromwell and Chatham to Lincoln, Roosevelt and Churchill, confronted the requirements of power in their day. The political leader starts with a feel for power, and an image of leadership taken from the historic figures who came closest to the accidents of his own biography and the needs of his personality. Thus, Churchill got his image from Chatham, De Gaulle from the classical heroes, Roosevelt from Jefferson and Lincoln, Kennedy from Roosevelt, and a host of Communist leaders—from Mao Tse-tung to Khrushchev and Walter Ulbricht and Fidel Castro—got it from Lenin.

There is always the danger of making an end and ikon of power itself. When it becomes short-circuited with a neurotic personal drive, or some manic dream of replacing the omnipotence of God, its destructiveness in an age of overkill can become incalculable. But the great dangers of the use of power come not in such regimes as the United States and Russia, which are habituated to it and saturated with it, but in the regimes and traditions that have been power-starved. The attitude of the unneurotic leader toward power is receptive, matter-of-fact and instrumentalist, without obsession or rancor. He knows that power is what leader and people make of it.

He knows, further, that all dominations and powers may prove futile in the face of apocalyptic events over which he has little control.

One thinks of Robert Frost's admonition to President Kennedy, to cultivate "poetry and power." For amidst the rigors of the world's iron age it is power alone which can make the survival of poetry possible, while it is poetry alone which can give verve to power, and meaning to human survival. But Frost should have added that the poetry may have a tragic strain. The simplicities and grandeurs of the Old Testament war-horse captain or the warrior-leaders in the *Iliad* and the Icelandic sagas are no longer at home in a world invested with pathos, guilt, anxiety. The unneurotic leader cannot avoid facing them, but he must give them a new tragic dimension.

We have come, several critics have told us, to the end of tragedy in the theater. That may be because tragic possibility had to shift from the world of the stage to the stage of the world. The political leader is expected to bear the burden of the sick conscience of humanity. He is saddled with responsibility for all inequities, and he feels obliged to repair everything that has gone wrong in the past and make it right quickly. He faces opposition, revolution, possibly war, or—perhaps worse—the fear of falling behind and of being isolated and beaten without a fight. Locked in an *agon* of encounter with rivals, enemies known and unknown, intangible forces, specters and myths which may prove the greatest realities, he wrestles at once with them and himself. It is the wrestling with himself which places him among the loneliest men in history, alone with his anguished decisions.

I take it that the term "decision making," which has become the barbarous darling of the political scientists, is simply the point at which the leader must take the plunge, the point of final testing for good or ill, when everything painfully prepared and kept in readiness must be ventured. It is the point at which he must evoke whatever boldness and maturity he has and the crisp command of men and the knowledge of their springs of action. The decision may of course prove the wrong one, as with President Kennedy's ill-conceived, ill-prepared semi-invasion of Cuba, and when it is wrong its consequences may be disastrous and perhaps irreversible. Faced by this chasm of possibility, a political leader runs the danger of becoming punch-shy and overwary, and rather than make the wrong decision again he will make no decisions at all—which is in itself a form of blind decision.

To make decisions with insight, the political leader must have learned to know himself and to master his identity. Lincoln had his near-decade of vegetation, self-doubt and despair before the Doug-las debates brought him forward as a national figure. Roosevelt had his struggle with polio, when he tasted the ashes of nothingness; Kennedy had his brush with death in the PT boat in the Pacific, and the long struggle to regain his health; Gandhi had a period of bleak-ness after his return from his law studies in England, and Nehru a period of dawdling and indecisiveness before he threw himself into the Congress movement; De Gaulle went several times through the ordeal of withdrawal-and-return; Lenin languished in Swiss exile and spent himself in seemingly futile pamphleteering and faction-alism before the event came which took his train to Finland Station; Mao Tse-tung had not only to hold together the thinned-out cadre of his men on the Long March of the Eighth Route Army, but to hold desperately to his belief in himself; Nkrumah, Kenyatta, Bourguiba —like Gandhi and Nehru before them—had long stretches in jail when they searched the recesses of their being for the assurance that they were equal to the tasks ahead; Tito was repeatedly on the brink of having his Partisan detachments wiped out by both the Nazis and the Chetniks during his guerrilla years; Castro had to huddle in the Sierra Madres with his little band, scrambling for a toehold on the bare, unlikely rock of survival.

It was in those long watches that each man discovered the fortress of identity within himself. The leader is on this score more fortu-nate than most men, whose lives are likely to form a series of iden-tity crises as their life roles change; the political leader must make the hard confrontation once and for all if he is to survive. This does not exempt him from the later crises, but they become lesser foot-hills alongside the forbidding peak he had to scale for self-discovery. There is an element of sadness here, for—whatever the triumphs which adorn his victorious later course—his nostalgic memories are likely to cluster around his days of wrath and despair, when he was the elusive figure in the hills, always pursued, always slipping out of the net, or when he ate the bitter bread of sickness and isolation. Nothing that happens to him later can ever quite match the acrid sweetness of that memory, when he was alone but not lonely, for he had a whole generation to express and a world to win.

Unfortunately the inevitable loneliness of the leader may have to be paid for by the people and leaders of later generations. Some-times what they pay for is not the fact that he expressed his own insights but that he shared too closely those of his intellectual gener-ation. The figure of Franklin Roosevelt, which will defy adequate analysis for years to come, is a modern instance. He and his New Deal generation of lieutenants and advisers faced the crisis of the Depression and later of the Nazi world threat, mastered events, rode the whirlwind and commanded the storm. He was great in these crises because, in his swaggering way, he expressed the traditional dynamism and optimism of American life and gave a whole generation an antidote to its anxieties. But he also drew, for the decisions which he made and carried into action, upon the necessarily limited insights of the very generation whose symbol and leader he became. Himself little of an intellectual, he leaned upon a number of semi-intellectuals (Hopkins, Sherwood, Ickes, Corcoran) who were the mediators between himself and the liberal-radical creative elite of the time.

As it turned out, the insights of the generation, which were adequate for the New Deal domestic policies and the winning of the war against Hitler, proved inadequate for the settlement which laid the foundations of the future. The Yalta formula, which has been branded a betrayal and defended for its wisdom, was neither a betrayal nor wise, but quite simply naïve. True, it may have saved Italy from a postwar Communist regime. But the incredible decision to leave Berlin an island in the sea of a Communist East Germany was part of a larger blindness which needlessly left Eastern Europe to the "people's democracies" of Communism and failed to use Western military and political power effectively. At fault was not only the sentimental political romanticism of the American non-Communist Left, which thought the Russians would behave better if they had a cushion of antifascist states around them, failing thus to understand the nature and assertiveness both of Russian nationalist expansiveness and of the Communist Grand Design. At fault was also Roosevelt's assumption that he could woo and cajole Stalin into reasonableness.

It was part of Roosevelt's strength as a leader to express the most generous energies of his time; but the element of weakness in that strength—at the point where he might have transcended his time— can no longer be denied. His weakness was that he was not radical enough about the democratic destiny. His generation was somewhat awed by the revolutionary *élan* of Communism and accepted it as part of the march of history; it did not think of adopting the same stance of inevitability for the free democratic society whose vigor the New Deal had underlined.*

* For an earlier discussion of the problem, see Chapter II, Section 5, "The Ice Age and the Political War." Roosevelt's task was burdensome, and his overall

That is why leadership is more than the decision making of one man; it is all the sense and sensibility and insight of the commanding and creative elite whose spokesman he is. Every so often you get a man who isolates himself from both elites and from the "spirit of the time," as De Gaulle did when he cut himself off not only from the Left wing French intellectuals but from the army officers of the Right wing as well; but it is the rarest of rarities that this self-isolation should succeed. For better or worse, the leader is usually part of his time. The biggest fact about Roosevelt was that at a particular point of history he was *there*. Very often the great fact about a leader is not his decisions or actions or insights, but his *presence*. The trauma at the death of a great political leader, as at Lincoln's, Roosevelt's, Lenin's, Gandhi's, Hammarskjöld's, is the ultimate tribute of the generation to him. But whether it is also history's tribute may depend upon whether he mirrored or transcended his time.

3. *Commanding and Creative Elites*

THE LEADER and his advisers, I have suggested, cannot give direction to a viable society unless they come out of the creative forces in that society and release its best energies.

It may seem a choice bit of irony to speak of creativeness in an era of 50- and 100-megaton nuclear explosions, of strontium snow and of fall-out shelters, of space weapons and potential space warfare—an era obsessed with destructive power. Yet not so ironic, since the only war the nuclear powers dare fight at present—the political war—will be decided not by the balance of destructive power but by the balance of brains, will, vision, commitment. The decisive race is not the weapons race but the intelligence race; and even in the weapons race it is a scientific intelligence that counts. If the weapons are to be kept from dooming the world to a common massacre, it is the collective social intelligence, pooled from the conscience and creativeness of every society, that will count in the race against entropy.

---

place in history is still a towering one despite my strictures above. He had a war to win; he was determined to nail down the ensuing peace by methods more realistic than Wilson's moralism; he felt that only a Concert of Great Powers could do it. Hence his reliance upon a strategy of tentative trust. There are indications that shortly before his death his trust in the Russians had been deeply shaken. Had he lived out his term he would doubtless have given his great resourcefulness to the beginnings of political war.

I use the "elite" concept despite its accrual of overtones of snobbism, privilege and antidemocratic values during the 1920s and 1930s, when in American and European intellectual circles, the idea of an elite carried the same horrendous freightage of meaning as the idea of aristocracy did among intellectuals of the late-eighteenth century. This is the more curious since it was exactly the intellectual elites who prepared the way for the American and French revolutions and the Reform Acts in Great Britain, and in our own century furnished the motive power for every sweeping social change, including the Russian Revolution, the Nazi adventure, the New Deal, the Chinese Revolution, and the liberation movements of Asia and Africa.

For a period, especially in the shadow of Rousseau's "general will" and of Marx's obsession with class struggle and with the historic creativeness of the proletariat, the intellectuals were bent on ignoring the creative role of other elites and denying their own. The most brilliant exception was the tradition of Italian thought from Machiavelli to Vilfredo Pareto and Gaetano Mosca, which focused on the rise and fall of ruling groups, their conduct and tactics, their "circulation," their relation to power and to revolutions, and (in the case of the allied French thinker Georges Sorel) the myths by which they rule. In time contemporary thinkers rediscovered and applied their insights and began to talk of managerial and administrative elites, of military elites, of party elites, of religious elites, of communications elites, of intellectual elites, of the rivalry of elites in nuclear and space technology, of the need to train the elites of the developing countries.

Unfortunately, too much of the weight of elite theory has been placed upon the strategic, manipulative and power elites, not enough on the analysis of creative elites, and of their recognition, accessibility, training, replenishing and commitment. Confronted with the nuclear destructive potential and with the Grand Design as a political religion, a viable democratic society and a viable world are not possible except through the interplay of the commanding and creative elites in both. Leadership, as one phase of the commanding elite, will be futile unless it is linked with the creative energies of the society as a whole; these energies, if they are to be effective, require the purpose, will and vision which I shall be calling *élan;* and, if they are to be meaningful, they require the commitment to basic life purposes and life style which I call *ethos.*

I shall be dealing comparatively with the role of these elements in the Communist and free-world power clusters, and in the undeveloped world. But my emphasis in this chapter will be on whether and how there can be a Grand Design for democratic man, sharply different from the Grand Design for Communist man, yet adequate to its challenge. My concern throughout is with the convergence of a *democratic creative elite, a revolutionary* élan, and a *radical humanist ethos,* to shape a viable society and a viable world. What I am dealing with is neither democratic nor Communist theory alone, but what I venture to call *viability theory.*

To start with, the distinction I draw between the commanding and creative elites is not meant to seal them off tightly from each other. The commanding elites are those that rule, direct, manipulate, govern, possess and use power, command the energies and dispose of the destinies of men. It is not fruitful to think of them as a ruling class, for the ruling middle class of eighteenth- and nineteenth-century Europe and the ruling proletarian class of twentieth-century Russia and China will yield, under analysis, to the commanding elites (whether of business, party, church, army, government bureaucracy) that sit in the seats of the mighty, and the larger class membership which shares little of their command, and is passive, compliant, resentful or indifferent. Nor is it fruitful, while making the separation between class and elites, to think of the latter as a single, unified, self-perpetuating "power elite." The groupings are loose and shifting. What holds them together is that they form, in every culture, the dominant minority.

If I use the concept "creative elites" instead of the more familiar *intellectuals* or *intelligentsia,* it is to place them more readily side by side with the commanding elites, and observe the parallels, contrasts and overlappings. The commanding elites have talent, but what defines them is their power and rule, not their talent. The creative elites may at times have power, especially when their skills or insights are drawn upon by those who make decisions; but again, what defines them is their talent, not their power. Some may come from lower-class origins, some from gentry and aristocracy or business groups; some may be absorbed with the world of contemporary events and some detached from it. Some may be innovators, others critics and practitioners. Some may be primarily involved with science and technology, others with their own versions of truth and beauty, God and justice, the known and unknown. But what ties them together is their concern with words, image, or idea, with whatever can be wrought, thought, asserted, represented, believed. In every culture they form not the dominant but the creative minority.

I am not as bold as Plato, who said that a state is best in which philosophers are kings. Although Jefferson and Madison were good Presidents as well as great political thinkers, and Woodrow Wilson made the transition from college professor to Chief Executive, it is best to use the brain-trusters for their brains, at which they are professionals, rather than for their feel for power, at which they are at best amateurs.

But nothing can be said for the suspicion and scorn which the commanding and creative elites have had for each other in many societies, including the American, during long stretches of their history, or for the alienation of both from the people as a whole, and of the people from them. Obviously this has not been true generally or at all times. But, to the extent that this scorn and alienation have existed, they have weakened the society. A viable society will have to overcome the anarchist strain of hostility toward whoever is in power, as it will also have to overcome the anti-intellectualism which regards ideas and their possessors as dangerous, the arts as a frippery, and the creative mode of life as a dispensable indulgence when it is not a scandal. And it will have to clear the paths of access and replenishment that lead between the people and both elites.

This is to ask much. But a few examples from recent history will illustrate how disastrous it is not to make the attempt. I take a single instance from each of four countries which are today crucial to the survival of the free-world power cluster: Great Britain, France, Germany, the United States.

The English war poetry of World War I (Brooke, Sassoon, Wilfred Owen, Isaac Rosenberg) is torn between love of country and recoil from the horrors of war, but the generation that came after the war generation went all the way with the recoil and was willing to forget and forgo the love of country. It found a just cause for anger in its anti-fascism in the between-the-wars period, thrilled to the Spanish Civil War, found much that was sympathetic in Communism, excoriated Neville Chamberlain for his Munich betrayal. But as George Orwell noted, waspishly but truly, in his essay, "England Your England," the generation that lambasted Chamberlain for knuckling under at Munich had made his surrender inevitable by its unreasoning pacifism, its constant intellectual negativism, its merciless caricaturing of the Colonel Blimps. A hardier spirit and more astute mind than Chamberlain's—Churchill's, say—would not have traveled Chamberlain's humiliating road, but even he would have had to face the fact of British unpreparedness for the show-down with the Nazis, for which the attitudes of the creative elite were so largely responsible. As it turned out, Churchill was always far more in touch with the British people than the Leftist elite was; their estrangement from the military elite, from the governing elite, from England itself, was to cost them and England another harvest of blood in World War II. Yet, as I write, although the main corps of Labour Party leadership understands well the meaning of what Orwell wrote, the mournful unilateralists and the angry-for-anger's-sake young writers are treading the old path toward estrangement and destruction.

The German case was even more tragic. There was no adequate reason in the German mind itself nor in German history—despite the totalitarian strain in both—why the nation should have dropped into the abyss of Nazism. The inflation-*cum*-paralysis-*cum*-hysteria which eased Hitler's capture of power was not inevitable if a strong regime had taken over in the revolutionary situation following World War I. This would have meant a Socialist-New Deal regime, much like that of Roosevelt later in the United States. What made it impossible was that the long indoctrination in Socialist dogma, from Lassalle and Marx to Kautsky to Liebknecht and Rosa Luxembourg, had set for the trade-union elite a standard of militancy for which the German working class and the leaders themselves were unprepared, and had conditioned the intellectuals to a contempt for militancy in the democratic state itself and a hatred for the army elite without which such militancy was inconceivable. If the Socialist leaders of postwar Germany had not been so imbued with a hatred of militarism, and the military elite so fearful of a socialism which it equated with Communism, and if the intellectuals had faced the realistic task of building a militant democracy instead of finding solace in Communist political romanticism, Hitler might never have happened.

One might add, as a wry footnote, that as a consequence of Nazi repressions a whole generation has dropped out of the intellectual elite. The generation which was born in the 1920s, coming of age during the war years and having only tyranny, sadism and tragedy during its formative years, has simply not come to any creative fruition.

The French case is again one of the corrosion of will the intellectual elite suffered by embracing the Marxist doctrine of *raison d'histoire* and the myth of historical inevitability. There followed an estrangement from the people and from those members of the commanding and creative elite who still believed that the French nation had a future and that that future lay with the rediscovery of European man and with the free-world power cluster. It was not the loss of France's imperial possessions which undercut its prosperity or power; at the turn of the 1960s France shared the general prosperity of Europe despite a depleting Algerian war. What counted was a creeping debility of will which pervaded most of the creative elite and much of the commanding elite. Of the two great leaders who sought to counter it, Pierre Mendès-France had the support of the intellectuals and the people in sustaining the Fourth Republic but lacked the confidence of the commanding elite, while Charles de Gaulle started with the support of the military elite, won the people, then cut himself off from both groups of elites and, therefore, from the essential base for his Fifth Republic. Nothing could illustrate better than the history of these two men that the leader as an individual is not enough, even if he knows how to maintain a dialogue with the people; if the elites do not share his will, vision and conviction, or if he does not know how to express theirs, all will be futile, and the viability of the nation will end.

The special importance of the French case is that the brilliance of its creative elite in philosophy, the novel, the theater, painting, architecture, could not save it from its sense of powerlessness. It was too humanist, despite its massive Communist party, to accept wholly the Grand Design of the Russians; but it was too bemused by the Marxist version of America's fascist potential to put any will or belief into free-world unity. Except for men like Malraux, Camus, Mauriac, Sperber, Raymond Aron, Bondy and the group around *Preuves,* the prevailing French intellectual mood was the sense of being trapped—not so much by the bomb but by an incapacity for belief in viability—by having (as an editor from the Catholic Left put it to me toward the end of 1961) "to support the very causes and ideas which we know, to our dismay, will overthrow the West." The reader may recall my speaking, in my Foreword, of the enchanted wood in which the animals are held as in a mesmerized dream.

The case of the American creative elite is different from any of the three above. It suffers, to be sure, as do the European elites, from a deep sense of guilt about what the Western imperial powers did to the colonial peoples, and it has the additional guilt of an acquisitive and affluent economy to atone for, not to speak of the more recent guilt about Hiroshima. Over a long period it maintained a contempt for the business and political elites, just as they were themselves riddled with anti-intellectualism. But the New Deal experience under Roosevelt resolved one set of these antipathies and gave the creative elite and the people a new trust in political leadership, as it gave the political elite a new belief in the life of the mind. The strength of the American tradition of civilian control of the military saved America from the disastrous experience of the Germans and the French with their army officers. As for paralysis via Communist thought, the combined Utopianism and pragmatism of the American radical tradition proved effective in the end, after a brief flirtation with the image of the Soviet solution during the early Depression years. After all, the core of American radicalism lay in its healthy Utopian conviction that the American dream had been lost, mislaid or betrayed; the American intellectuals were therefore quickly disenchanted, learning of the purges and brutalities of the Stalin police state, with the betrayal of the humanist and even the Marxist dream under Communism. Their open-mindedness to fact reinforced their inveterate Utopianism of conviction.

The real danger to American viability came from a double source: on the one hand from a lack of tragic experience in American life which, along with its clinging to Babylonian standards of living, made segments of both the business and intellectual elites fearful of nuclear terror, and led them to prefer survivalism to the difficult and stoical pursuit of the good life. But even more the danger came from the frustrated segment of the middle class with its chauvinist nationalism, its inexpungeable suspicion and hatred of the creative elite, its cult of tangible action and contempt for the intangibles in national policy, its status fears and life frustrations, its paranoid delusion of being surrounded by enemies at home. From McCarthyism to Birchism, the threat to American viability has come from radicals of the Right, who have been panting for a home-grown tyranny, far more than from the weak reactionary Left, which has been complacent about a foreign tyranny. The deepest hurt that America's primitives have inflicted upon it has been to poison with suspicion the atmosphere of confidence that must exist between both elites and the people. During the decade of the fifties there was a steady draining away of the recruiting of the best young talent, whether for science or diplomacy, because of the anti-intellectualism that ran like an ugly scar across the face of American awareness.

I am not arguing for complacent acceptance of everyone by everyone. It is natural for American intellectuals, both in defending their status and as part of their committed task, to despise popular culture. No one can deny that much of the product of the big media is slick, sleazy and homogenized, where it is not simply mindless. But too few intellectuals, despite their professed identification with the "common man," are aware that in sheer technical terms the big media give many of the low-income and less-educated groups a window opening on a world hitherto inaccessible to them, and thus serve an important function of social cohesion. Nor do they seem aware that a genuine democratic aesthetic cannot despise its own raw material except at the risk of eroding the soil within which the roots of elite culture can alone flourish.

If I understand the sickness of popular culture aright, it lies in the essential facelessness of the grand market, which in the case of the big media does not sell the product to a particular buyer but sells a mass audience to someone who in turn wants to sell a product—an advertiser or sponsor in press, TV or radio, or a movie magnate buying an audience through a famous movie star and intent on making sure that the theme and treatment of the picture will not interfere with its sales appeal. I speak of "facelessness" because an audience viewed in these terms is an aggregate of faceless units, impersonal and interchangeable. It does not make much difference, except for the subtleties of market research, who they are as individuals, but it matters crucially how many they are.

But every society has also, in addition to its mass culture, another culture whose carriers are the creative minority, in whatever area they may find themselves, from governing to the ballet or archaeological research. While I like Margaret Mead's phrase for it, the "spearhead culture," with its suggestion of a spearhead leading the whole society into the future, I prefer to call it the *creative culture*. Its cultural product has meaning in itself, but takes on an extension of meaning by being made available to the people as a whole, just as its creators come from the people and are cut off from them only at their peril. It is also, in one sense, an autonomous culture—not in being separated from the people or the nation as a whole, but only in not being tied to church, state, army, business, advertising, public relations, but deriving from the exercise of the creative and critical intelligence.

The whole Western intellectual tradition consistently averted its gaze from power. At the beginning of the modern state it was a kill-the-tyrant strain, then it became a leave-the-state-alone strain, which had as its corollary another proposition: let the state fend for itself; we owe it no service and want no part of it. The last of these themes has been carried over into the brainpan of almost every thinker and artist. At the source of it is probably the early division between contemplation and action, going back to the Greeks and maybe earlier, and strengthened by the intellectual elite of the Christian clerks who were specialized to the spiritual life and the next world, while the commanding elite of the medieval knights were specialized to action and the temporal world. The split between the idea and the act is, in terms of a viable society, a paralyzing one, leading to privatism on the one side and mindless atomism on the other.

One way of regarding Communism is to see it as the reorienting of the intellectual elite toward power. This is also to grasp some of the secret of its strength. But the cruel jest which history played on the reoriented intellectuals was to push their new-found engagement to history and power all the way to the edge of the annihilation of their autonomy. The intellectual elite in Russia has become a servant of the commanding elite, and specifically of the party.

Thus the beat and counterbeat of the atrophy and hypertrophy of power. The Communist experience illustrates what happens when, in recoil from its power atrophy, the creative elite dons the strait jacket of power hypertrophy, and is locked into it by a party elite which uses the intellectuals for their skills but rejects the ferment of their ideas, and takes a revenge upon them for their condescension of centuries. There remains to the intellectuals, as their counterrevenge, only one course—which they are taking in Russia and generally in Eastern Europe, although evidently not yet in China. We may call it *disengagement,* using the word not in a military but in a psychological sense. Having been by turns unengaged and overengaged in their attitudes toward power, the intellectuals in Russia have largely become disengaged. They are "spiritual emigrants"; they stay physically where the party places them, but intellectually they have retreated to a universe of their own. While they give obedience to the party elite and perform the obeisances, they lock up their minds and suspend judgment on every issue on which the commanding elite clamors for a clear and single response. It is a curious ending of a curious road.

I trust the reader will not conclude that undying hostility to power is, after all, the best course for a creative elite. What has happened to intellectuals under Communism has happened because of the essential view that Communism holds of man, history and society. Within the frame of another view, it need not happen —provided that the creative elite remains constantly and critically aware of the dangers of the hypertrophy of power.

For Americans there may be a specific danger of the "military-industrial complex," against which President Eisenhower warned in his farewell to the Presidency. Under analysis it becomes a triple-elite axis—that of the Pentagon, Wall Street (and Madison Avenue), and the industrial and university laboratories. It is the danger that the men who invent the great weapons of tomorrow, those who organize and profit from their production, and those who are specialized to their use, will strike a pact of interest and power, obstruct changes of policy on war and peace, and perhaps even take over the society they are meant to serve.

The danger is doubtless there, the more dangerous because the periodic waves of political primitivism which wash over the American mind may weaken the resistance to such a power thrust. Yet the combination strikes me as unlikely. The turning of a military craftsman into a political general, which has flourished on the European continent and has a hold on the developing nations of Latin America, Asia and the Middle East, is not a habit in a society with a tradition of civilian control of the military. I recall a session at the Army War College, with several hundred men destined to become general officers, and their genuine shock when someone brought up the possibility of a military take-over of America. To be sure, the American officers have suffered some of the frustrations of the European officers, especially the French, because of the elusiveness of victory. The political Right is always alert for an officer-martyr. And in the current American situation there is a constant temptation for some "man on horseback" fanatics to make common cause with the True Believers in anti-Semitism, white supremacy, and salvation by nuclear war. But without the prestige of the military, these groups remain crackpots, and the tradition of political command over the generals is still stronger than the scattered instances of the political engagement of the generals.

As for the elite of industrialists, I need only add that without the generals they would be powerless in a showdown, and without the scientists (modern warfare being what it is) both the generals and industrialists would be helpless. In the confrontation of President Kennedy and Big Steel in 1962, the steelmakers were isolated. The scientists have acted on the whole with reflective maturity, doing what they must do for the defense of their country and the viability of their world, yet always maintaining a vigil against the possible use of the weapons they have created.* There is always, of course, the minor danger that industrialists, generals, Congressmen and scientists with a vested stake in particular weapons will exert pressure for them as against rival weapons and arms strategies, as happened in 1962 in the agitation for keeping the B-70's. But this is part of the traditional pressure politics in America, applied now to the politics of arms strategy. It does not—nor does any foreseeable combination of elites—menace the nation with a take-over.

The problem of the elites, from the angle of a viable society, lies not so much in the danger of tyranny by any or all the commanding elites, as in the need for bringing into being a great democratic elite, in both its commanding and creative strains.

4. *The Education of a Democratic Elite*

TO START WITH the lineage of the phrase above, I go back to Jefferson's emphasis on "an aristocracy of virtue and talent." The reader will find it in the long correspondence between Jefferson and John Adams after both men had retired from public life and had sunk their political enmity in a common concern for the future of the fledgling democracy. That Jefferson should use the term "aristocracy" in this context was itself striking. As a revolutionary thinker, he hated the aristocracy of privilege, blood and position as he had seen it operating in the Europe of his time, and he might have been expected to hate all aristocracies. But he had studied the rise and fall of civilizations to some effect, and he was not one to be frightened by a phrase. He did not believe, as Andrew Jackson was to believe after him, that the tasks of government took no special training or competence, and that any man could learn to perform them. He believed, with Adams, in a "natural aristocracy," and my guess is that as a revolutionary thinker he got a special pleasure out of asserting that the old aristocracies were exhausted and that only an aristocracy of virtue and talent could save the great venture of democracy.

It is still true today. With the Communist regimes and the nationalist revolutions, new elites have come in and taken over from

* For a further discussion of the scientists, see Chapter VI, Section 7, "Fear and Conscience in Atomic Man."

the old privileged aristocracies.* They have released the untapped talent of a whole generation, and they pose the question whether there is a democratic dynamic that can do the same.

The Russian Revolution set off an explosion of political talents. A double process was at work—the attraction which the revolutionary movement exercised for generations on the energies of fierce and dedicated Russian youth, and the urgencies of the new regime. Once the new people came to power, there was an imaginative outburst in political and economic reconstruction, in rebuilding the army, in staffing a new diplomatic staff, in fashioning an administrative apparatus. Add to this the tapping of talent among the peasants and industrial workers, to whom public careers had formerly been closed.

In effect, the call was out: if a youth had ability, ambition, ruthlessness and cunning, there was scarcely a limit to what he could achieve. There was, of course, a big proviso. He had to watch his step politically, learn wariness and the skills of maneuver, trust no one, suffer humiliations, learn silence in the face of injustice, guess right about where to place his loyalty and whom to betray, know how to land on his feet when others around him were being toppled. Out of this fiery furnace he would come, with all his weakness and most of his humanity burnt out of him, much like the Communist agitators whom Bertolt Brecht admiringly described in *Die Massnahme* (The Measures Taken).†

The weakness of this talent-recruiting system is its wasting of material. It is a tribute to the profusion of talent in Communist Russia that it survived the succession of purges. In one sense, curiously, the Great Purge of 1939 served to consolidate the regime, not only by destroying the potential opposition, but also by opening so many places at the banquet of power to the younger generation which had been waiting hungrily below the salt. The same process happened, without any purges, when the Roosevelt-Truman Administrations in the United States were succeeded by Eisenhower's, and Eisenhower's in turn by Kennedy's. In Russia the generation corresponding to Kennedy's is waiting. There is no proof yet, except perhaps in science and technology, of whether it is capable of the ferment of action which the early generations of a revolution achieve.

* For the Communist Party elite, see Chapter III, Section 6, "Winds of Communist Doctrine." For the elite in developing nations, see Chapter IV, Section 6, "Color, Heroes, and Elites."

† For an earlier discussion of this theme, see Chapter III, Section 6, "Winds of Communist Doctrine."

Several things are clear, however, about what happens to talent and how leadership is shaped under the two systems. Under Communism, talent is a monopoly of the state and party, which can pre-empt and, in effect, conscript young people into the commanding elite and the lower posts of the public service. One of the things open in an open society is the direction in which talent will flow—wherever it will find the best rewards, whether money and advancement, or security, prestige, power, and the excitement of the work. The Communists use much the same incentives, but their distribution is controlled by the party; thus, if the state stands in need of scientific talent, the party channels the extra rewards (pay, honors, car, *dacha*, relative freedom of work) in that direction.

The open society leaves the offering of incentives to each of the competing segments of employment—to business, science, the professions, the army, the churches, teaching and the universities, the arts and the world of entertainment. Government service and the political career must take their place among the competitors for talent, and their competitive pull is weakened by the traditional belittling of politics and by the harassments that attend government employment and public-office holding. The final striking of a trial balance is left to the individual; and while in some cases he makes his choice early and holds to it, more often his career is an experimental series of shiftings before he finds where his life chances and life choices converge. The result is probably a more satisfying life for the individual and a more diversified deployment of creative talent in an open society, but a more effective channeling of talent into the commanding elite in a Communist society. Moreover, in an open society the ordeal of choice and training for the commanding elite is haphazard and fragmented.

In a Communist society the ordeal is not the election campaign, but a prolonged struggle to survive in a series of party posts from a small factory or collective farm unit to the higher command posts and planning agencies. It is a jungle ordeal in which those who outlast jealousy, treachery and purge, and all the hydraulic pressures of the internal struggle for survival, are likely to be, in Darwinian terms, the "fittest" for the world political war as well: the tough-fibered, cunning, tenacious, unscrupulous, disciplined in a combat of nerve and will, with a flair for political drama and timing. Stalin's career, or Khrushchev's, will show how the qualities of aggrandizement and survival were developed in the harsh school of Communist rivalry. Once the commanding elite reach their top posts under Communism, moreover, they are likely to stay and fight off any challenger elite, nor are they subject to the legal limitations of tenure which will turn a man like Kennedy out of the top leadership exactly when he has reached the maturity of experience and is at the summit of his powers.

The issue I am probing is not one of abstract choice and advantage as between open and closed societies, or between monolithic and pluralist structures of power. It is rather what an open pluralist society can do to make itself also a viable one in a time of overkill and of world political struggle. The Communist state and party have not only the total talent pool of the society at their disposal, as a captive elite, they have also a reserve army of external elites who serve them in the Communist "apparatus" in other societies, drawn to them either by some predicament of personal history or by the mystique of revolutionary romanticism. This network of True Believers serve both as new recruits and as cadres and trainers of Communist elites. They cannot be matched by anything comparable in an open society.

Don't think that a creative elite comes into being full-blown, or that once in being it can be sustained without taking thought of the *how*. There is, if you will, a natural history that may be roughly applied to the talent elites, both in their power phase and their intellectual phase. There must be a social climate in which the potentials for talent are released, there must be access to the elites for every group in the population, there must be ways of training and educating that will make them effective, there must be ways of replenishing their ranks, there must be a resulting commitment of the elites to their calling and society. *Release, access, training, replenishment, commitment*—my concern here is not with the mystery of how talent comes or flowers in the individual, but with the problem of how the talents of various individuals can be channeled and made effective for a viable society.

As for the release and channeling of talent, there will always be a margin of mystery about why particular segments of a society achieve a summit creativeness in it. To take India and West Asia as an example, how did it happen that the Buddhist, Hindu, Jain and Sikh religious founders should have come in so oppressive a society, where the bristling divisions between conquerors and conquered, rich and poor, belongers and nonbelongers might be expected to stifle sensibility? Why did the Jewish and Christian founders come out of a narrow, unlikely strip of coast between Asia and Europe, among small farmers, sheepherders, fishermen, artisans?

How account for the solitary phenomenon of Mohammed at Mecca, rising from not only a physical but an intellectual desert? Why did the sequence of great Persian poets come when it did, never to be paralleled in the same culture? Or, to shift to a wholly different kind of talent, what brought into being the series of great Mogul conquerors and emperors, what explains the energy (in a society which undervalues energy) of the Rajasthan feudal fighters who resisted the Moguls, and of the Punjabi and Sikh soldiers? How explain the localizing of Bengali intellectuals and Mawari business creativeness? How, finally, explain the talent explosion in the 1920s and 1930s in India which, after centuries of stagnation, produced the close-knit group of Gandhi, Nehru, Rajagopalachari, Kripalani, Jayaprakash Narayan—a group as talented as, and far more humanist than, the commanding elite turned up by the Russian Revolution?

In some instances the clue to an answer is clear. Talent in a society is released by the triple convergence of a great event, a demanding need, and some personal constellation of genes and nurture. The great event may be war or revolution, disaster or triumph, the great need may be for building a new society or fortifying the best elements in a continuing one; the convergence of genes and nurture in a particular biography may have been aided by the cross-fertilizing of good biological and cultural strains. In the American instance, the release of talent by the events of the American Revolution and the founding of a new society follows the familiar pattern of a similar release in Periclean Athens, Elizabethan England, Renaissance Italy. But the theory that war and tragedy bring an inevitable release of talent was not, except for Lincoln, Lee, Grant, and Whitman, true of America during and after the Civil War years. Nor is it easy to explain why the three important periods of the American Renaissance should have come where and when they did—in the New England and New York of the 1830s and 1840s; the turn-of-the-century period before World War I; and the present generation, when American vitality in a number of widely removed fields from painting to science challenges the comparable work in Europe and outstrips the Communist world.

I put this in as detached a way as I can, without succumbing to my own cultural nationalism as an American, and I stress it because of what may be called the fallacy of creativeness. To use the parallel of the growing-up years, love for the child within the family is indispensable, but "love is not enough." Nor is creativeness enough in a society. It must be recognized, welcomed, enlisted; and it must be talent which is put to the service of a viable society. The Greek city-states had creative talents but the city-states went under. The British and French have in various ages released great creative energies; yet, as societies, they reached a declining arc of effectiveness, which they are now trying to overcome. It may well be that no nation-state today, however creative, will survive if all of them do not surmount the narrow perspective of national power. But if the American open society can muster its best talents in every area and put them to the service of the society as a whole, it may also give the lead in confronting the necessary means for world viability.

A natural aristocracy today* can have no concern with the irrelevances of color, birth, religious belief, or income. Its concern is with "virtue and talent"—that is to say, with character and personality, with merit and ability. This courts the dangers of a "meritocracy," a theme on which Michael Young has written a witty and withering attack. But the true dangers in today's and tomorrow's world are not that intelligence will have more than its due, but that it will not have anything like its due, and will be crowded out by privilege, monopoly, bigotry (both religious and political), brute force, and blindness. The task in any society is to find the carriers of promise, wherever in the social structure they may be located, and give them a chance to develop their potentials. They are often to be found in the unlikeliest of places—not necessarily in the old aristocracy centers like Boston, Newport, Richmond or Charleston, or in the newer ones from the Westchester suburbs to Nob Hill in San Francisco, but among the lowly and rejected. Wherever they may be, the task of recognition and the provision of access cannot be neglected.

I stress access, because it needs to be distinguished from a crude egalitarianism. Despite the Declaration of Independence, men are not created equal in the sense of being created with equal ability. Increasingly we are aware of the fact of individual differences. But in its best sense, the idea of equality is to provide equal access to equal opportunity, so that doors open to some children will not be shut for others, and life chances available to some will not be denied to others. Only thus will human potentials best be tapped and will each individual develop his unequal ability. The meaning of an open society does not lie in a general leveling, but in the

---

* In the remainder of this section I have drawn upon the argument of my little book, *Education and a Radical Humanism* (Ohio State University Press, 1962).

widest possible openness of access to the elites and to the fullness of life they offer.

One could, in fact, define the natural aristocracy of Jefferson and Adams by sloughing off whatever is irrelevant to it: class and caste, race and ethnic origin, political preference, region, religion, family income. What remains is ability, character, promise, and what Carlyle called the "fire in the belly." Even brightness in the form of capacity to do well in general and specific testing is not what finally counts. Sometimes the late-bloomers prove of greatest value in the garden of creativeness. I am not arguing here for a particular form of education, but describing only what a society can least afford to lose by shutting off access. There is a scar left on the hearts of individual children by the doctrine of irrelevant exclusion. But what counts for a viable society is not only the individual scar, but the fullest use of the reservoir of potential ability.

This sets the frame for the education of a democratic elite. I prefer the term "education" to "training," because the latter implies a narrower approach. To *train* someone is to transmit skills to him, to induct him into the mysteries of a craft; to *educate* him is to provide him with the tools, knowledge, exposure, and insight into self which he will need for shaping his own thinking and personality. In this sense, no state with party-line truth as its objective dares educate its young; fear goes with the ideological territory. The state trains and indoctrinates them, but that does not add up to educating them.

The American public-school system was revolutionary in a triple sense: It was universal, compulsory, and (for a minimum number of years) free. When this educational revolution emerged it fitted the needs of a polyglot society into which had poured streams of immigration from every corner and country of the world, each with its own cultural heritage. It achieved the purpose of civic education, in preparing young people for jobs, business and the minimal requirements for voting, and in furnishing a common cement of national cohesion.

The wild dream of the educational thinkers and administrators of the early nineteenth century was the dream that the son or daughter of the lowliest immigrant family could, through schooling, help make poverty and bigotry and war archaic. Nor was it an ignoble dream. But today it has paved the way for a second educational revolution, going beyond the common denominator of culture for the mass, and dealing with the education of a talent elite. This involves paying a double price—setting aside a greater portion of the national income, by federal taxation and appropriation if necessary, for the development of the real wealth of the nation, and, perhaps more difficult, giving up holdover attitudes from the past which prevent the total enlistment of the nation's best talent.

Americans might have taken much longer to enter this second revolution if they had not been prodded by Russian strides in training their young. The Russians telescoped the two educational revolutions in one. They made a great effort at conquering mass illiteracy and giving the ethnic and religious populations a substratum of cohesion. But they also trained their carriers of promise more purposively and effectively than was true of the United States, with a more solid base of general knowledge and skills in the early years before specialization starts. They worked their children hard in the schoolrooms, set up competitive standards, eliminated anything not bearing directly upon the survival and power of a Communist world. They turned out scientists by the thousands, engineers and technicians by the hundreds of thousands.

The thinker who best expressed the democratic educational revolution which grew out of universalism was John Dewey. His revolt against the mechanical methods of teaching in his day was a healthy revolt. He emphasized the relation of education to the experience of the culture and of the child. He urged teachers to let children learn by doing rather than by being told. He concentrated upon the study of the child—its growth, motivations, fulfillment. The result was a child-oriented educational system which has drawn the fire of critics upon Dewey as well as upon the overpermissive methods of teaching he helped to shape. He was a revolutionary thinker, but his best thinking was done before the turn of the century. Dewey's thinking, crucial for the first educational revolution, is no longer adequate for the second. The problem is to set up standards of excellence at every level of ability, to refashion the curriculum to meet those standards, and to stretch the intellect at every level to the full limit of its potentials. Thus the new battle cry has become not "educational democracy," not "experience," not a "child-centered school," not "life adjustment," but the kind of unsparing excellence which will develop the best talents for the life purposes of the individual and his culture.

The bearing of this upon the viable society ought to be clear enough. Recoiling from Plato's conception of education as an instrument of the state, American thinkers abandoned wholly the core of what was valid in it. We must reject the use of education as an instrument of power by a state or a party or a commanding elite, and the deliberate distortion of social reality through the Platonic lie under the guise of party-line truth. But this should not mean rejecting education as a way of sustaining the vitality of the society as a whole. A universalist philosophy of education, suspicious of what will be subtracted from the ordinary child by a concentration upon the more promising ones, needs to be rethought in terms of the crisis of the free-world societies. In the case of America, for example, there are talent needs of great urgency to be met in science and technology, in the political and military leadership at every level, in the diplomatic services, in the schools and universities, in every profession. Despite a persisting unemployment among the unskilled and semiskilled, America is long on shortages in posts demanding high skills, new perspectives, innovating capacity. Hence the task becomes one of the most effective education of a democratic elite.

I stress the adjective as well as the noun. The trouble with much of elite theory is its emphasis on the power of the elites, without much concern for their relation to the society as a whole. While there must be the widest access to the elites for every group, the danger is that, whatever the source from which they come, the elites will harden into an Establishment and what Pareto called the "circulation of the elites" will be slowed down and all but stopped. In an open society, the obstacles to the replenishment of the talent groups are much the same as the obstacles to the original access to them. They are the persisting ethnic and social discriminations, the undervaluing of both the life of the mind and the importance of the teacher, the inequalities of life chances, the unwillingness to place the nation's financial resources at the disposal of the nation's human resources, the failure to will the means while willing the ends.

The Communists argue that there can be release, and presumably replenishment, of talent energies only by class revolution and the setting up of a society which for the first time taps the talents of the underlying population. But a party Establishment rapidly sets in, and the atrophy of its power dries up the channels of replenishment except under the terms of the existing party elite. In an open society, circulation is attained by freeing educational opportunity from every consideration except potential ability, and opening every job —public and private—to the competition of ability. In totalitarian and directed states, it is achieved by a directed competition, mainly within the ruling party, in which political reliability is part of the screening process. In a Communist society, the talent is siphoned off and sprayed all over the social landscape as it is in a democracy, running into every area where it will be rewarded and welcomed best. In the circulation of talent, a Communist society is at a disadvantage, since whatever iron there is in the "iron law of oligarchy" will settle in the channels for distributing ability, and make them less fluid as the original revolutionary group settles down to enjoy its perquisites of power.

The right of revolution, which the Communists celebrate, seems to end with the Communist state, which presumably marks the end of history. The problem of the replenishment of talents gets short-circuited with the problem of the succession to power, and it falls to the mercies of internal party factionalism, with its secret maneuvers and public condemnations and confessions, its tortures and purges. Much of the best talent is cut off either by exclusion and exile or by the "spiritual migration." Hence the paradox that a regime which came to birth by a revolt against the class Establishment may in time explode in violence or die by arteriosclerosis because of the hardening of the party Establishment. An open society carries many defects and burdens, but to the extent that it remains open—once the widest possible access is established—the replenishment of the elites can continue to be achieved.

There are revolutions which do not carry either class or nationalist violence with them, and which bear on the problem of replenishment. In a remarkable set of essays which may seem to weigh against my theme, H. A. Innis has shown how the changes in the history of communication have come about despite elite resistances. There is always a Vulgate of the masses, he says, to the Latin of the educated classes. It is true that mass education was fought in the England of the early nineteenth century by those who had a vested interest in restricting the spread of communication, but the revolution of the word—of movable type on pulp—was too strong to be held back. Journalism, which started as the adjunct of the coffee houses in England, has become the adjunct of the department store, and the need for daily fresh advertising to move goods has made daily publication imperative, thus reinforcing the tendency to see only the linear time-scheme of events instead of their weblike complexity and their extension in depth. Today television has become the new Vulgate, and the electronic tube producing an instant moving and speaking image is replacing the dominance of movable type on pulp.

I have tried to show, in my way of putting the analysis, how it reinforces my theme. The revolutions in communication are always resisted by the existing educated elite, but it loses, and new revolutionary ways enter history, new roads of access are opened to groups which had hitherto been shut off from education and the elites. It is in this revolutionary way that an open society best manages the circulation of its elites.

Yet it would be a mistake to write off the persisting importance of movable type on paper cheap enough to reach everyone. The reading revolution of the paperbacks in America not only has brought with it a flood of how-to-do-its and whodunits, but also has made the treasures in the gallery of ideas another "museum without walls," as with paintings themselves. There are knowledge generations as well as weapons generations in history, and they are also moving with dizzying pace, making obsolete much of what was once held to be effective knowledge and piling up mountains of new and esoteric knowledge to be mastered. Exactly because it is so esoteric it makes greater demands upon a new educated elite; but by that fact it also makes imperative its constant replenishment from the ranks of the people themselves. The reading revolution makes this replenishment possible, just as the TV revolution (despite the obsessive scorn for it on the part of the existing educated elite) opens new worlds for those who depend primarily on its Vulgate, and adds a new education tool for the mass education without which any creative elite breaks its touch with the people.

This brings us to the final phase—that of commitment. There is a passage in Gibbon, in the concluding section of the *Decline and Fall,* about the Rome of his own day, and how "the beauty and splendour of the modern city may be ascribed to the abuses of the government, to the influence of superstition," since the palaces of "the fortunate nephews" of the Pontiffs became "the most costly monuments of elegance and servitude." Depicted in Gibbon's elegance of language, as a member of the creative elite of his own time and culture, the beauty of modern Rome is seen as the product of a privilege elite, almost of an iniquity elite.*

I draw a line between a privilege elite and a productive elite. The privilege elite of which Gibbon wrote produced nothing and was committed to nothing. True, it had a creative elite in its service, which worked in the setting rays of what had once been the fierce

* I write these lines in a small piazza in the working-class section of Rome. It is a good place in which to reflect upon the death and life of civilizations, the succession of class dominations and powers, the surviving beauty wrought by the commanding and creative elites of the past, and the present fragility of these cities of beauty in the face of an encroaching Spartan power cluster, with the chance of nuclear overkill always present.

sun of Christian faith, and in the dawning rays of a reborn spirit of classical antiquity which ushered in the modern era. But whatever commitment the creative elite had, it was not a commitment to the people or to the society as a whole, and the privilege elite had none except to its own comfort and aggrandizement. I do not mean to belittle *quattrocento* Rome. In a God-haunted society, the creative elite was preoccupied with the great themes of the nature and faces of God, in the secularized Europe which followed the Reformation it was haunted by the theme of the nature of history and the experience of Nature, in the latter-day twentieth century it is likely to be haunted by an anxiety about survival and a concern for the viability of society and man. The new commitment of the creative elite must be not to the past and its certainties but to the possibilities of the future. Yet it must be none the less a commitment, carrying with it both a daring for innovation and an ardor for vocation.

I have written of the education of the new elite, and my premise has been that education is possible. Yet, a sentence from Talleyrand, one of the most resourceful members of a commanding elite of the past, challenges it: "What I have learned," he said, "I have forgotten; what I know, I have guessed." There will have to be much forgetting and unlearning of what is no longer so, and much guessing about what can be, by the few who have an innovating daring. There will also have to be a sense of vocation. Writing about the "committee politics" of scientists, C. P. Snow has spoken of "the intricate labyrinthine and unassuageable rapacity, even in the best of men, of the love of power." The only thing that can temper power for the commanding elites, and replace it for the creative, is the doctrine of work as calling and fulfillment. The demand for talent will, in the years ahead, grow greater than ever. Many are chosen, but few are called.

5. *The Death and Life of Civilizations*

WHAT IS IT that decides when a civilization dies, or whether it will live? I don't mean what immediate events, like an assassination, an electoral defeat, a political blunder, the loss of a battle, which may topple a governmental regime, but the long-term forces which circumscribe the destiny of civilizations. Thus far I have assumed that whether or not a society is viable depends primarily upon will and intelligence. This is a voluntarist view, a "will-theory," as it were. It is humanist in the sense that it puts its stress upon human beings and their actions, rather than upon impersonal determinants like God or history. But I must ask in fairness whether there may not be something in the determinist view—whether there may not, in fact, be an irreversible trend locked up in the historical process, which makes the defeat and death of the free-world societies and the victory of world Communism inevitable. If this were so, then my discussion of leadership, decision, and the elite has been pretty much of a waste, and the later sections of this chapter, dealing with the *élan* and ethos of a democracy, will be futile.

There are two major forms of determinist theory—one cyclical and repetitive, as with Spengler; the other an unfolding of some principle inherent in history which works out its effects as a law of social development, as with the materialist dialectic of Marx and Engels. I shall be quite summary about the first, and say it is too late in the day to revive the discredited Spenglerian scheme of cycles of springtime, maturity, decay and death in civilizations. By Spengler's view, Hitler should have triumphed, praetorian governments should now be in control in every developed capitalist democracy, and modern industrialism should have spawned formless mass states instead of the managerial elite states—whether Communist, democratic, or national-socialist—which have actually taken over. As for the Marxist dialectic, I have paid my respects to it in dealing with its doctrine and its myth of inevitability.* I don't put much stock in the idea of impersonal forces which decide such things and against which men cannot struggle. That may do as a substitute marijuana dream for True Believers, to make their universe orderly and keep them from having to think for themselves. But in the real arena of world history, within a general frame set by geography, resources, population and technology, what happens to civilizations is mainly shaped by what their people think and feel and do—their political leaders, their talent elites, their common man.

There is an alternative to tracing cycles or working out the development of some immanent principle in history: it is to seek causes. One thing that saves Toynbee's work, for all its cycle tracing, is the seriousness with which he searches for the causes of the birth and strength, the weakness and death of civilizations. My own impulse, in asking about causes, is to put the problem of death

---

* See Chapter III above, especially Section 6, "Winds of Communist Doctrine," and Section 9, "A Stick, a Plan, a Myth."

ahead of that of life. For in the study of society, as in medicine and psychiatry, it is best to start with malfunctioning; the healthy organism is best described not in *a priori* terms of an ideal abstraction, but in terms of what keeps it from getting sick and breaking down.

One clue to the death of civilization is rigidity. There may set in, at the height of a successful civilization, what Ortega called an "arteriosclerosis of belief"—a hardening of the intellectual and moral arteries of a civilization, so that it can no longer adapt itself to drastically changed situations, much as the prehistoric monsters died out as species because they could not adapt to the great changes of climate and physical environment. Partly, this rigidity may be the result of a failure of replenishment in the elites. Or the civilization may become the victim of its own success, suppressing anything from the outside that might disturb its complacency, and making an ikon of its master institution, whether slavery or militarism, capitalist power or the monolithic party, social caste or feudal or religious hierarchy.

I find this an engaging lead, and there are many who think it the decisive one, believing that America's greatest danger lies in an inner rigidity which prevents it from adapting itself to the changed power distribution resulting from the Communist and nationalist victories. If it means an adaptation to Communist power, with constant one-sided concessions to the constant push and urgency of Communist expansion, then the result will be not death-by-rigidity but death-by-surrender. But if it means the need for adapting the techniques of survival to the nature of the new world's challenge, then it makes sense to condemn rigidity and practice plasticity. For the plasticity becomes then not one of panicky concession but one of ways and means for maintaining the life of the civilization. President Kennedy's Inaugural sentence, "We will never negotiate from fear, but we will never fear to negotiate," repudiates both panicky adaptation and panicky rigidity. Plasticity is all. What it does not express is the paramount plasticity which, by devising a whole armory of new ways and means for the political war and for peacemaking, can give a strong strategic position for viability to those who negotiate in its spirit.

The second clue lies in overreaching. Spartan man died of rigidity, but fascist man—whether in the version of Mussolini's inflated neoimperialism or of Hitler's dream of a thousand years of world domination or of Admiral Tojo's predatory "coprosperity sphere" under the Japanese military elite—died of attempting too much too fast, and of becoming an overreacher. Will that happen to Communist man? It is unlikely, but who would say it is impossible? Stalin attempted too much too fast, and made an almost fatal mistake as an overreacher when his nonaggression pact with Nazi Germany opened the way for Hitler's gamble with a war. The whole civilization pattern in Russia was saved from destruction only by the hairbreadth of the Churchill-Roosevelt decision to give the Russians all-out aid. Khrushchev has repudiated Stalin and consigned him to a second death by removing his corpse from its position next to Lenin's; it may have been a way of reassuring the Russian people that he would not replay Stalin's role of the overreacher and bring on the ruin not only of Russian civilization but of a good deal more besides.

The chances of free-world leaders playing the overreacher, and courting thereby the death of their civilization, seem to me far less. If it were to happen it would be as a consequence of the rigidity principle, almost as a phase of it, rather than through the principle of *hubris* which is at the root of overreach. What rigidity does in a civilization is to keep its elites and people from the resourcefulness which explores modes of viability other than war. If the free-world regimes, faced by an expanding Communist power cluster, and unable to muster the strength of the lion or the cunning of the fox in meeting it, were to find themselves isolated and at bay, they might reach beyond their actual strength and stake everything on nuclear war. But in that case the free-world civilization would have lost its viability anyway. It would have died first on an arc of inner moral decay before it died outwardly on a descending arc of power.

A third clue is the "failure of nerve," to which Gilbert Murray attributed the fall of classical civilizations. The essence of it lies in the recoil of the civilized, the comfortable, the possessors, from the specter of the advancing "barbarians": the Greeks could not face the Roman legions, with their crude strength, their organizing skill, their belief in their imperial star; the Romans, in turn, having absorbed and been absorbed by Greek culture, could not face the thrust of the tribes beyond their walled fortifications.

There is little question that the fear of the barbarian continues through world history; Europe, which thinks of itself as Greece, has felt it about the Americans-as-Romans, the Americans have felt it about the Russians, and the Russians in turn now feel it about the Chinese, who may some day feel it about still another power thrust. But it does not follow that it is the fear of the barbarian which dooms the civilization. In fact, one could as readily say that the appearance of the barbarian may act as a tonic to the older civilization, awakening it from its deep dream of peace and bestirring it to call upon its reserve resources. Thus the threat of the new barbarians may serve to rebarbarize, as it were, the older civilization. It happens in a man's life that a sharp crisis may evoke this unsuspected reserve strength, calling it up from levels of resolve he believed long buried. There are times of great danger when an animal awareness and directness of response cuts through the overlaid crust of apathy. It is also well known that, for groups and societies, the collective potential stretches unimaginably in disasters. The question is why it might not also stretch before the disaster, in confronting its danger.

To say "collective potential" is to go beyond the failure-of-nerve idea. The latter strikes me in any event as a less happy concept than one could wish, despite its literary cachet, since it suggests the nervy bravado of teen-agers calling "Chicken" at each other in a head-on confrontation of jalopies. The question is not really one of nerve or of individual courage or heroism, but quite simply of collective potential and will. The response to the challenge of a dangerous new rival to be met—what I have called "rebarbarization"—need not take the form either of savagery or of bluster, but of the organization of social energies. Historically Americans are conditioned to thinking of individual will, and they find something a little sinister about the idea of a collective will, as if it were a negation of the individual. There is, to be sure, a traceable sequence from Rousseau's "general will" to the ant society of the Chinese commune. But to abandon the idea of collective will to the Communists for that reason is like abandoning to them the idea of a talent elite, or to the fascists the idea of great leadership, or to the Machiavellians the idea of power. These are all neutral concepts in the sense of being vessels into which a varying content may be poured.

One may take William James's "will-to-believe," which was an individual matter and has been carried far too far toward a straitjacket compulsion, and transform it into a collective will-to-live. I said earlier that each of the great power centers of today represents an energy system built up over the course of centuries. Such an energy system does not question its own survival—at least, not until it faces an abrupt challenge. Once that comes, an energy system which is more than a chance collection of individual energies has a good chance to transform itself into a will-system, with a collective will-to-live as its core. The Communists never had to undergo this change, since they started as a will-system. Yet I wonder whether the advantage is wholly theirs. The Russians achieve their collective action by party-line concealment and distortion of reality; consequently their intellectuals have ended by refusing to believe in anything, retreating to their private interior world. Americans, with their tradition of personal will, are slower to act for common ends, but whatever gains they make in their fumbling toward a collective will are likely to stick.

I have spoken of rigidity and of overreach, of failure of nerve and of defect of collective will. There remains to speak of a factor which shares something with each and subsumes them all. It is the failure of self-knowledge, which is a distortion or vacuum of identity. A civilization which is rigid through hostility, overaggressive, guilt-ridden, fear-obsessed, loses its sense of identity just as a person does who has a distorted image of himself because he does not dare face the real image. That is why the American tradition of self-criticism of the society is good, provided it does not end there but is used as a starting point for a healthy self-acceptance.

If the revolutionary nationalisms of our time are identity revolutions, why should the quest for a collective identity be limited to the anticolonial movements? At a time when a bitter political war and a looming *auto-da-fé* of civilization compels every civilization to examine itself, each of them is thrust into an identity crisis, in which it may sink forever or from which it may emerge with a greater self-knowledge. I don't equate this crisis with the fear of the nuclear bomb in itself, nor with the naked drive of the individual to live—although that is not a negligible fact. The identity crisis applies to the civilization as a whole.

The rigid civilization, with its compulsion to repeat its crisis experiences and its blunders, has little plasticity and, therefore, little capacity to make a radical change in its image of itself; rather than change the image, it will break and go under. The overreacher civilization will fear to arrest its conquering course, lest it have to ask what the conquest will cost and what it is for, just as the success-seeking personality fears to pause for the question that may turn it to stone. The civilization that lacks a collective will is like a person for whom the day is a witless sequence of atomized incidents, and for whom, therefore, a crisis which cannot be grasped as such an incident is unthinkable.

Yet it may none the less be possible (although history is chary of examples) for a civilization in the full course of its life, when brought to a halt by a lion in the path, to experience something very like a rebirth of self-understanding. It would not be the sickly self-consciousness of Hamlet's communing with his doubts, nor will it come about merely through an epiphany of high resolve at a sacred moment of insight. It will be a groping, stumbling affair, and will extend over what seems an unconscionable time. And it will often seem at best an ambiguous business. America, for example, will have to perform day after day a double miracle, of resolving to live but of learning how to face potential death, of beating the Communists at their own game of political war but also of learning how to live with them for decades and perhaps centuries to come, since there can be no total victory for either side.

6. Élan *as Vision and Drive*

I MIGHT ADD, as an epigraph to the discussion just ended, a remark which Finley Peter Dunne ascribes to his philosophical Irish saloon-keeper, Mr. Dooley, about "the post-mortem kind of history." "It tells ye, Hinnissey," says Dooley in one of his bursts of social criticism, "what a country died iv. But I'd like to know what it lived iv."

I am interested in both and consider each a part of the other. But Mr. Dooley's stricture carries the right emphasis. One cannot take the vital processes of a civilization for granted. There is always something a people lives of, and when that *élan vital* ceases, the civilization dies. At the turn of the 1960s a malaise spread among American intellectuals regarding the lack of a "national purpose" and "national goals"; a National Goals Commission went to work to formulate them, and representative Americans wrote eloquent statements of the National Purpose. I prefer Bergson's term, *élan*, for one may state the goals or the purpose readily enough, but what counts most is the drive behind them. The road signs may be there, and the intent to make the journey; the *élan* is the gas in the engine, that gets you to your destination.

I hope I shall not be misunderstood. Despite our mechanistic age, which makes the gas-and-engine figure a natural one, *élan* goes far beyond the drive, to include the vision that gives it meaning and direction. Every civilization embodies somewhere a vision—of man's image, of what is progress and what is tragedy and disaster, of Nature and of God, of life and death and human possibility. The Americans have recognized this vision as the crucial element of what gave their whole national enterprise its start; hence the "American dream," which they outwardly deride (witness Edward

Albee's farce-satire of that title) but have inwardly never quite given
up. It is a very personal vision, of success and the good life for
yourself, of a glowing future for your children even if your own
life chances have been exhausted, but it also embodies a sense of
what has been possible through the common action of the nation.
In essence it has been a folk myth, and as such it has served the
needs of social cohesion in an age of great ferments.

Along with it has been a tradition of social dynamism which is
the one common element in the thinking of Americans, whatever
their class and status and whatever their regional and political
differences.* When a young Presidential candidate, in 1960, repeatedly returned to the theme of "Let's get moving again"—of the
restoration of American prestige and the recovery of national purpose and of American dynamism—he found himself in the deepest
harmony with his campaign audiences. He had touched a chord in
the American experience deeper than any other. What John F.
Kennedy was appealing to was the American instinct for the recovery of *élan* ("Let's get moving again") , just as Franklin Roosevelt's slogans ("We have a rendezvous with destiny"; "We have
only just begun to fight") made essentially the same appeal. The
vaunted father image to which FDR's continued popularity has always been attributed was a security image, but without the sense of
dynamism (going somewhere), the sense of security would not have
been enough to account for the excitement he engendered. It was a
case of the American people feeling,

> I know where I'm going,
> And I know who's going with me.

For a people to know where it is going is the meaning of national
élan.

Civilizations die, I have said, of rigidity and overreach, of failure
of nerve and will, and of the vacuum of identity. They live by the
vision and will of their people and leaders. If the dream and
vision go, then the whole power structure becomes blind, like Sam-
son among the pillars of his own temple, which he must pull down
to save his self-image. If the drive and the will are to go, then
not only America but the centuries of history which it and the free
world embody will go down with it.

The reader may say this is nothing but mystique. I agree that it is
a kind of mystique, which is why I have deliberately adopted Berg-

* I have dealt with this in an earlier book; see my *America as a Civilization,*
Chapter I, Section 7, "American Dynamism."

son's phrase. What his charisma is to a leader, its *élan* is to a civilization—something indefinable that sets in motion all its forces and resources, stretching each to the utmost and giving the ensemble its meaning. No army can march or win, no people can survive, without it. "It was a possibility not studied in our war academy," said the battle-scarred German General von Kluck, of the French attack at the Marne after ten days of exhausting retreat. And von Moltke, paying the French the tribute of using Bergson's own term, noted that "French *élan,* just when it is on the point of being extinguished, flames up powerfully."

You cannot indoctrinate a people with it, but you can, under the right conditions and conditionings, find the trigger that releases it in them. It is to be found in the experience of a civilization, deeply buried in the residues left in the unconscious after all the specific actions and passions have been washed away by events. Nor will the statement of "goals" and "purpose" in themselves release it. If the drive is there, and the right people to release it, then the goals— whatever they may be, and even at a heartbreaking cost—become accessible. "If we will it," said Theodor Herzl of the charge that his goal of Zionism was unrealizable, "then it is not a dream." The mystique may be vested in the institution (as with kingship or the British or American Constitution), or in a particular leader, or in the people themselves and their history, but somewhere it must be. In the recovery of this mystique the people experience a rediscovery of their identity.

Much of the discussion of *élan* has in the past run in terms of battles. General Maxwell Taylor went back to a chapter in *Corinthians:* "For if the trumpet give an uncertain sound, who shall prepare himself to the battle?" Justice Holmes, recalling the Civil War days, remembered that "in our youths our lives were touched with fire," and the experience deeply affected his whole philosophy about the springs of national greatness. Henry Adams continued to believe for a long time in the need for an enemy: "Fifty years ago," he wrote in a 1910 letter, "we fought—God knows why, but we believed in it. Whom ought I to fight now? I wish I may be hung up another fifty years to dry utterly out, if I have the smallest notion whom I ought to fight. . . ."

It is in the nature of national and revolutionary struggles to require an enemy, as it is in the nature of religions to require some principle of evil without which the good—or God—cannot be defined. The Communist political religion is deeply rooted in the idea of constant struggle, and the Marxist credo has given religious overtones to secular effort by its mythologies of the continuing capitalist-imperialist enemy and the new nationalist-proletarian hero. If, as Tocqueville said, it is difficult for a democracy to carry out a "fixed design," it is not only because of the struggles in the popular arena, but even more in the separation of religious intensity from the collective image. It is democracy-as-skepticism that makes it difficult, not democracy-as-common-decision. The centuries of modern skepticism had corroded the very principle of belief, and men were left with the technology of questioning, but with an unsatisfied hunger for belief and for greatness. Only those who could cut through the questionings—as Marx did with his doctrine of man's transformation of his environment and himself and, therefore, his inevitable progress—seemed worth following. The rest of the world was left and America especially, with the doctrine of a lost Arcadia, which made the sense of the loss of belief all the more insufferable.

This hunger for belief is also a hunger for greatness—the greatness of the theme, be it country or love or God or humanity, on which the belief is fixed. I can only scorn those who still apply little criteria to vast enterprises and think we can meet the intensity of a political religion with no intensity of our own. They recall another remark of Mr. Dooley: "Th' enthusyasm in this counthry, Hinnissey, always makes me think iv a bonfire on an ice floe. It burns bright so long as ye feed it, an' it looks good, but it don't take hold somehow, on th' ice."

As a practical people the Americans have a fear of political myth, which is in its roots the political expression of the pervading American fear of being "taken for a sucker." This is the more curious since the strain of Utopian thinking is so strong in American history, and the idea of America as Arcadia runs through its thought from Jefferson and Jackson to the latest antitrust order of the Department of Justice. The distinction is between Arcadia as something lost and Utopia as something still to come. The Utopian thinking of Communism is centered in the political religion of the age of plenty and of statelessness in the years ahead. It may well be, as Daniel Bell has suggested, that the modern age has come to "the end of ideology" and has exhausted its passion for blueprints and vast intellectual schemata, but has it exhausted its sense of mystique and political mythmaking? Every idea must become something of a myth if it is to be an effective idea.

But if the *élan* of the free world is to have this mythmaking capacity, stirring men to belief in their future and fulfilling their hunger for greatness, it cannot be an *élan* which goes back nostal-gically to the past or clings to the *status quo* in order to keep the past from wholly slipping away. This is the trouble with the "new conservatism" of the young American intellectuals, quite aside from their programmatic blindness in domestic and foreign policy. It is hard not to have some feeling for the power of the conservative idea in a world of wild flux, where every landmark is going and where the best conservatism wants to hold on to what has been built so painfully and at so high a cost over the centuries. But conservatism, whether Edmund Burke's or Russell Kirk's, tries to hold on to what was achieved in past centuries by men who were not salvaging something but building something. If the conservative tenets had prevailed during those centuries of striking out for the new, the results to which conservatism now clings would never have been achieved in the first place. Even the constructions of the past cannot be held by men who, as Tawney put it, walk into the future backward.

Americans have almost stopped thinking of themselves as the "new men" of a new world. Now they must remember to remem-ber that it was as revolutionaries that they took an open continent and built on it an unparalleled open society, setting in motion universal currents whose consequences are still incalculable. As the progenitors of the great revolutions of the modern world, the Amer-icans must stop being afraid of the idea of revolution. I recall my students and audiences at Indian universities whose image of Amer-ica was that of a fat but fearful civilization, with the highest living standards in the world but also with the lowest threshold of panic at the convulsive events of a revolutionary age. I agreed that this America existed. But I told them also of another and different America—that of the revolutionary tradition of a little handful of bold men not content to remain colonials, that of Jefferson and Jackson, of the Abolitionists and of the Lincoln who signed the Emancipation Proclamation, of the Populists, of the New Freedom and the New Deal. This other America, of the authentic modern revolutionary tradition, was one with which they could identify. In fact, for some of them it helped revive the lost *élan* of their own nationalist revolution which, with the old sense of the enemy gone, had all but lost its drive. In the world political war, which is a war of ideas and myths even more than one of guerrillas, space achieve-ments, economic aid, and UN Assembly votes, the vision and drive of a democratic revolutionary *élan* may count for more than any other single factor.

I know that I am speaking primarily in terms of the intangibles of myth, mystique and *élan*—that is to say, of political psychology—and omitting the hard facts of economic planning, rate of economic growth, the allocation of resources, the fierce world rivalry of trade and aid and currencies. Some of these I have already discussed at length in an earlier chapter. But my plea is that it is the political, psychological and moral factors that count. Once they are in motion, on an ascending arc, the seemingly Himalayan difficulties of the more tangible elements become surmountable and accessible.

But there are treacheries, not only verbal but actual, in the uncritical use of the idea of revolution. There are reactionary as well as radical revolutions—reactionary in the sense that they take potential change which could have been turned into the channels of the radical insurance of freedom and of humanist values and (like the Cuban revolution or the North Korean, or the Chinese, or the revolutionary movements which set up the East European Communist regimes) damage the potential humanist values and all but snuff out the chances of freedom. Such reactionary revolutions distrust and despise the people and are permanently estranged from them. The truly radical revolution is not always one by violence, although that is not ruled out; it is one whose humanist ends are matched by a humanist concern for freedom as a means as well as an end.* When a revolutionary leader like Sukarno speaks of his "romantic intoxication with revolution," he is speaking as a man who craves stimulants, and, like drunks or addicts, he exercises no critical discrimination. But those whose business is not with romantic absolutes but with the hard facts of the world power struggle and the world danger must make the critical distinction between the cult of revolutionism and the concern for radical humanism.

7. *The Battle of the Ethos: Life Style and Personality Type*

IT WAS SURELY a disease of the romantic imagination to believe that universal civil war could bring about fraternity, that human progress could be advanced by brother shedding brother's blood, that you could get more freedom for people by depriving them of the freedom they had, that you could efface an old tyranny by setting up a new one, that you could bring about the good life by turning

* For an earlier discussion of this theme, see Chapter III, Section 2, "The Two Faces of Revolution."

your back on what had painfully been achieved over the centuries in building a human ethos.

It may well be that the viability of free-world society will depend on the competition of ethos as well as of weapon and *élan* and idea. If *élan* is vision and drive, ethos is commitment to values—at once what sustains the struggle and what gives it meaning. The overriding Marxist emphasis on historical necessity makes the ethical norm a measure of the power survival of the party elite and the class state. But if we say that the ethos of the free world will be a decisive factor in its survival, what is the difference between this instrumental view and the Communist instrumentalism? It can be put quite sharply. In the Communist view, what is good for the Communist state and the commanding elite is valid for ethics. In the view of radical democratic humanism, what is valid for the ethos of free man is by that fact good for the society as well. And I add, what the reader may regard as much shakier, that what is valid for the ethos of free man and the good life is also highly likely to be effective in nailing down the viability of the free society. But that is not why it is valid. It gets its validity from its own autonomous fiber, as the product of centuries of human experiment and experience.

In one sense, Communism too is an experiment, and a radical one. I don't mean in its effort to set up a class dictatorship, which is only another variant of the old and weary principle of using maximum coercion as the stuff of social cement. I am thinking, rather, of its attempt to reach down to the foundations of human nature itself and create Communist man as a new personality type and life style. There are not many basic life styles in human history; the list would vary in content, depending on whether one uses the Dionysian-Apollonian-Faustian-Promethean categories or the pastoral-agrarian-feudal-ascetic-industrial categories, or a combination of these and others, but in any event it would not be much longer than a half dozen. The Communists are now adding Communist man as a new personality type. The basis for their hope of success is Marx's doctrine that in the process of transforming his environment man also transforms himself, but their actual method is to help and prod history by drastic measures of effacing the undesirable and evoking the desirable traits. What is true of changing the old Russian personality style and character to a new one is true even more strongly in China, where ancestral and family ties, which might have been expected to be more resistant, were among the elements to be effaced. It is a tribute to the strength of the effort at shaping a Communist man that it has been able to cut across two national characters and two sets of traditions as diverse as the Russian and the Chinese.

While the program cannot yet be called a success, the important fact is that after two generations in Russia and a generation in China it has not yet failed. The Russian and Chinese leaders are at least attempting the task, remembering perhaps that the willed power systems of the past, from Alexander through Napoleon to Hitler, failed because they did not even make the attempt. It is an effort to fuse doctrine, culture and psyche. Note that we are dealing here not with the naïve enthusiasm of a spontaneous new religion but with the planned and willed effort to structure a system of power in the personality by an assault on the mind and a manipulation of an ethos.

I have already spoken of the guiding ethical principle of historical necessity; if anything is possible for man, then nothing is excluded in reaching it.* The Chinese are more radical in the acceptance of this principle, because they are farther from the Western humanist tradition. True, Russia in its history skipped both the Renaissance and the Reformation, but it did not skip the Enlightenment, and in its own form of Christianity it recaptured some of the spirit of Christian primitivism which the Roman Catholic Church in its prosperity missed. These factors helped to lead it to Communism, but they also tempered its absolutism; an intellectual community exposed to Shakespeare, Pascal and Mill was able to produce its own Tolstoy, Dostoevsky and Pasternak. But the Chinese had almost none of these exposures, in the absence of which they were ready for a movement which combined the exuberance of the Renaissance, the moral intensity of the Reformation, the crusading cruelty of the Counter Reformation, the subtlety of the Jesuit fathers, the ascetic devotion of the monastic orders, and the sense of a Heaven revealed of the primitive Christian Church.

The ethos of a society can be best gauged not by what it teaches and preaches but by the questions which, even if not always articulately asked, pervade it. These are the questions that are symbolic of the enveloping atmosphere within which the children grow up, and which form the "inarticulate major premises" of the logic of their personalities. The question in Russia has been Lenin's famous *Kto kovo?—Who whom?*—suggesting better than any treatise in the dialectic of Marxist ethics what the ethos-in-action is like. Who outmaneuvers whom? Who rules whom? Who purges and exiles whom?

* See above, Chapter III, Section 5, "Reason of State and Reason of History."

Who sentences whom? Who survives whom? They are the questions of the political and social jungle, and their message is reinforced by every sanction of the power and comfort of the successful and the wretchedness of the failures. This does not mean that the doctrinal fanatics inherit the earth, which is more likely to be inherited by the pragmatist armed with the right doctrinal text—"right" only because it is quoted by the survivors.

As for brotherhood, which goes back as a revolutionary motif to the French Utopians, its flourishing in a who-whom atmosphere is minimal. The comradely values of the human connection have been eroded in the Soviet society of today, to the extent of disillusioning any enthusiastic foreign visitor who comes to it with dreams of humanism—a materialist humanism, to be sure, but still humanism. What remains of the brotherhood strain in the Soviet ethos is likely to come as a heritage from the Tolstoyan and Pan-Slavic mystics, and is better expressed in the *Zhivago* of Pasternak, a Jew-turned-Christian mystic, than in any product of Communist creativeness. The real mystique of Communist man, wherever he may be, is the mystique of science, and it is more safely established in what science can do *for* the countless millions of the impoverished and unliberated than what Communist man can do living *with* them. It is this mystique which furnishes whatever religious element there is in "socialist realism" as a credo for writers and artists.

The Unknown God whom the Communists worship is compounded, thus, of a new fanatic jungle Darwinism where political death is the principle of natural selection, a new instrumentalism which rests on the unflagging pursuit of the end through flexible means, and a vague mystique of what science and technology can do in providing the good life for all.

Note that I do not include a Spartanism of life in this portrait of Communist man. Puritanism, yes, but not Spartanism in the sense of spareness of living standards for the elite. The Russians are prepared to take over the world, and in the process to take over also its comforts. Their diplomats in every country live in high style and scarcely miss a cocktail party, their commanding elite in Russia drives about in fine cars, eats sumptuously, vacations in luxurious villas. If the archetype of Communist man in his ruthlessness and instrumentalism was Lenin, then his archetype in a peasant's envy for fine living was Stalin, and Khrushchev continued the tradition of flexibility and comfort. As Russia moves into a consumers' economy, social changes take place which make the old ethos of fanatic spareness and simplicity of life archaic.

But not with the Chinese, who represent a kind of Comteist society of compulsive flat rationalism in its purest and most primitive form. That also describes the kind of society envisaged by the Communist regimes or parties of North Vietnam, North Korea, Indonesia, Malaya, Thailand, Burma and, to a great extent, Cuba and the African nations, most of whom have either operated in the Chinese orbit or are closely sympathetic to it. They are militant True Believers who, like the Christians at some epochs of their history, and like the Moslem emperors, aim at either persuading or exterminating the unbelievers. They sleep in barracks, eat like soldiers on a march, work round the clock, and are lit by the inner fires of belief in their victory. What will happen when they gain the victory and set up their own regimes, and then later when they achieve consumers' economies, is another matter. Thus, the ethos still clings to the idea of austerity. But not, one should add, of renunciation. One of the problems of the Communist ethos in Southeast Asia is that its materialism unfits it for the centuries-old doctrine of renunciation. There may be for a brief temporary spell, as with the Chinese, a Spartanism of life and an ascetic denial of creature comforts, but there is never renunciation of the world itself or of power in it.

In one respect the Russian and Chinese models of the emergent Communist man share the same ethical quality—the absence of any inhibiting scruple in aiming for the Communist goal, and scorn for the recklessness and decadence of the "paper tigers" who will the end and not the means. The zeal with which the commissar or *apparatchik* will dehumanize himself and accept dehumanization in the name of the deferred goal suggests the doctrine of the Sabbatai Zevi, the false messiah of Jewish tradition, who taught that man must become wholly corrupt before he can become wholly pure. The chief hindrance of the West, in fighting the world political war, is not its affluence, or even its conservatism, but the burden of guilt it bears, so that every move in the power struggle is judged by a religious ethos which comes close to an absolute standard of morality. *Do I approach Thy shrine, O Lord, with clean hands?* is the constant torturing question of the Christian conscience, which may have had its origin in the recoil from the vengeful tribalism of the society to which it was first addressed. This is perhaps less true in Catholic countries, which have trafficked with secular circumstance through the mediation of dogma and found ruses for living with an imperfect world. As Charles Peguy put it, with summary honesty, the way not to dirty your hands is to have no hands. The leadership of the free world in the political war has fallen, however, on the Protestant societies, where the individual conscience is the test of public actions, and where the necessary prudent means are accompanied by agonies of guilt.*

Communist society does not suffer from this guilt, nor does it have the disease of conscience; its religion is not that of the valuing individual who has to face himself in the solitude of his psyche, but a political religion which squeezes out everything but the collective triumph, and whose symbol is not the eye of the needle but the juggernaut of the logic of history. The danger with such a jungle ethos is that the society committed to it may end in self-slaughter. But the Communists expect to have world victory long before that happens, and they are willing to take the risks involved in their own intramural games.

But the *kto-kovo* routine is only the segment of the Communist ethos which shows most obtrusively, especially to free-world feelings about police-state toughness. The more important segment, less visible, operates not through direct violence and coercion but through the indirect pressures of the society upon the nonconformists. The "ritual of liquidation," in the physical sense, is overshadowed by the ritual of the extirpation of identity. The Chinese have carried this farthest, partly in the corrective procedures of "social rehabilitation" for the doubters and those of independent mind or queasy conscience; partly in the refusal of the social group itself—village, factory, collective, university, laboratory—to let the sinner fall from grace. This is reflected in the conditioning of the child in the growing-up years. His fear is that he may be excluded from the group, and since all his identity is based on its accepting him and making him part of itself, to be excluded means to be cut away not only from them but from himself.

The conformity pressures on free-world man are also strong, of course, but in a pluralist society the pulls are from many directions, and identity lies inside the self which is enriched by the net of relations but remains itself even if they are cut. In a wholly politicized society where no independent associations are allowed lest they be power rivals, and where not only party-line truth but party-line ethic holds a monopoly, the danger is that there will be no identity outside what the party approves.

The question about every society is what it holds to be fulfilling and delightful, what intolerable. For Communist man, *delight* is a word scarcely in the lexicon, the fulfilling lies in what gives him par-

---

* For an analysis of how this guilt operates in the context of nuclear weapons and deterrence, see Chapter VI, Section 7, "Fear and Conscience in Atomic Man."

ticipation in the group, the intolerable consists in being excluded. The ideal goal in all Communist societies is to have the growing-up years under the all-seeing tutelage of the state. The family system is a danger to emergent Communist man, since it is always an independent—and hence an unreliable—agency in shaping him. But the substitution of state for family, and of socially coerced cooperation for the natural play of hostility and affection, means an intolerable conflict between psychic expressiveness and social duty; the result is an emotional isolation which makes Communist man bleak in himself, as his society is dreary. If Communist society is not destroyed in a general world holocaust, along with free-world society, it is likely to die of sheer boredom and emotional starvation.

The one way of preventing this emotional isolation is the deliberate separation ("migration") of the inner personal self from the outward social one. Since the whole Pavlovian conditioning of Communist man is aimed at drowning his ego in his superego, not so much through conscience as through the fear of ostracism and the conflict of duty with emotion, the way to keep the ego from drowning is to develop a capacity for living underwater. They have learned, at least some of them, that what has been presented to them as party truth does not match their experience. As a result some withdraw into their privatism, develop a protective fiber, and manage to survive with sanity by distrusting every generalization and value, whether by the regime or against it. They are not autonomous men—that would involve a core of belief which they have arrived at for themselves. But neither are they automata. The Communism which started them on the road to belief by asking them to shed their disbelief and embrace a faith, has ended by leaving them no choice except to suspend their belief—in everything, permanently. They are limbo men, suspended between a belief they can no longer hold and an unbelief they dare not embrace, uncommitted to anything and anyone except their own private determination not to be committed.

Is free-world man in a better case? Certainly he has been more critical of himself and his society than Communist man. I have said that the dominant question for Communist society, which informs the envelope in which the child grows up, starts out as "Who whom?" continues as "How can I keep from being excluded?" and ends as "What can anyone believe any more?" The dominant question in free-world society, notably in America, has been not "Who whom?" but "Who gets what?" and "What's in it for me?" It is not the question of society as a political jungle but as an economic market place where everything is vendible, and where the crucial life goals are money and success, and the power, prestige and security based on them. These are not adequate life goals for a viable society. If you add to them the hedonic life goals, as implied in the questions "Are you happy?" and "Did you have fun?" the sum is still inadequate. The ethos of vendible values, the happiness ethos, and the ethos of the fun imperative, may be superior to the ethos of the political jungle, of coercion-by-exclusion and of the limbo of uncommitment, but they will not do.

I have written elsewhere* of the corrosions of these life goals upon the American personality. But, whatever the differences in the battle of the ethos, the diseases of the two systems are not wholly unlike. They are the diseases of social pressures and inner insecurity, of mass man with the emotional equipment of his heritage from the primates, of the desensitizing of man and the dehydration of his personality. But in every aspect I have mentioned, Communist man carries the disease so much farther that, to use a favorite Marxist expression, a change in quantity becomes a change in quality. This may be because he carries to their logical conclusion the tendencies of modernization, especially in the cynicism about means, the politicizing of every value, and the extirpation of identity, with all the stops removed. What I mean is that the whole freightage which Western man has built up to check and inhibit the full operation of these tendencies is removed—the play of ideas, freedom, the valuing of the individual. Even with that freightage the human condition in an age of overkill is difficult; without the freightage it becomes potentially monstrous. Thus, I should say that the contrast is not so much between the open and the closed societies as between the open and the closed personalities—and that in turn may be pushed back to the contrast between the notion of a finished society that has found the answers and need only apply them, and an unfinished society which is still in ferment, and where the interplay of answers and questions—each suggesting a new form of the other, neither ever ended—goes on.

Let us glance more closely at the nature of what I have called the freightage of the modern condition. Leaning heavily on the mystique of Soviet science, Khrushchev went to great pains at the Twenty-second Soviet Party Congress in 1961 to depict the good life to come under Communism. But, by his own witness, he was enter-

* See my *America as a Civilization* (1957), Chapter IX, Section 8, "Life Goals and the Pursuit of Happiness," pages 688-94.

ing Communist society on a race where the free-world society had the advantage, so that at best he could not overtake it until 1975 at the earliest, by which date there would either be a system of world law or no world left. Even more important, he made the mistake of moving over into the universe of free-world values, among which the value of the good life has been (along with freedom) the most underscored and the most successful. It is another instance of the unconscious homage paid to the Western tradition, even by those who are most insistent upon a sharp breakaway from it.

But Khrushchev made another mistake as well. The same Twenty-second Party Congress for which he had prepared the broadside to announce the Second Coming in Plenty was at the last minute turned into an occasion for launching the Second Death of Stalin, and to that end all the party elite was hauled up to the platform to denounce Stalin's crimes of secret assassination and mass murder, in such detail that they make the pages of Gibbon on the corruption and murder practiced by the Roman emperors seem pallid. He had his reasons for this shift, and they must have been good reasons. But the result was to set off the claims about the Second Coming in Plenty within a frame far more meaningful than he could ever have intended. What he was saying was that the price of the promised living levels and consumers goods to come was a high one, measured in conflict and blood.

If I may venture my own scheme of the basic needs of a viable human society, I should put bread (or *plenty*) somewhere on the list, but certainly not at the top. Above it I should place the ferment of ideas, the play of creativeness, the exposure to the best of what has been achieved and experienced in history, using *openness* as my key word—openness to ideas and experience, and the freedom to grow with both, toward diversity and identity. Side by side with that, because they are related to it, I should put love and the *expressive life,* including the erotic drives and the whole range of affectional and emotional needs. At the top (or the base?) I should put the sense of belonging and of solidarity—the *human connection.*

If the battle of the ethos is to be waged, free-world man need not feel disheartened about its probable outcome. In none of these basic life needs does Communist man even see the nature of the values involved, and in none—except with respect to security welfare—does he even make claims and demands on the future. I have spoken of the good life in terms of living standards, where the battle strength of Communist man ought to be greatest, but where it is not quite strong enough. In terms of experience in the sense of cultural creativeness and the enrichment of the individual by it, the condition of Communist man is bleak; in scarcely a single sector of human experience have a generation of Communist man in China and two generations in Russia made the creative contribution one has a right to demand. However repressive may have been the regimes that preceded them, their level of cultural creativeness made the successor regimes seem bleak. True, there was progress in applying science to technology, and in literacy and the transmission of skills to the mass of people; but this is (except in a few areas) a process of spreading someone else's butter, not of making it.

On the issue of freedom for the personality, I have already tried to draw a portrait of the fear of diversity and the hollowing-out of identity in Communist man. On the issue of Eros—of emotional and affectional expressiveness—an ice age is settling over Communist society, and a new Puritanism of repressive morality threatens to hold Communist man in its glacial grip for centuries to come. It is the hope of men like Herbert Marcuse, who has done some good thinking about Eros and civilization, that the repressive morality will also vanish. As hopes go, it is a good hope, but there is little current evidence either in China or Russia to warrant it. Erich Fromm, who also cares about Eros, sees the repressive morality as organic to both capitalism and Communism, and seems to imply in his latest writing that a *modus vivendi* between the two which will allow a humanist socialism to take their place will also provide a greater freedom for the release of the arts of loving.

My own view is that, whatever the ills of Eros in the free-world society under capitalist and mixed economies, they will have to be healed by some means other than the victory of Communist man, or of his closely related brother in the national socialisms of societies like the Yugoslav and the Egyptian. Only a radical humanism can heal them, as indeed only a radical humanism can win the battle of the ethos. I use "radical" in the sense that man is always the root, and "humanist" in the sense that human welfare and the human connection must be the measure and test of all actions.

CHAPTER VI

Beyond the Power Principle

1. Beyond Power—To What?

2. Dialogue Against Death

3. Negotiation Without Illusions

4. The New Federalists

5. UN: The Dynamism of the Order Principle

6. Toward Collective Will in an Open World

7. Fear and Conscience in Atomic Man

8. Death Urge or Life Force?

Beyond the Power Principle

1. Beyond Power—To What?

ADAPTING Freud's provocative phrase and book title, "Beyond the Pleasure Principle," to man's current dilemma in the Age of Overkill, I suggest that we shall have to move beyond the *power principle*. But to what? Freud made it clear that going "beyond" the libidinal and ego instincts did not mean denying them or leaving them behind; it meant taking them along, but going further, so that what you take along becomes transformed. A living organism never leaves any phase of its existence behind. When we go beyond youth, we carry along with us the scars and experience of youth into some sort of maturity. We carry sorrow with us to the grave, yet if we did not transcend the sorrow we could not live. A writer viewing the pathos of life knows, if he has any depth, that he must go beyond compassion to the tragic meaning of what he has seen, but he carries his compassion along.

Thus with the power principle. I find it as impossible to agree with those who think we can say "Good-bye to All That," and bid farewell to power—as the young Englishmen in the 1920s so cheerfully did—as to agree with those who think that power is the only thing that counts, now and forever, to world's end. Power is one of the three imperatives which serve as frames for what goes on in the world of men and nations—power, order and creativeness, and the greatest of these is creativeness. But there can be no creativeness in today's world without world order, and there can be no world order without power in some form.

But in what form? Surely neither nation-state power nor imperial power. There are men who say that what lies beyond power is *more* power; that thus it has been since the world's beginning and thus it will ever be; that the way to have peace is to have bigger and better arms than the enemy; and that anyone who thinks differently is tender-minded. The trouble is that the history to which they point for confirmation is one that confirms the wrong thing. True, the world has always organized for war, but then the world has always got the war it organized for, and has had to pay for it. The payment this time will be intolerably high, which is why overkill has transformed the power problem.

The fact is that the nation-state has ceased to be a viable unit of world order exactly because it cannot get along without at some point using its showdown war power, which it dare not do under overkill conditions; yet, when faced with a threat to its identity and survival as a nation, it dare not *refrain* from invoking its war power, however powerless it be. Thus I return to where I left the first chapter of this book—the passing of classical world politics. Actually the nation-state no longer exists in any sovereign sense, except in its diplomatic abracadabra and in its formal voting in the UN and other international bodies. The working power units have become the power systems, which operate from power centers, hold a moving power equilibrium in the world which it is the function of diplomacy to break or restore, and which are increasingly the basis even of the work of the UN.

I am not suggesting that the power principle can or will be discarded soon. In the weapons race, in nuclear diplomacy, and in the world political struggle, it is still the power principle that is dominant. But these are short-range perspectives, and for the first time in history the commanding elites know it. They know that time may be running out on all of them. Partly they are caught in the power rivalry, partly (as with the Chinese) they tell themselves that it will always be thus until there is a Communist world, partly they either dream (as do the Russians) of being able to lay down the terms on which the power principle will be liquidated, or hope against hope (as do the Americans) that somehow the transition can be made before the world has blown up.

The persisting dream of empire is a desperate dream in an age of overkill. True, it is the seductive dream of peace through power— and, in the end, of the dethronement of the power principle, because with universal empire and no rivals there will no longer be any need for it. This was, of course, the rationale of the *Pax Romana* in the Augustinian age, and of the *Pax Britannica* and the *Pax Teutonica*. I suppose that relatively sane men still play with the idea of getting universal peace through universal empire, whether under the Russians, the Chinese or the Americans. I may note in passing that this is the only kind of peace which logically the unilateralist disarmers can hope for, since the camp that doesn't surrender its weapons will pretty well be able to run the whole world show. But, unilateralism aside, the road to world empire is unlikely to be achieved except by a world nuclear war—which might mean that there would not be very much of a world to enjoy the blessings of universal peace. "A peregrination of the catacombs with guttering candle" was the description Keynes once used to impale protectionist doctrine. Its underground image has even more relevance when applied to the peace-through-empire dreamers.

Is it not possible then to get the leaders of all nations to renounce power altogether? Since the power principle is the principle of evil, and since its application today must lead to irreparable destruction, why not, then, end the political war and live together as peoples without weapons and without war? This has of course been the dream of moralists and religious leaders for centuries. You will find a strong strain of it in the Christian pacifist movements, and an even stronger one in India and Southeast Asia, with their Hindu-Buddhist tradition. The thinking of Gandhi and of Schweitzer, on the sanctity of life, the strength of spiritual power, and the morality of the means, has left a considerable impact on world thought. The core idea is Gandhi's *satyagraha*—the use of the force of mind and spirit rather than of weapons of death. Or, adapting Herbert Croly's rather smug phrase about the "righteous use of superior force," this moralistic approach stresses the forceful use of superior righteousness.

This has the merit of being logical, but not much more. Gandhi's *satyagraha* worked against the "Europeans" in South Africa and against the British in India, in both cases against people who had inherited the tradition of the Western conscience. It would not have worked against Hitler, as Gandhi understood when he called for support of the British in wartime. It did not work against the Chinese when Nehru made a *satyagraha*like pact with Mao, and both sides agreed to the *Panch Sheel* code. It would not work today against either Russia or China. For the *satyagraha* principle works only when it is applied against a commanding elite by an overwhelming weight of the population, as in India under Gandhi. It does not work between governments when it is only a one-way street.*

Gandhism has its uses but, as Gandhi would have been the first to understand, it also has its limits. In the form of nonalignment it

* As I write (1962) it is still not clear whether the *satyagraha* principle will work as used by Rev. Martin Luther King in his "Albany Movement" for civil-rights enforcement on the local level for American Negroes. What is being tested is the truth-force of a minority, backed by the Federal government and "outside" opinion, against a local government and an overwhelming local majority.

may be the right policy for undeveloped and uncommitted nations in their international posture; it is not a principle of world order, because moral force must be embodied in some form of collective power before it can meet the threat of nuclear force. What I have called the surplus power of the nuclear weapons cannot be displaced by the surplus moralism of *Panch Sheel,* relying only on the shakiest deficit morality of the world powers who might have little concern with the appeals of men of good will.

I do not mean to brush aside the power of moral codes as a principle of international conduct or a force in world affairs. It is an important and even indispensable ingredient of any progress toward world peace, and without it no plan for peace can work. Even world law will be meaningless until and unless it expresses the operative moral conviction on the part of people throughout the world. The problem is how that moral conviction can be channeled into a strong world force. But even when it is so channeled, it will operate only as a kind of motive power behind world law. It cannot operate by itself, and those who dissociate it from the movement toward world law, in the belief that it can somehow work like a disembodied cloud of hope and anger in the no-osphere, are not doing a service toward either world law or world morality.

The unilateralists are doing an even greater disservice in draining off the moral force which could, given time and circumstance, be directed toward a movement for world peace through law. Philosophers cannot always be trusted to understand very much about what goes on in the minds of ordinary men. When Bertrand Russell launched the unilateralist movement he may have been trying to come full circle back to his youthful martyr days, when he served a prison term for his pacifism during World War I, and close his life with an even more heroic challenge to the commanding elites of today. Encouraged by the response of students, clerics and artists, as well as the professional support of interested Leftists, he may have felt that the movement would snowball into an irresistible force and would frighten the little men out of their chancelleries. But when he raised the "Better Red than dead" banner, the moral force which is needed to meet the problem of overkill was poisoned at the source, for it ran afoul of the will to freedom, of the will to national survival.

There are elements of *satyagraha* in the unilateralist sit-down movement which recall the Indian sit-downs on railroad tracks during the Gandhi days, even in the face of the *lathees* of the police. If only one could sit for peace, just sit, and win it by applying one's seat tenaciously to the hard cold ground, all would be well. But suppose the fellows on the other side don't sit? And if you count on the infection spreading around the world to them the answer is that it will not spread. For the two things that can sweep a people are the infection of freedom and the infection of national survival; where both have been offered for sacrifice, like Isaac and the lamb together by a stern Abraham to whom God has spoken in the burning bush, there is not much left for moral fuel except individual skin-saving which, even when multiplied on a world scale, is not enough. Thus, what is true in unilateralism is not particularly new —the *satyagraha* principle, the compassion for human victims and the reverence for human life—nor has it ever proved effective except as a drive behind law; and what is new about unilateralism— the indifference to the moral values of freedom and of national survival—is not morally true. Think of where Gandhi would have got if he had shrugged his shoulders about either India or freedom.

Thus, if we ask, "Beyond the power principle—to what?" the answer of the all-outers for ideological empire is, "Peace through universal empire," the answer of the moralists is, "Peace through morality," and the answer of the unilateralists is, "Peace through the infection of laying down our weapons," which in essence means "Peace through survivalism-as-morality." Of these three the first tries to cure the power cancer homeopathically by the cancer of more power; the other two, in their recoil from the immorality of the weapons spiral, jump to the immorality of exposing the free world to the near certainty of subjugation, if not of destruction.

I fear I have not been wholly just to one proposal for world order —that of the *modus vivendi* school, which understands both the viciousness of the weapons spiral and the need for the power principle in some form. One wing of this school takes a no-nonsense approach to the problem of world order; since Russia and America are now the two great conservative world powers, it says, and since nothing in the world could resist them together, why should they not combine and impose on the world a *Pax Eborica-Americana?* They could thus make the UN work as a great-power agency, practically corner power, exercise restraint in their development and use of weapons, prevent the spread of nuclear weapons to irresponsible hands, and impose a lasting peace and order upon the world—or else. It is a vision which can boast of a beautiful simplicity.

Aside from how it might feel to have peace imposed on you by two bullies instead of one, there is only one thing wrong with this vision—its question-begging fallacy. The question it begs is the greatest power question of the era of overkill: How can the Russian and American power clusters reach an agreement to suspend hostilities? The *Pax Eborica-Americana* does not answer the question, but only assumes the answer. If the Russians and the Americans were willing to make a pact to divide the world, thereby incidentally putting an end to Russia's own dreams of a single world hegemony, why would they not be equally ready to make a pact to leave others and themselves alone, and swear each to guard the security of the other and learn to live together forever after, whether happily or unhappily? Thus, the assumption which would make a Russian-American combine possible would also make it unnecessary.

There is another wing of the *modus vivendi* school. Stillman and Pfaff, in their *New Politics,* believe that while the nuclear weapons and the cold war have dislocated the relations between the Russians and Americans, the aim now should be to "re-create the conditions of an international balance of power." Erich Fromm also hopes for a *modus vivendi* between the two systems, stressing, however, the need for a controlled disarmament agreement as a condition of its working. I agree heartily that a *modus* must be found, not only between Russia and America but between Russia and China and between America and China. It can be found only, for the time being, in the principle of power equilibrium between the two (or three?) power clusters. But it is in the nature of an equilibrium that it offers a continual temptation to disarrange it to your advantage. Every power equilibrium is thus a *moving* equilibrium; but if that is so, what else then is the definition of the world political war except the struggle to throw off the balance of power before it can be restored at the new level?

Thus, the trouble with a *modus vivendi* as a long-range principle of world order is that it depends upon attaining and maintaining a power balance, and the trouble with the balance-of-power principle is that it is constantly subject to change without notice, and to sudden death. If it swings too far one way or the other, the temptation to restore it by any and every means may prove too strong to be resisted. If one asks further why it might swing too far, the inevitable answer is that the Grand Design of world Communism is not aimed at security through power equilibrium but at world dominance by upsetting the equilibrium. Thus the *modus vivendi* principle and the balance-of-power principle come up against the hard fact of the Grand Design.

In fighting the political war, each side keeps its eye on the balance of power. But beyond it lies another goal, without which there can be no peace—that of collective world security through a code of world law which is backed by world force. To achieve this kind of world law is to move beyond power but not to leave power behind; it is to move beyond an isolated morality, but not to dispense with it; it is to move beyond the nation-state but not to do away with it; it is to move beyond national interest, but to serve the national interest in a new way because of the new circumstances.

It is not the nation-state but the relation between nation-states that is dying. Nor can power or morality or national interest be dispensed with. The world must move beyond the nation-state power principle to a collective-security power principle. Since the classical system of nation-states no longer can serve as a principle of world order, another principle must be found—the power of a world force backed by a collective world will. Within this frame of world order the nation-state can flower as never before, because all the conditions of its flowering are now abundantly available.

This, then, will be man's most perilous assignment: to prevent undreamt destruction in wars starting in unpredictable ways with unpredictable weapons, and to do it by releasing unknown springs of consent, so that in time an unparalleled organization of world will can come into being.

2. *Dialogue Against Death*

IF THE WORLD is to move beyond the nation-state power principle to the collective-security power principle, what will it use for ways and means? Since the danger is unparalleled, must the ways of averting it also be new and unexplored? Not wholly. The war against war has to be a simultaneous three-front affair. One is the disarmament dialogue, carried on mainly between the two big nuclear camps. The second is political negotiation at every level, especially at the crucial trouble points. The third is the building of personnel and precedent for collective action to police aggression.

As I write* the disarmament dialogue has not quite stopped, nor has it quite begun. If this is a paradox, most things about disarmament are paradoxes. The United States made the first proposal for limiting and inspecting atomic weapons in the form of the Lilien-

* In September 1962.

thal-Baruch Plan in 1947, and since then both sides have proposed and counterproposed plans, backtracked, sidetracked, grandstanded, debated, and just plain shammed. There have been talks at Geneva, talks at the UN in New York, talks between the nuclear powers, talks in a larger UN disarmament committee, talks between informal teams of scientists and political experts from both sides. Even when massive testing was resumed by the Russians in 1961 and by the Americans and the Russians together in 1962, neither side dared to take the responsibility for letting the talks break down wholly—which is why I say the dialogue has not quite stopped. Yet it has not really begun in any sense of a will to reach a meeting of minds.

Never in history has so much depended on the success of negotiation, nor has so much technical virtuosity been invested in it. The disarmament business is Big Bureaucracy, employing an army of experts making short-range and long-range studies, specific and general. But on each side it must serve three masters: the military chiefs, who judge every disarmament move by what it does to their place in the weapons race; the foreign-policy chiefs, who judge it by what it does to the balance of power and the political war; and the people themselves, who want peace, however they can get it best.

Of all expert dialogues this one is most hedged about with wariness—not only because everything must be secret, but also because even the seemingly innocent technical matter may be a trap from which disentanglement is hard. It is also, of all diplomatic dialogues, the one most vulnerable to military opinion, pressures and vested interests, even when the agency is, as in the American case, formally independent. In no other aspect of the Age of Overkill is its essential character of trapped irreconcilables so clearly revealed: the military weapons are there, not to be used but to give the nation or power cluster advantage in the political war; but in the process of disarming, in essence a process for political decision, the military impact is paramount. Thus, the military is necessarily politicized, the political constantly militarized. Thus the dialectic of death between a megaton diplomacy and disarmament decisions in which the defense chiefs are the puppeteers.

Whether this dialectic can be broken will depend largely upon three factors—coverage, inspection and trust. On coverage, the Russians took high ground with Khrushchev's sweeping proposal for total disarmament, which won him a resounding political-warfare victory. Eisenhower blundered in his wary and halting response. Kennedy corrected the blunder and has kept asking for immediate talks on total nuclear disarmament, with progress on disarmament and inspection going hand in hand, as suggested by the informal meeting of the Pugwash group of American and Russian nuclear experts in Moscow in December 1960.

Total disarmament before inspection will have consequences for the relative position of the two power clusters in the political war. The Russians and Chinese have, as it were, an inside track on insurrectionary and guerrilla warfare, with their world network of linked parties for conspiracy, agitation and underground activity. They can use their political weapons for stirring up trouble in widely removed areas, from Laos and South Vietnam to Cuba, Ecuador and Brazil. They need not export either their own soldiers or their own weapons; the guerrillas can always be organized on the spot with some leadership by professionals. America, Britain and France, on the other hand, must export weapons, and sometimes even soldiers, to keep another part of the political map from being annexed by the hostile power cluster. If they gave up all arms and armies—ships, planes, and the rest—they could no longer offer an umbrella of protection, whether nuclear or conventional, against Communist encroachment. The Communist risk might seem just as great, because there would no longer be Russian tanks to move against a national liberation movement in one of the satellites, as happened in Hungary. But, obviously, the Russians would never agree to disarming the "People's Police" within their satellites, and while not always reliable they would be a considerable insurance against insurrection.

We must ask, What is the specific danger and what is the remedy for that danger? The danger does not lie in armies and armaments as such (the world has survived them for centuries), but in nuclear weapons, their carriers and their manufacture. Those are what must be banned, under adequate safeguards. To ban all arms and armies is to make more trouble than you mend by the additional coverage, for it leaves at least half the world jittery about the use of actual violence in the other half, in the crevices of the agreement. It might also mean that, in the absence of armies, the nations with the largest mass of manpower and the will to use it, like China, could overwhelm the less populous nations whose higher industrial development would be useless in defending them. If there were an outlawry of aggressive war in any form, enforced by an international authority, a good deal of what is dangerous about total disarmament could be remedied. In that event, however, there would be no great danger in retaining conventional weapons anyway, for immediate defense and internal order.

The problems of inspection and trust are closely related. Even if trust existed, inspection would still be necessary, as is true in the internal legal system of a nation. But the absence of trust makes inspection at once difficult and imperative. A national leadership may take calculated risks on many things, but not on something where treachery could mean the life and death of a nation.

It is an interesting question, why the Communists are so reluctant to accept effective inspection. Very largely it is because Russia and China form the heartland of a potential world dominion, and the very vastness of their expanse and its relative impenetrability by spies gives them an advantage of secrecy which the West European and American countries, open to every random eye, do not possess. Why should they surrender it? It may also be that when regimes have lived on secrecy for almost a half century and have kept their people alert by the myth of capitalist encirclement, it is hard for them to give up their accepted stance. Along with the fear of spying eyes, there is also a fear of the infection of the people by alien ideas. A closed society is what it is because it is closed and resists being opened for whatever purpose.

The best chance of developing trust as well as of getting controlled disarmament is to start with some concrete steps and go on at a steady gradual pace, having the degree and tightness of inspection increase with every new step in disarmament. A single failure, even repeated failures, need not lead to despair—only to greater caution. The method itself is a sound one, like the use of first-aid amateur surgery in a life-and-death emergency, for a quite simple reason: no other method is available. The two armed camps will have to start with confidence-building measures in disarming, because the alternative is for both to die.

For those who regard disarmament as a cure-all for the world's ills there is a simplicity about it which few other measures possess: since the world's danger comes from arms, get rid of the arms. Alas, the problem is not so simple. Hans Morgenthau has put the difficulty well: "Men do not fight because they have arms. They have arms because they deem it necessary to fight." If you do not remove the causes and occasions for fighting, it solves little to give up the arms themselves. Even if both sides gave up their arms tomorrow, if the need came the cunning of hand and brain which brought the weapons into being to start with could breed them again. "We have eaten of the fruit of the tree of evil," an Indian scientist told me, "and we shall carry the knowledge of it wherever we go." The greatest creativeness our age demands is not in fashioning weapons nor even in contriving ways by which they might be given up, but in persuading the commanding elites of both systems that they have less to fear from halting the weapons race than from letting it continue.

There is a school which believes this can be accomplished only by the infection of example, and that if the American government were to take a number of concrete actions in giving up military or political advantages it would set in motion a responsive course of action from the other side. It is what Charles Osgood calls "graduated unilateral disengagement," and it goes beyond nuclear weapons to the whole psychological context of the arms-fear spiral. Its dynamics would seem to turn on the idea of retaliatory goodness, both out of an awakened sense of inner shame (as with the Christian psychology of meekness to evoke countermeekness) and out of a contest for the world's good will. Unfortunately, as with Gandhism and nuclear unilateralism, this takes account neither of the reality of the Grand Design nor of the calculated unsentimentality of the personality structure to which Communism has sought to adhere. Possibly, if the Communist elite felt there was little hope for the success of the Grand Design, and if it were shaken in its efforts to build Communist man, it might respond to the campaign of goodness; but almost certainly, under the conditions of looming triumph, it would regard such moves on the free-world side as simply a confession of weakness or a psychic trap and would only move in on the kill.

In a debate between two American scientists, Leo Szilard and Edward Teller, each indicted the doctrine of the other as possibly leading to a paralysis of will. Teller spoke of "irresponsible trust" of the Communist leaders, and Szilard answered that there could be "irresponsible mistrust" as well. Each was right, but it would be hard to cite any Russian spokesmen who could be accused of paralyzing trust of American intentions, except in the view of the Chinese-Albanian axis. There must be trust in world affairs as there must be hope, if men are not to abdicate the survival effort wholly. There can be a paralyzing mistrust as there can be a paralyzing despair. But within any realistic appraisal of the Communist mentality and ethos, the trust and hope must take the form of a belief that the Communist elite may follow a more, rather than a less, enlightened self-interest.

Within this frame, and given the conditions of the world political war, the best hope is not for universal and total disarmament tomorrow or the next day, but for a dialogue tomorrow and the next day about how to achieve universal and total *nuclear* disarmament in time, and how to take the immediate arms-control steps toward that goal. The assumption behind this species of trust and hope is that the Communist leaders are torn between their Grand Design and the prevailing great fear of apocalyptic destruction, and that if they believe arms control will buy them time for carrying on indefinitely the political war they are equipped to win, they will accept an earnest part in this dialogue against death. This much trust, on the basis of wary self-interest on both sides, may not be *much* trust, but it will have to do for a time. The same goes for hope. And in time there may develop even the requisite trust and hope for an acceptance of a frame of collective policing to insure a continuance of legitimate political rivalry without nuclear aggression or accident.

3. Negotiation Without Illusions

THERE IS another phase of the dialogue against death—that of political negotiation. The two are interdependent, since the ending of either would reach to the deepest sources of mistrust and irrationality on both sides and spur the ending of the other. "If we can't trust them to make or hold to agreements on our territorial and political quarrels," the Americans (or the Russians) may say, "how can we expect them to make or hold to agreements on arms control, or on anything?"

A theory of trust is incomplete unless it is supplemented by a theory of communication. Unless communication is open, there can be no transmission, from one power center or power system to the others, either of what is needed to make deterrence deter or to build mutual trust. It is not only the hostilities of the weapons spiral and the political war which tend to close up communication. It is true even between friendly peoples who carry on their minds the "mental scratches" distorting the actual images that might otherwise come through, and who replace them with conditioned ones. The very walls that enclose a civilization, giving it identity, also shut it off from others, and shut others off from it. In vast polyglot countries, like India, often with a heavy bureaucratic load at the center, this is true even of internal communications and internal walls. How much truer is it of peoples between whom an initial hostility and a continuing rivalry exist!

I do not mean to treat this as if it were wholly a problem in semantics, as if the removal of verbal confusions and blockages would cause the hostilities to dissolve. There are real substantive clashes of interest involved in the world struggle, but why should they be made worse by the breakdown of communication? Similarly, at the other end of the tender-and-tough-mindedness scale, I am aware that conflict has its uses, in clarifying choices and evoking the requisite *élan* to make them. Yet the more serious problem today is not atrophy but hypertrophy of conflict. The virtues of conflict come from the direction of the challenge and spur they offer, whereas the present conflicts present the possibility of a world so desolated that no challenges will be able to operate. I know that communication between political and military enemies is at best hard to achieve, but the effort must be made. I suppose that there are, as Max Ascoli has suggested, "negotiationmongers" as well as warmongers. But if the negotiation dialogue breaks down wholly, what is left of trust, hope, and possibility for peace?

The real choice is not between negotiation and nonnegotiation but between illusioned and relatively illusionless negotiation. A man who, using the freedom of free-world expression, cries in and out of season that every problem must be negotiated, regardless of terms, timing, mood, and tensions between the allies within the free world, is doing almost as great a disservice as one who cries day after day that no problem can or should be negotiated. They have both lost the quality of prudent judgment and the faculty of discrimination. President Kennedy has come closer to the heart of the matter in saying, "We shall always feel free to negotiate, but we shall never negotiate freedom," which in turn was a variation on his Inaugural sentence, "We shall never negotiate out of fear, but we shall never fear to negotiate." These were formula answers, of course, both to those (a minority in America, but one with psychic intensity) who regard all negotiation with Communism as "appeasement," and to those (in other parts of the free world, and among the neutrals, but also in America) who cling to the belief that the "cold-war mentality" prevents America from negotiating at all.

These are questions of intellectual maneuver, and I am less interested in them than in the question of effective negotiations. To be effective, negotiations must be held in an atmosphere without illusions on either side, they must generate trust in the sense of suspending total disbelief by appealing to enlightened self-interest, they must be held on every level, and they must use international agencies like the UN, both for drawing the rest of the world into the great-power agreements and for furnishing the frame in which these can be nailed down.

Can these imperatives be in any degree fulfilled? When they are put in a moderate way, as I have tried to do, I don't see why they should not. The leaders of both the major power clusters are tough-minded men, accustomed to struggles of maneuver and persuasion inside their own parties and nations; they have been brought up in the school of negotiation. Both Khrushchev and Kennedy have shown a bent for getting free of red tape and hierarchy, and finding ways of addressing themselves to each other and sometimes even over each other's head to the people on the other side. Khrushchev has been notably without tender-minded illusions about America and the free world, although he is still saddled with the equally dangerous illusions—taken from a mechanical Marxism—that America is governed by its big businessmen, and that its internal contradictions will make it an easy prey. Kennedy's illusions have tended to be not those of a too-rigid dogma, but those of wishfulness about specific desired events which he had never thought through within a rigorous-enough frame of doctrine. But he has had to learn in the school of experience, and he is ready for a fruitful negotiation dialogue which takes account both of the Grand Design and the Communist ethos, as well as the internal problems of the free-world power cluster.

Given a realistic confrontation, what can be relied on to bring about agreements? Mainly the self-interest arising from the intangibles in the political war and from fear of the tangibles. At the start of 1962 the central friction points between America and Russia were four: the Laos-South Vietnam area, where the stakes were not only those countries but the whole of Southeast Asia; the chaotic areas of Africa, whether the Congo today or Angola tomorrow, and their relation to UN moderating efforts; thirdly, Berlin, as both symbol and handle of a still potentially unstable power-balance in Europe; fourthly, Castro's Cuba, which had become a Russian sphere within a free-world power cluster, and which was being used by both Castro and the Communists as a bridgehead for neutralizing Latin America.

I call them "crucial points" because upon them depends the power balance of a whole area or even continent, and they can thus be decisive for how the political war is going and how the world is going. It is interesting to note that in all four cases the heat comes from the Soviet cluster, not from the free world. It is interesting, too, that except for the case of Berlin each has proved an arena for the classic Soviet tactics in the political war—massively organized propaganda on a world scale; guerrilla warfare, and a Soviet airlift of men and supplies (in Cuba's case a heavy economic and military investment) to aid the military posture; and infiltration into the educated elites in order to overthrow a regime and secure one closer to the heart's desire.

In all these conflicts, a negotiation dialogue has a number of healthy functions. It clarifies for each side how high the stakes are for the other, and how earnestly it regards them, without forcing either of them to the dangerous point of sending battleships and planes or moving armies. It explores what concessions each is willing to make. It is thus a test both of the will to fight and of the will not to fight. Most of all, after moves have been taken—as in the case of American and Russian tanks confronting each other across a hundred yards at "Checkpoint Charlie" at the Friedrichstrasse gate —which are too close to brinkmanship, each side is enabled to move away from the brink without loss of face. We live constantly on the edge of history. The question for political leaders is, at times, how close to the edge they can come without disaster; but, once the edge is reached, the question is how far from the edge they can get, and how fast, and with how much grace and face. That is where negotiation comes in. It is part of the self-interest in the whole dialogue. It gives scope to what Khrushchev, speaking of Berlin, once called "the recognition of our grandeur." It allows the leader to talk tough, for the benefit of his image with his people and perhaps his self-image. But it also allows him to retreat with some gains.

Note that I say *some* gains. Neither side can win if the negotiations are on some impasse issue. Once a problem has reached the point of needing resolution by the top leaders, it is beyond a hundred-per-cent victory for either. To put it in the now too-fashionable language of games theory: nuclear war today is, as Thomas Schelling has shown, a game in which neither side can win; negotiation to prevent war becomes a game in which each must win something, but neither can win the whole stake. This again is a matter not of good will but of self-interest.

Whoever carries on such negotiations will have to be a diplomat and must be called one, whether he be career officer, head of mission, technical adviser or President. There has been much unfruitful discussion about the merits of traditional diplomacy as against "summitry." Something interesting is happening to the emerging diplomat. The days of the giants who presided over the classical system of world politics—men like Talleyrand, Disraeli, Bismarck—are past, and the diplomat has had to change. When he operates through traditional channels, he must master a range of technical knowledge unknown to his forerunners and be prepared for hardships and dangers. There was a period when the indictment, made in *The Ugly American,* of the ignorant, spineless, bewildered American diplomatic corps, living in an enclave of provincialism, stuck like a burr and was as uncomfortable. But increasingly America has been prodded into sending abroad diplomats who are good technicians, and technicians who have become good diplomats, both of them compelled into a new awareness and having to learn strange languages and outlandish cultures.

Another thing has happened as well: the heads of state have had to become, as Lord Bryce once described Theodore Roosevelt, a "combination of St. George and St. Vitus." They must show a crusading fervor, whether for Communism or for freedom or for national self-determination, and their goings and comings, their flittings and perchings, are reminiscent of the dance of St. Vitus. Where America once had the itinerant preacher, doctor and teacher, it now has the itinerant statesman, and other heads of state are similarly unremitting. One wonders why they do it, why this febrile pace, these long jet hops, these inedible banquets and incredible parades, these unending talks that are inevitably countered by other talks, these crowded days and sleepless nights, these joint communiqués that say nothing, and these tired eyes and furrowed faces that say everything? The reason is that they can't help it; the head of state has become a symbol of the political war, but—since nuclear war is so dangerous—he also must take personal charge of negotiations on issues that might lead to it. The age of negotiation leads inevitably to summitry, and the age of summitry is necessarily also an age of consultation preceding and following the summit.

There are, of course, perils in summitry, as the collapse of the Paris summit showed in 1960. I am not speaking only of the idiocy of a too-protracted U-2 surveillance followed by total confession, but of more integral dangers. As the hour of confrontation approaches, it sends tremors through the whole power cluster, especially of the free world, which is more sensitive to tremors, but also of the Communist world. Every interest becomes fearful of being betrayed. As the public debate goes on, the issues get sharper than they need be. There is always also the chance that the top leaders, amateurs at everything except leadership, may ignore something of vital moment to a subordinate who knows everything about something. But there are two incomparable advantages to summitry—the personal touch in the meeting of minds, and the widened frame of perspective. When men who have dealt with each other only at several removes can sit across the table for some time, they take each other's measure, and if there is any chance for a meeting of minds this is it. As for perspective, this is a meeting not of technicians or specialists, but of generalists. The experts have a mastery of their expertise, but the political leaders have a consciousness of the total world as frame, and a responsibility for world peace. The crucial weaknesses of summitry are the weaknesses also of a concert of powers, namely, that a few men who divide the world power can also decide the world destiny. The fact is that this is the era of the "nuclear super powers." Until a genuine frame of collective world will is shaped, there is no alternative to the effort to get a meeting of minds by negotiation between them.

In one important sense the nuclear powers are limited: they are having to all but give up the traditional diplomatic ultimate weapon, that of the credible threat of war. In the drive for the power they don't dare use, they are at times forced to assume positions they cannot maintain without using the inept violence they must abstain from using. This gives the secondary and tertiary nations, especially in the UN, an interstitial role in the world power structure they would not otherwise have.

I see no need for choosing between traditional versus summit diplomacy. They are both necessary, and so is UN mediation and debate as a form of negotiation. Each has its time and function, and a productive alternation between them is one of the things the diplomat-leaders must master. What must be avoided is so much delay and build-up toward the summit that it becomes in itself the point of convergence for every pressure, and an arena in which the protagonists become champions rather than reflective leaders meeting for a settlement. If this can be avoided, the arts of summitry can clear away enough of the political issues to give the disarmament dialogue a chance, and that in turn may be able to ease the tensions which lead to one political impasse after another.

I see both the disarmament dialogue and the political dialogue as ways of buying time. But something must be done with that time.

One way to use it is in building a world body like the UN, relatively neutral and detached, which can serve as the core for an eventual collective world will.

4. The New Federalists

MAN, WROTE ROUSSEAU IN *Émile*, is born not once but twice: the first time when he comes into existence, the second when he comes into life. Rousseau was of course speaking of the development of the frame of life's meaning which we call an "education." This is true in a different sense of power systems as well. The Communist power system came into existence in 1917 (in Russia) and 1949 (in China), but it is now growing into an ordered frame of relations in Russia and Eastern Europe and is just beginning to grow into such an ordered frame in China. The free world, especially in Europe and the Americas, came into existence as a power system during and after World War II; it is now beginning to reach a fuller consciousness of its intent and strength, and to shape a frame of constitutional order.

A good deal of the world's future will be contained in the question of how effectively the two systems organize their internal relations both in the struggle of the political war and in the struggle for world peace. This is more than a question of their resources and power, with which I have been concerned earlier.* Each will need, for survival, not only a power frame but also a constitutional frame, and with it a cultural-emotional cement to act as a cohesive element. It may well prove that in the process of shaping these frames of order for themselves the two antagonist systems will (if they do not destroy themselves in the meantime) clear away some of the present obstructions to a more far-reaching world constitutional frame.

I have already discussed some aspects of the rift inside the Communist power cluster, especially between Russia and Hungary and between Russia and China, and the tensions inside the free world power cluster, between America and France and also between America and its Latin-American neighbors. But it is far more important to inquire what affirmative efforts are being made and can be made within both systems to resolve their problems of unity and diversity and to build comprehensive constitutional systems.

For the time has come when the political war needs something

* See Chapter II above, "Power Center and Power Cluster."

more than day-to-day improvisations and "contingency plans," more even than long-range projections of foreign policy planning. In speaking of a constitutional frame, I do not of course mean a written one but an operative one, although the latter is likely to find formal expression in treaties, conferences, and resolutions. There was a NATO Treaty, but without the collective will to defense as a living reality it would mean little. There was a Rome Treaty of 1957, marking a crucial stage in the progress toward a European Common Market, but without the living reality of operative understanding between the older and newer member states since 1957 this treaty would mean little.

This is one area in which the Communist power system has allowed the free-world system to take the initiative, and—especially in the case of Europe—has had to content itself with responding to free-world actions. The collapse of the Comintern, which was at once overambitious and too cynically an instrument of Russian policy, left a constitutional vacuum in the Communist camp which the short-lived substitute Cominform could not fill. The Russian response to the Marshall Plan was almost schizoid in its ambivalence, although the response to the military NATO through the military Warsaw Pact was a decisive one. The COMECON (Council for Economic Mutual Aid), formed at the end of the 1940s, was largely dormant in the 1950s but has recently been revived as a parallel structure to the Common Market. Yet its actions hitherto have been halting and feeble. At present writing the Soviet leaders show some of the same ambivalence in meeting the Common Market that they showed earlier in meeting the Marshall Plan.

Despite the importance of Asia, Africa, and Latin America in the overall political war, Europe has proved the great battleground on which the struggle of the two systems for a constitutional order is being fought out. It is there that the Marshall Plan, the Coal and Steel Community, the Common Market, and the plans for a federated United States of Europe have taken shape. It is in Europe that the Russians had to meet their early tests of unity and flexibility in their international systems—the tests in Yugoslavia, East Germany, Hungary and Poland. These formed a scarring ordeal for the Soviet leaders and furnished the school in which they learned some bitter lessons about how not to keep an ideological empire in order. Yugoslavia confronted Stalin with the problem of controlling heretical diversity, and his resolution through cajolery and terror proved a dismal failure. The East German strikes were met by repression, but they never became more than a form of economic protest, and they fell short of doctrinal diversity. The "National Communist" heresy of Prime Minister Nagy of the rebellious Hungarian regime posed a more serious problem, and was met at first by temporizing and in the end by bloody repression. The Polish heresy of Gomulka was resolved by a mixed formula of relative autonomy on domestic issues and orthodoxy on issues of foreign policy. This is likely to be the formula which Khrushchev and his successors will use in the years ahead, since it is the only one that will work. The distance between the Yugoslav and Polish solutions measures the range of discipline and tolerance within the Communist international system.

The case of the conflict with Chinese communism involves problems that were not posed in the European cases. For the Chinese commanding elite has not been content merely with making a bid for an independent ideological stance, nor even for a national communism within the larger frame of Communist world power. In actuality it has been a rival bid for leadership of the total world Communist camp. The Polish solution, satisfactory as it has proved in Europe, is thus not adequate for the case of China. Yet it would be a mistaken hope of the free-world system if it counted upon a permanent cleavage between Russia and China. As Z. K. Brzezinski has put it, it is hard to "promote heresy in a church to which one does not belong." There is a kind of self-sealing process at work in the ideological conflicts within a doctrinal system like that of world communism, which is reluctant to give the common enemy a chance to exploit its differences of principle and power and tends therefore to close up cleavages wherever possible on the ground of overall survival policy. In the event of an actual power showdown between the Communist and free-world power systems, there is no question that Russia and China would stand together. The real question is whether their sense of common danger will lead them not only to hide their problems from the world and perhaps even reach some temporary modus vivendi, but actually to build a set of constitutional rules which will resolve future problems as well. This kind of constitutional structure, as between the claims of Russia and China, seems an unlikely one in the calculable future.

The real difficulty lies in the relation between the commitment to expansionism and the commitment to a one-party commanding elite at home. Such a commanding elite can justify the absolutism of its power, and the sacrifices it calls upon the people to make, only by an appeal to the expansion of its power. To be sure it is always possible to speak vaguely in terms of a common ideal of world communism. But what is really at stake is not only whether world

.communism will expand in its power, but specifically which nation
and which commanding elite will be the agent for that expansion.
This is one of the difficulties with seeking historical parallels as
modern instances. Brzezinski's* interesting comparison between the
effort of the Papacy in the seventeenth century to contain and control Jansenism as a deviant form of universal Catholicism is highly
suggestive, yet one misses in it the stakes of world power which are
involved in the Sino-Russian conflict. I do not say that there was no
power involved in the struggle against Jansenism, especially since it
identified itself with the Gallic sense of independence; but there
were no problems of survival as against a rival political power system, as is true now in the confrontation of the Communist world
and the free world.

Even more important is the question of whether the Communist
system can develop, in the relations between member states, the
kind of flexibility and sophistication which it tends to practice at
home. The case of Russia, in its shift from Stalin's ruthlessness to
Khrushchev's sophistication, is very much in point. But one must
note that the new Russian tactic toward deviant doctrinal claims on
the part of other members of the Communist cluster has carried
along with it a weakening of the police-state system inside of Russia and, even more, an erosion of doctrinal commitment both inside
and outside of Russia. This is the great dilemma of world communism. If it is doctrinally rigid it runs the danger of power splits
along national lines. If it is doctrinally flexible and underplays the
importance of orthodoxy in dogma, it runs the danger of ideological
erosion. The Russian leaders seem to have chosen the second danger
rather than the first. It was the only sensible choice to be made if
there was to be any hope of a constitutional frame for the Communist world system.

Let us be very clear about it: It is such a world system, and not
simply a temporary collection of nation-states with similar interests.
In a painstaking analysis George Modelski† has spelled out the tests
of an "international system" and has concluded that communism

---

* See his article, "Deviation Control: A Study in the Dynamics of Doctrinal
Conflict," *American Political Science Review*, Vol. 56 (March 1962), pp. 5-22. For
what is easily the most comprehensive discussion of the general problems of di-
versity and cohesiveness in the Communist world system, see his *The Soviet
Bloc: Unity and Conflict* (Rev. Ed. 1961), especially the epilogue on "The Sino-
Soviet Dispute" and Appendix One on "The Organization of the Communist
Camp."

† See his provocative study, *The Communist International System*, Research
Monograph No. 9, Princeton University Center of International Studies (1960).

fits them. I would very strongly agree that it is at present more than an alliance or a bloc, but an incipient form of world organization, which the Communist commanding elite hope to complete as quickly as possible. It is interesting that the Communists themselves call it a "world Socialist system," and that the recent Czechoslovak constitution states formally that "the Czechoslovakian Republic belongs to the world Socialist system."

The nub difficulty in any effort to shape a constitutional frame for world power lies in harnessing ideological discipline and unity of action with the passion of nationalism and the doctrine of national sovereignty. If either the free world or the Communist world succeeds in doing this on a grand scale—assuming the victory of one or the other in the political war—it would mark the first such successful effort in history. For the great empires of the past *were* empires—that is to say, they operated out of a power center, with a centralized administration of provinces and satrapies; and the Universalist church of Christendom had its heyday before the rise of the nation-state and of nationalism.

Given this almost wholly new task, the free-world system stands a better chance than the Communist system of resolving it, since it has a more intrinsic respect for national diversity and less commitment to doctrinal conformity. The recent tensions between America and several of its European partner-nations, notably the French and the Germans, have been in part an expression of this valuing of nationalism on both sides. In the history of liberal-democratic thought, which paralleled the growth of the modern nation-state, there developed alongside of nationalism a basic respect for individual and national diversities. More absolutist in temper than the liberal-democratic tradition, the Communist system began with the advantage of a stronger appeal to those who were looking for a faith to die and live by, but also with a handicap in the long-range resolution of the problems of unity and autonomy.

Curiously, each of the systems made the same initial mistake by its oversimplification of the importance of the economic theme. Much of America's strategy in the political war, when faced by national resistances, operated on the premise that you can always buy compliance, if not affection, by grants of military and economic aid. The new reliance of American policy on such autonomous efforts as the European Common Market, while still embodying a basic economic approach, is a far subtler one, with its emphasis on self-help and on mutuality of obligation and gain. The Communists under Stalin, in their haste to build a base rapidly for Russian industrial and military power, practiced a crude exploitation of the industrial resources and manpower of their satellites. The Khrushchev regime has had to move away from this, but the memory of it is a burdensome heritage for any common planning for trade and production in the Communist camp which carries binding obligations with it.

The logical next step in the shaping of a Communist world system is the integration, if not yet the outright fusion, of the various national economic plans of the member states. This is simply an extension of the basic inner drive toward planning which forms the logic of Communist growth and expansion. Yet such a step would almost inevitably awaken fears that the Russians, at their power center, would use the overall world plan as a way of giving advantage to their own industries and their own plan at the expense of the weaker nations. Russia will somehow have to win the confidence of its sister nations in the Communist power system exactly in this area of economic egalitarianism, where its accusations against the Capitalist democracies have been most damning. Failing that, it will have to abandon the idea of overall planning and accept a system of its own patterned after the European Common Market, where the commitments lie mainly in the trade area and each national economy is left to make its own adjustments in its own way.

While the Common Market does not call for integrated planning, and while it uses indirect strategies to reach its purpose, it is nevertheless a Grand Design. By removing tariffs, subsidies and cartels which have been obstacles to the free flow of goods and raw materials—and even of manpower—it not only allows each economy to focus on what it can produce best: it also serves, in the popular mind, to link the idea of accepting inroads into national sovereignty with the idea of greater prosperity. If this linkage gets firmly established in the minds of Europeans, it will be an important first step toward a collective world will, since people may in time come to associate peace as well as prosperity with the inevitable inroads into national sovereignty. I am suggesting that what counts about sovereignty is not the question of its untrammeled freedom but the question of its equality. The European experience has already shown that nations will accept limits upon their theoretically unlimited power of national decision if these limits are equally imposed upon all. It is inequity that is galling, not limits in themselves. To give up an academic freedom of action in order to gain a more authentic freedom of economic and social growth within a frame of world peace is a gain which must in time recommend itself to people of every national conditioning.

The European experience has again shown that national hatreds, carrying over from past wars and rivalries, can be muted just as they can be intensified, depending upon the purposes to be served. The Russians have used and strengthened the anti-German feelings of their people—and also of the Poles and other East European peoples—in order to solidify the common psychological front against America, and not only against Germany. The Americans in turn have used the fear of Chinese Communist extremism and vaguely of Chinese "hordes," to solidify the free-world feeling not only against China but against Russia. The Chinese in turn have played upon the anti-American feelings of their people not only in their struggle with the free world but also with Russia. Yet one must also note that France and Germany, who have been the most deeply chauvinist traditional enemies, have managed to play down their historic hostility on both sides, mainly because de Gaulle and Adenauer each felt that it was in the interest of his country to do so. Inevitably the cleavage between Great Britain and the European continent will heal as the logic of economic interest for each of them dictates such a healing.

If there is an escalation principle in modern warfare, as I have noted earlier, there may also be an escalation principle as applied to European unity. The European leaders, like Jean Monnet, were careful to start with very specific projects like the Coal and Steel Community. They escalated this into a Common Market, and they are in process of overcoming the Six's and Seven's. In the face of this trend it is hard to conceive of the continuance of NATO in its old form; there is bound to be an autonomous system of military defense paralleling the system of economic welfare. The next logical step is that of a United States of Europe, which is already being discussed. In fact, Walter Hallstein, the President of the European Commission, has gone to the heart of the matter in saying that "our Economic Community already contains pronounced political features. These are evident in all the regulations of a constitutional nature. . . . We should not forget that the main thing pooled by the Rome Treaty was not the "economies" of our nations . . . but the economic policies of the participating countries. In other words, it is not the citizens who are making a sacrifice to the Community . . . but the Governments. . . . The significance of our Community lies in this political aspect." This accents the crucial fact that the steps taken toward economic unity are in themselves deeply political, and that they must lead—if they are to be completed—to an overall effort at a new constitutional structure for Europe which will parallel the effort of the American states in 1789. Beyond this prospect lies still another—that of an Atlantic Federation linking a United States of Europe with a United States of America, especially on basic economic policies and foreign policies. If the United States can achieve this, the way will be opened toward a similar linkage with whatever autonomous federal organization can emerge from the OAS in Latin America.

These are far vistas, and they are bound to be called Utopian, yet they are nonetheless in the realm of possibility. The people who are concerned with them now are in a deep sense the new Federalists. From the standpoint of the Communist world, which is working away at its own problems of constitutional structure, there must be a similar group which is undergoing the travail of innovating ideas and institutions.

Yet the analogy with the American experience in 1789, which has been much emphasized in some of the commentaries on both sides of the Atlantic, is not a complete one. For Madison and Hamilton and the other shaping minds of the Constitutional Convention, the problem was to find the best form of constitutional relations between states relatively unthreatened by destructive war and with a common—whatever their local divergences—cultural base. The major concern of the Federalists was how to achieve effective government while preventing internal tyranny from developing. But in the case of the new Federalists, both within the free world and the Communist systems, the major concern is to form a constitutional structure that will insure at once survival and victory while avoiding a destructive nuclear war. Nor does the common cultural base exist for them, as it did for the American states in 1789. It would be as foolish to ignore these differences between the framers of the American Constitution and those who are seeking to build new federal structures today as it would be to ignore the underlying parallel. For in each case there is a problem of survival, of effective government, and of innovating institutions.

Something should be added that goes beyond economic plans and political frames of unity. I mentioned it earlier when I spoke of a cohesive cement which every constitutional system needs if it is to be a living entity. What Justice Holmes called the "inarticulate major premise" applies in the case of cultural cohesion. If there is in fact an entity that can be called "Western civilization," then its reality lies not in what men consciously believe but in what they take on faith without examining their own belief. The revolutionary effect of Marxism as an intellectual and emotional movement was to call into question these unexamined major premises. What holds the Marxist system of world power together today, along with its apparatus of force, is the fact that the young men in every Communist party have developed a set of such unexamined premises.

One of the core problems in developing a free-world constitutional system is to find some cement of cohesion which goes beyond the now hackneyed slogans of fighting for the survival of freedom. In confronting this task the great obstacle is the "culturalist" one —that is to say, the fact of existing cultural divergences which mean that each culture has a different set of unexamined major premises. The difficulty is less in the case of an Atlantic partnership than it would be if the United States were to attempt the same kind of partnership with the Latin-American states, since the gap between the Spanish-Indian tradition of those states and the polyglot culture of the United States is greater than the gap between Europe and America.

It would be unwary however to assume that there is no culturalist problem even within Europe itself in moving toward a United States of Europe. The Europe of Spain and Portugal, of Great Britain, of the Mediterranean countries, of Turkey, of the Scandinavian countries, of such marginal Iron Curtain countries as Hungary and Poland, of France, of Germany—these are separate historic entities which have developed cultural traditions of their own that will not easily be fused into a collective one. The harsh test of European unity will come when the more obvious gains to be achieved by a Common Market have already been taken and further unification runs into cultural resistances. It will be one of the tasks of the Europeans themselves to explore, both in their history and in their present situation, whatever common cultural elements there are which they can rely upon when such tests approach. It may well be that they will discover the core of something that has been a common European civilization, and can become even more so. "Why did the Middle Ages and the Renaissance," asks Karl Mannheim, "produce entirely different types of man?" What Mannheim suggests here is that, whatever the cultural divergences between the European peoples, there are facts and trends about a historic epic which corrode divergences and produce a common mood and spirit. One of the great questions of our time is whether a new European man can develop—and perhaps a new transatlantic man, and a new Communist man—to bridge the gulf between the present danger and some constitutional world frame that lies ahead.

5. UN: The Dynamism of the Order Principle

IF THE CHANGES I have suggested are to be achieved, the United Nations, which began as a concert of the Great Powers and has become the forum for the new small nations, must move from its history as an international agency to a new role as a transnational one. The UN, despite its ordeal as an actual organization, has come painfully to embody an idea of greater potential importance for a viable world than any other idea of our time. It is the idea of a world interest as distinct from national interests, of a world conscience as distinct from national honor or sensibility, of a world sovereignty and law as distinct from national sovereignties and legal systems, and finally, of a world policing and executive body limited to the tasks of preventing aggressive warfare and serving transnational welfare and cultural needs.

When it was first formed at San Francisco, amidst universal skepticism, the UN was in one sense a triumph of order over chaos and of reason over unreason. After Wilson's shattered dream of a League of Nations, Franklin Roosevelt was certain of his diagnosis in ascribing the League's failure to the disagreements among the Great Powers, and Stalin had his own reasons for agreeing. The United Nations was to be what the name suggested: a group of nations that did not give up their sovereignty, and were to be united for ends that did not conflict with the vital interests of any of the Great Powers. The conclusion was that it would work as long as the Great Powers avoided imposing the will of the new body upon any of their members. The Assembly became largely a thing of rhetoric, an unglorified "parliament of man"; the Secretary General was to run the technical work of the functionaries but make no executive decisions; the crucial agency was the Security Council, where the great powers had permanent seats, and each had a veto power to preclude hurt to its vital interests.

Then came the three great events under whose intense heat the UN idea was twisted into strange shapes to fit the mold of the age. One was the new weapons, the second was the new continents, the third was the political war. The new weapons, and the shadow they cast upon the world, gave the UN the heavy task of finding a frame of world order before their use would decimate man; but the weapons for the first time also offered a means of world policing which, if it were once adopted, would free an international army from the burden of mass recruiting and prolonged fighting. The nationalist revolutions shifted the axis of concern and decision in the UN from Europe to Asia and Africa; the nation-state explosion proved also to be a UN explosion. With the entry of scores of new nations in a few brief years, they came not only to dominate the Assembly voting but to set the intellectual and emotional climate of the UN. The Assembly meetings and the Delegates' Lounge became a seismograph of changes in the ideas and feelings of a number of national elites under the impact of events. After the death of Hammarskjöld an Asian, U Thant, was chosen Secretary General, and the only serious competitor was an African Moslem, Mongi Slim, who became Assembly President. Thus, the locus of majority decision, if not of power, moved steadily eastward and southward.

The political war, especially in its intense cold-war phase, turned the UN into an arena of conflict and made it the target of both world power clusters as they struggled to turn it to their uses. Before the nation-state explosion the United States started with a numerical advantage in the voting, and so tough-minded a geopolitical thinker as Nicholas Spykman, who scorned most intangibles in the struggle for the world, was realist enough to see the UN as one of the free world's most important weapons. The doctrine of a militant UN scored a triumph when (the Russians having made the blunder of being absent from the Security Council) the UN voted to send troops to repel the invasion of South Korea. The action marked the end of a phase in the UN's history. The struggle to get a UN consensus for decision was transferred from the Security Council to the Assembly, where the role of the new African and Asian nations as neutralists transformed a legislative chamber into a massive courtship operation.

In another sense also, this marked the end of a phase for the UN. Although the Korean War was a messy affair, it set a precedent for using the UN dynamically to prevent situations of potential chaos from triggering a world war. Korea was followed by the Suez crisis which, along with the Arab-Israeli war earlier, left a residual deposit of a UN policing operation in the tortured boundary problems of Arabs and Israelis. That in turn was followed by the Congo crisis, in which Secretary General Hammarskjöld played for high stakes, lost his life, and failed in his specific Congo plan—yet gained for humanity at least a glimmer of a hope, in the form of a precedent for preventive action by a UN executive which interprets its mandate flexibly.

If the UN leadership were to wait for crises to arise and run their course before rousing itself to write their epitaph, it would doom the organization to the death-in-life that the League of Nations suffered. The immediate problem is to keep the channels of UN action open so as to anticipate where the great crises will come and minimize their impact. It is the choice between trying to prevent a ship fire and trying to put it out once the boilers have exploded and the hatches are in flames. Khrushchev's *troika* principle, by which the UN Secretariat was to represent the three ideological camps, with the unanimity principle built in, would mean adding a new veto in the Secretariat to the old veto in the Security Council, to paralyze the administrative agency as the deliberative one has been paralyzed.

The heart of the matter lies in the conflict of two conceptions of the UN's functioning. Dag Hammarskjöld, in his clairvoyant and classic Fifth Annual Report to the Assembly, called it a conflict between the "static" principle of conciliating a crisis after it has exploded, and the "dynamic" one of anticipating its growth and coming to meet it. Clearly, the latter was bound to run afoul of the nations which felt they had a monopoly of dynamism and meant to use it in sponsoring conspiratorial action whenever it suited their drive to world power. Hence the shoe-brandishing vendetta of Khrushchev against Hammarskjöld and his principle, setting in motion a series of attacks which debased, as it were, the currency of UN exchanges, introducing a note of violence in language and gesture. And the violence of these explosive passions was in itself a symbol of the fact that man, who had contrived such ingenious modes of mastering the laws of space, had not moved far in mastering the turmoil of his own power drives.

One could make a case for Khrushchev's position. The fact is that the UN Charter had not provided for a real executive. The Secretary General was meant to be an administrator running the show, not an executive with the power of deploying armies in trouble areas over the face of the earth. Khrushchev is in effect asking for a return to the original Roosevelt-Stalin conception of the UN as a gentlemen's agreement among the great powers, each with a veto over the actions of the others.

But what happened in the Congo crisis, as well as at the time of Korea and Suez, was that the UN Charter—viewed as a living constitution, not as a dead mockery of a document—was stretched to meet the world's needs. The Secretary General did not displace either the Assembly or the Security Council as a policy-making (legislative) body; but no group as large as the Assembly, or as torn in many directions as the Security Council, can initiate policies. It is as adviser to the UN policy makers and as an initiator of policy that the Secretary General performs one phase of his function; the other phase lies in the latitude with which broad UN declarations of policy are applied to a situation which could not possibly have been predicted with clarity. For each new situation the existing mandate must be stretched to embrace it; out of each crisis come new insights which the Secretariat must take the initiative in translating into a new tactic, perhaps a new mandate, for the future. This is a creative process in the government of world disorder and order—perhaps the most creative potential governmental development in the world.

This suggests why Dag Hammarskjöld's work was as difficult as it was. He was a pioneer in the still-uncharted arts of fashioning a frame of accepted order within which peace would have a built-in security, instead of having to be sweated for whenever the passions of contending nations threatened war. He had no body of world law to work with. His only chance was to build one as he went along, brick by brick, using each incident as a new case for applying the working principle of peace, and each case as a precedent for the next. This is the method that worked in the history of the Anglo-American common law, without the need for framing a judicial code. The student of the United States Supreme Court decisions knows how important it is to build up a body of judicial opinions, applied to case after case to fit the varying circumstances, which can be subjected to merciless criticism by the professionals and amateurs in constitutional law.

There are bound to be objections to such a world force; they will come from whatever national interest at the time gets a bloody nose from it. At one point it may be the Arabs, at another the Israelis, at one point Tshombe's Katanga, at another Adoula's Congo, at one point the Russians, at another the Western allies. But the UN instrument cannot be ignored. The violence of the Russian attack was best deflated by Adlai Stevenson, saying that when the leader of a member state wanted a place where he could bang his shoe on a desk and get world attention he had to come to the UN. Khrushchev made the mistake of downgrading a symbol which meant much to the leaders of the African nations, with their status hunger and their craving for a world stage on which they would be recognized as equal actors with the old and great names. The UN also furnishes for them, as for others, a school for training diplomats which is unparalleled in the breadth of its exposure and the cross-section character of its experience, but which trains them for the new rather than the old diplomacy. It was therefore a mark of the shortsightedness of the small and unaligned nations, chiefly from Africa and Asia, that they did not stand up to the defense of the UN instrument which had become their greatest reliance and protection against great-power politics. They seemed caught in the enchanted wood, under the spell of the anticolonial slogans which had helped liberate them but could not furnish a frame of world order.

The attitude of the great powers too toward the UN has had an element of blindness. For a time the Western powers felt that the UN was a convenient voting machine in which they almost always managed to get a working majority for their purposes. But with the nation-state explosion and the rise of Left neutralism the axis of UN power has shifted, and the balance of voting power in it is a thin one on either side. This quality of the UN constitutional structure, in giving as much weight to Yemen as to India or France, is what lies behind much of De Gaulle's scorn for it. One can see why it irritates the Russians and the Americans, both, who find themselves having to set aside the power principle for that of persuasion. The Americans have accommodated themselves to the new situation, and while they must sweat to hold their own in the contest for votes, they regard the UN as an indispensable instrument for keeping communication open between the member nations, for negotiating and settling concrete problems, for conducting the world contest of prestige, and for moving beyond power toward some world rule-of-law principle.

The Russians find themselves caught between a fear of accepting the implications of a functioning UN and a fear of the consequences of scuttling it. To have to carry the responsibility for scuttling it would be to alienate marginal and perhaps decisive world opinion; it might also increase the chances of a nuclear war which the Russians would not welcome. The nation-state explosion and the new Left-neutralist and national-socialist trends made the UN a more tolerable fact of life for them, made the voting contest more manageable and the politicial atmosphere of the UN debates more hospitable. But what the Russians found alarming in the current of UN development was exactly the quality that Dag Hammarskjöld found indispensable to its future effectiveness—the conception of it not as a static cluster of procedures but as a dynamic principle of order. For such a principle might well interfere with the Communist use of revolutionary nationalism arising out of the anticolonial movements. Once it became clear that the overkill weapons were not as a practical matter usable, the Russians had to count chiefly on using and fomenting the revolutionary fires in area after area. This was their brand of dynamism, and unless they could use it they might fear for their Grand Design and even for their national security. But the UN in turn could not survive a succession of fires unless it moved to control them early or prevent them by timely action. This was to confront the dynamism of unrest-into-revolution by the counterdynamism of order. It was here that the UN presence in the trouble areas, and the UN instrument as a fact of contemporary history, most troubled the Russians.

As for the Chinese Communists, they had reason to be hostile to an association of nations from which they had been excluded since they came to power; and they could add a touch of bitterness to their essential dogma that the UN is (as the Chinese official organ, *Jenmin Jih Pao* put it) a "voting machine for it to pursue its policies of aggression and war." Moreover, in their contest with the Russian Communists, they found it useful to express their scorn for the bourgeois parliament—still "bourgeois" even though it was a parliament of nations—which the Russians had allowed themselves to get caught in; while the Russians in turn felt impelled to prove to the Communist world that this was not mere parliamentarianism they were engaged in, but the "highest form of class struggle"— which may shed some light on the deliberate violence of Khrushchev's classic assault upon Hammarskjöld in September 1960, and his insistence upon revolutionizing the UN by applying the *troika* principle throughout its Secretariat.

In its present functioning the UN thus suffers from the double disability of being caught in the political war between the great power systems and being caught in the bind of the bitter memories and resentments of the former colonial peoples. It has suffered from both, but its great danger comes less from the batterings of conflict than from the erosions of injustice. There is a growing sense, which the record confirms, that a double standard is being shaped, one to apply to the claims and to the sins of commission and omission of the older member states, the other to apply to those of the new. If this trend is maintained it is a fault for which the UN will grievously answer. For while it may survive the tactical assaults of its enemies, it will not survive the moral apathy of those who would wish to be its supporters. And the moral energy which it needs for its support can only be generated if there is a belief that it can become an objective and independent body.

Beyond the tactical perspectives there is a fundamental difference of philosophy which separates two sets of attitudes toward the UN. Khrushchev has insisted that there are no neutral men, echoing Maxim Litvinov's remark, "Only an angel can be neutral, and there are no angels." If they are right, then there is no possibility for the UN as a presence in trouble areas, an instrument for dealing with conflicts, or a potential for world order. For if the objective mind is impossible, then it is impossible to build a body of men whose working and thinking loyalties are not to the nation of their origin but to the instrument which seeks to go beyond nationalist allegiance. In that case one would have the spectacle of men with their own nationalist interests, prejudices and passions seeking to sit in judgment upon conflicts involving these very interests, prejudices and passions. If that were so, then the *troika* principle would make sense as an effort to acknowledge the national and ideological loyalties, represent broadly each bloc of them, and give each a veto against injurious actions by the others.

The answer is, of course, as Dag Hammarskjöld put it clearly in his notable Oxford address in May 1961, that an international civil servant cannot cease being human, but he can guide himself by the mandates and precedents of the UN, reducing the area of his discretion as far as possible, and then striving hard for a self-critical effort at evenhanded, independent judgment. He must be aware of his "human reactions," and "meticulously check himself so that they are not permitted to influence his actions"—an attitude which makes the international career service "politically celibate," if not "politically virgin." And Hammarskjöld added, "Is not every judge under the same obligation?"

In relation to neutralism, the basic distinction one must make, for clarity, is between being fair-minded and being without a standard of values. "The only true detachment," Lord Acton has said, "is that of the dead: they no longer care." This is to define "detachment" as the lack of feeling and values, which is a self-defeating definition, since it makes no differentiation between the valuing person who is a fierce partisan and the valuing person who is capable of evenhanded justice without giving up his humanity or resigning himself to quietism. A man may have values, as indeed every UN Secretary General has had, and live and act on those values, yet rid his mind of prejudice and cant, refuse to prejudge any issue, and thus be neutral as a good judge is neutral, in the sense of being just.

This is the final battleground of the idea, upon whose outcome not only the UN's future but that of man may hinge. Hammarskjöld demanded much of himself, and perhaps, therefore, too much of others. Only a lonely man, as he was, could endure the ordeal of standing outside the structure of all political and tribal allegiances, which the head of a transnational organization must do. Perhaps he was not enough aware of how frail most men are in their dependence not only on their national allegiance, but on the accepted frame of personality in their culture. He felt deeply hurt when his own UN aide, Georgi P. Arkadyev, acted secretly to convene a Security Council session on a Cuban complaint, putting Russia's stake in the Castro regime ahead of his own commitment to the UN and to his chief. Yet he scarcely need have been surprised, for ethical relativism is a cardinal principle of the Communist perspective: since there are no inherent values anywhere (they say), don't make a pretense of transcending the demands of your ideological system—which means, after all, making an absolute of the ideological values and thus abandoning relativism.

Yet, while he asked perhaps too much, what Hammarskjöld asked was in the right direction. I should define the direction as that of moving beyond the *national* outlook, and even beyond the *international* (in the sense of relations between or among nations) to the *transnational,* by which I mean cutting across the claims of the nation-state. Hammarskjöld knew that this was lonely and dangerous work. "Working at the edge of the development of human society," he said at the University of Chicago Law School, "is to work on the brink of the unknown." And he added that we must have faith in "the ultimate result of the creative evolution" of which that work is part. This requires, I suspect, more than the creed of "political celibacy" that Hammarskjöld saw in it. For those who forswear the nationalist allegiance, it is not enough to take the oath of chastity in abstaining from any other. It took centuries to create modern Western democratic man. The Russians and Chinese have made strides, in two brief generations, in creating Communist man. There can be no success in bringing a new world order and a new transnationalist outlook into being unless one makes an effort to bring into being a new personality type and life style which one may call transnational man. He would not be politically celibate; he would be married to the creed of speaking not for a nation but for man, and of putting the claims and interests of mankind as a whole ahead of the claims and interests of any segment of it.

6. *Toward Collective Will in an Open World*

WE DO NOT have to start wholly at scratch in our effort to build an enduring peace. The UN has shown itself flexible enough on the whole to meet situations never envisaged when the Charter was signed. And a force-in-being exists, in the form of soldiers who have watched over trouble areas and fought under UN insignia, from the time of the Korean War on, but especially in the Congo. I dare even speak of the historic function which the UN casualties in the Congo fighting have performed. Every great achievement of world history has had to be paid for in blood. The UN casualties in the Congo fighting have done something more than serve notice on individual governments that the maintenance of the "brush-fire peace" involves risks as well as stakes. They are also getting people in many countries accustomed to the idea of a UN military force which is more than the sum of its national contingents, and which can be counted upon in world crisis.

I spoke earlier* of moving beyond the nation-state power principle to the principle of world collective security. I then examined the three actions which must be pursued simultaneously on three fronts, to buy time and a favorable climate for this principle—the struggle for arms control, the dialogue of political negotiation, and the development of the UN presence and the UN instrument into a dynamic peacemaking force. We are now ready to come back to the nature of the collective-security principle, and how it may be nailed down to provide some calculable measure of peace.

Collective security, as a concept, has been worn thin as part of the currency of internationalism since the time of the League of Nations. The League experience with it was a hapless one. In any realistic terms there is a double key to effective collective security. The first requirement is that there be some central agency through which force ("sanctions") can be used against any nation taking aggressive action which breaks—or threatens to break—world peace. The second requirement is that the obligation to contribute to this force, or assent to its use, should be binding on every nation, instead of being left to the voluntary decision of individual nations.

In its succession of crises in the 1920s and 1930s the League foundered always on the second of these. The League itself, through its Council, could have been used as a central agency for applying the

* See Section 1, above, "Beyond Power—To What?"

requisite force when it was judged that a violation of the Covenant had taken place. But while the Council, under Article 16, had to recommend to the member nations what military contribution they should make toward this force, the duty to recommend proved a frail reed on which to base a system of transnational law. The 1921 resolutions of the League Assembly, interpreting Article 16, interpreted it out of existence. "The unilateral action of the defaulting State," the resolution read, "cannot create a state of war. . . . It is the duty of each Member of the League to decide for itself whether a breach of the Covenant has been committed." That did it. Except for the halfhearted application of sanctions against Italy in 1935, when it invaded Ethiopia (the measures likely to be effective, like banning oil shipments to Italy and closing the Suez Canal to it, were never taken), no collective sanctions were applied to any of the test cases: against Japan in its invasions of China in 1931 and 1937, against Paraguay in the Chaco War in 1934, against Russia in its invasion of Finland in 1939.

In the United Nations, as provided in Chapter VII of the Charter, the Security Council marks a considerable stride toward a system of collective security, since it is the judge of whether an act of aggression has taken place, it can decide upon economic sanctions, and it can call for military sanctions. But here again there are lumps in the porridge. One is that the extent of the military contribution of any member state is left (by Article 43) to an agreement it reaches with the Security Council, which means that each member state can limit its contribution, making it minimal and even token. The second is the veto power built into the Security Council, applying to each of its five permanent members. The General Assembly sought to circumvent this, in November 1950, in its "Uniting for Peace" resolution, which empowers it to recommend collective action to the member states in case of a Security Council veto. But whatever it does still remains in the moral and hortatory realm, not in that of committed power.

The problem is one of getting a force-in-being, whose use will not depend upon assent by the member states individually but upon objective standards for deciding whether an act of aggression has taken place. This will mean, in turn, a code of world law-in-being, whose agencies of conciliation, interpretation and decision can move fast enough to deal with events in swift motion, stopping what they have been unable to prevent, punishing what they have been unable to stop, and thus able to prevent or stop exactly because they are able to punish.

This is not the place for a detailed plan: forests have been felled to provide the paper for the numberless plans already proposed, and other forests will be needed for the plans still to come. In my own view the essence is for a start to be made by an international police force (or army, if you will) which will have at once inspection and surveillance functions and punitive functions. I see no reason why one branch of it should not administer the highly technical inspection system for the disarmament agreements, while another branch is in charge of political surveillance to prevent planned aggressions; and both in turn will be charged with the task of cracking down on actual aggression. The size of such a force will depend upon the degree of completeness of disarmament; if all armies have been leveled, except for internal police, the world police force could vary from a quarter to a half million. If disarmament is less complete, but the national armies have been stripped of nuclear weapons, it would be good policy to give the world police force a small stock of such weapons for their monopoly use. With such a monopoly right, they would have a margin over any nonnuclear force which a recalcitrant nation or group of nations could muster; and if these nations held on to a secret stock of nuclear weapons, or tried again to build them, the world police force would remain uncowed by them.

Such a force-in-being should be recruited afresh under world auspices, as volunteers, instead of having national units assigned to it, as under the UN today. It should be trained under its own officers, who in turn must (in time) be prepared for their mission in training schools where the whole atmosphere is one of neutrality-with-values. It should be paid for by revenues derived from taxes on goods and services collected throughout the world, independently of the national governments. It should act only after decisions by a mixed political-judicial tribunal which would function much like a world Supreme-Court-*cum*-Executive; these decisions, in turn, must be backed by reasoning and precedent, and subjected to public scrutiny as the only way in which a responsible body of guidance and law can be developed. Since every military force—national, international, or transnational—needs civilian control of some sort, this one will be no exception: its composition and leadership should be subject to the decisions of the political-judicial tribunal, perhaps with the consent of whatever Assembly the world authority functions with.

Note that I am not speaking of a "parliament of man," nor a new debating society, nor an international agency at the mercy of the individual will of the member states. I am speaking of a *world authority*, created by the nation-states but independent of their changing moods and power configurations, with a *force-in-being* which acts after the proper deliberations, on the basis of world conscience and law, brought into being by that conscience and law and in turn giving them effectiveness. I am speaking not of collective security in the old sense of an assembly of individual national wills to provide either a coalition force or an international force against an aggressor, but of a *collective world will* operating through independent transnational agencies and an independent world force-in-being.

There are, of course, many possible objections to such a world design. The practical mind will ask more questions of *how* than I have just considered; but the resourcefulness of the human mind is unending, and once we accept a basic approach the *how*s can get ironed out. The revenues, the recruitment of men and officers, their training, the combining of inspection and surveillance with the punitive, the dismantling of armies and national nuclear stores, the building of a compact nuclear power as a monopoly of the world authority—these problems open vast areas for differences in techniques. I know that the questions of *how* are the essence of polities. But I must add that every great era of constitution-making has been made possible by a thrashing out of the issues of ends and means—goals and institutional approaches—and that once we are clear about the *why* and the *to what end* and the broad questions of means, the problems will yield in time to detailed techniques.

Yet, several far-reaching questions remain which are questions not of technique but of principle. The most difficult is: Why should either Russia or America, not to speak of China, allow a world force to come into being which could be used not only against its rivals and enemies but quite possibly against itself?

True, the American and Russian commanding elites have known for some time that they risk self-destruction by piling up weapons in a lawless world. But always in the minds of each group of elites there is the self-serving hope that something will happen in the weapons race which will give them the advantage they need in order to set up their own unilateral system of power, and get world order through empire; or perhaps only the desire to improve its world position in the political war before making a showdown bid for world law. Always also, on each side, there is the fear that the world authority, whether the UN or some outgrowth or alternative, will be under the control of the other side—the Americans heavy-hearted as they watch the axis of the UN shifting to the Left-neutral-ist nations, the Russians recalling the days when the UN was almost a concert of Western powers, and mindful of the fact that the West-ern power centers are still the centers of intellectual ferment and political creativeness which may exert a suction force upon a world authority. Most of all, from the Russian side and even more from the Chinese, there is the fear that a rule of world law will arrest and freeze the revolutionary ferments upon which the Communist power cluster depends for ultimate victory without either a nuclear war or a world authority.

If this analysis is valid, then the chances of getting such a world authority in the calculable future are slight indeed, barring a dras-tic change of heart on both sides or a surge of world fear of war which would overcome the current preoccupations with the politi-cal war and with revolutionary nationalisms. What makes the pros-pect even dimmer is the fear of the tyranny of a world authority, which almost balances the fear of war. Men tend to project their fears from the known past into the unknown future. The past fears have been those of the tyranny of a foreign power, usually one that is known and envisaged from past deeds. Take these fears and pro-ject them into an unknown future, on a scale of world power hith-erto unknown, and with national military power leveled almost to the vanishing point—and you begin to glimpse the dimensions of this new fear.

I doubt whether this fear is contained within the compass of the debate that is being waged over national sovereignty. This is an old debate, using worn terms that no longer have much meaning for today. There is no real question about "dividing" sovereignty. The fact is that, functionally, sovereignty is being divided constantly. It is a mockery to speak of the sovereignty of the Communist puppet states of Eastern Europe, and only a little less so to speak of the sovereignty of Finland, or—on the side of the American power cluster—of South Vietnam or of Thailand. Where a nation is under the military and political "protection" of another, the final deci-sions which are the nub of sovereignty are scarcely its own. Nor is this only a result of what may be called the "new colonialism." Even the free nations in an age of overkill are likely to remain free only to the extent that they trade some of their sovereignty for com-mon decisions made in common councils. This is notably true of NATO as a pooling of military sovereignties, as it is true of the European Coal and Steel Community, and also of the emerging Common Market—in fact, of the whole struggle to unite Europe. It is true, in a different area and from a different viewpoint, of the OAS—Organization of American States—which is an effort at hemisphere collective security. Each member state commits itself to the joint action which the OAS as a whole resolves to take, whether in the field of economic development or in that of economic or even military sanctions. By doing so it commits at least a segment of its sovereignty to the decision of a body over which it has at best only the limited control of its own vote.

Here then, ranging all the way from good-neighbor cooperation or big-neighbor umbrella to regional economic and political groupings, is the strong current drive to bolster the weakness of the nation-state by bunching aggregates of them together. The incentive is not volition of sovereign power but the facts of geopolitical life, which operate through pursuit of a common interest or fear of a common doom. I do not say that these aggregates of nation-states embody the principle of a collective world will. I do say that in their limited way, clinging always to the forms and illusions of national sovereignty but having to embrace the functional necessities of collective action, they are fumblings toward a world will. The road leading to it is not one to be wholly hacked out of the jungle of national sovereignties. Some clearings of it have been made.

As for the problem of the inviolability and indivisibility of national sovereignty, my suggestion is that it is being violated and fragmented every day. The real question about it is to what purpose it will be committed. Wendell Willkie used to say that sovereignty is not something to be hoarded, but something to be spent. This cuts to the heart of the matter. The classical economists talked of a "wage-fund doctrine," a fixed fund out of which alone wages could come, so that every wage increase moved toward a depletion of the fund. More enlightened economic doctrine has learned that wage increases can mean wider prosperity, thereby making possible higher profits and wages together. There is a danger of getting stuck with a kind of "sovereignty-fund" doctrine, such as underlay the thinking of the Connally Amendment—the "self-judging clause," which reserves for American authorities the right to decide what disputes are "essentially domestic" and therefore outside the jurisdiction of the International Court of Justice.

Its reasoning here was that to acknowledge the sovereignty of a world authority of any kind is to impoverish the sovereignty of the nation. This is the hoarding theory. But the truth is that only by spending some of its sovereignty and pooling it with others can America or any other nation make possible the survival of any sovereignty. Nothing will ever recall the old power—which probably was a light that never shone on sea or land—of sole final decision for each nation as an independent entity. What can be saved, however, by committing some of the warmaking power to the purposes of peacemaking, is a chance for each national culture to fulfill itself in its basic life purposes within an ordered world.

I know that analogies are likely to be tricky, and the analogy between the law behind a world police force and municipal police law has often been attacked. Yet it has enough validity in it to be worth repeating. Which of us has not had the experience, on his job at the factory or office, in business or profession, on a university campus or in a church or neighborhood, of working and living alongside someone whom he hates and who hates him? Which of us has not at some point had murder in his heart? But only rarely is the murder committed. Not because the intent or hatred is lacking, but because the punishment would be swift and decisive. There is a framework of municipal law which makes possible a framework of tolerable order. I do not say that punishment is the only deterrent to murder or even the crucial one. The judicial and penal systems have developed alongside systems of moral values, inhibitions, repressions. But the punishment administered under the civil law is the end-product as it is the symbol of the whole constellation of sanctions that have developed over history. Some such development has already begun in the world arena, toward a world order. It will have to go farther.

But (some will argue) municipal police order is a product of law, and behind both is the local and state government. Doesn't this mean that a world police authority is impossible without a world state? This may be largely a matter of verbal difference. Certainly there must be a body of world law, but it will not cover every subject as does municipal law; it will be restricted to murder and sudden death, to offenses of aggression by one state against others. To the extent that a world policing authority possesses a punitive power, it will embody the state machinery and institutions covering that authority, but it need not embody any more of a state apparatus than that. I see no reason for jumping all the way from a world of nation-states to a single world-state, nor do I regard it as desirable if it could be achieved. The purpose of a world military authority is not to displace the nonmilitary functions of the nation-state but to make it possible to pursue them free of the shadow of terror hanging over them.

I would agree with Walter Millis, whose *World Without War* is a sharply and boldly portrayed analysis of a viable warless world, in saying that the removal of the nuclear shadow would energize the nation-state into a genuine competitive struggle for economic, political and moral stakes which are today dwarfed by the military struggle. A warless world would certainly not be a world without nation-states; it might prove to be the one type of world in which alone the nation-state could survive and find a genuine function to fulfill. Nor would it be a world without power. Arms are not the only form of power, although the classical system of world politics made a showdown by arms the final test of power. There are other forms of power—the power of economic systems, of ideas, of ethical and value systems, of life styles and personality types, of myths as visions-of-possibility, of beliefs, of faiths. The only power form that would be denied to the nation-state would be the warmaking power, simply because it has become a principle of disorder rather than of order and is now unthinkable except in its transformed use as a world police power.

If a world authority would not mean the end of power struggles, neither would it mean the end of ideological struggles. The conflicts between Islam and Christianity, between Catholics and Protestants, have continued long after the religious wars; for the most part they have had to take other forms than man killing man. Thus, too, the conflict between the Communist and the free-world ethos is likely to continue, but it cannot be allowed to continue in the form of nation destroying nation, because the consequences would be endless destruction. We know in our own internal world, within the frame of an orderly nation-state, how much expressiveness we give to continuing conflicts, and how creative the conflict principle can be within this frame.

This leads to the question, which strikes me as basically an academic one, of a world society. Like the argument that there can be no world force without world law, and no world law without a world state, it is argued that there can be no world state unless it is the power skeleton of a world society. Again I must disagree. I cannot go along with those whose animus against the nation-state jungle is so great as to push them into the fallacy of seeing the root of evil in the conflict of national cultures. It is true that dynastic war states have tried to turn the national culture into a military instrument, and nowhere more so than in ideological states like those of Hitler and Stalin. But it does not follow, because a national culture can be thus twisted, that it is, therefore, inherently a poisoned well which must be closed up and marked out of bounds. Cultures should be viewed not as means, whether for war or for internationalism, for religious creeds or for secularism, but as value-systems and, to that extent, as ends. One of the functions of political order is to make cultural creativeness possible. It would be a wayward waste of such creativity if one of its principal forms and impulses —the sense of identity within a national culture—were to be removed.

In a well-meaning speech before the UN, President Eisenhower expressed the hope for an eventual "world of open societies." Not only was this a futile hope, but it violated the basic principle of the right of each nation to have its own kind of society, provided that it is not guilty of aggressions against others. He would have been better advised to say "an open world of diverse societies"—the open societies of the West European-American model, the closed Communist societies of the Russian model, those of the Chinese model, the more-or-less-open societies with a measure of military rule, the national-socialist societies not explicitly Communist, the variants of each, and a number that do not fit into any of the categories.

Adapting John Stuart Mill's theme, in his *On Liberty*, that much of the meaning and savor of life lies in the diversity of individual differences, one might say that much of the meaning of world history lies in the diversity of national cultures. The instinct of the herd is toward the ironing-out of diversities. It would be ironic if the means for averting nuclear world destruction were to result in a monolithic cultural uniformity for the world thus saved.

7. *Fear and Conscience in Atomic Man*

WHEN THE NEWS CAME of the Los Alamos bomb Winston Churchill called it the "Second Coming in wrath," and Robert Hutchins spoke of the "good news of damnation." Both men saw that fear too —like love and hope and the drive to power and the spur of need or greed—may have its uses in politics. If all men feel they are damned together, such knowledge may give perspective to their conflicts and bring about a new consensus of effort in the face of a common democracy of death. One may apply to our time the great sentence of William Blake, "The tigers of wrath are wiser than the horses of instruction." But they will have no wisdom unless they can awaken the conscience of atomic man—not only American and British and French, but Russian as well—to the necessary means for his salvation.

In the course of its history, mankind has known many fears, genuine and spurious alike. What is new about the present fears is that for the first time they are ultimate and all-inclusive. Fear as a force in world politics has not been adequately thought through. Although a single word, fear is a double agent: it can galvanize or paralyze a people. Not all fear is destructive—only fear as a pervasive drive, the habitual fear of the fearing personality; but where there is a threat of danger which will wreak harm unless you summon your will and resources to meet it, then the fear which jolts you into confronting the world of reality is to that extent a healthy force and can be beneficent of life and protective of the state. In Freudian terms, fear can recall a people to the reality principle. If this confronting of reality can move world opinion to the kind of operative moral code on which world law can be based and a collective policing agency can be established, then the "Second Coming in wrath" may have served man well.

One might, I suppose, contrast with the fear of real dangers a fear of phantoms arising from one's own neurotic drives and anxieties. Yet it is hard to call the fear of world destruction a phantom; it is real enough. It is not fantasy fears one must now oppose to reality in world politics, but panic fear. It is the fear that paralyzes because it is absolute, and in its absolutism it produces an incapacity to meet reality in its total context. For the reality includes not only the overkill weapons with all their destructive potential, but also the Communist power system with its domination effect. There are in actuality two great dangers, not one; there is the danger that the world will become a mound of radiated ashes, and there is also the danger that it will become an ant colony, under a commanding elite that is ready to rule it thus for the calculable future and does not hesitate to use the conscience of atomic man for its own power purposes.

We live in an era when the prevailing attitudes toward the weapons of the time have themselves become a form of weapon. Nor does history lack examples of such political instrumental use of attitudes toward war and peace. Woodrow Wilson tried to use the war weariness and pacifism of the Germans toward the end of World War I as a revolutionary weapon and partly succeeded. Lenin was even more successful with the war weariness of the Russian peasant, whom he wooed away from both the war and the state with the slogan, "Peace, Bread and Land." After World War II, the war weariness of the American people led to a haste in demobilizing their armies in Europe, a haste from which the Russians benefited, which their Communist partisans encouraged, and which laid Europe bare to the advance of the Communist armies. To take the most dramatic incident, the pacifism of the Oxford Pledge before World War I led to an unready Britain and doomed many of its undergraduate generation to a needlessly wasteful death when the war did come.

There is a moral absolutism that has developed toward the overkill weapons, based on the proposition that they are an expression of the dehumanizing of mass capitalist-democratic culture; that no sane and humane man can tolerate the thought of using them; that people who wish to build or live in a sane society must first wash themselves clean of the guilt of the radioactive shadow now resting on mankind; and that only a unilateral laying down of the overkill weapons, in the absence of an agreed disarmament, can save man either physically or morally.

The political reasoning behind this view rests on a high valuation of survival in itself and a low valuation of the differences between the open society and the totalitarian one as compared with the difference between the life and death of mankind. If world destruction were a certainty it might be arguable ("better Red than dead") that man might gamble with the chance of being ultimately able to reform or overthrow a coercive Communist world state from within, and that he should prefer that gamble to the certainty of human extinction. Actually, however, there is no certainty in either term of the contrast; both are gambles. There is an element of considerable risk in pushing the political war over a protracted period of time, with all the chances of war by accident or miscalculation. There is also a considerable element of risk in counting upon the overthrow of a well-entrenched and consolidated system of Communist power, especially when no alternative system is left to challenge it. My own tendency, when confronted by the *either-or* of a world of radiated ashes or a world which has become an ant society, is to replace it with a *neither-nor*. I fall back upon the very considerable possibility that we shall be able to buy time enough for a meeting of minds which will avoid both evils.

Yet, the moral absolutism on which the position of unilateralism is based is a fact and a force in the world today—at least, among the nations of the free world. As with all moral absolutisms, this one evokes a passionate commitment to its cause, with a readiness for personal sacrifice and a demand that others should also subordinate everything else to human survival.

One may ask why this movement should have come up first and most strongly in England, especially since the British tradition, with its historical talent for compromise, has not been as much given to moral absolutisms as the cultures of continental Europe or of Asia. Perhaps it is because, after losing some of the best elements of their youth in a succession of wars, along with their power base, the British have been receptive to absolutism in the form of antiwar conviction. As a vulnerable isle, studded with American missile sites and Polaris bases, Britain would be a natural first target for the Russians in a nuclear war. Thus, while the apocalyptic vision is that of the world's death, the immediate vision is a limited Apocalypse— that of the death of England as a chosen first victim.

At its deepest, the movement expresses a profound moral revulsion against the meaningless stupidity of mass death. Yet, in political terms, whatever the underlying moral energy, it adds up to a will to surrender. This is not peculiar to Great Britain, or to the equivalent American movement, which at present writing has not gone much beyond a "graduated unilateralism," deriving from a more subtle psychological analysis than is to be found in the dry and rationalist thinking of Bertrand Russell. The anxieties and fears out of which pacifist absolutism grows are world-wide, and the potentials of the movement are also world-wide. What is most lacking in all these movements is a tragic sense about the human condition. Anyone with tragic depth will refuse to be caught in a death trap, but he will not accept as a likely solution the unilateral stripping by a nation of its weapons of resistance. He will use his nerve to sustain himself in danger and his will to keep the trap from closing while he contrives a way of getting free of it.

It would be curious if the Russians did not adapt their strategy in the political war to the fact of the agonized debate within the conscience of atomic man. Much of the Soviet nuclear diplomacy, in underscoring rather than minimizing the terror of Russian nuclear weapons, has been directed against this prevailing fear of man's destruction, especially in Western Europe. In this sense, fear becomes an instrument for political maneuver, and the manipulation of the human conscience becomes one of the important facts of world politics today.

I am not suggesting that conscience is any less operative in the minds of the Russians than in the minds of the British or the Americans. Certainly, the Russians, with the devastation and death of World War II still fresh in their memories, have a passion for peace with which their leaders must reckon, just as the free-world leaders must reckon with pacifism among their own people. The difference is that these drives of fear and conscience cannot be politically challenged and expressed in the Soviet Union as they are in the free world; they are not debated in newspapers and magazines, in books, from lecture platform and pulpit; they are not made dramatically manifest in mass demonstrations and sit-downs. Thus, they are not translated into an active climate of political opinion, as they are where such debate and demonstrations are not banned.

The result is something that may be called a *conscience differential* between the two power systems. It is this differential which is used as one of the effective weapons of psychological and political war by the Communist leadership. The fact of this use is, of course, not a decisive argument against the position itself in an open society. It is simply a fact of life in the unremitting struggle of the political war. It serves thereby to strengthen the critique of this kind of moral absolutism—a critique which would be valid without it.

For what is needed is not so much moral absolutism as a prudent morality which will serve man's purpose both for survival and freedom. The important element to be salvaged from any humanist tradition is the stress on man's moral capacity to will his destiny and keep himself from being trapped in a mass death. Because the shadow of death today is a total one—not just the weak and helpless minorities nor the subject peoples, but man himself, caught for once in the full democracy of death as a leveler—the response must be sharp and strong, but it must be a response in the total context of world forces. Never in history has man been so completely threatened. Never, therefore, has it been so possible for him to weigh against possible death not only the trivia of party, property and power, but his freedom itself, and his chance to use that freedom in the fulfillment of his aims and dreams. Seen thus the truly radical morality is that of freedom, human development and the good life. It is the task of leaders and people alike to move, as prudently as they know how, toward a future in which they will have a chance at these goods.

Like a condemned prisoner in a death cell, man has had to face the imminence of the worst. Nothing can any longer terrify him, because he has endured the utmost terror that hangs over him. It is in this sense that a glimpse of freedom becomes possible—the freedom to seek survival without abdication, in a mood at once compassionate, realistic, stoical. The Bertrand Russell who wrote *A Free Man's Worship*—who saw that man is only a tiny figure caught in a universe inhabited by billions of galaxies, spanning only a fraction of a second in an infinity of time, but who saw also that this man can assert his intellectual and moral freedom, understand his minuscule and transitory place in the universe, yet remain in command of that understanding—that Russell is still the more relevant one.

To whom can we turn for the decisions which may save mankind? Some say that only the scientists who created these nuclear weapons have it in their power to prevent their use. Sir Charles P. Snow, in a speech to a convention of American scientists, spoke of the "moral unneutrality of science" and called, in effect, for a syndicalist rebellion of scientists against the arms decisions of the state which run counter to their moral values and their sense of humanity. "Soldiers have to obey," says Snow; "that is the foundation of their morality. Scientists have to question and, if necessary, to rebel." He goes on to point out that the basis of the morality of the scientist is his knowledge of the consequence of his weapons. This knowledge, says Snow, enables the scientist to make his moral choice.

The trouble with his reasoning is that the scientist has no monopoly of the knowledge of what the overkill weapons mean. One needs no technical knowledge today to understand the consequences of the weapons. Yet the choice of political and moral strategies is still a hard one. With the same knowledge, a man like J. Robert Oppenheimer said No to the H-bomb, while a man like Edward Teller said Yes. It is then not a question of knowledge but of values, and when it comes to values, the scientist is no more expert than anyone else. I agree with Snow that the scientist, like the rest of us, must be able to say No to those whom he regards as the powers and principalities of evil. But again the conscience differential enters. I suspect that the Western scientist who says No will scarcely be able to reach the Russian scientist who has no will to say No, and no way to say it even if he had the will.

One further word on No-saying: Pushed far enough, every No has a Yes potential in it, as shown by the willingness of the atomic scientists to work at Los Alamos, even though they knew what might result from their task; they were unwilling to have the Germans solve the secret of the atomic bomb first, and so what they did at Los Alamos was a race against tyranny and a Yes-saying to freedom. Similarly every Yes has a No potential in it; there is little question that most of the American scientists working on nuclear weapons today would lay down their work if a ruthless fascist government were to come to power in Washington. The difference does not lie between moral choices by scientists and nonscientists, but in the alternatives for moral choices offered to valuing men.

In the end, I suspect, the decisions must be essentially political ones. Scientists must use their knowledge and insight to guide them to their own best choices, but aside from their knowledge they have nothing unique to offer to the community as a whole. Moral leaders must use their best wisdom, and they can do much to clarify the nature of the choices, as men like Jaspers and Barth, Buber and Niebuhr have done. But the final decision must be made by the people through their political leaders. Even if it were possible for the philosopher to become king, he might be less sensitive to all the pulls and pressures of a real world than the man who is specialized to them and fuses his feel for the common experience with his feel for power. There is no way of transferring the burden of decision from the political leaders and the men upon whose expertise they call. One might wish that they had a more piercing vision of the future and a more tragic perception of man's plight. They may have to pay heavily for both; yet there is more trust to be put in them than in the ideologists of either camp. Instead of pursuing abstractions, they are likely to act in a real world, and they are likely to act with less absolutism and greater prudence.

8. *Death Urge or Life Force?*

THERE REMAIN more questions than any book can answer. When the news of heavy casualties in the Crimean War came to England, John Bright noted that the Angel of Death was "abroad in the land," and he spoke of almost hearing "the whirring of his wings." But those were traditional casualties in a conventional war, and the Angel of Death was doubtless fitted with orthodox wings. D. H. Lawrence's premonition of a "vast Death-happening" came closer to the mood of our overkill era. I have said that the world will have to move beyond the nation-state power principle, and I have suggested some of the mechanisms which might make it possible. But by what motive force will we be moved, if at all? What conception of human nature is likely to furnish a base for it? With what mood and philosophy can the transition take place? What are the chances of buying time enough for waging the political war until a disarmed world can be brought into being?

The crucial question here is that of man's basic nature and the drives in it that bear on war and peace. With terrifying prescience, yet also with curiously blinkered vision, Sigmund Freud has posed for us the problem of whether we can survive the Age of Overkill, and he has done it with the radical pessimism which has affected the

intellectual climate of our world. In his middle sixties, during the
two emotionally bleak years following World War I, after the war
had driven a wedge through his life and released him for specula-
tive thinking beyond the strictly clinical, Freud advanced the bold
idea of a death instinct which operates not only in human life but
throughout life, in the very constitution of the universe. In a little
book called *Beyond the Pleasure Principle,* which has, almost without exception, pained the psychiatrists while it has delighted the
philosophers and imaginative writers, Freud wrote that the deepest
instinctual drive in every form of life was the drive to revert to the
original state of inorganic matter, of nothingness. He became preoccupied with the repetition-compulsion principle, as he noted it in
children, even in acts extremely unpleasant to them. Without
wholly abandoning the *Lust-prinzip* (pleasure principle) he now for
the first time went beyond it as a central drive and saw it as tied in
with the death instinct. The brutality and the destructive aggressions of World War I had clearly left their impact on him, as perhaps also had his personal experience of the death of a beloved
daughter. But these were secondary; what counted was Freud's
preoccupation with death all through his life, and his persistent,
courageous attempt to place it in his "metapsychology." He went so
far as to say that the purpose of all life is death.

Implied in this view was the conviction that just as the life of the
individual and the cell moves toward death, so does the life of nations and of civilization itself. A decade after *Beyond the Pleasure
Principle,* Freud—then in his middle seventies—wrote *Civilization
and Its Discontents,* whose theme is that civilization is a socially
necessary framework for repressing the instinctual life of man, and
that out of these repressions flow the discontents through which the
aggressive-destructive death instinct erupts into the barbarism of
war.

"*Homo homini lupus:* Who has the courage [asked Freud] to
dispute it in the face of all the evidence in his own life and in history? This aggressive cruelty . . . reveals men as savage beasts to
whom the thought of sparing their own kind is alien." He goes on
to pose, more sharply than in the earlier book, the struggle between
the two great primal instincts: that of Eros, "which aims at binding
together single human individuals, then families, then tribes, races,
nations, into one great unity, that of humanity"; and the death
instinct, "the hostility of each one against all and of all against each
one." Together Eros and Death "share rule over the earth." Freud
continued to be fascinated by "the struggle between Eros and

Death, between the instincts of life and the instincts of destruction, as it works itself out in the human species . . . And it is this Battle of the Titans that our nurses and governesses try to compose with their lullaby song to Heaven."

Several years later Freud returned to the same theme, in his open letter to Albert Einstein, who had asked him publicly whether there was "any way of delivering mankind from the menace of war." Freud's answer was refreshingly free from the kind of cant which had crept into Einstein's letter—which may be why Fromm was later to complain that "Freud manifests in his letter to Einstein a political attitude far to the right of liberalism." Summing up his two books on the death instinct, Freud gave Einstein little nourishment for hope. "There is no likelihood," he wrote, "of our being able to suppress humanity's aggressive tendencies." In fact, he insisted, the death instinct is sometimes turned inward to destroy the living human being; the human conscience itself is the product of the "turning inward of the aggressive impulse." If this happens on a massive scale it becomes a morbid fact, whereas "the diversion of the destructive impulse toward the external world must have beneficial effects." Hence the "biological justification for all those vile, pernicious propensities which we are now combating. . . . They are really more akin to nature than this, our stand against them, which, in fact, remains to be accounted for."

He ends by holding out a glimmer of hope: that the process of civilization itself, with its "strengthening of the intellect" and its "mastery of the instinctive life," along with the "well-founded dread of the form that future wars will take," would "work against war." At the end of *Civilization and Its Discontents* he had expressed something of the same thought: "Men have brought their powers of subduing the forces of nature to such a pitch that by using them they could now very easily exterminate each other to the last man . . . And now it may be expected that the other of the two 'heavenly forces,' eternal Eros, will put forth his strength so as to maintain himself alongside his equally immortal adversary." Written fifteen years before Los Alamos, it was a remarkably prophetic insight.

I have gone into Freud's views on the roots of war at such length because no one has better stated the case against a tender-minded view. In its deep and far-reaching pessimism, what Freud's thinking about man in his collective relations comes down to is that the individual neuroses may be healed by a tracking-down and confronting of their roots in the life history, but that the great collective neurosis that comes from man being trapped within the death instinct cannot be healed or resolved. It is firmly built into man's essential nature, and while it may be possible to control and postpone for a time the death of civilizations and of civilization itself by invoking the leadership energies of an elite who will master the instinctual death drive by the sovereignty of reason, the chances of the whole of mankind becoming such an elite are minimal. The trouble is that Eros itself, the drive toward the linking of human beings with each other through the libidinal tie in ever widening circles is infected at the source; crossing with the aggressive drive, it tends to turn inward into a self-destructive urge which becomes intolerable until the destructiveness is again channeled outward. Thus, while we may aim at restoring the healthy forces in the psychic lives of individuals, the creation of a sane society—especially a sane world society in a warless world—is something quite different.

This view has been reinforced recently from the angle of the new discoveries in the prehistory of man, stretching back to the Pleistocene and even Pliocene ages among man's ancestors in the apes and ape men and early not-yet men of the African plain. Building especially on the work of L. S. B. Leakey in the Olduvai Gorge, in Tanganyika, and on the researches of Raymond Dart, Robert Ardrey's *African Genesis* (despite some critical pages on Freud's "romantic fallacy") reinforces Freud's conjectural death instinct by the evidence of man's instinctual endowment from the centuries of human evolution. We are, says Ardrey, Cain's children, and we carry Cain's heritage. If the human emergence took place, as now seems likely, in the bleak wastes and savannas of East Africa, you can study man's instinctual endowment by studying the animal mentality in the great game preserves where the African animals are in their natural habitat. Hunger, territoriality (the defense of the animal's territory), the sexual possessiveness that goes with the territory, the need for enemies as well as for friends (the enmity-amity complex), the drive to fight for his territory and for his status in the animal group—these are the basic drives one finds in the context of animal behavior. Ardrey calls man in his origins "the most sophisticated predator the world has ever known."

The recent events in the new nations of Africa, where young men for the first time had guns in their hands and the freedom to kill, the hacking of a group of innocent young Italians in a medical team in the Congo, the inhumanity of man to man in South Africa, the killings in the tank-dominated streets of Budapest and the even worse killings in the "liquidation" of the "counterrevolution" behind the scenes—if anything were needed after the history of the Nazi destruction of Europe's Jews to underscore the persistence of the destructive element in man, these episodes have surely supplied it.

Think of what this perspective on man's nature and inner drives means in the new context of overkill weapons, of revolutionary nationalism, and of territorial struggle with new idea-weapons in the world political war. Assuming, with the neo-Darwinians, man's psychic heritage from his animal origins and his African prehistory, assuming, with Freud, that life moves inevitably toward a return to the original nonlife in the cellular structure of all living matter, and assuming, with Freud, also the unequal struggle between death and Eros—then strength is added to the pessimist view that there is little likelihood of being able to prevent civilization from careening to death and expiring in a bloody radiated stain left by the idiot weapons which "man's presumptuous brain" has created.

And yet, and yet, I must confess that I am far from content, in my own thinking, to let it rest there. In studying Machiavelli I found that he had brought into the European intellectual climate of Dante's world, which ran in terms of what ought to be, a new modern intellectual climate running in terms of what is. But I found also, especially when I studied *The Prince* and *The Discourses,* that there is a realm between the "ought" and the "is"— the realm of the "can be." As I look at man's calculable future I do not think in terms of either pessimism or optimism, but of possibilism. It is a stoic and tragic possibilism, yes, but there is no inherent doom discernible in the record of human history when you view it as the creative unfolding of human possibility. The Freudian conjectures, like those of Schopenhauer before him, are impressive and deeply moving; yet, until the last record is written, there is nothing certain about man's nature which shuts the door upon human possibility for contriving the resources of survival as well as for contriving the weapons of destruction. "Mankind," Romain Gary has said, "is born. Humanity must be created."

Freud was fascinated by the rigidity he saw in the repetitive-compulsive behavior of children. Yet every student of the creativity in the child's growth must also be fascinated by the plasticity of the human material shown in that growth. The students of paleontology and prehistory are absorbed with human evolution from the standpoint of its animal origins. But there is another way of looking at the same perspective: to sweep the succession of the

ages of man and to see that within the broad limits of his instinctual life man has had to break the mold of what he called "human
nature" from age to age and from culture to culture and has had
to go through a series of cultural transformations and psychic
leaps-into-the-dark in order to survive as a species. Meditating upon
his remarkable "rule of phase" and on the political implications
of entropy in the Second Law of Thermodynamics, Henry Adams
wrote a friend his prediction of "the immediate dissolution of the
world." He added, "My brother Brooks grumbles that I can't make
it sooner." But these apocalyptic visions of world dissolution have
been the stock material of religions ever since the Babylonian story
of the Flood; they need not be taken as the final datum on man's
past or future.

I prefer Susanne Langer's way of putting it: "Because our moral
life is negotiated so largely by symbols, it is more oppressive than
the morality of animals. . . . Animals react only to the deed that
is done or is actually imminent. . . . The story of man's martyr-
dom is a sequel to the story of his intelligence, his power of symboli-
cal envisagement. For good or evil, man has this power of envisagement, which puts on him a burden that purely alert, realistic
creatures do not bear—the burden of understanding. . . . So he
must conceive a world and a law of the world, a pattern of life, and
a way of meeting death."

Where I break with the intellectualists, as indeed with Freud too,
is in the premise that this power of envisagement—which is closely
related to Freud's emphasis upon what man can do in his higher
cerebral centers of the "sovereignty of Reason"—is basically rational. I prefer the way Jung puts it, in a preface to an anthology
of his writings, *Psyche and Symbol:* "The instinct to survive is
aroused as a reaction against the tendency to mass suicide represented by the H-bomb and the underlying political schism of the
world. The latter is clearly man-made and due to rationalistic distortions." These distortions, he is confident, can be overcome by
an appeal to the fundamental life instincts. "As nowadays we are
threatened by the self-destruction of mankind through radioactivity,
we are experiencing a fundamental reassertion of our instincts."

I do not mean to invoke authority on a matter where I don't
suppose there are authorities of any sort. But two of the great minds
of our time have wrestled with the problem of the irrationals imbedded in the human psyche and in human history, and neither
has come up with an answer wholly bleak. Freud died believing

that the struggle between Eros and Death would always go on and would always be unresolved, although at every decisive point Death was bound to triumph. Jung died, unrepentant about positing a collective unconscious in which all the important human enactments take place, and believing that the very fact of man's mad rush to death is what has already begun to evoke a new strength in the life instincts within him. Of the two "envisagements"—both mythical, both symbolic—Jung's seems to me nearer to the truth of human possibilism. It may be what Joyce meant when he saw his hero going out to "forge in the smithy of my soul the uncreated conscience of the race."

What strikes me most about these insights is that they do not depend wholly on the superstructure of man's rationality, but reckon with his instinctual endowment and his deep nonrational drives of the life force itself. Man has not reached the end of history unless, deep within the river bed of his unconscious striving, he believes that he has reached the end of history. I prefer to say that he has reached the point where he must with his whole being decide whether he is capable or incapable of ending what he has begun. He began it, in our time of overkill, with his technology of death. But he has always made it a point to live with his technology, ever since the conjectural time when (according to Raymond Dart) he picked up an antelope bone and fashioned it into a weapon to use against his fellow man. His problem now is not to destroy his weapons, but to localize their use as power instruments in the hands of a group who will use them for collective power through world law. If this be thought an incredibly creative leap, there have been other leaps in man's history—in the use of fire and the tool and the wheel, in the idea of law and of freedom and of the good life— which have been more creative and more exacting of human resourcefulness. The new element is that of collective will. Never in the history of man's transformations has he had to take so great a leap across the chasm of chaos into the collective will. He may not make it, but he is bound to attempt it.

He is reaching today to explore possibility in three major directions: into space and other realms of physical exploration; into what Teilhard de Chardin calls the "no-osphere," which can stand as a symbol for the more subtle aspects of his increasing self-awareness and self-knowledge; and, most crucially, into the possibilities of collective action that will cut across his tribalisms and reach into his humanity.

Of one thing I am certain: At some point man will fashion something like the collective policing agency, with a monopoly of the more lethal weapons, which I have described as crucial for survival. There is only one real question: Will it be before, or will it be after, the great "Death-happening" of an overkill war?

A Note on Reading

(This is not meant as a bibliography of the principal literature on world politics; it is only some notes on books and articles which I have found especially evocative, and which I therefore suggest the reader may pursue.—M.L.)

Foreword: The Enchanted Wood

On the use of words in political thinking, see T. D. Weldon, *Vocabulary of Politics* (1953). On the nature of political thinking, including the concept of the "public" and the rational, nonrational and irrational elements in politics, I have drawn on my own essays in *Ideas Are Weapons* (1939), *Ideas for the Ice Age* (1941), and *The Unfinished Country* (1959), especially Part V, "The Underground River," pp. 627-733. See also Graham Wallas, *Human Nature and Politics* (1908); H. Stuart Hughes, *Consciousness and Society* (1958); Ernest Cassirer, *The Myth of the State* (1946) esp. ch. XVIII; Daniel Lerner, ed., *The Human Meaning of the Social Sciences* (1959). On the power concept see Robert Dahl, *A Preface to Democratic Theory* (1956), and Bertrand de Jouvenel, *Power: Its Nature and the History of Its Growth* (1949), two very diverse books but with a tenacious realism in common. On the use of metaphors in social theory see Stanley Edgar Hyman, *The Tangled Bank: Darwin, Marx, Frazer and Freud as Imaginative Writers* (1962), with rich material on poetry, metaphor and myth in those writers.

Chapter I: The World of Overkill

For the system of classical world politics and its study, see Hans Morgenthau, *Politics Among Nations* (third edition 1960); Louis J. Halle, *Men and Nations* (1962); Stanley H. Hoffmann, *Contemporary Theory in International Relations* (1960); A. F. K. Organski, *World Politics* (1958); Frederick L. Schuman, *International Politics* (sixth edition 1958); Stillman and Pfaff, *The New Politics* (1961); John G. Stoes-

singer, *The Might of Nations* (1961); Ludwig Dehio, *The Precarious Balance: Four Centuries of European Power Struggle* (1962).

For the overkill weapons and the deterrence system, see Herman Kahn, *On Thermonuclear War* (1960) and also his *Thinking About the Unthinkable* (1962); Henry Kissinger, *The Necessity for Choice* (1960); Pierre Gallois, *The Balance of Terror* (1962); Thomas C. Schelling, *The Strategy of Conflict* (1960); Glenn H. Snyder, *Deterrence and Defense* (1961); Donald Brennan, *Arms Control, Disarmament, and National Security* (1961); Albert Wohlstetter, "The Delicate Balance of Terror" in *Foreign Affairs*, Jan. 1959; Oskar Morgenstern, *The Problem of National Defense* (1961); Anatol Rapoport, *Fights, Games, and Debates* (1960); W. F. Hahn and J. C. Neff, eds., *American Strategy in a Nuclear Age* (1960).

For the sharpest criticism of some of the above works on deterrence and "games" theory, see J. R. Newman, *The Rule of Folly* (1962); Erich Fromm, *May Man Prevail?* (1961); H. Stuart Hughes, *An Approach to Peace* (1962); Arthur Waskow, *The Limits of Defense* (1962); and any of Lord Russell's voluminous writings, of which I have found *Common Sense and Nuclear War* (1959) and *Has Man a Future?* (1962) most useful as summaries. The important exchange of articles in the debate between Sidney Hook and Lord Russell in the *New Leader* will be found in Hook, *Political Power and Personal Freedom* (1959). See also, for an over-all view of the moral and political imperatives which follow upon the new weapons, Norman Cousins, *In Place of Folly* (1961), and Karl Jaspers, *The Future of Mankind* (1961).

309

For the "Great Decision" on the Hiroshima bomb and later nuclear policy, see R. C. Batchelder, *The Irreversible Decision, 1939-1950* (1961); Knebel and Bailey, *No High Ground* (1960); Teller and Brown, *The Legacy of Hiroshima* (1962); Lewis L. Strauss, *Men and Decisions* (1962). For one of the earlier books on this theme, see Michael Amrine, *The Great Decision* (1959).

For summaries of a set of research studies made for the Senate Committee on Foreign Relations, by thirteen Foreign Policy Research Centers, see J. H. Cerf and Walter Pozen, *Strategy for the 60's* (1960). One of the best of these studies, made by the Washington Center of Foreign Policy Research, of Johns Hopkins University, under the direction of Arnold Wolfers, will be found in a report to the Senate Committee: *U. S. Foreign Policy: Developments in Military Technology and Their Impact on U.S. Strategy and Foreign Policy* (1959).

On the chances of nuclear war, and the typology of situations which could lead to it, the best discussion is in the two books above by Herman Kahn, especially *Thinking About the Unthinkable*. On the development of the Faustian Question in the history of ideas, see E. M. Butler's trilogy: *Myth of the Magus* (1947), *Ritual Magic* (1949), and *The Fortunes of Faust* (1952).

Chapter II: Power Center and Power Cluster

On the nature and transformation of classic imperialism, see John Strachey, *The End of Empire* (1959); Rupert Emerson, *From Empire to Nation* (1960); Lenin's *Imperialism: The Highest Stage of Capitalism* (1915); and John Hobson's *Imperialism* (1905). See also Louis L. Snyder, *The Imperialism Reader* (1962); E. M. Winslow, *Pattern of Imperialism* (1948); and the special number of the *Journal of Economic History* devoted to imperialism. The Schumpeter essay in the text will be found in Joseph Schumpeter, *Imperialism and Social Classes* (1951). An original treatment of the whole matter

will be found in Reinhold Niebuhr, *The Structure of Nations and Empires* (1959), which deals searchingly with universalist-utopian imperialisms. For the roots of these imperialisms in European intellectual history, see J. L. Talmon's *Origins of Totalitarian Democracy* (1961) and his *Political Messianism: The Romantic Phase* (1960). For the "Third Rome" theme in the history of pan-Slavism, see Hans Kohn, *Pan-Slavism* (1960).

There are as yet no sustained discussions of the history of either the Russian or the American imperium as an energy system. I have profited from Michael Florinsky's *Russia* (2 vols., 1953), supplemented by Georg von Rauch, *A History of Soviet Russia* (1957), and E. H. Carr's masterful volumes on *A History of Soviet Russia* (6 vols., 1951-1960). For American history as the story of empire-building, see Charles and Mary Beard, *The Rise of American Civilization* (1930). See also, among a number of important recent studies to a greater or lesser extent in the Beard tradition: Hofstadter, Miller and Aaron, *The American Republic* (2 vols., 1959); William Miller, *A New History of the United States* (1958); William Appleman Williams, *The Contours of American History* (1961); Henry F. May, *The End of American Innocence* (1959); Dumas Malone and Basil Rauch, *Empire for Liberty* (2 vols., 1960); Ernest R. May, *Imperial Democracy* (1961); Brooks Adams, *America's Economic Supremacy* (1947); R. W. Van Alstyne, *The Rising American Empire* (1960); In my *America as a Civilization* (1957), Chapter XII, "Among the Powers of the Earth," I have tried to apply the distinction between imperialism and imperium to contemporary American history.

For the cold war and the political war, see John Lukacs, *A History of the Cold War* (1961); W. W. Rostow, *The United States in the World Arena* (1960); Edmund Stillman and William Pfaff, *The New Politics* (1961); George Kennan, *Russia, the Atom and the West* (1958) and his *Russia and the West Under Lenin and Stalin* (1961); Robert Strauss-Hupe, *Protracted Con-*

flict (1954) and Robert Strauss-Hupe and others, *Forward Strategy for America* (1961); Herbert Agar, *The Price of Power* (1957). Three works which are examples of intense American self-criticism in the political war with world Communism are Fred Warner Neal, *U. S. Foreign Policy and the Soviet Union* (Center for the Study of Democratic Institutions, 1961); D. F. Fleming, *The Cold War and its Origins* (2 vols., 1961); and F. L. Schuman, *The Cold War: Retrospect and Prospect* (1962). For a vigorous defense of a humanized capitalism as a weapon in the political war, see Calvin Hoover, *The Economy, Liberty and the State* (1959). For a perceptive recent trial balance, see Thomas Wilson, *Cold War and Common Sense* (1962).

For three early basic studies, see Nicholas John Spykman, *The Geography of the Peace* (1944); Chester Wilmot, *The Struggle for Europe* (1952); W. T. R. Fox, *The Super-Powers* (1944).

There is no reader oriented specifically to the political war, but the following will be found useful: Robert A. Goldwin's three volumes, *Readings in World Politics* (1959), *Readings in Russian Foreign Policy* (1959), and *Readings in U. S. Foreign Policy* (1959); N. H. Mager and Jacques Katel, *Conquest Without War* (1961); A. Dallin, *Soviet Conduct in World Affairs* (1960); Robert V. Daniels, *A Documentary History of Communism* (1960).

For Indian neutralism, see Michael Brecher, *Nehru* (1959); Frank Moraes, *India Today* (1960); Vincent Sheean, *Nehru: The Years of Power* (1960). For the earlier background of British rule see John Strachey, cited above, and Philip Woodruff, *The Men Who Ruled India* (1954). For the transition period see V. P. Menon, *The Transfer of Power in India* (1957) and Leonard Mosley, *The Last Days of the British Raj* (1961).

For the arts of diplomacy in the political war, see Charles W. Thayer, *Diplomat* (1959); Sir William Hayter, *The Diplomacy of the Great Powers* (1961); Gordon Craig and Felix Gilbert, eds., *The Diplomats* (1953). For

an appraisal of the work of American Secretaries of State in the 20th century see Norman A. Graebner, Ed., *An Uncertain Tradition* (1961).

For the internal problems of the free world and the Communist world power clusters, see Zbigniew Brzezinski's *Ideology and Power in Soviet Politics* (1962) and his *The Soviet Bloc* (1961); Donald Zagoria, *The Sino-Soviet Conflict 1956-1961* (1962); Robert R. Bowie and John K. Fairbank, *Communist China 1955-1959: Policy Documents with Analysis* (1962); Joseph Kraft, *The Grand Design* (1962). There is a rapid obsolescence rate in historical and descriptive books on Communist China. Among those which I have found useful are Charles Patrick Fitzgerald, *Revolution in China* (1952); William Stevenson, *The Yellow Wind* (1959); and Edgar Faure, *The Serpent and the Tortoise* (1958).

For Hungary, see Leslie B. Bain, *The Reluctant Satellites* (1960) and Paul E. Zinner, *Revolution in Hungary* (1962), based on interviews with Hungarian refugees.

For the role of the German problem in the political war, see Gerald Freund, *Germany Between Two Worlds* (1961); Hans Speier, *Divided Berlin* (1961); Fred Warner Neal, *America and the German Problem* (1962).

Of the many books on the Castro revolution and recent Cuban-American relations, the best is Theodore Draper's *Castro's Revolution: Myths and Realities* (1962).

For the U-2 incident as a weapon in the political war, see David Wise and Thomas B. Ross, *The U-2 Affair* (1962).

Chapter III: Grand Design as Political Religion

For the history and anatomy of revolutions, see Crane Brinton, *The Anatomy of Revolution* (1957); Franco Venturi, *Roots of Revolution* (1960); Robert J. Alexander, *Prophets of the Revolution* (1962); Albert Camus, *The Rebel* (1956) and *Resistance, Rebellion, and Death* (1961).

On the elements of domination and accommodation in Soviet policy, see the divergent viewpoints in the writings of Alexander Dallin, *Soviet Conduct in World Affairs* (1960) and Barrington Moore, *Terror and Progress in the U.S.S.R.* (1954) and his *Soviet Politics: the Dilemma of Power* (1950). A useful group of essays will be found in Ivo J. Lederer, ed., *Russian Foreign Policy* (1962). See also Louis Fischer's new introduction to the Vintage edition of his classic study, *The Soviets in World Affairs* (1960), and George F. Kennan, *Realities of American Foreign Policy* (1954).

On Marxism and Communism, see Alfred Meyer, *Marxism: The Unity of Theory and Practice* (1954) and also his *Leninism* (1962); Erich Fromm, *Marx's Concept of Man* (1961); T. B. Bottomore and Maximilien Rubel, *Karl Marx* (1956); Adam Ulam, *The Unfinished Revolution* (1960); Hannah Arendt, *Between Past and Future* (1961); George Lichtheim, *Marxism* (1961); Daniel Bell, *The End of Ideology* (1960), especially the material on the early "humanist" Marx and the concept of alienation. Also Robert V. Daniels, *The Nature of Communism* (1962) and his *A Documentary History of Communism* (1960); Herbert Marcuse, *Soviet Marxism* (1961); Isaac Deutscher, *Russia in Transition* (1957) and his massive biography of Leon Trotsky, of which two volumes, *The Prophet Armed* (1954) and *The Prophet Unarmed* (1959), have already appeared. See also the extraordinary appendix on Lenin's theory of the State which appears as Note A in Volume 1 of E. H. Carr's *A History of the Russian Revolution* (1951); and Stanley Page, *Lenin and World Revolution* (1959). For a highly original view of the origins of Soviet Communism, see Karl A. Wittfogel, *Oriental Despotism* (1957).

For the pre-history of Communist theory in 18th and early 19th century Europe, see J. L. Talmon, *The Origins of Totalitarian Democracy* (1961) and his *Political Messianism: The Romantic Phase* (1960); Frank E. Manuel, *New World of Henri Saint-Simon* (1956) and also his *Prophets of Paris* (1962); Kingsley Martin, *Rise of Liberal Thought* (1959). Among earlier discus-

sions of Soviet Communism as a political religion I have profited from works as diverse as Carl Becker, *The Heavenly City of the 18th Century Philosophers* (1932), and Harold J. Laski, *Faith, Reason and Civilization* (1944). For a discussion of how John Stuart Mill was first drawn to rationalism as a cult turned into a faith, see my Introduction to the Bantam Classics edition of *Essential Works of John Stuart Mill* (1961).

On the development of Communist Party doctrine in Russia, see Leonard Schapiro, *The Communist Party of the Soviet Union* (1959) and John S. Reshetar, Jr., *A Concise History of the Communist Party of the Soviet Union* (1960).

On the history of the American Communist Party, especially in its relation to Soviet controls, see Theodore Draper's two volumes, *The Roots of American Communism* (1953), and *American Communism and Soviet Russia* (1960), and also Lewis Coser and Irving Howe, *The American Communist Party: A Critical History* (1957). See also Clinton Rossiter, *Marxism: The View from America* (1960).

On this whole array of problems I have profited from the divergent views in the writings of Sidney Hook, Bertram Wolfe, Louis Fischer, Isaac Deutscher, E. H. Carr, Herbert Marcuse, Barrington Moore, and Daniel Bell, especially on the internal development of Marxist theory within the Soviet Union.

For an early view of my own on the distortions of Marxist theory, see *It Is Later Than You Think* (1939)—"Marxism: Six Errors," pp. 67-72.

Milovan Djilas' criticism of Communist society is contained in two of his books, *The New Class* (1957) and *Conversations with Stalin* (1962). See also his *Anatomy of a Moral* (1959). For an already classic portrayal of the position of the intellectual in a Communist regime, see Czeslaw Milosz, *The Captive Mind* (1953).

For excellent studies of the case of Yugoslavia, see J. B. Hoptner, *Yugoslavia in Crisis: 1934-1941* (1962) and George W. Hoffman and Fred Warner

Neal, *Yugoslavia and the New Communism* (1962). For the internal problems within the Communist power cluster, see Z. K. Brzezinski, *The Soviet Bloc: Unity and Conflict* (rev. ed. 1961).

For recent books on culture and personality in the Soviet Union, see Raymond A. Bauer, Alex Inkeles, and Clyde Kluckhohn, *How the Soviet System Works* (1961); Raymond A. Bauer, *Nine Soviet Portraits* (1955); Klaus Mehnert, *Soviet Man and His World* (1962); Joseph Novak, *No Third Path* (1962).

On reason-of-state and reason-of-history: the classic discussion of reason-of-state is F. Meinecke, *Die Idee der Staatsräson in der Neuren Geschichte* (1925), translated as *Machiavellianism: the Doctrine of Raison d'Etat and Its History* (1957); see my essay, "Machiavelli and Machiavellianism" in *Ideas for the Ice Age* (1941). For reason-of-history, see Albert Camus, *The Rebel* (1954) and Hannah Arendt, *The Origins of Totalitarianism* (1951).

For Communism as a political religion, see the works of J. L. Talmon cited above. See also the same author's *Utopianism and Politics* (1958).

Chapter IV: The Undeveloped World

On the revolution against imperialism, see the reading suggested under Chapter II, especially Strachey and Emerson. For a basic theoretical analysis, see Daniel Lerner, *The Passing of Traditional Society* (1958), and Everett E. Hagen, *On the Theory of Social Change* (1962). Two broadly informative works are Vera M. Dean, *The Nature of the Non-Western World* (1957) and Barbara Ward, *The Rich Nations and the Poor Nations* (1962). For the problems of economic growth, see W. Arthur Lewis, *The Theory of Economic Growth* (1955); W. W. Rostow, *The Stages of Economic Growth* (1960); J. K. Galbraith, *Problems of Economic Development* (1962); A. O. Hirschman, *The Strategy of Economic Development* (1961); A. O. Hirschman, ed., *Latin American Issues: Essays and Comments* (1961); P. T. Bauer and B. S. Yemey, *The Economics of Undeveloped Countries* (1957), Robert E. Asher and others, *Development of the Emerging Countries: An Agenda for Research* (1962), a study for the Brookings Institution, especially the paper by Everett E. Hagen and the comment by A. O. Hirschman. See also the essays by Hagen and others in *Economics and the Policy Maker* (1959), which is also a Brookings study; L. W. Shannon, *Underdeveloped Areas* (1957); Irma Adelman, *Theories of Economic Growth and Development* (1961); and Alan M. Sievers, *Revolution, Evolution and the Economic Order* (1962). For a strongly Marxist analysis, see Paul Baran, *The Political Economy of Growth* (1957). For the discussion, in the text, of the political consequences of a high tempo of capital formation, see the provocative and too-neglected book by Sidney Lens, *A World in Revolution* (1956).

On Woodrow Wilson and self-determination, see Arno J. Mayer, *Political Origins of the New Diplomacy: 1917-1918* (1959); John M. Blum, *Woodrow Wilson and the Politics of Morality* (1956); Arthur Walworth, *Woodrow Wilson: World Prophet* (1958), the second volume of a two-volume biography. For Lenin's views on nationalism and world revolution, see Stanley Page, *Lenin and the Idea of World Revolution* (1961); Alfred Meyer, *Leninism* (1962); and E. H. Carr, *A History of Soviet Russia* (6 vols., 1951-1960), especially the appendix on the Bolshevik doctrine of self-determination, which appears as note "B" in Volume One, *The Bolshevik Revolution: 1917-1923* (1951).

For the political aspects, the best general surveys are G. A. Almond and J. S. Coleman, *The Politics of the Developing Areas* (1960); Braibanti and Spengler, eds., *Tradition, Values, and Socio-Economic Development* (1961); and Max F. Millikan and D. L. Blackmer, eds., *The Emerging Nations: Their Growth and U. S. Policy* (1961). For a biographical survey, see Vera M. Dean, *Builders of the Emerging Nations* (1961). For the Asian nations, there are two good studies of Indonesia: Louis Fischer, *The Story of Indonesia* (1959) and George Kahin, *Nationalism and Revolution in Indonesia* (1952).

For Burma, see L. W. Pye, *Politics, Personality, and Nation Building: Burma's Search for Identity* (1962), and Louis J. Walinsky, *Economic Development in Burma 1951-1960* (1962). For India, see Myron Weiner, *Party Politics in India* (1962); Richard L. Park and Irene Tinker, *Leadership and Political Institutions in India* (1959); and Selig S. Harrison, *India: The Most Dangerous Decades* (1960). For Africa, see G. H. T. Kimble, *Tropical Africa* (2 vols. 1960); Immanuel Wallerstein, *Africa: The Politics of Independence* (1961); G. M. Carter, *The Politics of Inequality: South Africa Since 1948* (1958); J. Duffey and R. A. Manners, eds., *Africa Speaks* (1961); A. Keppel-Jones, *When Smuts Goes* (1947); Arnold Rifkin *Africa and the West* (1962); H. J. Spiro, *Politics in Africa: Prospects South of the Sahara* (1962); Margery Perham, *The Colonial Reckoning* (1962); Louis Lomax, *The Reluctant African* (1960); and D. E. Apter, *The Political Kingdom in Uganda: A Study in Bureaucratic Nationalism* (1961); and Bascom and Herskovitz, *Continuity and Change in African Cultures* (1958). For the Middle East, see Keith Wheelock, *Nasser's New Egypt* (1960); N. Safran, *Egypt in Search of Political Community* (1962); and Morroe Berger, *Arab World Today* (1962). For Latin America, see the Hirschman studies above; also R. J. Alexander, *Prophets of Revolution* (1962); Richard N. Adams and others, *Social Change in Latin America Today* (1960); Dexter Perkins, *The United States in Latin America* (1961). For a sharply Marxist position on the Castro regime and Cuba, see Huberman and Sweezy, *Cuba: Anatomy of a Revolution* (1960); and C. Wright Mills, *Listen, Yankee* (1960). For a critical position, see Theodore Draper, *Castro's Revolution: Myths and Realities* (1962). For a history of the Bay of Pigs episode, see Karl E. Meyer and Tad Szulc, *The Cuban Invasion* (1962).

On some of the psychological aspects of revolutionary nationalism, see Eric Hoffer, *The True Believer* (1951) and his *The Passionate State of Mind* (1955); and Max Scheler, *Ressentiment* (1961), ed., Lewis Coser. See also L. W.

Doob, *Becoming More Civilized: A Psychological Explanation* (1960), Bruce Crozer, *The Rebels* (1960), and the remarkable study by O. Mannioni, *Prospero and Caliban* (1956).

A number of books above discuss the theory and politics of economic aid programs. See also C. Wolff, Jr., *Foreign Aid: Theory and Practice in Southern Asia* (1960) and J. S. Loeber, *Foreign Aid: Our Tragic Experiment* (1961).

Chapter V: The Viable Society: Elite, *Élan*, Ethos

For the role of the leader in history, see Isaiah Berlin, *The Hedgehog and the Fox* (1953); Sidney Hook, *The Hero in History: A Study in Limitations and Possibility* (1955); E. H. Carr, *What is History?* (1962). For the tragic in history, see "Tragedy and the New Politics," a discussion by Scott Buchanan and others in a pamphlet issued by the Center for the Study of Democratic Institutions (1960); Hans J. Morgenthau, "The Trouble with Kennedy," (*Commentary*, January 1962). Also, for an interesting perspective from literary history, George Steiner, *The Death of Tragedy* (1961). For the power-aspect of presidential leadership, see Richard Neustadt, *Presidential Power* (1960). For identity as an element in leadership, see Erik Erikson, *Identity and the Life-Cycle* (1959) and also his *Childhood and Society* (1950).

There is no room to list all the many studies of great modern leaders. Lincoln has been well studied by David Donald in *Lincoln Reconsidered: Essays on the Civil War Era* (1961); Franklin Roosevelt by J. M. Burns, *The Lion and the Fox* (1956), and in *The Coming of the New Deal* (1959) and *The Politics of Upheaval* (1960) by Arthur M. Schlesinger, Jr. Churchill and De Gaulle have written so much on themselves that it has proved hard for biographers to compete with them. For Churchill, see Peter de Mendelssohn, *The Age of Churchill: Heritage and Adventure, 1874-1911* (1961), for the first of what will be a massive three-volume biography. For De Gaulle, it is still necessary to rely on his three autobiographical volumes, *The Call to Honor* (1958), *Unity* (1959), *Salvation* (1960), comprising *The War Memoirs of Charles de Gaulle* (1958-60); see also his earlier reflections on military leadership, *The Edge of the Sword* (1960). There is as yet no adequate biography of Khrushchev, but I have found Konrad Kellen, *Khrushchev: A Political Portrait* (1961) and Lazar Pistrak, *The Grand Tactician* (1961) stimulating. The same is true of Gandhi, but see Louis Fischer, *Gandhi* (1954) and Vincent Sheean, *Lead, Kindly Light* (1949). For Nehru, see Michael Brecher, *Nehru* (1959). The earlier Russian leaders have been well studied: see Bertram Wolfe, *Three Who Made A Revolution* (1948); Isaac Deutscher's biography of Trotsky, mentioned above, and his *Stalin* (1960). The best analysis of Lenin is to be found in the first four volumes of E. H. Carr's *A History of Soviet Russia* (1951-54).

On the great elite theorists, see James Burnham, *The Machiavellians, Defenders of Freedom* (1943); H. Stuart Hughes, *Consciousness and Society* (1958). Harold Lasswell and Daniel Lerner are responsible for much of the recent spurt of interest in elite theory: see their *Policy Sciences: Recent Developments* (1951). My reference to George Orwell on the British intellectual elite is to the title essay in his collection, *England, Your England* (1953). For one phase of the history of the American creative elite, see Daniel Aaron, *Writers on the Left* (1961). The classic analyses of the surrender of European and American intellectuals to the Communist idea, especially in the 1930s, are R. H. Crossman, ed., *The God That Failed* (1950). See also Raymond Aron, *The Opium of the Intellectuals* (1957) and Albert Camus, *The Rebel* (1954). For a different view, emphasizing the affirmative path which the Communists betrayed, see John Strachey, *The Strangled Cry* (1962). For the political Right see Daniel Bell, ed., *The New American Right*, in a revised edition (1962) with a brilliant new introductory essay by Bell.

For the military elite, see Samuel P. Huntington, *The Soldier and the State* (1957); S. P. Huntington, ed., *Changing Patterns of Military Politics* (1961); and also Edwin Lieuwin, *Arms and Politics in Latin America* (1960). For the scientific elite, see the reading suggested under Chapter VI below.

On the education of a democratic elite, see my *Education and a Radical Humanism: Notes Toward a Theory of the Educational Crisis* (1962). The recruiting and training of the Russian elite is discussed in George Z. F. Bereday and John Pennar, *The Politics of Soviet Education* (1960), and Richard C. Renfield, *Soviet Education and the New Soviet Man* (1962), a pamphlet for the National Education Association. See also Richard Pipes, ed., *The Russian Intelligentsia* (1961). For considerable light on the conditions under which the Soviet commanding elite is recruited, see Bauer, Inkeles, and Kluckhohn, *How The Soviet System Works* (1960), and Merle Fainsod, *How Russia is Ruled* (1953). For the reference to Jefferson's letter in the text above, see Gordon C. Lee, *Crusade Against Ignorance: Thomas Jefferson on Education* (1961). See also Paul R. Hanna, ed., *Education: An Instrument of National Goals* (1962). For a lengthier analysis of Dewey's thinking, see Lawrence Cremin's *The Transformation of the School* (1961), and also my *Education and a Radical Humanism*, cited above, as well as George R. Geiger, *John Dewey in Perspective* (1958). The recent emphasis on excellence as a test of the creative elite is best discussed in John W. Gardner, *Excellence* (1961); and Jacques Barzun, *The House of Intellect* (1959). My reference in the text to the writing of Harold A. Innis is to his book, *Empire and Communications* (1950).

For the death and life of civilizations, see Oswald Spengler, *The Decline of the West* (new condensed edition 1962); also H. Stuart Hughes' study, *Oswald Spengler: A Critical Study* (1952). See also Arnold J. Toynbee, *A Study of History* (11 vols. 1934-1959), along with a twelfth volume, *Reconsiderations* (1961). I have touched earlier on this theme in my last chapter

of *America as a Civilization* (1957).
On *élan* and national purpose, see
Hans J. Morgenthau, *The Purpose of
American Politics* (1960). On the issue
of the ethos, see Charles Frankel, *The
Case for Modern Man* (1955), especially
the section on liberalism and the imagination of disaster; Iris Murdoch, "A
House of Theory," in Norman MacKen-
zie, ed., *Conviction* (1958); and Ed-
mond Cahn, *The Dilemma of Democratic Man* (1962). There are a number of insights bearing on the problem in David Cooperman and E. V.
Walter, *Power and Civilization: Political Thought in the Twentieth Century* (1962); Charles Morris, *Paths of
Life* (1956); Simon Daniger, ed., *The
Nature of Man in Theological and
Psychological Perspectives* (1962); Crane
Brinton, *A History of Western Morals*
(1959); Elting Morison, ed., *The A-
merican Style* (1958), especially the
chapter by Clyde Kluckhohn on the
recent transformation of American
values. For a perceptive criticism of my
own discussion of the American ethos
in *America as a Civilization* (1957),
see Clyde Kluckhohn's review in *World
Politics* (January 1959), reprinted in
Abraham S. Eisenstadt, ed., *American
History: Since 1865* (1962).

Chapter VI: Beyond the
Power Principle

On the transcending of the nation-
state as a principle of world order, see
Norman Cousins, *In Place of Folly*
(1961), and his earlier *Modern Man
Is Obsolete* (1945). On universal empires as a basis of world peace, see
Arnold J. Toynbee, *A Study of History*
(11 vols.), especially Volume Seven
(1954); and Reinhold Niebuhr, *The
Structure of Nations and Empires*
(1959). On the renunciation of power
as a road to world peace, see Louis
Fischer, *Gandhi* (1954); Homer Jack,
ed., *The Gandhi Reader* (1956). On the
role of morality in international politics, see Hans J. Morgenthau, *Politics
Among Nations* (1960); Louis Halle,
Men and Nations (1962); and Stanley
H. Hoffman, *Contemporary Theory in
International Relations* (1960). On unilateralism as embodying a principle of

world order, see John C. Bennett,
*Nuclear Weapons and the Conflict of
Conscience* (1962). On a Russian-
American modus vivendi as the basis
for a dual division of world power,
there is a good discussion in Erich
Fromm, *May Man Prevail?* (1962); also
see F. L. Schuman, *The Cold War:
Retrospect and Prospect* (1962), already
cited. For the over-all Soviet view of the
structure of world power, see Elliot
Goodman, *Soviet Design for a World
State* (1960). On a free-world concert of
powers as a basis of world peace, see
also an important article by Senator
J. W. Fulbright, "For a Concert of
Free Nations," in the October 1961
issue of *Foreign Affairs*. For the emergence of a new Europe, moving toward
economic and political confederation,
see Joseph Kraft, *Grand Design* (1962),
and for historical accounts see Hans A.
Schmitt, *The Path to European Union:
from the Marshall Plan to the Common Market* (1962), and Arnold J.
Zurcher, *The Struggle to Unite Europe, 1940-1958* (1958).

The recent literature on disarmament and arms control is massive.
Among those I have found most useful (for the historical background) are
Bernhard G. Bechoefer, *Postwar Negotiations for Arms Control* (1961);
for the dynamics and controversies of
the current problem, Thomas C. Schelling and Morton Halperin, *Strategy
and Arms Control* (1961); Ernest Le-
fever, ed., *Arms and Arms Control*
(1962); Louis Henkin, ed., *Arms Control* (1961); James J. Wadsworth, *The
Price of Peace* (1962).

For the role of the UN in the building of peace, see Joseph P. Lash, *Dag
Hammarskjold* (1961). Hans J. Morgenthau, *Politics Among Nations* (third
edition 1960) has a good comparative
treatment of the mechanisms for collective security and peaceful change under the League of Nations and the
United Nations. For a history of the
process of forming the United Nations,
see Ruth B. Russell, *A History of the
UN Charter: The Role of the U.S.
1940-1945* (1958). For overall appraisals
see Ernest A. Gross, *The UN Structure*

for Peace (1962); Benjamin A. Cohen, *The UN: Constitutional Developments, Growth, and Possibilities* (1961); Leland M. Goodrich, *The UN* (1954); Inis L. Claude, *Swords into Plowshares* (second edition 1954).

On proposals for changing the UN, see F. O. Wilcox and H. F. Haviland, Jr., eds., *The U.S. and the UN* (1961); F. O. Wilcox and C. M. Marcy, *Proposals for Changes in the UN* (1955); and Grenville Clark and L. B. Sohn, *World Peace Through World Law* (1958). See also the issues of the bulletin *Intercom* put out periodically by the Foreign Policy Association.

For collective security through world law, the three basic books are Clark and Sohn, mentioned above, and M. S. McDougal and F. P. Feliciano, *Law and Minimum World Public Order* (1961); and Quincy Wright, William M. Evan, and Morton Deutsch, eds., *Preventing World War III* (1962), a perceptive and balanced anthology of proposals for peace. See also F. L. Schuman, *The Commonwealth of Man* (1952); Arthur Larson, *When Nations Disagree* (1961); W. W. Wager, *H. G. Wells and the World State* (1961). Three pamphlets written for the Center for the Study of Democratic Institutions deal with this problem: Walter Millis, *A World Without War* (1961); Walter Millis, *The Might of Nations* (1961); William O. Douglas,

The Rule of Law in World Affairs (1961). For the moral debate on atomic weapons see John C. Bennett, *Nuclear Weapons and the Conflict of Conscience* (1962) and John C. Batchelder, *The Irreversible Decision: 1939-1950* (1961). There is also a remarkable roundtable discussion on "Western Values and Total War" by Sidney Hook, H. Stuart Hughes, Hans J. Morgenthau, and C. P. Snow in the October 1961 issue of *Commentary*. For the role of the scientists in war and peace see in general the files of the *Bulletin of Atomic Scientists,* published monthly in Chicago; see also J. S. Dupre and S. A. Lakoff, *Science and the Nation* (1962), and Don K. Price, *Government and Science* (1954).

On the psychology of war and peace, I have profited most from several of Freud's works, especially *Beyond the Pleasure Principle* (1922) and *Civilization and its Discontents* (1930). See also Ernest Jones, *The Life and Work of Sigmund Freud* (3 volumes, 1953-57), especially Volume Two (1955). For Jung's views see his preface to Violet De Lazlo's *Psyche and Symbol: A Selection from the Writings of C. G. Jung* (1958). My reference to Robert Ardrey is to his *African Genesis* (1961). The exchange between Freud and Einstein will be found in *Einstein on Peace* (1960), edited by O. Nathan and H. Norden (pps. 185-202).

A Note of Acknowledgment

I AM INDEBTED to my colleagues at the Indian School of International Studies, at New Delhi, especially the Director, Dr. A. Appadorai; to the students in my seminar at the school; to the faculties and students at the universities at Chandigarh, Bombay, Poona, Mysore, Madras and Lucknow, where I first presented the theme of this book; to the directors of the Ford Foundation, who made my year of teaching and studying in India possible; to my editor, Henry Simon, for his criticism and help; to my assistant, Roslyn Mass, for critical suggestions, large and small but always helpful, as she saw the ms. through its successive drafts; to my Brandeis assistant, Georg Fromm, and to the students in my class in World Politics at Brandeis University during the years 1960-62, whose questions and comments made me aware of the weaknesses in my analysis; to my former student, Stephen Solarz, for help with the Note on Reading, and to Frances Reichman for help with the Index; to Brenda Grossman, Secretary of the Politics Department at Brandeis, and to Pauline Deacon, for bringing typing order into the chaos of my ms. revisions. I am grateful to President A. L. Sachar and Dean Clarence Berger of Brandeis University; to Edwin G. Cohen of the National Educational Television and Radio Center; to Hartford N. Gunn, Jr., Greg Harney, Virginia Kassel, Donald Hallock, and the staff of WGBH in Cambridge, Mass., who enabled me to present the main argument of the book in a series of thirteen TV lectures in the winter of 1960-61. Also to Professor Robert E. Martin and to the faculty and students of Howard University where I delivered the substance of this book in four Sidney Hillman Foundation lectures. I want finally to thank my fellow students of world politics—Daniel Bell of Columbia University, Merle Fainsod of Harvard University, Alfred J. Hotz of Western Reserve University, Samuel P. Huntington of Columbia University, Herman Kahn of the Hudson Institute, Hans J. Morgenthau of the University of Chicago, Milton Sacks of Brandeis University, Frederick L. Schuman of Williams College, and Adam Ulam of Harvard University—for their generosity in reading my manuscript and for their criticisms, both general and detailed. Their devotion to the cause of scholarship, cutting across their agreements and disagreements with me, is warrant that those who dream of a similar political disinterestedness in a possible transnational world are not wholly wrong.

Index

A

access, 182, 224-226
accommodation effect, 102-104
Acton, Lord, 285
Adams, Henry, 238, 306
Adams, John, 219
Adenauer, Konrad, 200
Africa, 11, 76, 143, 150-152, 174-180, 304
African personality, 194
African socialism, 194
Alexander the Great, 97
alienation, 119; of elites, 212-218
alliance system, 21, 62
ambiguity, 41
America: as energy system, 67-73; as great power, 67-73; diplomacy of, 88; foreign policy of, 38-40; history of, 88; intellectuals in, 214-216; American Revolution, 89, 100
Angola, 48, 88
anti-colonialism, 145-146
Ardrey, Robert, 304
Arendt, Hannah, 117
aristocracy, 219
Arkadyev, Georgi P., 286
armed doctrine, 61, 127-132
arms control, 33, 259-264
Aron, Raymond, 10
Ascoli, Max, 265
Asia, 11, 76, 80, 169, 180
Ataturk, Kemal, 184, 188
Atlantic Partnership, 78, 276-278
Ayub Khan, 81
Azikiwe, Nnamdi, 186

B

Bacon, Francis, 127
balance of power, 11, 12, 22, 30, 51
balance of terror, 11, 28-33, 42, 46, 51
Balewa, Sir Abubakar, 184
Baran, Paul, 61
BCR weapons, 34, 35
Bell, Daniel, 239
Ben-Gurion, David, 184, 187
Bergson, Henri, 236-238
Berlin, 40, 75-76, 208, 267
blackmail, 36, 37
Blackmur, R. P., 130
Blake, William, 295
Blanquism, 131
bloc, 62
Botsford, Keith, 188
Bourguiba, Habib, 184, 186, 207
bread-or-freedom fallacy, 166-167
Brecht, Bertolt, 220
Brennan, Donald, 27
Bright, John, 301
brinkmanship, 38, 40
Brzezinski, Z. K., 272-273
Bukharin, N. I., 191-192
bureaucracies, 161
Burke, Edmund, 61, 127, 180
Burma, 187, 188
Burns, James M., 203

C

Caesar, Julius, 97
Caliban and Prospero, 176

Camus, Albert, 102

capital: export of, 59; investment of, 59

Carlyle, Thomas, 202

Carr, E. H., 146

Castro, Fidel, 40, 155-156, 207; *see also* Cuba

catalytic war, 43

Catholicism, 63

caudillo regimes, 185

change, social, 180-181

Cheka, 115

"chicken," 37, 38

chiliastic principle, 130

China, *see* Communist China; *see also* Formosa

Chou En-lai, 105

Christianity, 60, 128

church-state relations, 182

Churchill, Sir Winston S., 30, 49, 57, 73, 87, 90, 198, 213, 295

circulation of the elites, 227

civilian defense, 37

civilian-military relations, 182, 212-215

civilizations, 230-236

class struggle, 59

classical economics, 19, 20, 22

classical world politics, 10, 19, 20, 22, 23, 51

Clausewitz, Karl von, 38

closed society, 37

coalition, 62

cold war, 39, 51, 73-79

collective will, 234-235, 287-295

colonial administration, 181-182

color, 174-180; color consciousness, 174-180; color revolution, 145

COMECON, 271

Comintern, 271

commanding elite, 9, 11, 209-219; *see also* elite

Common Market, 271, 274-278

Commonwealth, 84, 87

communications revolution, 228-229

communications theory, 26

Communism, 37, 101-102, 110-114, 116-132, 271-276; as energy system, 71-73; Communist elite, 72, 217-219; Communist ethos and

man, 242-247; Communist mystique, 135; Communist Parties, 122-123, 171; Communist Power Cluster, 55-57, 92, strategy of, 35, 132-136; as a world system, 273-274

Communist China, 36, 42, 46, 49, 50, 55, 62, 80-83, 84, 92, 103, 105-107, 115, 126-127, 166, 173, 242-247, 284; personality structure in, 242; Chinese Revolution, 71, 109, 134

Comte, Auguste, 129

conformity, 246

Congo, Belgian, 48, 88, 147-148, 152

Connally Amendment, 292

conscience, 298-299; conscience differential, 299

Constitution, American, 277

constitutional imperium, 89-90

containment, 31-32, 39, 74

counterforce capability, 28

creative elites, *see* elite

credible first-strike, 26, 28, 35; credibility, 31

Croly, Herbert, 255

crystallization, 77

Cuba, 36, 48, 63, 93, 155-156, 206, 266-267; *see also* Castro

culturalist movements, 148-149

Czechoslovakia, 274

D

Dachau, 47

daemon, Communist, 104-114

Dart, Raymond, 304, 307

deadly spiral, 33-38

death urge, 301-308

de Chardin, Teilhard, 307

decision making, 206-209

De Gaulle, Charles, 49, 65, 84, 85, 87, 90-91, 200-202, 204, 207, 209, 214

democracy, 67, 182-183, 187

democratic class struggle, 59

democratic elite, *see* elite

deterrence, 25-28, 31, 35, 38, 40, 41, 49

De Tocqueville, Alexis, 116, 139, 230
developing areas, 141-194; developing polities, 180-188; developing societies, 188-194
Dewey, John, 226
dialectic of history, 110-114
dictatorship, 187
diffusion, nuclear, 11, 41-46
diplomacy, 12, 86, 88, 264-270
disarmament dialogue, 12, 259-264
Djilas, Milovan, 112, 124-125
dollar diplomacy, 59, 88
domination effect, 102-104
"Don't Touch Me," 38-41
"Dooley, Mr." 236, 239
Dostoevsky, F. M., 127, 130
Drury, Allen, 203
Dunne, Finley Peter, 236
Dutt, Palme, 61
dynamism, 64
Dzerzhinsky, I., 101, 115

E

economic aid, 39, 85, 153-163, 190-191; economic growth, 153-163; economic imperialisms, 60
economics, 153-163; *see also* classical economics
educated elite, *see* elite
education, 219-230
Einstein, Albert, 303
Eisenhower, Dwight D., 48, 199, 218, 295
elan, 236-241
elite, 110, 111, 174-180; colonial, 87; Communist, 69, 106, 123-125; creative, 209-230; democratic, 219-230; educated, 132-136, 178-179; theory of, 210-211, 227
Emerson, Ralph Waldo, 148
empire, 55-57, 61-67, 69, 70, 83-94, 254, *see also* imperium
enchanted wood, 14
enemy, 21
energy systems, 67-73
Engels, Friedrich, 114, 122
equilibrium, 22-23, 30, 51
Erikson, Erik, 148

Eros, 126, 250
escalation, 26, 35, 36, 41, 44, 45
espionage, 37, 39, 86
Establishment, 10, 227-228
ethos, 241-250
Etzioni, Amitai, 29, 188
Europe, 55, 74-76, 78, 83, 148, 271, 274-278

F

fail-safe, 26, 28
failure of nerve, 233-234; failure of will, 234-235
fallacy of the isolated polity, 189-192; fallacy of the isolated technology, 189-192
fanaticism, 60
Faustian Question, 47-50
fear, 21, 35, 37, 296-301
Federalist Papers, 43
Fedin, Konstantin, 117
five-level analysis, 192-193
Fontenelle, Bernard, 117
food failures, Communist, 36
force-in-being, 288-289
Formosa, 40, 48
founding-father regimes, 184
Fourteen Points, 168-169
France, 49, 62, 84, 85, 213-214; French Community, 62; French intellectuals, 213-214; French Revolution, 100-101, 114, 127
Frazer, Sir James G., 14
Frazier, E. Franklin, 179
freedom, 67
free world, 67; free-world ethos, 247-250; free-world power cluster, 55-57
Freud, Sigmund, 51, 253, 301-308
Fromm, Erich, 250, 258, 303
Frost, Robert, 206

G

Galbraith, J. K., 157-158, 161
Gallois, Pierre, 25
games theory, 27, 28, 34, 36

Gandhi, M. K., 80, 149, 190, 201, 207, 209, 223, 255-257
Gary, Romain, 305
Genet, Jean, 179
Germany, 62-63, 213; intellectuals in, 213
Ghana, 62
Gibbon, Edward, 98, 229-230, 249
Gide, André, 172
Goethe, Johann W., 50
good life, 248-249
graduated unilateralism, 263, 298-300
Grand Design, 11, 20, 35, 39, 66, 74, 75, 82, 97-99, 101, 105, 116, 179
Great Britain, 49, 62, 84, 88, 212-213, 297-298
Great Leap Forward, 166
Greek culture, 233
growth, idea of, 154; Communist plan for, 154-157; democratic plan for, 157-163; economic, 163-168
guerrilla warfare, 36, 76
Guinea, 83, 193

H

Hallstein, Walter, 276
Hammarskjold, Dag, 81, 175, 209, 280-286
Harlan, John M., 175
have and have-not nations, 42, 160, 165
Hegel, G. W. F., 202
heroes as leaders, 174-180
Herzl, Theodor, 238
high-consumption economy, 59, 139, 158
Hiroshima, 24, 25
history, 114-116, 230-236; determinist theory of, 231-237; inevitability in, 231-232
Hitler, Adolf, 69, 98-99, 107
Hobson, John A., 56, 57-58, 59-61
Holmes, Oliver Wendell, Justice, 238, 277
Hugo, Victor, 143
human connection, 244, 249

Hungary, 48, 93; Hungarian Revolution, 40
Hung Ch'i (Red Flag), 106
hunger, 147, 167; hunger revolution, 144
Hutchins, Robert, 295

I

idealist school, 22
identity, 207, 235; revolutions of, 10, 11, 141-194
ideology, 65, 94
impact aid, 190
imperialism, 11, 55-57, 57-61, 85; classical, 59, 87-88; ideological, 61; types of, 60-61; imperial style, 83-94
imperium, 56-57, *see also* empire
incentives: for talent, 221-230; under Communism, 221-222, 227-228
incongruity effect, 193
India, 48, 62, 63, 149-150, 172-173, 181-182, 187, 240
Indochina crisis, 40; war, 45
Indonesia, 87
Innis, H. A., 228
inspection, 262
instrumentalism, 126-127
intellectuals, 132-136, 211-218; intellectual elite, 211-218; *see also* elite
intelligence race, 38, 209
intervention, nuclear, 44-45
investment, 162
Islam, 60
Israel, 184, 187; socialism in, 194
Italy, 62-63

J

Jackson, Andrew, 219
Jackson, Stonewall, 200
James, William, 234
Jansenism, 273
Japan, 24, 62-63
Jefferson, Thomas, 219-230

Jews, 47, 305
John Birch Society, 37
Joyce, James, 131
Jung, C. G., 306-308

K

Kahn, Herman, 27, 28, 29, 38
Kashmir, 48
Kennan, George, 74, 109, 159
Kennedy, John F., 32, 91, 199, 201-
    202, 206, 207, 222, 232, 237, 265,
    266
Kenyatta, Jomo, 207
Keynes, John Maynard, 157, 255
Khrushchev, Nikita S., 48, 102, 105,
    110, 111-114, 119-120, 121-123,
    126, 199-200, 201-202, 266-267,
    281
kingship, 183-184
Kissinger, Henry, 27
Korea, 48; Korean War, 40, 45
Kripalani, J. A., 223
"kto kovo," 101, 103, 243-246
Kuusinen, Otto, 105

L

Ladakh, 45, 80, 83
laissez-faire, 20
Lambo, T. Adeoye, 177
Langer, Susanne, 306
language, 150
Laos, 48
Laski, Harold, 128
Latin-America, 66, 93
Lawrence, D. H., 301
leader, death of, 209; leadership,
    186, 197-209; leadership style,
    197-204
Leakey, L. S. B., 304
leapfrogging strategy, 36
Lenin, Nikolai, 21, 56, 58, 59-61, 70,
    71, 72, 75, 98-99, 100-102, 104,
    107, 111, 119, 131, 133, 134, 146,
    168-174, 207, 209, 243, 296
Lewis, W. Arthur, 157-158

liberation policy, 40
life force, 305-308; life-purposes, 247-
    250; life style, 241-250
Lincoln, Abraham, 207, 209
Litvinov, Maxim, 285
Liu Shao-Chi, 49
locomotive of history, 110-114
Lomax, Louis, 175
Lyautey, Marshal, 181

M

MacArthur, Douglas, 201
McCarthy era, 37
Machiavelli, Niccolo, 11, 22, 24, 33,
    38, 39, 210, 305
MacLeish, Archibald, 33
Macmillan, Harold, 200
McNamara, Robert S., 36, 44; Mc-
    Namara doctrine, 44
Madison, James, 43, 277
Malthus, Thomas, 159
managerial elite, 218-219, *see also*
    elite
Mann, Thomas, 203
Mannheim, Karl, 278
Manuel, Frank, 114
Mao Tse-tung, 49, 120, 134, 207
Marcuse, Herbert, 250
Marlowe, Christopher, 50, 107
Marshall Plan, 39, 74, 160
Martin, Kingsley, 117
Marx, Karl, 38, 101, 111, 114, 116-
    127, 146, 239; Marxism, 38-39,
    101-102, 116-127, 230-231, 277-
    278
massive retaliation, 31, 36
Mayer, Arno J., 169
Mead, Margaret, 216
Mendes-France, Pierre, 214
Menon, Krishna, 80
meritocracy, 224
merit service, 182
metaphor, 33, 34, 192-193
Mexico, 155-156
Middle East, 48, 180
military: elite, 46, 212-219; imperial-
    isms, 60; military-industrial com-
    plex, 218-219; principle, 121-

122; regimes, 184-185; stalemate, 29-30; strategy, 28-29
Mill, John Stuart, 129
Millis, Walter, 293-294
miscalculation, nuclear, 45
missiles, 25; missile-fear spiral, 33-38; missile gap, 34
Modelski, George, 273
modernization, 149-153, 179-180, 186, 190
modus vivendi, 250, 257-258
Monnet, Jean, 276
Monroe Doctrine, 68
Moraes, Frank, 151
morality, 299; and world order, 255-257; moral absolutism, 299; moralism, 255-257
Morgenstern, Oskar, 27
Morgenthau, Hans, 30, 200, 262
Mosca, Gaetano, 210
moving equilibrium, 32
multi-stable deterrence, 32
Murray, Gilbert, 233
Mussolini, Benito, 107
Myrdal, Gunnar, 157
myth, 15, 128, 139, 239-240

N

Nagasaki, 24
Napoleon Bonaparte, 98
Narayan, Jayaprakash, 150, 223
Nasser, Gamal Abdel, 157
nation-state, 19, 21, 51, 64, 254, 259; nation-state explosion, 10
national interest, 22
nationalism, 64-65, 109-110, 132, 186; revolutionary, *see* revolutionary nationalism
national purpose, 236-241
national socialism, 10
NATO, 75, 84-85, 90
natural aristocracy, 219-230
negotiation dialogue, 12, 36, 264-270
Nehru, Jawaharlal, 76, 80-83, 150, 162, 184, 187, 207, 223
Neustadt, Richard, 205
neutralism, 79-83, 283
New Deal, 172, 208

New Federalists, 270-278
Ne Win, 188
Niebuhr, Reinhold, 61
Nigeria, 62
Nkrumah, Kwame, 184, 186, 194, 207
North Korea, 187
nth nation, 42
nuclear weapons, 108; blackmail, 36; monopoly, 42; spiral, 10; testing, 260
Nyerere, Jules, 183, 184, 186

O

obsolescence, 35, 36
Oedipus, 203
Olympio, Sylvanus, 186
open world, 287-295
Oppenheimer, J. Robert, 300
order principle, 279-286
Organization of American States (OAS), 292
Ortega y Gasset, José, 232
Orwell, George, 212-213
Osgood, Charles, 263
overkill, 51, 260; factor, 10, 23; principle of, 51, 107-108
overreach, 102, 107; overreachers, 232-235
overtake, 163-168, 248-249
Oxford Pledge, 297

P

Pakistan, 48, 81
Pan-Africanism, 175
Panch Sheel, 80, 256
Pan-Slavism, 66
Pareto, Vilfredo, 210, 227
Pasternak, Boris, 244
Pavlov, I. P., 91
peace strategy, 28-29
Peacock, Thomas Love, 74
Peguy, Charles, 245
permanent revolution, *see* revolution

personal rule, 180-188

planning, economic, 163-168; Communist, 138-139; socialist, 138-139

Plato, 212, 226

pleasure principle, 302

Plessy vs. Ferguson, 175

Poland, 272; Polish Revolution, 40

Policy of the Hundred Flowers, 106

political: negotiation, 264-270; religion, 66, 99, 127-132, 178-179, 198, 238-239; romanticism, 100, 208, 241; style, 198-204

political war, *see* war, political

polities, developing, *see* developing polities

polycentrism, 32, 65-66, 270-278

popular culture, 216

population problem, 159-160

post-office socialism, 161

power, 20, 22, 51, 63; as ikon, 204-205; principle of, 9, 12, 15, 30, 253-308; scarcity of, 20, 24; struggle for, 36, 63; surplus of, 24

power centers, 14, 55-57, 62-73; power clusters, 10, 14, 32, 55-57, 61-67, 86, 270; power clusters, cohesion and division in, 86

power elite, 210-211, *see also* elite

power politics, 23, 43

Powers, Francis Gary, 37

power-systems, cohesion and division in, 270-278

preemptive war, 45; preventive war, 39

public, the, 13; public opinion, 13

public school system, 225-226

Pugwash Conference, 261

Puritanism, 126, 244, 250

R

radical humanism, 250

radicalism of the right, 215

raison d'état, see Reason of State

Rajagopalachari, C., 223

rationalism, 129

readiness effect, 181

realist school, 22

Reason of State, 11, 21, 114-116; Reason of History, 11, 114-116

religions, 128

religious imperialisms, 60

Renaissance, 19

responsible government, 181-3

ressentiment, 165

revolution, 99-102, 110-114, 241; limited, 100; permanent, 20, 70, 112; of rising expectations, 144; revolutionary nationalism, 10, 35, 43, 63, 79, 82-83, 141-194; revolutionary situation, 170; types of, 100-102

rich and poor nations, *see* have and have-not nations

rigidity, 232-235

Rome, 229-230

Roosevelt, Franklin D., 37, 39, 73, 90, 172, 197, 198, 201, 207-209, 215, 237, 279

Roosevelt, Theodore, 268

Rostow, W. W., 157-159

Rousseau, Jean-Jacques, 270

rule of law, 182

Russell, Lord Bertrand, 37-38, 256, 298-300

Russia, 42, 67-73; and China, 11, 92; as energy system, 69-73; as great power, 69-73; foreign policy of, 91, 102-104; intellectuals in, 217-218; personality structure in, 242-247; Russian Revolution, 69-73, 169, 220; science in, 72; social change in, 113-114

S

Sabbatai Zevi, 245

Saint-Simon, Claude, 129

Sargant, William, 91

satellites, East European, 110, 122

satyagraha, 80, 255-257

Schelling, Thomas B., 27, 34

Schumpeter, Joseph, 60

science, 117; cult of, 116-118; mystique of, 36, 116-118, 130, 244

scientists, 12, 300-301; scientific elite,
    218-219; scientific-military elite,
    11, *see also* elite
secrecy, 21, 25, 262; neurosis, 36
Security Council, *see* United Nations
Seeley, Sir John, 88
self-determination, 152, 168-174
self-fulfilling prophecy, 46
Senghor, Leopold S., 184, 186
Shaw, G. B., 184
showcase aid, 190
Shute, Nevil, 43
sinews of strength, 21
Sino-Indian border, 40, 45, 48
sky surveillance, 37
Slim, Mongi, 280
Smith, Adam, 20, 22
Snow, Sir Charles, 159, 230, 300
Snyder, Glenn H., 27
socialism, 162; in one country, 70,
    112, 164; pattern of, 162
soldier-leaders, 184-185
Sorel, Georges, 128, 210
Souphanouvong, Prince, 184
South Africa, 48
South America, 48
South Korea, 48, 187
South Vietnam, 36, 48
sovereignty, 11, 19, 21, 51, 292-293;
    national, 64
Soviet Union, *see* Russia
Spengler, Oswald, 231
Sputnik, 72
spy-hunting, 37
Spykman, Nicholas, 280
stable deterrence, 41
Stalin, J. V., 39, 48, 65, 70, 73, 99,
    102, 107, 164, 165, 191-192, 199,
    249
Stalingrad, 72
Stendhal, M. H. B., 77
Stevenson, Adlai, 282
Stimson, Henry L., 24
Strachey, John, 55, 61
Strategic Air Command, 44
Suez War, 40, 45
Sukarno, Achmed, 241
summit conferences, 105; summit
    diplomacy, 267-269
Sumner, William Graham, 159

Supreme Court, U.S., 120-121
Szilard, Leo, 263

T

take-off, 158
take-over, 163-168
talent, 220-230
Talleyrand-Périgord, C. M. de, 230
Tawney, R. H., 240
Taylor, Maxwell, 238
technological-military elite, 35; *see
    also* elite
technology, 11, 176-177, 188-190
Teller, Edward, 44, 263, 300
Third Rome, 66
Tibet, 48, 80, 83
time and timing, 204-205
Tito, J. B., 39, 75, 102, 207
Tkachcv, T. Y., 131
Tojo, H., 107
Tolstoy, Leo, 176
Torgau, 75
totalitarian liberals, 116
totalitarian revolution, 101-102
Toure, Sekou, 83, 184, 186, 193, 194
Toynbee, Arnold J., 137, 185, 231
traditional society, 192-194
tragedy, and leadership, 203-206;
    sense of, 30, 203-204, 215
tribalism, 150-152
troika principle, 281
Trotsky, Leon, 71, 112, 113, 164;
    Trotsky-Stalin controversy, 112-
    113
true believers, 245
Truman, Harry S, 24, 38-39, 48, 74,
    198-199, 201; Truman Doctrine,
    39
trust and mistrust, 262-263
Turkey, 188

U

U–2, 37, 268
undeveloped areas, 141-194; unde-
    veloped countries, 141-194; un-
    developed world, 14, 78, 141-
    194

unilateralism, 297-300
United Arab Republic, 62
United Nations, 10, 81, 176, 279-286, 287-295
United States, *see* America
United States of Europe, 267-268, 271
universal church, 98; universal empire, 66, 254-255; universal peace, 254-255
unlimited revolution, 100-102, *see also* revolution
unreadiness effect, 180-188
U Nu, 184
U.S.S.R., *see* Russia
U Thant, 280

V

viability theory, 210-211, 242; viable society, 197-250
violence, 48
vocabulary of politics, 14
Von Neuman, John, 27

W

Wallerstein, Immanuel, 179-180, 193
war, 23, 25, 38, 108; art of, 28; atomic weapons, 28; by inadvertence, 43, 45; inevitability of, 105; limited, 49; of ideas, 10, 77; political, 14, 35, 36, 41, 73-79, 86, 132-136; psychological, 36; pushbutton, 27-28, 44

Warsaw Pact, 75
weapons, generation, 10, 24, 35; race, 24, 26, 27, 32, 34, 51, 209, 259-264; revolution, 24-25
welfare states, 139
West, 66
West Germany, 75
"who whom," *see "kto kovo"*
Willkie, Wendell, 292
Wilmot, Chester, 39
Wilson, Woodrow, 69, 156, 168-174, 296
Wittfogel, Karl, 137
Wohlstetter, Albert, 27
Woolf, Virginia, 130-131
world authority, 289-295, 308; and constitutional frame for, 270-279; world law, 12; world order, 12-13; world police force, 12, 289-295, 308; world society, 12; world state, 12
world politics, 9, 22
world revolution, 71
World War I, 69
World War II, 69

Y

Yalta, 73, 208
Young, Michael, 224
Yugoslavia, 39, 63

Z

Zionism, 238

ABOUT THE AUTHOR

MAX LERNER, *author, teacher, and columnist, received his B.A. at Yale in 1923 and his Ph.D. at the Robert Brookings Graduate School of Economics and Government in 1927. He has taught at Sarah Lawrence College, Harvard University, and Williams College. At present he is Professor of American Civilization at Brandeis University and a regular columnist for the New York* Post. *He has frequently appeared on television and radio and has written numerous books on politics, law, education, and social theory.*

Mr. Lerner spent the academic year of 1959-60 in India, teaching in the Graduate School of International Studies at the University of Delhi, and will be in Europe in 1963-4 under a Ford grant for research and study. The Age of Overkill is his first full-scale book since his now classic work, America as a Civilization.